THE BOOK OF BURTONIANA
VOLUME 3: 1887 to 1924

The Book of Burtoniana

Letters & Memoirs of Sir Richard Francis Burton

Volume 3: 1887 to 1924

Edited by Gavan Tredoux

© 2024-01-08 2:52 AM Gavan Tredoux.
http://burtoniana.org.

The Book of Burtoniana:
   Volume 1: 1841-1866
     Volume 2: 1867-1886
       Volume 3: 1887-1924, Register and Bibliography

Contents

List of Illustrations ix

1887–1890 1

1.	1887. Anna Bonus Kingsford via Edward Maitland	1
2.	1887/01/10. Richard Burton to John Payne.	1
3.	1887/05/08. Richard Burton to A. G. Ellis..............................	2
4.	1887/05/27. Richard Burton to Leonard Smithers.	2
5.	1887/09/14. Richard Burton to A. G. Ellis..............................	2
6.	1888. Walter Thomas Spencer.	3
7.	1888/01/16. Charles Montagu Doughty to Richard Burton. ...	4
8.	1888/02/09. Richard Burton to Leonard Smithers.	4
9.	1888/—/—. Ouida to Isabel Burton.	5
10.	1888/03/04. Richard Burton to John Payne.	6
11.	1888/06/14. Isabel Burton to Ouida.	6
12.	1888/06/14. Richard Burton to Ouida.	7
13.	1888/07/18. Richard Burton to the *New York Herald*............	8
14.	1888/07/22. Richard Burton to Leonard Smithers.	9
15.	1888/07/27. Richard Burton to Leonard Smithers.	10
16.	1888/08/08. Richard Burton to Leonard Smithers.	10
17.	1888/08/13. Richard Burton to A. G. Ellis............................	11
18.	1888/08/18. Richard Burton to A. G. Ellis............................	12
19.	1888/08/22. Richard Burton to Leonard Smithers.	12
20.	1888/09/20. Richard Burton to H. S. Ashbee.......................	13
21.	1888/09/26. Richard Burton to John Payne.	13
22.	1888/09/30. Richard Burton to Leonard Smithers.	14
23.	1888/10/20. Richard Burton to Leonard Smithers.	14
24.	1888/10/22. Richard Burton to Leonard Smithers.	15
25.	1888. A. H. Sayce..	16
26.	1888. Verney Lovett Cameron.	16
27.	1888-1890. Harold Nicolson.	17
28.	1888-1890. George Bainton.	17
29.	1888/10/25. Isabel Burton to Lynn Linton............................	19
30.	1888/11/04. Richard Burton to Leonard Smithers.	19
31.	1888/11/04. Richard Burton to Colonel Chaillé-Long.	20
32.	1888/11/08. Richard Burton to John Payne.	21
33.	1888/11/14. Richard Burton to Leonard Smithers.	21
34.	1888/11/21. Richard Burton to John Payne.	22
35.	1888/12/02. Richard Burton to Leonard Smithers.	23
36.	1888/12/24. Richard Burton to Leonard Smithers.	23
37.	1889/01/31. Richard Burton to Leonard Smithers.	24
38.	1889/02/17. Richard Burton to Leonard Smithers.	25
39.	1889/04/03. Richard Burton to Leonard Smithers.	26
40.	1889/05/01. Richard Burton to Leonard Smithers.	27
41.	1889/05/08. Richard Burton To A. G. Ellis.	28

#	Date	Description	Page
42.	1889/05/08.	Richard Burton to H. S. Ashbee.	28
43.	1889/05/13.	Richard Burton to Leonard Smithers.	29
44.	1889/05/22.	Richard Burton to Leonard Smithers.	30
45.	1889/06/02.	Richard Burton to Leonard Smithers.	31
46.	1889/06/26.	Richard Burton to Leonard Smithers.	32
47.	1889/07/11.	Richard Burton to Leonard Smithers.	35
48.	1889/08/29.	Richard Burton to Leonard Smithers.	35
49.	1889/09/13.	Richard Burton to Leonard Smithers.	36
50.	1889/11/14.	Richard Burton to Leonard Smithers.	37
51.	1889/11/17.	Richard Burton to Leonard Smithers.	37
52.	1889/11/20.	Richard Burton to Leonard Smithers.	39
53.	1889/12/11.	Richard Burton to Leonard Smithers.	40
54.	1889/12/20.	Richard Burton to Leonard Smithers.	41
55.	1890/01/08.	Richard Burton to Leonard Smithers.	42
56.	1890/01/16.	Richard Burton to Leonard Smithers.	43
57.	1890/01/28.	Richard Burton to A. W. Thayer.	44
58.	1890/01/28.	Richard Burton to John Payne.	45
59.	1890/02/07.	Richard Burton to Leonard Smithers.	46
60.	1890/02/12.	Richard Burton to A. B. Ellis.	47
61.	1890/02/20.	Richard Burton to Leonard Smithers.	48
62.	1890/03/05.	Richard Burton to Leonard Smithers.	50
63.	1890/03/26.	Richard Burton to A. B. Ellis.	51
64.	1890/05/10.	Richard Burton to Leonard Smithers.	52
65.	1890/05/11.	Richard Burton to Leonard Smithers.	53
66.	1890/05/12.	Richard Burton to Leonard Smithers.	53
67.	1890/05/15.	Richard Burton to Leonard Smithers.	54
68.	1890/05/—.	Richard Burton to John Payne.	54
69.	1890/05/19.	Richard Burton to Leonard Smithers.	55
70.	1880/05/20.	Richard Burton to Leonard Smithers.	55
71.	1890/05/28.	Richard Burton to Leonard Smithers.	56
72.	1890/06/18.	Richard Burton to Leonard Smithers.	57
73.	1890/06/26.	James Augustus Grant to Sir Samuel Baker.	58
74.	1890/06/26.	Richard Burton to Leonard Smithers.	59
75.	1890/07/15.	Richard Burton to Leonard Smithers.	60
76.	1890/08/03.	Richard Burton to A. W. Thayer.	61
77.	1890/08/08.	Henry Morton Stanley.	62
78.	1890/08/08.	Squire Bancroft.	63
79.	1890/08/15.	J. A. Symonds to Richard F. Burton.	63
80.	1890/08/18.	Richard F. Burton to J. A. Symonds.	64
81.	1890/08/27.	Richard Burton to Leonard Smithers.	65
82.	1890/09/03.	Isabel Burton to the Morning Post.	66
83.	1890/09/08.	Richard Burton to Leonard Smithers.	68
84.	1890/09/09.	Richard Burton to Colonel Chaillé-Long.	69
85.	1890/09/20.	Colonel Chaillé-Long.	70
86.	1890/09/24.	Richard Burton to Leonard Smithers.	71
87.	1890/10/04.	Richard Burton to Leonard Smithers.	72

88.	1890/10/19. Richard Burton to Leonard Smithers.	73

1890-1924 Posthumous 75

89.	1890/10/25. James Augustus Grant to *The Times*.	75
90.	1890/11/01. Sporting Truth.	76
91.	1890/11/02. G. W. Smalley.	78
92.	1890/11/29. John James Aubertin.	82
93.	1890. Francis Galton.	83
94.	1890. Verney Lovett Cameron.	84
95.	1890. Edwin de Leon.	88
96.	1890/—/—. Isabel Burton to A. W. Thayer.	94
97.	1891/04/11. Isabel Burton to Colonel Chaillé-Long.	94
98.	1891. Georgiana Stisted.	95
99.	1892/04/06. Isabel Burton to A. W. Thayer.	96
100.	1892. Albert Leighton Rawson.	97
101.	1892/11. Isabel Burton in *The New Review*.	115
102.	1893/06/05. Isabel Burton to A. W. Thayer.	130
103.	1893/12/30. Isabel Burton to Lady Paget.	131
104.	1894/01/05. Isabel Burton to A. W. Thayer.	134
105.	1894/05. John Theodore Tussaud.	135
106.	1895/09/27. Isabel Burton to A. W. Thayer.	137
107.	1890-1896. Edward Clodd.	138
108.	1890-1896. Augustus John Cuthbert Hare.	139
109.	1896/01/08. Isabel Burton to Lady Paget.	140
110.	1896/05. Raymond Blathwayt.	141
111.	1896. Bernard Quaritch.	144
112.	1896/12/09. W. J. Eames to the Editor of The Standard.	145
113.	1897. Eliza Lynn Linton to Georgiana Stisted.	145
114.	1898. Herbert Jones.	146
115.	1898. John Payne.	152
116.	1900. William Tinsley.	152
117.	1904. Sir Clements Robert Markham.	156
118.	1906. Ouida.	156
119.	1907. Richard Patrick Boyle Davey.	162
120.	1908? Francis Galton.	163
121.	1919. John Payne via Thomas Wright.	164
122.	1920. David Scull Bispham.	166
123.	1921. Archibald Henry Sayce.	167
124.	1921. Dr. Frederick Grenfell Baker.	168
125.	1922. Earl of Dunraven.	179
126.	1923. Lady Walburga Paget.	180
127.	1924. Luke Ionides.	180

Chronology 185

Register: A-J 198

128.	Abraham, Walter.	198

129.	Adye, Major-General Sir John (1819-1900).	199
130.	Arbuthnot, Forster Fitzgerald (1833-1901).	199
131.	Arnold, Julian Tregenna Biddulph (1860-1945?).	201
132.	Ashbee, Charles Robert (1863-1842).	202
133.	Ashbee, Henry Spencer (1834-1900)	202
134.	Ashby-Sterry, Joseph (1838-1917).	203
135.	Aubertin, John James (1818-1900).	204
136.	Austin, Richard (1832-1899).	204
137.	Babington, William.	204
138.	Back, Sir George (1796–1878).	205
139.	Badger, George Percy (1815-1888).	205
140.	Bainton, George (1847-1925).	206
141.	Baker, Frederick Grenfell (1853-1930).	206
142.	Baker, Martha Beckwith (1797?-1854.xii.10).	207
143.	Baker, Richard (1762-1824.ix.16).	207
144.	Baker, Sir Samuel White (1821-1893).	208
145.	Bancroft, Squire (1841-1926).	208
146.	Barth, Heinrich (1821-1865)	208
147.	Barnard, Charles Inman (1850-1942).	209
148.	Bates, Henry Walter (1825-1892).	209
149.	Bellamy, Henry Edward Vaux (1837?-1889).	209
150.	Bispham, David Scull (1857-1921).	211
151.	Bird, Alice "Lallah" (?-1921).	211
152.	Bird, Dr. George (1817-1900).	211
153.	Blunt, Wilfrid Scawen (1840-1922).	213
154.	Blumhardt, James Fuller (?-1922).	214
155.	Blackwood, John (1818-1879)	215
156.	Brassey, Anna Allnutt (1839–1887).	215
157.	Buckley-Mathew, Sir George Benvenuto (1807-1879).	215
158.	Burke, Luke (?-1885).	215
159.	Burton, Isabel (1831-1896).	216
160.	Burnand, Sir Francis Cowley (1836-1917).	217
161.	Burton, Edmund (1737.iv.04-1817).	217
162.	Burton, Edward (1747.iii.10-1794).	218
163.	Burton, Edward Joseph Netterville (1824-1895).	218
164.	Burton, Joseph Netterville (1782?-1857)	220
165.	Bushe, Charles Percy (1829-1898).	221
166.	Butler, Alfred Joshua (1850-1936).	221
167.	Butterworth, Alan (1864-1937).	221
168.	Cameron, Verney Lovett (1844-1894)	222
169.	Cautley, Philip Proby.	222
170.	Chaillé-Long, Charles (1842-1917).	222
171.	Clodd, Edward (1840-1930).	223
172.	Clouston, William Alexander (1843-1896).	223
173.	Coghlan, William Marcus (1803-1885)	224
174.	Coimbra, Dr. Augusto Teixeira	224

175.	Coke, Henry John (1827-1916).	224
176.	Colquhoun, Archibald Ross (1848–1914).	225
177.	Crane, Walter (1845-1915).	225
178.	Davenport, The Brothers.	225
179.	Davey, Richard Patrick Boyle (1848-1915).	225
180.	Dawson, Llewellyn Styles (1847-1921).	226
181.	De Kusel, Samuel Selig (1848-1917).	226
182.	De Leon, Edwin (1818–1891).	226
183.	Dennis, George (1814-1898).	226
184.	De Ruvignes, Charles Henry Theodore Bruce (1829-1883)	227
185.	De Ruvigny.	227
186.	Didier, Charles (1805-1864).	227
187.	Doughty, Charles Montagu (1843-1926).	227
188.	Drake, Charles Francis Tyrwhitt (1846–1874).	228
189.	Du Chaillu, Paul Belloni (1835-1902).	228
190.	Dunraven, Earl of.	229
191.	Eames, William. James.	229
192.	Edwards, Henry Sutherland (1828-1906).	229
193.	Edwards, John Passmore (1823-1911).	229
194.	Eldridge, George Jackson (1826-?).	230
195.	Elliot, Sir Henry (1817-1907).	230
196.	Ellis, Alexander George (1858-1942).	230
197.	Erhardt, Rev. Johann Jakob (1823-1901).	231
198.	Faber, George Louis (1843-1915).	231
199.	Fahie, John Joseph (1846-1934).	231
200.	Ferguson, Sir Samuel (1810-1886).	231
201.	Freeman, Edward August (1823-1892).	232
202.	Friswell, James Hain (1825-1878).	232
203.	Friswell, Laura (1850-1908).	232
204.	Furniss, Harry (1854-1925).	232
205.	Galton, Sir Francis (1822-1911).	233
206.	Geary, Grattan (?-1900).	233
207.	Gerard, Cécile Jules Basile (1817-1864).	233
208.	Gessi, Romolo (1831-1881).	233
209.	Gordon, Major-General Charles George (1833–1885).	234
210.	Grant, James Augustus (1827-1892).	234
211.	Granville, Earl (1815–1891).	234
212.	Graves-Sawle, Lady (1818-1914).	235
213.	Hale, Richard Walden (1871-1943).	235
214.	Hamerton, Atkins (1804-1857).	235
215.	Hamilton, James "Abbé" (?-1868).	236
216.	Hankey, Frederick (1821-1882).	237
217.	Hare, Augustus John Cuthbert (1834-1903).	243
218.	Harris, Frank (1856-1931).	243
219.	Herne, George Edward (1822?-1902).	243
220.	Hockley, Frederick (1809-1885).	243

221.	Hodgson, Colonel Studholme (1805-1890).	244
222.	Hooker, William Jackson (1785-1865).	252
223.	Hooker, Joseph Dalton (1817-1911).	252
224.	Hunt, George Samuel Lennon.	252
225.	Hutchinson, Thomas Joseph (1820-1885).	252
226.	Hyndman, Henry Mayers (1842-1921).	253
227.	Ionides, Luke (1837–1924).	253
228.	Iturburu, Atilano Calvo.	253
229.	James, Frank Linsly (1851-1890).	253
230.	Johnston, Sir Harry (1858-1927).	254
231.	Jones, Herbert (?–1928).	254

Portraits 255

Register: K-Z 272

232.	Kingsford, Anna Bonus (1846-1888).	272
233.	Kirby, William Forsell (1844-1912).	272
234.	Kirk, John (1832-1922).	272
235.	Kirkwood, Roy.	273
236.	Krapf, Johann Ludwig (1810-1881).	273
237.	Larking, John Wingfield (1801-1891).	274
238.	Laughland, Edward.	274
239.	Leighton, Frederic (1830-1896).	277
240.	Levant Herald.	278
241.	Leveson, Henry Astbury (1828-1875).	278
242.	Lynslager, James (1810-1864).	278
243.	Mackenzie, Kenneth Robert Henderson (1833-1886).	279
244.	Mann, Gustav (1836–1916).	279
245.	Markham, Sir Clements Robert (1830-1916).	280
246.	Martin, Sir James Ranald FRS (1796-1874).	280
247.	Massey, Gerald (1828-1907).	280
248.	McCarthy, Edward Thomas (1856?–1943).	281
249.	McCarthy, Justin (1830–1912).	281
250.	McCarthy, Justin Huntly (1859-1936).	282
251.	Milnes, Monckton (Lord Houghton) (1809-1885).	282
252.	Mitchell, Roland Lyon Nosworthy (1847-1931).	283
253.	Mitford, Bertram (Lord Redesdale) (1837-1916).	284
254.	Mohl, Mary Elizabeth (1793-1883).	284
255.	Money, Edward James (1822-1889).	284
256.	Moore, Noel Temple (1833-1903).	285
257.	Murchison, Sir Roderick FRS (1792-1871).	285
258.	Murray, Rear-Admiral Henry Anthony (1810-1865).	285
259.	Nichols, Harry Sidney (1865-1941?).	286
260.	Nicolson, Harold (1886-1968).	286
261.	Neville, Amelia Ransome (1837-1927).	286
262.	Notcutt, Oliver.	287
263.	Orton, Arthur (the 'Tichborne Claimant') (1834-1898).	287

264.	Ouida (Marie Louise de la Ramée) (1839-1908).	287
265.	Outram, Sir James (1803-1863).	287
266.	Paget, Lady Walburga (1839-1929).	288
267.	Palgrave, William Gifford (1826-1888).	288
268.	Parkinson, Joseph Charles (1833-1908).	289
269.	Paull, George (1837-1865).	289
270.	Payne, John (1842-1916).	289
271.	Quaritch, Bernard (1819-1899).	290
272.	Rashid Pasha, Mehmet (?-1876).	290
273.	Rathborne, Anthony Blake (1811?-1885).	290
274.	Rawson, Albert Leighton (1829-1902).	292
275.	Reade, William Winwood (1838-1875).	293
276.	Rebmann, Johannes (1820-1876).	294
277.	Rhys, Ernest Percival (1859-1946).	295
278.	Ricci, Dr. Hermann Robert (R. H. R.).	296
279.	Richards, Alfred Bate (1820-1876).	296
280.	Rigby, Christopher Palmer (1820-1885).	297
281.	Roscher, Dr. Albrecht (1836-1860).	301
282.	Rossetti, Dante Gabriel (1828-1882).	302
283.	Russell, Katherine Louisa (1844-1874).	302
284.	Russell, Lord John, Viscount Amberley (1842-1876).	303
285.	Russell, Odo William Leopold (1829-1884).	303
286.	Saker, Rev. Alfred (1814-1880).	304
287.	Sartoris, Adelaide Kemble (1815-1879).	304
288.	Sayce, Archibald Henry (1845-1933).	304
289.	Schroeder, Seaton (1849-1922).	305
290.	Schweinfurth, Georg August (1836-1925).	305
291.	Scully, William (?-1885).	305
292.	Seymour, Walter Richard (1838-1922).	305
293.	Seymour, Sir Edward Hobart (1840-1929).	306
294.	Shand, Alexander Innes (1832-1907).	306
295.	Shaw, Dr. Henry Norton (?-1868).	306
296.	Shelley, Major Edward (1827-1890).	307
297.	Shepheard, Samuel (1816-1866).	308
298.	Sheridan, Richard Brinsley (1806?-1888).	308
299.	Skene, James Henry (1812-1886).	308
300.	Sladen, Douglas Brooke Wheelton (1856-1947).	309
301.	Smalley, George Washburn (1833-1916).	309
302.	Smith, Laura A.	309
303.	Smith, William Robertson (1846-1894).	309
304.	Smithers, Leonard (1861-1907).	310
305.	Soldene, Emily (1838-1912).	311
306.	Speke, John Hanning (1827-1864).	311
307.	Spencer, Walter Thomas (1863-1936).	315
308.	Stanley, Henry Morton (1841-1904).	315
309.	Steinhaüser, Dr. John Frederick (1814-1866).	316

310.	Stevenson, Frederick James (1835-1926).	317
311.	Stisted, Georgiana Martha (1846?-1903).	317
312.	Stocks, John Ellerton (1822-1854).	318
313.	Stoker, Abraham "Bram" (1847-1912).	319
314.	Stokes, Sir John (1825–1902).	320
315.	Stroyan, William (1825?-1855).	320
316.	Swinburne, Algernon (1837-1909).	320
317.	Sykes, Colonel William Henry (1790-1872).	326
318.	Thorndike, Rev. Charles Faunce (1821-1915).	327
319.	Tinsley, William (1831-1902).	327
320.	Tootal, Albert (1838?-1893).	328
321.	Tussaud, John Theodore (1858-1943).	328
322.	Vámbéry, Ármin (1832-1913).	329
323.	Viator.	329
324.	Villiers, Frederick (1851-1922).	330
325.	Vizetelly, Henry Richard (1820-1894).	330
326.	Whistler, James McNeill (1834-1903).	330
327.	Wilson, Charles Rivers (1831-1916).	331
328.	Wilson, Frank.	331
329.	Wood, Sir Charles (1800–1885).	332
330.	Wright, William [Salih] (1837-1899).	332
331.	Wylde, William Henry (1819-1909).	333

Sources **334**
    Archives 334
    Microfilms 335
    Electronic Collections. 335

Bibliography **336**
    Books by Richard Burton 336
    Books by Isabel Burton 338
    Auction Catalogues 338
    General 339

Plates **342**
    Miscellaneous 342
    The East African Expedition. 348
    Trieste.   371

Credits **386**

Index to Authors and Correspondents **388**

List of Illustrations

Figure 1. Wilfrid Scawen Blunt	255
Figure 2. Dr. F. Grenfell Baker.	255
Figure 3. Samuel Selig de Kusel.	256
Figure 4. Earl of Dunraven.	256
Figure 5. Frank Wilson.	257
Figure 6. James Hain Friswell.	257
Figure 7. Joseph Dalton Hooker.	258
Figure 8. Sir Harry Johnston.	259
Figure 9. Colonel Chaillé Long.	259
Figure 10. Edward Thomas McCarthy.	260
Figure 11. Justin McCarthy.	260
Figure 12. The Tichborne Claimant.	261
Figure 13. Ouida.	261
Figure 14. Albert Leighton Rawson.	262
Figure 15. Algernon Swinburne.	262
Figure 16. Frederick James Stevenson.	263
Figure 17. Cecil John Rhodes and protégés, including Alex. Colquhoun.	264
Figure 18. Gustav Mann.	264
Figure 19. Julian Arnold.	265
Figure 20. Armin Vambery.	265
Figure 21. John Passmore Edwards.	266
Figure 22. Verney Lovett Cameron	266
Figure 23. Verney Lovett Cameron.	267
Figure 24. Francis Galton.	267
Figure 25. Lord Houghton (Monckton Milnes).	268
Figure 26. John Hanning Speke.	269
Figure 27. Lord Redesdale (Bertram Mitford).	270
Figure 28. Charles Francis Tyrwhitt Drake.	270
Figure 29. Dr. Norton Shaw of the RGS.	271
Figure 30. Sporting Truth.	342
Figure 31. Allen's Indian Mail Dec. 6th 1843.	343
Figure 32. Calling Card of H. S. Ashbee.	343
Figure 33. Mining Concession granted to Burton and Teixeira.	344
Figure 34. Speke Memorial Fund.	345
Figure 35. The Burton Exhibit at Madame Tussaud's.	346
Figure 36. Axim from the Gold Coast.	347
Figure 37: Illustration by Albert Letchford to Burton's Arabian Nights.	347
Figure 38. Zanzibar Town from the Sea.	348
Figure 39. Fuga, sketched by Burton.	348
Figure 40. Pangany Falls, sketched by Burton.	349
Figure 41. Pemba Island, sketched by Burton.	350
Figure 42. Mombas, sketched by Burton.	350
Figure 43. Shamba, sketched by Burton.	351
Figure 44. The Town of Wasim, sketched by Burton.	351
Figure 45. Fort of Tongway, sketched by Burton.	351
Figure 46. The Hills of Usumbara, sketched by Burton.	352
Figure 47. East Coast Scene, sketched by Burton.	352
Figure 48. A 'Savage of the Nyika', sketched by Burton.	353
Figure 49. The Ivory Porter.	354
Figure 50. Party of Wak'Hutu Women.	354
Figure 51. The Wazaramo Tribe.	355
Figure 52. A Village in Khutu. The Silk Cotton Tree.	356

Figure 53. Sycamore in the Dhun of Ugogi. 356
Figure 54. Explorers in East Africa. 357
Figure 55. The East African Ghauts. 357
Figure 56. Majiya W'heta, or the Jetting Fountain in K'hutu. 358
Figure 57. Ugogo. 358
Figure 58. Usagara Mountains, seen from Ugogo. 359
Figure 59. View in Unyamwezi. 359
Figure 60. Ladies' Smoking Party. 360
Figure 61. African House Building. 361
Figure 62. Land of the Moon. Loom and public house. 361
Figure 63. Navigation on the Tanganyika Lake. 362
Figure 64. View in Usagara. 362
Figure 65. My Tembe near the Tanganyika. 363
Figure 66. Head Dresses of Wanyamwezi. 363
Figure 67. African Types. 364
Figure 68. Snay Bin Amir's House. 365
Figure 69. Saydumi. a Native of Uganda. 365
Figure 70. Mgongo Thembo, or the Elephant's Back. 366
Figure 71. Jiwe la Mkoa, the Round Rock. 366
Figure 72. The Basin of Maroro. 367
Figure 73. The Basin of Kisanga. 367
Figure 74. Rufita Pass in Usagara. 368
Figure 75. The Ivory Porter, the Cloth Porter, and Woman, in Usagara. 368
Figure 76. African Implements. 369
Figure 77. Gourds. 369
Figure 78. A Mnyamwezi (l). A Mhela (r). 370
Figure 79. The Bull-headed Mabruki (l). African Standing Position (r). 370
Figure 80. Elephant Rock. 370
Figure 81. Burton, Baker, and Isabel at Folkestone, 1888. 371
Figure 82. Burton at work in his study, Villa Gosleth, Trieste. 372
Figure 83. Isabel at work, Villa Gosleth, Trieste. 372
Figure 84. Isabel, F. F. Arbuthnot and RFB in the garden, Villa Gosleth, Trieste. 373
Figure 85. Isabel talking to Richard in the Garden, Villa Gosleth, Trieste. 373
Figure 86. In the Garden, near the end. Villa Gosleth, Trieste. 374
Figure 87: Burton on his death bed. 375
Figure 88. Death mask and casts of Burton. 376
Figure 89. The Wake in Villa Gosleth. 376
Figure 90. The Smoking Divan in Villa Gosleth, Trieste, by Albert Letchford. 377
Figure 91. Room in Villa Gosleth, Trieste, by Albert Letchford. 378
Figure 92. Isabel Burton's Study in Villa Gosleth, by Albert Letchford. 379
Figure 93. Isabel Burton's Bedroom in Villa Gosleth, by Albert Letchford. 379
Figure 94. View of the Bay of Trieste from Villa Gosleth, by Albert Letchford. 380
Figure 95. Villa Gosleth, Trieste, scene by Albert Letchford. 380
Figure 96. View from Villa Gosleth, Trieste, by Albert Letchford. 380
Figure 97. View of the Bay of Trieste by Albert Letchford. 381
Figure 98. Burton, Letchford, and Isabel in the Dining Room at Trieste. 381
Figure 99. Alternative view of the dining room, with Burton, Letchford and Isabel. 381
Figure 100. Drawing Room, Villa Gosleth, Trieste. 382
Figure 101. The study, Villa Gosleth, Trieste. 383
Figure 102. Villa Gosleth, Trieste, in the 1830s, from an old print. 383
Figure 103. Burton in the 1880s. 384
Figure 104. Portrait of Burton by Madame de Benvenuti, Trieste, 1879. 385

1887–1890

1. 1887. Anna Bonus Kingsford via Edward Maitland.[1]

Anxiously sought information as to the best place to which to take her, consulting many persons and books. Egypt stood first with most authorities, Algiers next. But even about Algiers opinions varied greatly, one writer stating that he had lived there twenty-eight years, and had known twenty-eight exceptional winters, so unreliable was the climate. A visit paid us by Sir Richard and Lady Burton enabled me to consult him, when I found him a complete encyclopedia, and able to speak of most places from personal experience. Cairo he pronounced to have been spoilt for really delicate persons by its defective system of drainage: and only in the desert was pure air to be found. Pau, Tunis, Tangiers, and the Riviera all came under his ban. He most favoured Tenerife.

2. 1887/01/10. Richard Burton to John Payne.[2]

Address Athenaeum

Jan 10 1887

Private

My dear Payne

That last cup of tea came to grief. I ran away from London abruptly feeling a hippopotamus gradually creep over my brain, longing to see a sight of the sun and so forth. We shall cross over next Thursday (if the weather prove decent) and rush up to Paris where I shall have some few days' work in the Bib. Nation. There to Cannes, the Riviera etc.

At the end of my 5th vol. (supplemental) I shall walk into Edinb. Review the […] and the old ruffian Reeve.[3] You would do me a kindness if you would jot down in brief the gross blunders of the article &c. to show me that we both agree. Of course the move will be kept private.

I hope that you like Vol X and its notices of your works. I always speak of it in the same terms, always with the same appreciation and admiration. My wife joins me in kindest regards and best wishes, hoping to find you all fit next Spring, say April with the Chelidons[4]

---

[1] Edward Maitland *Life of Anna Kingsford* Part 2 (London: George Redway, 1896) p. 300.
[2] Huntington Library, Box 26, RFB 313. Postcard. Handwritten copy of MS by Thomas Wright. The location of the original MS is not known.
[3] Henry Reeve, editor of *The Edinburgh Review*.
[4] C. Urbanus, the House Martin, which winters abroad. Chelidon is Greek for

R.F.B.

3. 1887/05/08. Richard Burton to A. G. Ellis.[1]

Trieste May 8 '87

Excuse post card. The "Perfumed Garden" is not yet out nor will be for 6 months. The old version is to be had at Robson & Kerslake Coventry St Haymarket.[2] The Supplementary Nights you can procure from the agent Mr. O. Notcutt 4 Fairholt Road, Stoke Newington, London.[3] Many thanks: I am getting better and hope soon to be in full blast of work.[4]

R.F.B.

4. 1887/05/27. Richard Burton to Leonard Smithers.[5]

Trieste May 27 [/87[6]]

My dear Sir

I waited, before acknowledging yours of May 17, the receipt of the two volumes of Mickle's "Lusiad."[7] It came yesterday and is an excellent copy, for which you have my grateful thanks! I suppose you have found that missing vol. of Chavis and Cazotte (Heron's transl.)?[8] I propose to include ~~all~~ most of these tales in my Suppl. Vols. but they will be translated directly from the Arab. MS. in the Bibliotheque Nat^l Paris of which I have had a copy made. Repeating my thanks to you I am ev yrs faithfully

R. F. Burton

5. 1887/09/14. Richard Burton to A. G. Ellis.[9]

Sauerbrunn Rohitsch[10]

---

swallow.

[1] Royal Asiatic Society. RB 1/1/1. See the Register for Ellis.
[2] Booksellers.
[3] See Register for Oliver Notcutt.
[4] Burton was still recovering from his stroke and heart attack at Cannes in February.
[5] Huntington Library. ALS MS.
[6] Pencil annotation.
[7] William Julius Mickle *The Lusiad; or, the Discovery of India* (London, 1776).
[8] Dom (Denis) Chavis and Jacques Cazotte *Arabian tales : being a continuation of the Arabian nights entertainments, consisting of one thousand and one stories* translated from the French into English by Robert Heron (Edinburgh : G. Mudie, 1792; 4 volumes).
[9] Royal Asiatic Society RB 1/1/2.
[10] Hot springs in the Eastern Alps, in present-day Slovenia.

(direction Trieste)
Sept. 14

Dear Sir

You have been very kind and so has Mr. Kirby[1] in taking so much trouble about Scott's tale and I return you my best thanks. It must probably be sought in the Bodleian Library and the question must keep until my return to Town next spring.

Could you kindly tell me Mr. Blumhardt's[2] Christian name or names? A post card will do. I must quote him in my Supplem. vol. iii and do not want to betray any special ignorance.

Salute for me Mr. Bendall[3] and tell him how happy I shall be to see him at Trieste if he pass through that very foul port.

Again thanking you for your kindness I am

yours vy sincy
R. F. Burton

A.G. Ellis Esq.

6. 1888. Walter Thomas Spencer.[4]

Aubrey Beardsley came to my shop for the first time about the year 1890, before he was much known. He was such an extraordinary-looking man, exactly like the signed photograph hanging in my parlour, that I could not help wondering for long who he was. Then came an occasion on which he made a purchase and asked me to put the volume on one side for him, and at last I knew his name. Later on he suggested that he might illustrate a book for me to publish.

In those days Beardsley's beautiful decorative work was, I thought, a revelation in art. His later output, that with which everyone is familiar, was entirely different. He had come under the influence of Smithers—and, I must add, Sir Richard Burton.

About 1888 Sir Richard Burton was a frequent visitor to my shop, and I learned a good deal about what he called his "Yellow Breakfasts," held once a week at his rooms, close to my shop. Merry gatherings they seem to have been, and the guests generally included, I think, Swinburne and Whistler, Wilde and Beardsley. The gathering would have spent the night at some club or another, playing cards and drinking. Then they

---

[1] W. F. Kirby, see Register.
[2] James Fuller Blumhardt see Register.
[3] Cecil Bendall (1856–1906) of the Oriental Manuscripts Department of the British Museum (1882-1893). Later Professor of Sanskrit, first at University College London (1895-1902), then at Cambridge (1903-1906).
[4] Walter T. Spencer *Forty Years in My Bookshop* (London: Constable, 1923) pp. 245-6.

would adjourn at dawn to Burton's for breakfast.

Mr. Watts-Dunton told me that it was from this circle that he rescued Swinburne when he took him away to Putney. "Why," exclaimed Watts-Dunton, "the man couldn't drink more than three brandies without going under the table!" Sir Richard Burton told me that it was at one of these parties that Whistler first saw Oscar Wilde. "Who is this damned young Irishman?" he asked in a loud voice while he adjusted his monocle.

7. 1888/01/16. Charles Montagu Doughty to Richard Burton.[1]

Casa Napier [Alamo] 16 Jan

Dear Sir R^d Burton

Many thanks for your note especially when as I see you are very full of work. The 2 vols. <u>Arabia Deserta</u> will be pub^d by the Cambridge Univ^y Press this week & I hope may be almost immediately in your hands for the <u>Academy</u>, as the Editor wished me to send them on to you direct. I think you ask "what I would have particularly noticed in them?" I prefer to have them, without notes or comments, in your distinguished and generous hands. They are not only a [Journal] record but I believe will be new to Orientalists, though not perhaps to you as I know you once purposed to travel in Nejd.

Truly yours C. M. D.

The British Post Office in Beyrouth will find me for a year to come.

8. 1888/02/09. Richard Burton to Leonard Smithers.[2]

Hotel des Alpes Montreux
Feb. 9 [/88[3]]

Dear Mr. Smithers

I return with many thanks The Old Man letter-post, registered: please let me have a line acknowledging receipt, as such things are sometimes lost. See p. 3 within [p...] is for [principum]—Haykun 'l Sádát. In p. 7 I cannot understand the note ["alter aquam ..."] etc. The MS. is probably the work of a non-English writer, and the translation would have to be thoroughly changed before making an appearance in public.

I have two copies of the Arabic, one printed and one other litho'd;

---

[1] Huntington Library. Rare Books, 635407. Enclosure in Burton's copy of C. M. Doughty, *Travels in Arabia Deserta*. See also Kirkpatrick (1978), 1954, where the date is given as "10 Jan."
[2] Huntington Library. ALS MS.
[3] Pencil annotation.

and shall probably apply parts of it as notes to the S. Garden,[1] only I begin to fear an embarras de richesses.[2]

We have had here a still, quiet, foggy winter, but now horrid [...] has come down upon us just as the birds & the buds were expecting spring. Snow everywhere and no sign of St. Valentine. I am tired of the place and next Friday (15th) shall transfer myself to Lausanne (Hotel Gibbon) and after a week begin my return march for Trieste, arriving there early in March. With many thanks for the use of the MS., I am ever

Yours sincy
R. F. Burton

9. 1888/—/—. Ouida to Isabel Burton.[3]

Dear Friend

It is sweet of you to remember me. Our interview in London was too brief, & not a tete-tête. My talk with the Sheik was longer. I did not leave London till May but heard nothing more of you. I have really been doing nothing since then; and writing nothing except lines on Matthew Arnold[4] of which I send you a copy.

The Spring here is glorious after the winter's copious rains. I have had the pleasure of having the Windsors[5] here four months & Lady Paget three weeks. I think they will buy some place. I enjoyed England as a woman always enjoys a place where she is flattered and fêté—but life here is much more graceful, [parlée] and open to the impressions of Nature. Each existence is good for one in its turn but this [...[6]].

I am grieved the Tories have not more liberality of feeling towards you and appreciation of genius & originality in their treatment of so great

---

[1] Scented Garden.
[2] *The Perfumed Garden of the Cheikh Nefzaoui, A Manual of Arabian Erotology.* Burton had already issued a translation (from a French version) in 1886 and was working on a new and direct translation from Arabic sources, with extensive ethnological annotations in the style of the *Arabian Nights*, and an additional chapter on pederasty. This was eventually completed in 1890 but never published, and burnt by Isabel after his death.
[3] QK Collection, British Library. Add MS 88876 f. 121-128, 136-138. ALS MS fragment.
[4] Arnold had died on the 15th of April that year. See Elizabeth Lee *Ouida: a Memoir* (London: Unwin, 1914) pp.135ff for the verses on Arnold, which run "O Kai ! Thy master follows thee / Into the dread eternal night; / He whose fair hope and aim was light / Has sunk beneath the moonless sea." etc. Kai was one of Arnold's dachshunds.
[5] Lady Windsor, daughter of Lady Paget.
[6]

a scholar & traveller as the Sheik.[1] England has never even faintly comprehended the treasure she possessed in his vast and uncommon powers.[2]

10. 1888/03/04. Richard Burton to John Payne.[3]

Trieste Mar 14 '88

My dear Payne

I have been moving since yours of March 5 reached me and unable to answer you. Why? Because I had a copy of Zayn[4] etc., but it has been lost or mislaid or something and I have looked over a […] of papers in vain. I shall not forget it and will forward it if it turns up. But if you cannot wait my friend M. Hermann Zotenberg (Bib. Nation. Paris) will readily provide you another.

Delighted to hear that in spite of cramp Vol V Bandello[5] is finished and shall look forward to the secret being revealed. You are quite right never to say a word about it. There is nothing I abhor so much as a man entrusting me with a secret.

By the by a correspondent from New York who has every means of learning assures me that both your Nights and mine are admitted at the usual rate and although your 1st Vol was subjected to trouble &c that is now over. Is this good news?

My wife joins me in kindest regards

Ever yrs sincy

R. F. B.

11. 1888/06/14. Isabel Burton to Ouida.[6]

Grand Hotel Aigle Vaud
La Suisse
June 14/88

Dear Ouida

Thanks for your nice letter. Will you send the lines on Matthew Arnold here. The reason you did not see me after that one visit was, that I left London for good 2 days later, & have never been back I left on 5

---

[1] RFB.
[2] Subsequent MS text is missing.
[3] Huntington Library, Box 26, RFB 313. Postcard. Handwritten copy of MS by Thomas Wright. The location of the original MS is not known.
[4] Zayn Al-Asnam.
[5] Matteo Bandello (1480?-1652), whose novels were translated by Payne. Bandello wrote Giulietta e Romeo.
[6] QK Collection, British Library. Add MS 88876 f. 121-128, 136-138. ALS MS.

men's money.

The Administrator goes home fully resolved to state the facts uncompromisingly before the public of Great Britain, but, although the Administrator is an honest man, the influence of mediocre society ideas came trooping back into his brain, and so far from stating the fact, he stands up and declares that the missionaries are the cream of creation and the gospel is overspreading the land, while, if he mentions Islam, it is in a patronizing tone, as if the Mohammedans were mere cooks. This allows the unfortunate public no chance of learning the truth.

The narrator must be honest and honourable, but he dare not state the facts, nor has he the courage of his own opinions. If he did society would turn upon him with its usual, "Oh, we never mention him," and his name never would be heard unless accompanied by a snarl or sneer. The fact is, England's chronic disease is religiosity in the few and hypocrisy in the many.

RICHARD F. BURTON.
Hotel Meurice, Paris, July 18th, 1888.

14. 1888/07/22. Richard Burton to Leonard Smithers.[1]

St. James Hotel Piccadilly London
July 22 [1888[2]]

Dear Mr. Smithers

Yesterday I received your kind present. The "sketches" will be useful to me by reason of their date and I shall often want to quote from [Hoyland]. Have you seen our new Journal of the Gypsy Lore Soc.? Editor Mr. David MacRitchie, Archibald Place, Edinburgh?[3] I think it is going to be a success. Many thanks for informing me about Mr. Jacobs: today I will have a look at him and see whether punishment is required.[4]

---

[1] Huntington Library. ALS.

[2] Annotation in pencil.

[3] David MacRitchie (1851-1925) a folklorist and librarian, author of many books, including *Accounts of the Gypsies of India* (London: Kegan Paul, 1886), which has several references to Burton remarks on the Indian affinities of the Gypsies.

[4] Joseph Jacobs ed. *The Earliest English Version of the Fables of Bidpai* (London: David Nutt, 1888). Jacobs wrote "The prevalence of totemism is another proof of the intense interest of men in the hunting stage in the ways of animals, and if we may apply the inverse method and argue back from the infancy of the individual to the infancy of the race, we may notice that the 'gee-gee' and the 'bow-wow' are the first objects of interest to the little ones. Sir Richard Burton would even go further, and sees the essence of the beast-fable in 'a reminiscence of Homo primigenius with erected ears and hairy hide, and its expression is to make the brother brute to hear, think, and talk like him with the superadded experience of ages.' One hesitates to dissent

I am now hard at work with my Reviewers Reviewed which will contain some hard hitting.[1] Also, I am correcting Supp. Vol. VI and I have given Vol V over to the printers.

Yours very truly
R. F. Burton

Leonard C. Smithers Esq.

15. 1888/07/27. Richard Burton to Leonard Smithers.[2]

St. James Hotel Piccadilly
July 28 [27 1888[3]]

My dear Sir

I have failed to borrow Jacobs and don't want to buy him. Could you manage to lend it me for a couple of days as I want much to "whip" him.[4]

Yours very truly
R. F. Burton

Leonard C. Smithers Esq.

16. 1888/08/08. Richard Burton to Leonard Smithers.[5]

The Granville Ramsgate
August 8 [1888[6]]

My dear Sir

Many thanks for your kind letter of Augt 5. Romeike & Curtice who sent me the cutting give <u>June</u> 9; but they may be in error.[7] Mr. Clouston

---

from so great an authority as Sir R. Burton on all that relates to the bestial element in man …I owe this quotation and my knowledge of Sir R. Burton's views generally on this subject to an article by Mr. T. Davidson on 'Beast-Fables,' in the new edition of Chambers' Cyclopedia, which sums up admirably the present state of opinion on this subject, and a very confuted state it is. Mr. Davidson quotes section 3 of the notorious Terminal Essay of the Thousand Nights and a Night."

[1] "The Reviewers Reviewed" was published in the final volume of the *Supplemental Nights* (1888), which also reprinted Burton's rejoinder to Jacobs (see below).
[2] Huntington Library. ALS.
[3] Annotation in pencil.
[4] See 1888/07/22 above. Burton animadverted in *The Academy* (1888/08/11, p. 87) that Jacobs' remark was "uncalled for impertinence" by "this Maccabee", that his knowledge of Burton's views was entirely secondary, and that his work on Pilpay was "a little volume which, rendered useless by lack of notes and index, must advertise itself by the réclame of abuse".
[5] Huntington Library. ALS.
[6] Annotation in pencil.
[7] Henry Romeike operated a press clipping (monitoring) business on a

may not have written the ugly grumble; but it was necessary to contradict a false statement.[1] In my youth I served with Sir Charles Napier and learnt, from his career, never to be silent when the Press wants answering. I shall be glad to hear what you think of my "Reviewers Reviewed" which will end Vol. VI and the labour improves.

I shall be delighted to see the Priapeia, although some translation (French? or Italian?) was formerly known to me. And I will read without delay the "Turkish evening entertainments" if you can let me have them at once while we are here at Ramsgate.[2] We shall return to town (The Langham) on the 15th inst. Of course the Indexes etc. etc. will be in Vol VI, except in the case of those who decline going beyond Vol V.

Ramsgate is a fine place for air, much better, indeed, than Margate, and is doing both of us good after a feverish fortnight in London. With many thanks.

Yours very truly
R. F. Burton

P.S. I have this moment received yours of August 7 and of course accept Mr. Clouston's explanation. Sorry that you have had much trouble about the matter.

17. 1888/08/13. Richard Burton to A. G. Ellis.[3]

The Langham Portland Place
August 13

Dear Mr. Ellis

I have indented heavily upon your kindness by sending you Preface to my last Suppl. vol. and should be deeply obliged to you if you would run your eye over it and return it to this direction. You live in a magazine of learning where references are so easy and to us outsiders so difficult. Excuse this practical proof that need has no law and believe me ev

Yours very sincerely
R. F. Burton

P.S. Kirby has written to me from Hilden.[4] When will Blumhardt[5]

---

subscription basis.
[1] W. A. Clouston, see Register It is not clear what the "ugly grumble" referred to was.
[2] *Turkish evening entertainments: the wonders of remarkable incidents and the rarities of anecdotes by Ahmed ibn Hemdem the ketkhoda, called "Sohailee"*; translated from the Turkish by John P. Brown (New York: Putnam, 1850).
[3] Royal Asiatic Society RB 1/1/4.
[4] W. F. Kirby lived at "Hilden", Sutton Court Road, Chiswick, London. See Register.
[5] James Fuller Blumhardt, see Register.

return? My best regards to him.

18. 1888/08/18. Richard Burton to A. G. Ellis.[1]

Langham
Aug[t] 18[2]

Dear Mr. Ellis

One line to thank you for your kind corrections. Can you tell me if Brit. Mus. contains the Proverbes et Dictons de la Syrie par Carlo Landberg, Leide Brill & Co?[3]

Ev yrs
R. F. Burton

19. 1888/08/22. Richard Burton to Leonard Smithers.[4]

The Langham
Portland Place
August 22 [88[5]]

Dear Mr. Smithers

Today I return to your Sheffield direction the two volumes with many thanks. "Nile Notes" I read in '52 when it first came out.[6] The imitation of "Eothen" was then very distinct and the author added some neat peculiarities of his own such as Kushuk Arnem for [Korchuk Khanum]—[…]. Of the T. Even. Entertainments, I have [tran.] long notes which will be useful, as they repeat the stories of The Nights in a bare and barbarous fashion.

I hardly think that "thirty" can be the reading (p. 309); and as regards the two older sons, they were simply older than the hero.

Private. I think that Mr. Clouston[7] is quite right in providing an Edit. of The Nights, with his notes, etc. if any publisher will listen to the proposal. Nimmo's reprint of Mr. Scott is exhausted and he does not intend to re-issue.[8]

I await the Priapeia with extreme curiosity. Meanwhile

---

[1] Royal Asiatic Society RB 1/1/3.
[2] The envelope is postmarked "LONDON W./12/AU18/88/6."
[3] Carlo Landberg *Proverbes et dictons de la province de Syrie Section de Saydâ* (Leyde: E. J. Brill, 1883).
[4] Huntington Library. ALS.
[5] Annotation in pencil.
[6] George William Curtis *Nile Notes of a Howadji* (New York: Harper, 1851). There was a second printing in 1852, and many thereafter.
[7] See Register.
[8] Jonathan Scott *The thousand and one nights: the Arabian nights entertainments* (London: J. C. Nimmo and Bain, 1883; 4 volumes).

Yours very truly
R. F. Burton

Leonard C. Smithers Esq.

P.S. We shall be here till Sept. 1, after which we go to Oxford etc. returning on or after 15 Sept. Athenaeum or this direction will always find me. I am now working at the "Improprieties" of Sa'di.[1]

20. 1888/09/20. Richard Burton to H. S. Ashbee.[2]

Sept. 20, 1888[3]

Dear Mr. Ashbee

We returned yesterday to the Langham and shall be here till Oct 15—more or less. What are your movements?

You remember lending me one of Davenport's treatises.[4] Arbuthnot has lost his copy of the other and I want you kindly to let me have a loan of it. It shall be carefully returned after a few days. Or are there 2—a total of 3?

Ev yr sincy
R. F. Burton

21. 1888/09/26. Richard Burton to John Payne.[5]

No. 48 The Langham
26 Sept.[6]

John Payne Esq.
10 Oxford Road
Kilburn
N. W.

My dear Payne

Arbuthnot will be in town on Tuesday Oct. 2. What do you say to meeting him at the Langham 7 PM table d'hote hour sans façons and salad as you like. It will be our last chance of a meeting thus far we intend to flee on Oct. 15.

Yours ever
R. F. Burton

---

[1] Sa-di al-Shirazi *Al-Khabisat* (The book of impurities, 13th C.).
[2] British Library. Add MS 38808 C f. 42. Postcard.
[3] Athenaeum club embossed card.
[4] Presumably John Davenport (1789-1877) *Curiositates Eroticæ Physiologiæ: Or, Tabooed Subjects Freely Treated* (London: Privately printed, 1875).
[5] Huntington Library, Box 26, RFB 313. Postcard. Handwritten copy of MS by Thomas Wright. The location of the original MS is not known.
[6] Annotation: 1888.

22. 1888/09/30. Richard Burton to Leonard Smithers.[1]

Sept. 30 [:88[2]]

Dear Mr. Smithers

I have kept, as you allowed me, the printed papers for the purpose of showing them to a few select friends. Many thanks for putting down my name as a subscriber to the Priapeia. Where do you think I can get a copy of the Tableaux Vivants in case Mr. Nichols (to whom I have written) failing me?[3]

I am also curious about the Er. Bib. Society?[4] Have you formally established it, with list of members, annual subscription etc.? Or is it, like the Kama Shastra awaiting development? Something of the kind is very necessary to abate a yearly increasing abuse [by] the "bawdy publisher" who asks guineas for books which are worth only shillings and who booms the market only for his own benefit.

I am finishing my big task and working hard at the "Reviewers Reviewed."

Yours very truly
R. F. Burton

23. 1888/10/20. Richard Burton to Leonard Smithers.[5]

48 Langham Oct. 20 (direct Athenaeum)

Dear Mr. Smithers

Thanks for yours of Oct. 6—I waited till Mr. Nichols[6] had sent me Tab. Viv. (book came yesterday) before answering you. Thanks for details about E. Bib. Soc. Avery is a most prodigious rogue backed by someone more roguish. He pirated my friend Arbuthnot's book & our joint works. Now do I understand Rob. & Kers.[7] The "Scented Garden" is not finished nor will it appear before the end of the year. They tried

---

[1] Huntington Library. ALS.
[2] Pencil annotation.
[3] *Les tableaux vivants ou mes confessions aux pieds de la Duchesse. Anecdotes veridiques tirées de nos amours avec nos libertines illustres et nos fouteuses de qualité par un rédacteur de la R.D.D.M* ('Paris': 'Chez tous les libraires'). Sometimes attributed to Gustave Droz. Believed to be have been printed in Brussells circa 1870.
[4] Erotika Biblion Society, a vehicle for Smithers and his business partner Harry Sidney Nichols (see Register), used to (re)issue 'erotic' publications, including *Les tableaux vivants*.
[5] Huntington Library. ALS.
[6] Harry Sidney Nichols, see Register.
[7] Robson and Kerslake, the booksellers.

to sell "Gulistan"[1] as a pornographic book in order to make more money. […] The object is to "make" regardless of mode.

We start on Monday 15—Folkes., Boulogne, Paris and then a stop to Geneva. I shall always be happy to hear from you (via Athenaeum) and will undertake to answer regularly & keep our correspondence private. Ev yrs

R. F. B.

24. 1888/10/22. Richard Burton to Leonard Smithers.[2]

The Pavillion[3] Folkstone Oct. 22
(direct Athenaeum Club)

Dear Mr. Smithers

After a rude week of hard labour, we bolted from London on the 15th and have been resting here ever since. On the 25th we go on to Paris where I shall find the "Scented Garden" duly copied and ready for translation.

Priapeia not yet received. I like the idea of your four proposed prints—Ovid, Sterne & Stevenson, Noerins & Poggio, but I should most like Meursius' Aloisia Sigea.[4] Do you know anything of her (A.S.'s) history? Vols. V and VI of Supp. Nights are all ready, as far as I have to do with them. Please keep me au courant if you have time concerning Vizetelly & La Terre.[5] It is a pity that Priapeia did not proceed in time as in order the Tab. Viv.; but tears over spilled milk are to be avoided. I am now reviewing for Academy Lord Strat. de Redcliffe and that will be the last till The Garden is thrown open.[6]

Yours very sincly
R. F. Burton

---

[1] *The Gulistan or Rose Garden of Saadi Faithfully Translated Into English* Kama Shastra Society, 1888.
[2] Huntington Library. ALS.
[3] So spelled.
[4] Luisa Sigea de Velasco (1522-1560), a Latin teacher in the court of Maria of Portugal. The book *Aloysiæ Sigeæ Toletanæ satyra sotadica de arcanis amoris et veneris: Aloysia hispanice scripsit: latinitate donavit J. Meursius*, purporting to be written by Johannes Meursius (1579–1639), associated her with lesbianism. It has been argued that this work, also known as *The School of Women*, was actually written by Nicolas Chorier (1612-1692), a French historian—see *Des secrets de l'amour et de Vénus, satire sotadique de Luisa Sigea, de Tolède, par Nicolas Chorier* (Éditions l'Or du Temps, 1969).
[5] See Register.
[6] *Academy* Vol. XXXIV 1888/11/24, pp. 329-30; 1888/12/15, pp. 379-80.

25. 1888. A. H. Sayce.[1]

At Trieste I was welcomed by Sir Richard and Lady Burton, and the next few days were days of enjoyment. Burton was already suffering from the malady which killed him; but we still talked of the possibility of that journey which we had planned in earlier days from Tangier to Alexandria through the midst of the Beduin tribes of the Cyrenaica. ...

In the later part of the summer [1888] Burton came to Oxford in order to copy the unique manuscript of Aladdin which had been discovered in the Bodleian, and a translation of which he wished to include in a supplementary volume of his Thousand and One Nights. I asked him to stay with me in College, but he preferred putting up at the Mitre. "College," he said, was "a hotel of the ninth century" and dining with me twice a week. One Sunday he told me that he had gone to London the day before to see his doctor as he had had some twinges of gout, so when the dessert was placed upon the table and he was preparing to help himself to a glass of College port I put my hand on his arm and said: "Take claret instead; remember the gout!" "Oh," he replied, "the doctors now tell you that port is the best thing for the gout!" and before the evening was over he had drunk three glasses of it. On Tuesday morning while at breakfast, I received a note from Lady Burton "Do come and see us; Dick is down with the gout." I went to the Mitre and found Burton groaning in bed and Lady Burton packing up his clothes and preparing to carry him off to town. It was the beginning of the illness from which he never recovered. On one of the evenings that he dined with me he told me that when learning to speak a new language the first thing he acquired was "the swear-words; after that, everything is easy."

26. 1888. Verney Lovett Cameron.[2]

The last time I saw him was when he was in England, a little over two years ago,[3] and though then he was already an invalid, and the subject of loving and anxious care from his wife, his mighty intellect was still undimmed, as it was to the last, and it was a pleasure to sit and listen to him unfolding somewhat of his vast store of experience and knowledge.

---

[1] A. H. Sayce *Reminiscences* (London: Macmillan, 1923) pp. 26-7, 194-7, 216-7, 235, 243.

[2] Verney Lovett Cameron "Burton as I knew him" *Fortnightly Review* LIV (December 1890) pp. 878-884.

[3] Therefore, 1888.

27. 1888-1890. Harold Nicolson.[1]

The four years which Nicolson spent in Hungary were four years of boredom. ... For one summer he stayed at Fiume at the Villa Hoyos. A second was spent at Stübing in the company of Sir Richard and Lady Burton who had come up from Trieste. Burton would play amicably with the three Nicolson children, thrusting his dark face into theirs, shouting at the youngest baby, "Hallo, little Tehran!"[2] The child yelled: the memory of those questing panther eyes remained with this infant as a thrill of terror and delight.

28. 1888-1890. George Bainton.[3]

The names of Sir Richard and Lady and Lady Burton are here united because the following contribution is their joint work. Another reason for coupling them may be found in the fact of their loving comradeship in the literary calling. "We divide the work," says Captain Burton. "I take all the hard and scientific part and make her do all the rest." Lady Burton has won for herself an enviable place in the world of letters, while the number, the variety, and the quality of the Captain's works are truly remarkable. Readers of the interesting letter here given will learn what it has cost the intrepid traveller, who made the memorable pilgrimage to Meccah and Medinah, to raise himself to a level with literary men of the foremost rank.

Lady Burton writes to regret that so little can be said upon the subject.

"My husband dictates as follows:[4]

> His early youth was passed on the Continent, where, in addition to the usual studies of Latin and Greek, he learnt, instinctively as it were, French and Italian, with their several dialects, as thoroughly as he did English. In his native tongue he was ever fond of the older writers, and gave himself with great ardour to the systematic study of Addison. He knew Shakespeare almost by heart, and learnt to admire the thorough propriety of words which distinguished him. He worked hard at the perfect prose of the English translation of the Bible, and to this he added Euclid by way of shortening his style and attaining clearness of thought. When travelling in Central Africa he always carried

---

[1] Harold Nicolson *Sir Arthur Nicolson Bart* (London: Constable, 1930), pp. 78-9.

[2] Harold Nicolson was born in Tehran.

[3] George Bainton *The Art of Authorship: Literary Reminiscences, Methods of Work, and Advice to Young Beginners* (New York: Appleton, 1891) pp. 256-60.

[4] Indentation has been added here to clarify who is saying what – Ed.

with him the three bound up together in a single volume, with three clasps like a breviary, and used it to cheer his many dull and disagreeable hours, not spent in actual exploration. When picturing scenery it was his habit to draw from nature, as if painting a landscape. When describing character, he studied the man as completely as he could, and meditated carefully over his mental picture before he ventured to put it upon paper. He is thoroughly convinced that to express clearly, a man must think clearly, and must thoroughly understand what he means to express; and he would often pass the earlier hours of the night in reflecting upon the task of the coming morning. He felt that what is called unconscious cerebration was a great aid to his work. Having fixed in his mind exactly what he intended to say, he preserved himself from incoherent and unconnected writing. In India he passed stiff examinations in six languages, not to speak of Arabic and Pushtoo, the language of the Afghans. These studies again benefited his English style. Being forced to think of the foreign sentences before they were spoken, he applied the same process to English, and in that way gained no little clearness and point. In his many versions of Eastern authors, for instance, "The Thousand Nights and a Night," in sixteen volumes, he attempted to carry out his ideal estimate of a translator. According to him, the grand translator, Chaucer, was so-called by his contemporaries because he cast in thorough English mould the thoughts and language of Petrarch and of Boccaccio. Moreover, as no language is complete, and each has some points in which it can be improved he was ambitious of transferring from foreign tongues the idioms and turns of phrase which he thought might be naturalised and treated as welcome guests in English. Of course the process was viewed with different eyes by different people, some with friendly regard, whilst others characterised such efforts as "diverting lunacies of style."

Here my husband ceases to dictate, and I think I have given you as long an answer as you require. There is no doubt he is a master of English, and handles and plays with it skillfully; but to carry out his programme one must begin from childhood, and I doubt if it will serve what you want, whereas I think three very simple rules of my own might. One is, never to be ashamed to ask the meaning of anything, be it ever so simple, if one *ought* to know it. The second is, to read slowly, considering the words, and looking for the meaning of each different word in all its bearings. The third is, whether in speaking or in writing, to imagine you are relating a story to your friend by your own fireside, which gives a great charm to style, provided you avoid the jerky, or flippant, or question and answer style, adhering to flowing, earnest, natural, easy narrative, as you would in such case, quite devoid of shyness and restlessness."

I have inserted the above remarkable record here in order to illustrate the fact that obscurity is avoided and clearness gained only as a result of the most patient toil and constant care.

29. 1888/10/25. Isabel Burton to Lynn Linton.[1]

25 Oct. 88.
Folkestone.

Dear friend,

We are fully rested from London, & are looking forw^d to a nasty crossing tomorrow as the S.W. gales seem to be coming up. I heartily reciprocate, so does Dick—we all do, your kind words of affection & hopes for the future. We shall always <u>be true friends</u> & God willing will <u>never</u> neglect an opportunity of a happy meeting.

I ought not to ask you to write to me because I know how valuable your time is, but if you ever do, tell me about a Syndicate which Dr. Baker says takes up an authoresses book & brings it out in several paying magazines at the same time. I suppose country & popular mags & afterwards she may bring it out as a book. Is it true? Is there such a thing? I am thinking of my poor despised Edition of the Nights.

How I enjoyed the night you dined with us, but I could not get enough of you because Dr. Baker monopolized you. He says you are one of the very few of his Gods who have not disappointed him. The more he knows you the more he will like you I say—for when you are a friend you are a real one.

Au revoir not goodbye & God bless you & take care of you

Yr. affect. friend

Isabel Burton.

30. 1888/11/04. Richard Burton to Leonard Smithers.[2]

Hotel National Geneva
Nov. 4 [/88[3]]

Dear Mr. Smithers

We left Paris in fog and rain and reached this in fresh fallen snow (on the mountains) yesterday morn. Today the weather is perfection and we are resolved not to move Vevey-wards till the end of the month. I am now ready & anxious to see the Priapeia. What do you think of the

---

[1] Huntington Library. Richard Burton Papers, Box 26. RFB 216-219.
[2] Huntington Library. ALS.
[3] Pencil annotation.

Vizetelly business? and how will it affect the e. Bib & Kama Societies? I regretted that he pleaded guilty but he must best know his own business. The "cheapness" of his publications appears to have been the gravamen. At Liseux[1] I bought Cleland's Fanny Hill (an old acquaintance) (25 fr.)[2] and made all arrangements for copying the best MS. of the "Scented Garden." Hoping to hear from you soon. I am ev.

Yours very sincy
R. F. Burton

31. 1888/11/04. Richard Burton to Colonel Chaillé-Long.[3]

Hotel National, Geneva,
November 4th, 1888.

My dear Chaillé-Long,

Many thanks for a good long letter, dated last August, which has at length found me. The White Pasha may still be Gordon.[4] It is *aut*[5] Emin *aut* Stanley. As regards the latter, you, of course, understand that I do not admire him as a man or a geographer, but as one who has been Fortune's favourite, and who has done for Africa, what none of us have succeeded in doing, has bisected the Continent, and has given a new base whereupon to operate north and south. Voila!

You will have no chance of public recognition for your great part of the work in the solution of the Nile Source problem. You have Grant against you, who hates his idol to be touched by a hand profane, and the miserable X refuses your *Three Prophets* because it does not chime in with English ignorance. The R.G. Soc. will be interested in anything you do about Corea, but they will not have Africa stirred up. I still trust that Stanley is alive, but am almost certain that, as usual, he will not bring back a single white man. His committee seems to have bad news about him, but they do nothing beyond humbugging and blindfolding the public.

I do not quite understand what you propose to do in Corea, especially as the temper of the people seems to be adverse to trading and other industry. But I am delighted to read that you think of a return to civilization, and that there is a chance of our meeting again. We shall be

---

[1] The Parisian bookseller Isidore Liseux.
[2] John Cleland *Memoirs of a Woman of Pleasure* (London: Fenton, 1748). Burton means an old *reading* acquaintance.
[3] Colonel Chaillé Long *My Life in Four Continents* Volume 2 (London: Hutchinson, 1912) pp. 414-31.
[4] This is the idea that General Charles Gordon might still be wandering in Africa, having escaped from the Mahdi.
[5] or.

in Switzerland till March next, and then will go to Verona (Lombardy), Trieste, Athens, and back again to Austria for the summer. Let me hear from you when your plans are well worked up. My wife joins me in many salaams and the best of wishes.

Ev. Yr. sincere friend,
R. F. Burton.

32. 1888/11/08. Richard Burton to John Payne.[1]

Hotel National Geneva
Nov. 8

My dear Payne

I have just received enclosed from a correspondent, and thinking that you would like to hear about yourself in the J.[2] I enclose it. Please read and return. We shall stay here till end of November and then move on. Poste Restante Geneva all always find us.

How are you getting on in health and strength? Your winter must be truly beastly—to judge from ours. "The Scented Garden" now begun in real earnest. With united kindest regards. Ever yours

R. F. Burton

33. 1888/11/14. Richard Burton to Leonard Smithers.[3]

Hotel National Geneva
Nov. 14 [/88]

Dear Mr. Smithers

With the prospectus you sent me no address. I wrote at once to my agent:

Oliver Notcutt Esq.[4]
4 Fairholt Road
Stoke Newiqngton
London N

(Our weather has changed for the worse and today is our go of fog and rain—however, others are worse off.) He will pay my subscription to the Priapeia as soon as the Vol. is sent to him. Many thanks for your kindly offer of Ovid Travestie.[5]

---

[1] Huntington Library, Box 26, RFB 313. Postcard. Handwritten copy of MS by Thomas Wright. The location of the original MS is not known.
[2] Presumably 'Journals'.
[3] Huntington Library. ALS.
[4] See Register.
[5] Captain Alexander Radcliffe *Ovid Travestie. A Burlesque upon Ovid's Epistles* (1680), going through several editions The fourth edition of 1705

Aloisia Sigea and her sister were well known blue stockings at the Court of Portugal in Camoens' day. You will see their names mentioned in my biography of the poet.

The Pentamerone must wait till the Scented Garden is finished—say about next autumn. But the "final copy" only wants correction and subsequent recopying.

Pisanus Fraxus is H. S. Ashbee[1] of 53 Bedford Square London. I reviewed his Tunisia a few months ago.[2] He is a well-to-do merchant and has a fine collection of facetiae.

My review of Lane-Poole's Lord S.de R. is gone to Academy.[3] I cannot but speak well of the work.

Thanks for the details about Vizetelly trial—will it have any consequences? By this time you will have received Vols. V & VI of A. Nights & I want your judgment (candid) upon Reviewers Reviewed. The Liber Sadius in English will be atrocious as Fanny Hill shows our language is not fit for erotics.

Ev yours sincy
R. F. Burton

34. 1888/11/21. Richard Burton to John Payne.[4]

Hotel National Geneva
Nov 21

My dear Payne

I am glad too you like the gentle rebuke administered to Stead, Reeve and co.

You have your body[5] I have none or quasi none. You could greatly oblige me by getting down when you have a moment to spare the names of reverends and ecclesiastics who have written and printed facetious books. In England I have Swift and Sterne; in French Rabelais, but I want one more also two in Italian and two in German.

We are enjoying Geneva and magnificent weather and only wish you are here. With kindest regards from both.

Ever yrs sincy

---

was reissued by the Erotika Biblion Society in 1889. See James G. Nelson *Leonard Smithers: Publisher to the Decadents* (University Park, Penn.: Penn. State Press, 1990), p. 317.

[1] See Register.
[2] *Academy* Vol. XXXIII (1888-06-16), pp. 405-6.
[3] *Academy* Vol. XXXIV 1888/11/24, pp. 329-30; 1888/12/15, pp. 379-80.
[4] Huntington Library, Box 26, RFB 313. Postcard. Handwritten copy of MS by Thomas Wright. The location of the original MS is not known.
[5] Presumably a reference to the Villon Society.

R. F. B.

35. 1888/12/02. Richard Burton to Leonard Smithers.[1]

Hotel du Lac Vevey Geneva Lake
Dec. 2 [88[2]]

Dear Mr. Smithers

Only yesterday did I receive yours of Nov. 26 and all my attention was, at once, given to the Priapeia. It is (or rather will be) a scholarly publication and I have only one objection to the workmanship. The sting of the epigram should be in its tail e. g. ad costam tibi septimam recondam (no. V, p. 8) but the English version here fails and ends in the uninteresting "sting of the lyrics." When shall I receive other sheets?

Your opinion of my work is very flattering in the extreme—too flattering to admit except as the favorable estimate of a friend. Of course you understand that the phrase to which you take exception (the Cautious Canary) had no reference to any one individually and merely characterized a class. I am wholly ignorant of the business matters connected with The Nights and it never was my practise to sneer at a friend openly or covertly.

The "Scented Garden" flourishes but gives me much trouble. I am having chapter XXI copied from the Algerian MS. Have written to Algiers, […], Tunis, etc. for information & shall probably seek it personally next winter in Northern Africa. Meanwhile, we are here for a month & then probably return to Montreux.

Ev yr sincy
R. F. Burton

What is the address of Mr. Nichols.[3] I presume the London agents are Robson & Kerslake of […] Coventry St.

36. 1888/12/24. Richard Burton to Leonard Smithers.[4]

Dec. 24 '88

Dear Mr. Smithers

Yours of Dec. 21st received. Do not mistake me about the Priapeia: I like the first sheet very much and find it a scholarly performance; moreover it promises to become the one useful edition. You are quite right not to hurry the book through, but to humour the printers with their normal "heavy engagement."

---

[1] Huntington Library. ALS. Huntington Library. ALS.
[2] Pencil annotation.
[3] Harry Sidney Nichols, see Register.
[4] Huntington Library. ALS. Huntington Library. ALS.

On Jan. 2 we remove to Hotel des Alpes Montreux Lake of Geneva, which appears the only "fashionable" (i.e. crowded and uncomfortable) wintering place in Switzerland. I shall rub up against my kind there for a month or so and then plus voyages.

You will find Coynte in Chaucer. "Futter" is still common in Scotland, and the word is of noble family [...], futuv, foutuv, etc.[1] I have 2 copies of the "Return of Age to Youth-tide;" and I am sure that a literal rendering will be valuable—are you doing it? I should much like to see the translation.

It strikes me that Mr. Nichols[2] will be a useful man in the matter of the "Scented Garden" (which progresses well) especially if we have a list of 250 subscribers to the E. B. S. Beware of Rob. & Kers.[3] they are "on the make" as the Yankee hath it: perhaps it will be advisable to repudiate them in Mr. N's next issue. Best wishes for the Xtian Saturnalia—my fete is Dec. 27 when [God-dad] returns. Ev yrs sincy
R. F. Burton

37. 1889/01/31. Richard Burton to Leonard Smithers.[4]

Hotel des Alpes Montreux Jan. 31 [/89[5]]
(we shall be here till Feb. 15)

Dear Mr. Smithers

Yours of 23 recd. The missing word must be "nimble" ("or nimbly applied"—hand). In p. 36 I much prefer <u>peetras</u> to the silly <u>petra</u>. In XXXIV I think it is a pity not to preserve the original order "a girl who is many men etc." so many willow-wood pokers. In p. 41 one would prefer "never shaven" to <u>unshaven</u>, the latter suggesting to us moderns only a stubbly chin. These, however, are mere mistakes and I congratulate you upon reaching the half-way house without accident. Payne will also translate Zayn al Asnam.[6] Mr. Liseux (best type of old-fashioned "bawdy publisher") has been asking me 150 francs for a useless MS.[7] You need not believe a word he says about his translation (or anything else). I have not seen Cornazano.[8] Of course, I shall be my

---

[1] Copulate.
[2] Harry Sidney Nichols, see Register.
[3] Robson and Kerslake, booksellers, 23 Coventry Street, Haymarket, London. They advertised themselves as "dealers in rare English and foreign works."
[4] Huntington Library. ALS. Huntington Library. ALS.
[5] Pencil annotation.
[6] *Supplemental Nights*, vol. 3, p. 3. See also Burton's letter "The Thousand Nights and a Night" *The Academy* (1887) pp. 60-1, in which he announced that a Syrian MS had been located by Hermann Zotenberg in the Bibliothèque Nationale de France in Paris.
[7] Isidore Liseux.
[8] *Proverbs in jests, or, The tales of Cornazano* (Paris: Isidore Liseux, 1888).

own publisher and carefully eschew Rob. & Kers.¹ & Nic. and their whole lot. But I want as many names as possible of firms which take such volumes and I suppose Mr. N.² will make no secret of his South American house? He has given you very fair terms in the Priapeia. My only use of him as regards the Garden will be to send him an Advt. (when the volume or volumes shall be in the printer's hands) and find out how many copies he will take. I shall print a 1000 and might expect my old subscribers to take them up. But the public is a fickle catch and a manual of Erotology cannot have the interest of the Nights. It is however giving me the devil's own botherment and putting me to all manner of expense. The MSS. are so vile, defective in every page: I begin to see that a visit to Algiers will be necessary. The "Old Man" returns to you soon

Ev yrs sincy
R. F. Burton

38. 1889/02/17. Richard Burton to Leonard Smithers.³

Hotel Gibbon Lausanne
Feb. 17 '89

Dear Mr. Smithers

Yours of 12th recd yesterday: we shall be here for a week and afterwards must be addressed "Trieste", to be kept till called for. I must take measures about the wandering agent you kindly apprize me of (without, of course, pointing to you) or he will be playing some ugly tricks. I never expected Nichols to tell his South Amer. address. There is no chance of my employing him, beyond [placing a few copies: he showed the cloven foot at once and]⁴ would not forward me to my club Vol. I until I had paid. These fellows are all rogues and over-greedy (that is foolish) rogues.

And now to Pr. P. 49 […] I should have rendered by limper = flabbier: a good […] word. [XVIII] for "wanton girl" pathic girl one to be used fore and aft. LI full of punctuation-errors and at end "in the gardens which leaving you […] forsook" etc. (not "for the only thing which is left"). LIV is a puzzle; I think it […] the meaning.

I shall have nothing to do with Liseux's <u>Justine</u>. The French of De Sade is monotonous enough and a few pages chokes me off a bit, but what will it be in brutal Anglo Saxon? He is a greedy rascal like the rest. I proposed an exchange with him but he would have none of it—wanted

---

¹ The bookseller firms Robson and Kerslake, and Harry Nichols—see Register.
² Harry Sidney Nichols, see Register.
³ Huntington Library. ALS. Huntington Library. ALS.
⁴ Text appears to be missing from the top few lines of the scanned copy of the MS used.

ready money for a confessedly worthless MS.

Our winter came on Feb. 7th. It is always a snowy month in Switzerland, but it seldom sees such a snowfall as this, R.R. is[1] stopped and streets utterly and entirely beastly. I am collecting notices about old Gibbon and have already seen a host of relics.

Ev yrs sincy
R. F. Burton

39. 1889/04/03. Richard Burton to Leonard Smithers.[2]

Trieste April 3 '89

Dear Mr. Smithers

Yours of 28 ult. reached here yesterday & I lose no time in answering. The excesses (never mind these being "tinged," this is as it should be) please me immensely, they are thoroughly well studied. Allow me to suggest that you give Lat. list of names applied to the Yoni as a pendant to the Phallus terms. I should not allude to Tableaux Viv. p. 129.[3] Ruticliffe[4] considered as doggerel may amuse, but that is all. Why not conjecturally fill up brackets in p. 32. Priapus never, I believe, held a scythe: the sickle was for the purpose of amputating parts.

I am somewhat in a fix and want the aid of my friends. Can you assist me to a verse of Juvenal only whose garbled end I can give? "uda terit inguina barba"—speaking of one Ravola who is gamahucking his mistress.[5] The second want is more serious. I do not wish to pay that rogue Liseux 250 francs for his Aretino.[6] I require an extract from him (P. A.) with an account of his Figurae Veneris, and I must have the same from Forberg.[7] The Scented Garden has now reached a point where these are necessary to complete the <u>Historique</u>. As regards your hand press at 2d/ a page who finds paper, you or printer? Why do we not imitate the Yankees who colour their types and produce impressions so much sharper? I am sorry that you have had so much trouble about "Truth"

---

[1] Railroads.
[2] Huntington Library. ALS. Huntington Library. ALS.
[3] Tableaux Vivants.
[4] Possibly Alexander Radcliffe, author of *Ovid Travestie*.
[5] "Ravola dum Rhodopes uda terit inguina barba?" Juvenal Satire IX: 3-4. "Ravola's beard is wet from wearing the crotch of Rhodopes." See also *Ananga Ranga*, p. 13.
[6] Pietro Aretino (1492-1556) an Italian writer of pornographic literature, such as his *Sonetti Lussuriosi* and *Figurae Veneris*, who was potrayed by Titian.
[7] The German schoolteacher Frederick Karl Forberg (1770-1848) who published a commentary in 1824 titled *Manuel d'Erotologie Classique Texte Latin et traduction littérale par le Traducteur des Dialogues de Luisa Sigea*. on the latin verse *Hermaphroditus* by Antonio Beccadelli. H. S. Ashbee lists this in his *Catena Librorum Tacendorum*.

which was to me only une luxe.

Let me hear from you soon.

Ev yr sincy
R. F. Burton

40. 1889/05/01. Richard Burton to Leonard Smithers.[1]

Private

Trieste May 1 '89

Dear Mr. Smithers

Yours of 26 ult. reached me yesterday; & I have read the accompaniments carefully as usual. In […] / 60 surely it would be as well to fill up the blank. (N.B. Penelope to Ulysses is better than reverse). A Duchess was a troll etc. The notes did not fall off—quite the contrary. It is, of course, a matter of taste, but I should avoid all concessions to popular prejudice e.g. "foully disfigured" (enlivened?) (p. 162) and "infamous books" (priapistic?) (p. 165). All such peace offerings are only misjudged by the Publisher, qui l'excuse j'accuse is his motto. If we sit as judges and use the commanding tone Mr. P. is apt to feel crushed.

By the by in p. 134 l. 9 do you allude to receiving the old comic post or another n.?

A detailed note on Bestiality in Classical lit. would be exceedingly valuable. But perhaps you have written one at end of p. 176.

I do not think that the P.O. is directing its attention to Trieste, and if you want my book safely sent hence to England you could transmit it to me and I would forward at once. Attention seems too confined to France & Holland. I have my own dodge for sending home MS. About a week ago, I applied to Mr. Ashbee (directing to Coleman Street, not to his private address) but he has not yet answered. I have written direct to Mssr. Vizetelly. "Konima" is a rank blunder but hitherto I have not been able to trace the source. That will come in time. Does the surveillance over Mr. Nichols[2] affect you?

We are doing very well despite a most changeable season and an overdose of Sirocco: I hope that the "seasonable" Spring weather has not affected you. ~~I'll acknowledge Forberg when he comes~~. Forberg arrived safe this morn. Many thanks.

Ev yrs sincy
R. F. Burton

---

[1] Huntington Library, Burton-Smithers Papers, Box 2.
[2] Harry Sidney Nichols, see Register.

41. 1889/05/08. Richard Burton To A. G. Ellis.[1]

Trieste May 8 '89

Dear Mr. Ellis

I find it stated by Vicomte Delaborde "Marc-Antoine Raimondi"[2] that the Duke of Cumberland bought some fragments of Marc Antonio's engravings and that these after forming part of the Willett Collection[3] passed into the Brit. Museum. Could you kindly inform me if they are still there. The fragments are supposed to be part of the engravings made by M. A. from Giulio Romano's[4] series of "Postures" (I Modi[5]) which P. Aretino[6] is said to have illustrated by sonnets. You have so often assisted me in these small matters that I now apply to you without ceremony or apology.

After a ten months wander I found myself again at Trieste and very glad to be with my books once more. The spring was late and unpleasant but now all is blooming and people begin to talk of summer quarters. How has the time passed with you? What news of Mr. Blumhardt?[7] And your fellow-sufferer from leather emanations the Sanskritist?[8] Hoping to have a word from you. I am ev.

Yours very truly
R. F. Burton.

42. 1889/05/08. Richard Burton to H. S. Ashbee.[9]

Friday night, May 8, '89
Trieste

Dear Mr. Ashbee

Thanks for yours of 27th ult. Since then we have had Count Teleki

---

[1] Royal Asiatic Society. RB 1/1/5.
[2] Henri, vicomte Delaborde (1811-1899) *Marc-Antoine Raimondi: étude historique et critique suivie d'un catalogue raisonné des œuvres du maître* (1888).
[3] See Ralph Willett sale catalogue (His sale; Thomas Philipe, London, 12.vii.1812).
[4] Circa 1499-1546.
[5] The Positions. Also known as the "Loves of the Gods", or "De omnibus Veneris Schematibus," or "The Sixteen Pleasures"—engravings by Marcantonio of coital positions. They are in the British Museum.
[6] Pietro Aretino (1492-1556).
[7] J. F. Blumhardt, see Register.
[8] Cecil Bendall. According to Thomas Wright (*Life* Vol. 2, p. 202) the Manuscripts division at the British Museum was located on top of the book bindery, therefore the bad smell.
[9] British Library. Add MS 38808 C f 46. ALS.

here and he stayed a few days whilst sorting his collection.[1] He looks in first-rate trim, hard as nails and is getting over a bout of ague and fever caught (not in Masailand) but at Zanzibar. I hope to meet him again at [Ausee[2]] during the summer and have advised him as his chief object in visiting London is to show before the R.G.S., not to put in an appearance before the autumn. He is very grateful to you for your kindness and he wrote you a long letter—direct to Coleman Street—from Aden. You will rejoice to hear of his success.

We shall not see England this summer as the Garden[3] must be finished without delay. Tunisia is far too good to pay: you must be contented with the knowledge of having done excellent work for its own reward. "King Africa & his mines" would probably have paid you in coin.

My wife joins me in sending kindest regards to Mrs. Ashbee, and the demoiselles, not forgetting Miss Elsa.[4]

Ev. yrs
R. F. Burton

P.S. I enclose a note with my requirements. Arbuthnot wrote to me from Granada and I expect another chit soon.

43. 1889/05/13. Richard Burton to Leonard Smithers.[5]

Trieste May 13

My dear Mr. Smithers

In sheet 20 p. 153, 1 line from bottom I have only to note <u>one</u> <u>another</u> for each other.

Yesterday, I read your Introduction and return it today with my foreword. Please send duplicate proofs of both and if possible don't print off till they are returned corrected. I will not lose a moment.

Excuse the freedom of changing—I won't say correcting—and adopt only what you yourself like.

My friend Arbuthnot is now here & stays with us for seven days. Put him down for 5 (five) copies.

F. F. Arbuthnot Esq.
F.R.A.S. etc., etc.
18 Park Lane
London

---

[1] The Hungarian Count Sámuel Teleki (1845–1916), an explorer of East Africa.
[2] Possibly Lake Ausee in Austria.
[3] Burton's new translation and annotation of the *Perfumed Garden*.
[4] Ashbee had three daughters.
[5] Huntington Library. ALS MS. Burton-Smithers Papers, Box 2.

He will return to town before end of month & he has promised me to run down to Sheffield and have a talk with you. Better do nothing except correct proofs and register subscribers' names till he returns. Put off Rob. & Kers.[1] He and I see no reason why you should not issue copies to men well known as perfectly secure, especially as soon as Parliament is up. I say this because a question (by Mr. Smith?) in the House of Commons would entail disagreeable results to both of us.

I have two Lat. copies of Ausonius and now want the best English translation.[2] Hard work is cut out for us. Catullus is being rapidly licked into shape. Pity we did not begin with him.
ev yrs
R. F. B.

44. 1889/05/22. Richard Burton to Leonard Smithers.[3]

Trieste May 22 '89

Dear Mr. Smithers

Yours of May 11th safely to hand. I have no doubt you are right about "Turd". Mr. Clouston[4] has sent me his "Group" and a very dull group he has made of it. He seems to have worked out that subject. Messrs. Rob. & Kers.[5] lent me Aretino's sonnets by Liseux—60 francs is too much, but the vol. is very interesting.[6] I am attempting to "rehabilitate" the Aretino who was the perfect expression of the Renaissance epoch when Hellenism and Civilization were contending with [duty[7]] and barbarism. Mrs. Grundy will furiously rage, but she will have other matters to exercise what she calls her mind.

After a month of hideous Scirocco we have been having a few fine days with a north wind most grateful to unstrung nerves.

I have been carefully looking over your p.p. 133-135 and want you to "verify quotations," and to add information.

1 where have you found Trepsicles[8] (p. 135)

---

[1] Robson and Kerslake, the booksellers.

[2] Decimus Magnus Ausonius, the 4th Century Roman poet, is often referred to by Burton (e.g. *Camoens Life and Lusiads*, vol2., p. 656). His unpublished translation of the Epigrams (*Epigramata de diversis rebus*) of Ausonius was apparently burnt after his death.

[3] Huntington Library. ALS MS. Burton-Smithers Papers, Box 2.

[4] W. M. Clouston, see Register.

[5] Robson and Kerslake.

[6] Pietro Aretino, see above.

[7]

[8] Amatory pleasures. See *Terminal Essay to the Arabian Nights*, p. 201.

2. you quote P.P. anent Nico; but I cannot find the name either in Xenephon or in [Athen.] lib v.

These are <u>affaires de rien</u>,[1] but provide a handle to carping criticism when the book comes to be handled by experts and the notes are so good that they must be cleared of all carelessness.

p. 173 suggested to me that a classical note on bestiality esp. of the Gods & Goddesses might be useful. You could easily work up the subject.

I hope that my friends will keep me au courant of Vizetelly's business. It appears to me that the National Purity is going too far and that a reaction will presently set in.

Ev yours sincy
R. F. Burton

P. S. I find Forberg useful and only hope that I am not keeping it too long.

45. 1889/06/02. Richard Burton to Leonard Smithers.[2]

Trieste June 2 '89.

Dear Mr. Smithers

The Ovid[3] reached me some days ago and yours of May 27 yesterday. Thanks for the news concerning Vizetelly. As you say, these idiots are driving the trade underground to the detriment of everyone. But our Govt. or rather our public opinion will not even regulate prostitution—what can be expected from their absurd ideas of morality? (Weather here quite perfect and the same throughout Europe, apparently.) Mr. Clouston's last (I have read it through) is the mere sweepings of a Folklore shop and reads as if he had grown tired of his work or had exhausted himself.[4] I am sorry for him as he has a mother to keep besides himself.

You are unreasonably despondent about your volume. It is by no means a "poor amateurish piece of work" and had the beginning been equal to the end it would have been greatly valued. The commentary is excellent and I congratulate you upon it throughout. The 130 names of sexual organs may form a dull list but will be useful to students. You have said amply sufficient upon "postures" and as you say the subject

---

[1] making mountains of molehills.
[2] Huntington Library. ALS MS. Burton-Smithers Papers, Box 2.
[3] Captain Alexander Radcliffe *Ovid Travestie. A Burlesque upon Ovid's Epistles* (1680).
[4] W. A. Clouston, see Register. Burton must mean Clouston's *The Book of Noodles* (London: Elliot Stock, 1888).

needs a volume. Don't allow Nichols[1] (or anything else) to hurry you for his own private purposes; this is ever the fashion of such gentry—all for self. Your 250 copies will readily sell, and you should prepare one (at fullest leisure) for another and an enlarged edition which will certainly be called for. I hope in another year to be wholly free from engagements and will if you like trans. the prose translations of the Epigrams into verse. Meanwhile please don't forget <u>Niko</u> and <u>Trepsicles</u>. Sursum Corda![2] and no painting by the way.

Why should Vizetelly go bankrupt for a few hundred? Last time he fell without a blow and published his defense afterwards. I hope he will not do so now, but play bull (interview newspapers, write articles etc.) and raise Cain.

ev yrs
R. F. Burton

46. 1889/06/26. Richard Burton to Leonard Smithers.[3]

Trieste June 26[4]

Dear Mr. Smithers

Yours of June (?) rec^d, and envelope containing excursus and Introduction. I read the latter carefully & sent you a p-card to say that a change is wanted. Your p. xxxi set my wits working and I polished off a few lists of which I enclose 2 rough specimens. Hexams. and pentams. are a fine [brain-gymnastic] but hardly read like poetry in English. But the great point is variety and before I go farther we must meet and combine. The vol. I am sure will sell well & you must prepare for another day ordering the notes e.g., Yoni & Phallus in one place (not in 2 far distant). You must be very careful about index <u>i.e.</u> index every note.

I have no patience with Vizetelly: he ought to have fought the battle like a man and spent money upon the editors and critics. Now he has caved in without a blow & I suppose 6 months hence he will print his defense as before. Why not boldly quote the Bible & Shaks.? I have not seen Mr. Payne's Aladdin, but he will surely send it to me.[5] It is hard for me to believe that Mr. Clouston's huge dull book can pay and I am sorry

---

[1] Harry Sidney Nichols, see Register.
[2] cheer up.
[3] Huntington Library. ALS MS. Burton-Smithers Papers, Box 2.
[4] Pencil annotation: "/89".
[5] John Payne *Alaeddin and the Enchanted Lamp* (1889). Payne dedicated his translation to Burton: "My dear Burton, I give myself the pleasure of placing your name in the forefront of another and final volume of my translation of the Thousand and One Nights, which, if it have brought me no other good, has at least been the means of procuring me your friendship."

that he has made so bad a venture. I have puzzled out Niko & Trepsicles: the [Thes. Ent.] was right about the book no. v, but forgot the chapt. etc.

On Monday next, we start (with official leave) for our 2 weeks holiday, returning to my [remit] about Sept. 1. We shall stick to Styria and the neighborhood. Letters to Trieste (Consulate) will always be forwarded, only there will be some delay in my replying. When will Priapeia be out?

Ev yrs sincy
R. F. B.

To the Reader [...][1]
  always guiltless of garment and garb
So hide with thy tunic the part which is made
  to be mostly hidden,
or wi' what eyes see the part
  pleased by these lines to [...]

---

[1] Mostly illegible verses follow.

47. 1889/07/11. Richard Burton to Leonard Smithers.[1]

Graz, Styria July 11

One line to acknowledge yours of July 5 with excellent photo. We are on the loose till end of September, but anything urgent directed to Brit. Consl. Trieste Austria always finds me. Vive […]

R.F.B.
Abdullah[2]

48. 1889/08/29. Richard Burton to Leonard Smithers.[3]

Hotel Erzherzog Karl
Vienna (address Trieste)
August 29 '89

Dear Mr. Smithers

I arrived here yesterday after nearly two months of general discomfort in the Highlands of Styria, a July alternately roasting & chilling and an August as bad as yours in England. Many thanks for the last sheets of Priapeia which worthily end your work. My holiday has been spent in translating you and I enclose final copy. I should like it to be type written (if not to be had, copyist; but I prefer former—<u>of course at my expense</u>) and then to be carefully read by you and reviewed—no ceremony! you know that is by no means in my way. Lastly, I would have your corrected copy (<u>with original</u>) so as to give a final polish. This should be done, if possible, before Nov. 1, as soon after that time we shall be starting for winter in North Africa.

I am pretty sure that your volume will sell, so I have made all these preparations. Your idea of Lat. text prefixed and notes suffixed is good. For frontispiece let me suggest Hindu women in Moor's Pantheon[4] admiring the Linga-Yoni; it is (we must avoid everything "bawdy") delicate and artistic. The vol. must be large and handsome, a credit to Brit. "Pornology."

Under existing circumstances, I would not (if I were you) hurry on the printing of Aloisia Sigea[5] or we may draw down some molesting measures. The papers tell me that Vizetelly's[6] petition is refused, although good names were on it. I can't pity him: he gave up the game too tamely. If I am brought into court it will be with the Bible and Shakespeare and I will insist upon reading the passages which are at

---

[1] Huntington Library. ALS MS. Burton-Smithers Papers, Box 2.
[2] Arabic.
[3] Huntington Library. ALS MS. Burton-Smithers Papers, Box 2.
[4] Edward Moor *The Hindu Pantheon* (1810).
[5] See above.
[6] See Register.

point.

The effect of our English purists is to throw the hat into the hands of the French who get all the profit of our new modesty.

Write me a line to Trieste where we shall be about mid-September. The F. O. is complaining about my long and frequent absences—but I don't give a damn about the F. O.

Ev yours sincy
R. F. Burton

P.S. You will find it necessary to re-write almost all the excursus (e.g. names of male parts) and especially to "verify quotations." The latter point has taken me the devil of a time.

49. 1889/09/13. Richard Burton to Leonard Smithers.[1]

Consulate Trieste,
Sept. 13, '89

Dear Mr. Smithers

I rec^d y^{rs} of sept. 8, yesterday. Your having copied my "Arabic in Shorthand" without almost a fault is sufficient comment upon the ability of the copying expert.

All your alterations in red ink are marked improvements; in fact you have been set upon the true way—literalism and now all will go well. You will be quite right to subjoin all the shorter notes. I shall not leave for Africa till Nov. 15 (circa). In Tunis and Algiers I shall hear from you as at Trieste.

I have made no notes on Introduction or excursus; but shall be ready with a few lines of Foreword to my translation. What do you say to this title page? (I should like to see this in print)

> Cosmopoli 1890: Printed by the Erot. Bib. Soc. in one vol. 500 copies signed for private subscribers only.

> Priapeia, or The Sportive Epigrams of divers Poets on Priapus: The Latin text now for the first time Englished in prose and verse (the metrical version by the Translator of the "Book of a Thousand Nights and a Night"), with Introduction, notes explanatory and illustrations and excursus by (you must here adopt some nom de plume)

> Italian Frontisp. which is quaint and sufficient: Moor's is too Oriental.[2] Forberg is ready whenever you want him.

---

[1] Huntington Library. ALS MS. Burton-Smithers Papers, Box 2.
[2] The illustration from Moor's Hindu Pantheon that Burton had earlier proposed using as a frontispiece.

We must not hurry this affair but must allow full time for Mr. Nichols[1] to sell off 1st edit. When this is done I must find a new lot of subscribers. It is not my little game just at present (with "Garden," Pentamerone etc. in view) to be too prominent in the matter, but when time comes, I can work with old Quar.[2] Rob. & Kers.[3] Arbuthnot and a host of others. Let us say 500 copies at £3.3.0, 320 pp. with an outlay of £150-200 which we must share.

You are right to keep back A. Sigea till this matter is finished. I don't care a damn for the Saturday, the Pall M. and Co.[4]

For this Edt. you should prepare a short account of the translations into all the mod. languages of Europe, this proving the advisability of England not being left out in the cold.

I have a sneaking fondness for Brown-Sequard, one of the most original men known to me and his injection of spermatozoa deeply attracts me.[5] More of this presently. Payne's Aladdin has not yet reached me—patience! I shall winter in Malta, Tunis and Algiers, returning to Trieste end of April? (March?).

50. 1889/11/14. Richard Burton to Leonard Smithers.[6]

Trieste Thursd. Nov. 14 '89

Recd yours of 11th this morn. We start early tomorrow, will take Pros. to Brindisi & post it there after thinking it over. Also will answer letter. In p. 17 no. xv line 7 alter "youth" to "lad"—if not printed off. Otherwise no matter. Send letters to Trieste till further notice.

R. F. B.

51. 1889/11/17. Richard Burton to Leonard Smithers.[7]

Private

Brindisi Nov. 17
(direct Consulate Trieste)

Dear Mr. Smithers

According to promise, I return prospectus: you must have written it

---

[1] Harry Sidney Nichols, see Register.
[2] Bernard Quaritch.
[3] Robson and Kerslake.
[4] The *Saturday Review*; the *Pall Mall Gazette*.
[5] The Mauritian-born Charles-Édouard Brown-Séquard (1817-1894) was Professor of Experimental Medicine in the College de France. He claimed to be have been rejuvenated by injections of 'testicular fluid' harvested from animals.
[6] Huntington Library. ALS MS. Burton-Smithers Papers, Box 2.
[7] Huntington Library. ALS MS. Burton-Smithers Papers, Box 2.

in an unhappy hour and it sadly wants revision. However it solves one of my difficulties: I have now resolved to put "Translator of the 1000" etc. in the prospectus and Senex in the title-page of the volume. Pray take measures accordingly. I think you are right in not halting Edit. No. 1. But your Prospectus is far too long esp. with the additions you propose. So I send you a draft page which will cost little (and entail only somewhat more trouble in sending the long prosp. to bona fide) and efficiently fill the place of the long and expensive adv^t you propose. A morning's walk brought this conviction. All right about the index. You are right about the initials of lines, but after all it is a mere detail: we go in for matter rather than manner. Of course I paid through the nose for agency and was cheated accordingly: next time I shall consult you. Pickering & Chat[1], have promised me a set of illustrations and when I see them you shall have my opinion: don't buy till then.

Catullus gets on well (glad to hear that field of literalism is wide open). You shall see [Satyr.[2]] when finished. By the by what niche do you recommend for it (kindly think over it)? Please give me the metrical scheme which I have forgotten.

For Gr. & Rom. Sodomy see the great German encyclopedia quoted by me in Vol. X. I am told that the volumes are sold separately and that one need not buy the whole century. It is excellent upon purely classic pederasty. For Delepierre's "Point" you can apply to Quaritch, but 'ware prices.[3]

As soon as I see daylight through Catullus, I shall write to you in re Juvenal. I won't trouble you about copying Cat., but send you my text & transl. (like Priapeia) in one. Your handwriting is first rate for me, but I do not wish you to waste your valuable time in mere mechanicals.

I am glad that you see the advisability of not affiliating ourselves to any society. Let me hear from you soon.

yrs vy sincy
R. F. Burton

Print following upon these papers which will form an envelope.
Also make the gothics large & staring to attract the eye.

> The First English Translation (verse and prose) (Black Gothics) of (small type) <u>The Priapeia</u> (Red Gothics). The metrical part is by the translator of "The Book of the Thousand Nights and a Night," and the prose-postern is by "Juvanus" who

---

[1] Chatto.

[2]

[3] Joseph Octave Delepierre *Un point curieux des mœurs privées de la Grèce* (Paris, 1861). Delepiere was a member of Monckton Milnes' select Philobiblion Society.

has added notes explaining the text and long excursus on the pederasty of either sex, bestiality, masturbation, [...],[1] the cunnilinges, the figurae veneris (classical postures of coition), the habits of Roman dancing-girls, the tribadism of Roman women, the "infamous finger" and so forth.

The work will be completed in one volume (4°, large print and about ? pages), with etched frontispiece representing the classical Priapus and bound in antique boards. Five hundred copies will be printed (not published) for sale to subscribers only and the translators bind themselves never to reprint the work. The net price of the subscription to be paid when the work is ready for delivery (next 1890) (is £3.3.0) and applications should be addressed to the Agent Mr. ? ? of ? ?.

The Translators

52. 1889/11/20. Richard Burton to Leonard Smithers.[2]

Brindisi enroute to Malta
Wed. Nov. 20 '89

Dear Mr. Smithers

The day before yesterday, I sent back (registered) your Prospectus with a succedaneum: and I still think that the bigger text will be risking money and doing too much for an Adv^t. Please return enclosed for my friend Mr. Tedder (Librarian, Athenaeum) after taking from it anything you want. Keep an eye on Mrs. Besant as the case will be interesting to both of us.[3] What of the telegraph boys and Cavendish Square?[4] Catullus has reached No. XXIX and you will be pleased with it. I shall write again from Malta.

Yours sincy

---

[1] *immumatins*

[2] Huntington Library. ALS MS. Burton-Smithers Papers, Box 2.

[3] Annie Besant (1847-1933) then a leading figure in National Secular Society and Marxist (she was separated from a clergyman) but later a follower of Madame Blavatsky. She sued Rev. Edwyn Hoskins for libel, over a circular Hoskyns had published, accusing Besant of not being fit to administer children, on the grounds of her anti-religious positions and advocacy of family planning, when she was running for the London School Board in 1888. See the *Law Journal* Sept. 23 1889, p. 663. The jury could not agree on a verdict, and Besant declined a retrial.

[4] The "Cleveland Street Scandal" in which a brothel for pederasts employing telegraph messenger boys was uncovered in Cleveland Street. Many of the patrons were from the upper classes, including the Earl of Euston, and the Press promoted the scandal that followed its discovery. On the 16th September 1889 Euston had just been named in the *North London Press*.

R.F.B.

53. 1889/12/11. Richard Burton to Leonard Smithers.[1]

Malta Dec. 11 '89
(Direct Trieste)

Dear Mr. Smithers

Rec^d: 1 card Nov. 22.
   1 letter Nov. 25 with request for cheque.
   1 sheet proofs (all right)

I congratulate you on the event despite a streak of disappointment—which will quite disappear. Girls are more comforting than boys.[2]

Certainly let us say "Printed by the Translators" without "Soc." and now I have determined to place my identity in title-page "by the Translator of the 1000 Ns.". I must keep my few words of Foreword till all is finished so as to see what to say. The short page is in lieu of your long Prospectus which I cut up unmercifully: it will be for Introduction. Mind what you do with Quaritch and make no arrangement with him without consulting me. Of course, he will "take you up" (and us.)

No news about translations of Pr. as regards bibliography, I should mention only the marking Editions. No hurry whatever about Catullus (take him most easily): we must engineer Priapeia first. We will certainly print text (Ellis? Mueller?), our transl. & prose with notes & excursus. I shall send you final copy in Latin text as before. (Let me know when you find notes.)

With respect to the trade we must be guided by our subscribers' list. For The A. N. I paid the trade 10 percent: my wife (for her edition) 20 percent or so. Our main object should be to get as many private names as possible.

Again thanks for your kindness in the matter of copying, etc. The details as regards Nichols[3] are (alas!) perfectly intelligible. The A. N. pictures have not yet come and you will do wisely to await my opinion. The price is heavy and may be money quite thrown away. Clouston should do his best to become a journalist, pure and simple; these books will pay no more and his keenness in chase of coin would better suit a newspaper.

Today I have had a misfortune. We had taken passages for Tunis & yesterday the weather, which has been perfect summer, turned to the bad and this morning the wind (Scirocco) is awful, blowing big guns, it rains

---

[1] Huntington Library. ALS MS. Burton-Smithers Papers, Box 2.
[2] Smithers had just had a daughter born to him, Lena—she would only live a few years, dying on the same day that his son Jack was born in 1891.
[3] Harry Sidney Nichols, see Register.

and the sea is rough as rough can be. So we are obliged to spend another week in Malta and I am dead tired of the place. Next time, I hope to write to you from Africa.

ev yrs sincy
R. F. Burton

54. 1889/12/20. Richard Burton to Leonard Smithers.[1]

>Tunis (direct British Consulate Gen., Tunis, N. Africa)
>Dec. 20 (end of my yearly mourning : birth of Sun-god tomorrow; meanwhile, weather nasty.)

My dear Mr. Smithers

Yesterday I received yours of Dec. 4 returning the Sidda but no Aglae[2] and no proof of Adv^t. They will probably come by next mail and as you wrote to me here direct (for a month), the letter will not be a full fortnight on its way.

I got dead sick of Malta. Well civilized society, charming Hotel, first rate food, look out on dead hole across a street you could spit over and failed to get away as the weather was breaking. But last Thursday, I mustered up courage although not a little funking for my wife and set out in face of rain and Grigale (Eurakylon)?[3] we tossed a few but made this port yesterday morn. and in the evening got your letter. I am now answering the latter.

Mr. Ashbee will surely send you the book—he is very good in that way. You must see "Apprius".[4] Certainly insert a biographical list of Latin Edns. as complete as you can collect without over trouble or time-waste.

Don't hurry about Catullus. I am about half way through him—rough copy which will take a power of correcting and polishing. By the bye, I like your Scherzi[5] very well as Scherzi but not as translations. These according to me should be more serious e.g. Lesbia 7, VIII:

>*Caelius! That Lesbia ours, that Lesbia*
>*That Lesbia, she Catullus loved erst*
>*Than self more fondly and than all his kin—*

---

[1] Huntington Library. ALS MS. Burton-Smithers Papers, Box 1. Incorrectly dated there as 1888/12/20.

[2] *Aglae: An Idyll, An Erotic Fairy Story* ('Athens': Erotika Biblion Society, 1889).

[3] Eurakylon, or Grigale: a northeaster gale.

[4] *History of King Apprius* (Paris, 1728) (an anagram for Priapus).

[5] Jokes.

She now when four roads fork and alleys lurk
Gulps down th' high-spirited seed from Remus sprung[1]

And so forth

Don't begin Catullus till you are quite free from necessary work and then begin with a will. My part will be done about March.

I note the absolute injustice with which Mrs. Besant was treated by the Judge etc., and I propose to comment upon it. The Cavendish Sq^r. business appears to be compromising and one of the Princes is named in the matter.

As soon as Catullus is finished I shall take up Juvenal and Shaykh Sa'di, whose "practice" will make Brit. Pub.'s hair stand on end. He has his way more philosophically even than Horace.

If your weather is bad we are not much better off here, only it is dull sky and no sun for fog & snow. Of course, we grumble—that is human nature. Being amongst Moslems again is a kind of repose to me. The atmosphere of Christendom demoralizes and distresses me. Write as soon as you can.

Yrs very sincy
R. F. B.

55. 1890/01/08. Richard Burton to Leonard Smithers.[2]

Trieste (Direct c/o Consulate General Algiers) Jan. 8

My dear Mr. Smithers

Yours of Jan. 2 came yesterday. Post offices are Devil's Delights. You escaped a cheat-fee of 8d and we have just had to pay 3 francs for an open-end parcel of photos <u>because</u> a seal was on the string. No reason with these rascals.

Xmas to New Year et. seq. is a fortnight utterly wasted in England and the English world. I suppose, however, that your printers after the venal swinery are getting back into business. But I can pity the poor beasts: life in England for the poor working man is a mere Purgatory. So, by the bye, is the English Country house life for women: it is a standing marvel to me how they stand it. What would French or Italian

---

[1] The version Burton published has
"Caelius! That Lesbia of ours, that Lesbia,
That only Lesbia by Catullus loved,
Than self, far fondlier, than all his friends,
She now where four roads fork, and wind the wynds
Husks the high-minded scions Remus-sprung."

[2] Huntington Library. ALS MS. Burton-Smithers Papers, Box 1. Incorrectly dated there 1889/01/08.

women do under the circumstances.

Glad to hear the N. has shown such prudence. The Purity People sadly want a victim in order to quicken the Brit. subscriber and you must do your very best to keep the Ero. S. out of court.

I have done little with the Garden at Tunis where I expected so much. My French friends abound in promises, but apparently hold performance to be an affaire de luxe. Again today I am assured of "mountains and [mounds]" which will probably turn out midges & mole hills.

In Re Glubit, the orig. source of husking (corn) sets us pretty free to render as we please.[1] I prefer <u>sucer</u> because it is still so much the practise in France & Italy whereas "tossing you off into the gutter" is British & Northern. Moreover of our sources equally possible I always prefer the stronger and more exaggerated.

Juvenal will I agree with you make good work. Catullus progresses slowly but steadily.

Ev yrs sincy
R. F. B.

56. 1890/01/16. Richard Burton to Leonard Smithers.[2]

Consulate Tunis Jan. 16
(direct Consulate General Algiers)

My dear Smithers

By this time you will have got mine of Jan. 8, which crossed yours of 10th (yesterday received). I will notice parag. by para.

All right about the etching. £10 was an exorbitant price.

Mr. Notcutt as usual makes difficulties: he is a curse of Allah as an agent.[3] When you receive his list send it to me and I will carefully look over it and return by next post. You have answered him exactly as I could have wished.

Don't forget duplicate proofs of prospectus—one for me to keep. Before reading it I can hardly answer the question about February or March. There will be no reason for delaying the issue and I adopt once for all "By the Translator" etc. We must begin with circulars to private subscribers and end with the booksellers.

Of course, "notes in nonpareil" should be avoided.

But I should certainly make an erratum of "circumcise." If not, the enemy will have you upon the hip.

Certainly include Bibliography & Introduction. As regards

---

[1] Masturbation.

[2] Huntington Library. ALS MS. Burton-Smithers Papers, Box 1. Incorrectly dated there 1889/01/16.

[3] Oliver Notcutt, see Register.

Phallicism, Priapic cult etc. I should if I were you give (say a single page) about worship of Karma, Davenport's essay and other modern treatises, referring to them all the curious concerning the trite and well-worn subject.[1]

As regards the books (one & all) which you kindly offer to lend me I must await our return to Trieste in March. I accept with gratitude the Hecatelegium and shall keep it as one of my (few) treasures.[2]

Many thanks for the Abst.[3] of Hart-Davies:[4] I shall by no means follow suit. Is Robinson Ellis better?[5]

We should have left Tunis last Wednesday when my wife's Italian maid was violently attacked by influenza and rendered quite incapable of travel. So, much to my disgust we are detained here & probably shall not escape before March 20. I shall rush off to Algiers as fast as trains (40 hours) will carry us, keeping one day only for inspecting Constantine. The weather has been damnable—rain every night & most every day. Now, however, the glass has risen abnormally and we may expect a few dry hours before the spring rains of February set in. We are all disgusted with the climate & it is my 4th failure, the others being Tangier, Abbazia, Cannes & Montreux. Where the devil is one to go for a dry winter short of Canada or Tenerife?

At Algiers, I shall probably find a letter from you and will return it without delay.

Ev yrs sincy
R. F. B.

57. 1890/01/28. Richard Burton to A. W. Thayer.[6]

Hotel St George Algiers
Jan 28 '90

My dear Mr. Thayer yours of Jan. 9 reached me safely and found us

---

[1] John Davenport (1789-1877) *Curiositates Eroticæ Physiologiæ: Or, Tabooed Subjects Freely Treated* (London: Privately printed, 1875). The publication was apparently subsidized by H. S. Ashbee.

[2] Pacifico Massimo *Hecatelegium* (Florence, 1489), a collection of poems with frank descriptions of pederasty. "He was the King of Pederast; not a single scholar / Escaped his hands, so skilled was he." (quoted in Jacobus X *Crossways of Sex: A Study in Eroto-pathology* Volume 2, 1904). This book does not seem to have survived in Burton's collection, it may be been burnt by Isabel in the purge that followed his death.

[3] Presumably "abstract".

[4] Possibly *Catullus, translated into Engl. verse* by T. Hart-Davies (London: Kegan Paul, 1879).

[5] Robinson Ellis (1834-1913) Reader in Latin at Oxford University, author of *A Commentary on Catullus* (Oxford, 1876).

[6] Alexander Wheelock Thayer. Boston Athenaeum. Mss. L168.

still at Tunis, one of the most beastly places you can well imagine; so unwholesome that even Dr. Baker could not do a line of work. It lies between two fetid swamps and feels like a perpetual cold bath; the streets are grapevines and the roads impassable. We left it on Jan. 20 and took a week for the railway to Algiers, staying three days for Constantine. Here we are most comfortably housed (at the usual exhorbitant expense) and intend passing the rest of our leave returning by Marseille, the Riviera and upper Italy to Trieste. There's a report here that a new General order will compel Consuls to retire at the age of 65; in which case we get our marching orders.

Your last does not give a very good account of your head; let us hope that you have better news for us now. Of course you will not [...] Beethoven until you feel fit for the task—which must be terrible. Mr. Cautley[1] gives us a queer account of the weather at Trieste. What have you to tell us about the Jews? What more about [Mr. Joy] Your "anchor to windward" should have caught ground by this time, it will be a valuable protest against "received opinion" and at any rate arouse public attention. Have you written a line to Miss A. Edwards? I see she is making a great stir & deserves to make it, for her energy & perseverance. She will be the first to review you.

We were all glad to hear that you have had a visit from your nephew; 24 is a pleasant age for "self & party". You should keep the young gentleman for a time and look after his hygiene. Each and every of us "reciprocates" your kind sayings and we all look forward to a most pleasant visit in March. Meanwhile ever yours most truly

R. F. B.

58. 1890/01/28. Richard Burton to John Payne.[2]

Hotel St Georges
Algiers
Jan 28 1890

My dear Payne

I am answering yours of Jan 2nd: it reached me at Tunis and I kept it till we arrived at Algiers. Sorry that you have had such a bother about Aladdin. Why did not ask for my direction at Athenaeum Club? However I presume that all is now right and that they are keeping the book for me at Trieste. I have asked our friend Arbuthnot to take charge of the two Arabic MS.

    1. Zayn al Asnam

---

[1] Burton's Vice Consul, see Register.
[2] Huntington Library, Box 26, RFB 313. Postcard. Handwritten copy of MS by Thomas Wright. The location of the original MS is not known.

2. Aladdin

and he will bring them home in May. I regretted very much to hear that health prevented you visiting Tunis when at Cairo—the trip would have done you so much good. You should pass at least one winter out of England.

At Tunis I failed in procuring MSS for notes about the Scented Garden. Contacted all the booksellers in the bazar and people generally. No one knew anything about it. Today I am to see M. McCarthy of the Algiers Bibliotheque Musée; but I am by no means sanguine. This place is a Paris after Tunis & Constantine but like all France (and Frenchmen) in modern days duty is ditchwater. The [re…] is dead and damned, politics and money getting have made the gay nation stupid as Paddies. In fact the world is growing vile and bête. A vivant les chinois! A [new major enough] irruption would do Europe much good.

My wife joins me in kind regards and best wishes. Ever yrs sincy
R. F. Burton

59. 1890/02/07. Richard Burton to Leonard Smithers.[1]

Hotel St. George
Mustafá Supérieure
(direct Consulate General Algiers)
Feb. 7 '90

My dear Mr. Smithers

Yours of F. 1 reached me yesterday with list of names all right. I did not expect the latter and so my asking for it must have been badly expressed. The French post here is vile & I shall hardly dare to send it back to you before we reach Marseilles which will be early in March. Is this too late? if so we will risk it at once. Of course consult Mr. Notcutt[2] in any case of difficulty. The list is that of The Nights but it dates from 1884.

I have looked over Ch. 7. In p. 49 l. 16 ought to end with colon— "at the head:" not worthwhile cancelling page. But in p. 53 l. xlv there is a vile [metre] which should begin

"which lost mulct shall I pay of country" etc.[3]

I must either cancel page or put into list of errata. All the rest is quite right.

---

[1] Huntington Library. ALS MS. Burton-Smithers Papers, Box 2. A garbled version of this letter appeared in Young 1979.
[2] Oliver Notcutt, see Register.
[3] "Which lost shall I stand mulcted of country, and he that was …" *Priapeia*.

Thanks for [Catullus][1] of Ellis and Cranstoun: they are both detestable.[2] "Cybebe" is a very ancient reading which I shall retain when the original text has it.[3]

We had beautiful weather till Febr. 1st and since that a rainy spell which still continues. But the climate is not damp. The water runs off at once, and the wadi are dry half an hour after the heaviest downfalls. On 15th we propose to visit Hammám Righal, hot baths a few miles distant; direct Algiers as above. We are here in the outskirts of the city, about as oriental as Kensington Gardens and when I return, we shall move into a town Hotel. Algiers is a fine specimen of a French "Colony." A huge artificial Port, awfully expensive and quite desert of shipping. A splendid city doing nothing but doze on a hillside and look lovely. An Arab population thoroughly malcontent and "descolors" of the most squalid. Our old Austrian friend, Dry Rot, in full force. Roads except the main lines of diligence, detestable. Travelling arrangements, except feeding, thoroughly uncomfortable. Prices those of Paris and more so. A rule of [Magus], [Sorcerer] & [lie].

I have done little with the Garden although they still make promises. Have reached Catullus 7xviiii: the run in is now easy. After that correction—which is not. Let me hear from you soon.

Ev yrs sincy
R.F.B.

Dr. Baker[4] who is with me has a Ms. 450 pp. clean writing which he wants to print at his own expense. Proofs will have to be corrected from Trieste & sent back per return of post.

Paper must be good and type handsome. Could you manage to get me a rough estimate, taking average page and so forth.[5] After this we might discuss the binding and other particulars.

R. F. Burton.

60. 1890/02/12. Richard Burton to A. B. Ellis.[6]

Hotel St George, Algiers

---

[1]
[2] Robinson Ellis *The Poems and Fragments of Catullus* (London: John Murray 1871). James Cranstoun *The Poems of Valerius Catullus* (Edinburgh: Nimmo, 1867).
[3] Catullus used either Cybebe or Cybele as the name of the Phrygian Mother of the Gods, depending on the metre.
[4] F. Grenfell Baker, see Register.
[5] Frederick Grenfell Baker *The Model Republic*. This was eventually published by H. S. Nichols in 1895.
[6] Royal Asiatic Society RB 1/1/6.

Feb 12 '90
(direction c/o Consulate General)

My dear Mr. Ellis

Yours of Jan 29 followed me to this place. We have been passaging at Malta, Tunis etc. As regards "Changán" جبوك which I would translate "Bolo or Horseback" you seem to have looked up all the authorities known to me. You might, however, add to them the Thousand Nights (I have no copy here) where the index will save you the bother of wading through whole volumes. See the story of the Shi'ah who attempted to kill Haroun Al-Rashid. Sorry that I have not more to say.

As regards Taymúr al Wahsh[1] I have quoted (Unexplored Syria) the popular tradition known to every Damascene. Probably it is not historical, but it is firmly established in local folk-lore. Every guide book mentions "My Lord Iron's" nickname The Wild Beast and possibly the legend was invented by way of comment. He drove away all the Persian (Shi'ah) swordsmiths, and from his day no "Damascus blade" has been made at Damascus.

I have found these French colonies perfectly casual & futile. The men take months before making up their minds to do anything. A most profligate waste of time! My prime object in visiting Tunis was to obtain information concerning The Scented Garden, to consult Mss. etc. After a month's hard work I came upon only a single copy, the merest compendium, lacking also chapt. xxi my chief want.

From this place we go (Sat. next) to Hammám Ríghah (the absurd French "R'isha") for a week or ten days. Shall return to Algiers, steam for Marseille and return to Trieste via the Riviera and Northern Italy—a route of which I am dead sick.

Let us hope that the untanned leather bindings have spared you their malaria. You will not see me in England next summer, but after March 19 '91 I shall be free as air to come & to go.

I am yours very sincy
R. F. Burton

61. 1890/02/20. Richard Burton to Leonard Smithers.[2]

Hammam Risha (Righah)[3]
direct c/o Consul Gen. Algiers
Feb. 20/90

My dear Mr. Smithers

---

[1] Tamerlane.
[2] Huntington Library. ALS MS. Burton-Smithers Papers, Box 2.
[3] Hot springs.

Seduced by Guide-book lies, I came to this place (4 ^{hrs} rail & 1 coach) from Algiers and found it damnable. A half-finished country concern owned & managed by a French "Gentleman"—with all French cheek, meanness & bounce. Building ¼-finished. Advertises a hundred rooms but only some 40 furnished. Dining room like hall of work-house. Old piscina under the drawing room, making atmosphere like English stable—tempered for benefit of grooms. To make matters worse rain in torrents and all the world wet. I am dying to get away from this wet Hell.

And now to answer yours received Feb. 18. Mr. Notcutt always forgets when he sees no way to turn coin. My idea was to stamp "Translator of Arabian Nights" in blue ink upon the envelope so that the latter might have a chance of being opened. My wife's plan was not safe.

The list shall be returned to you from Marseilles. Here the Post Office cannot be trusted. Their delays are terrible and you never know when they lose. You are quite right about not losing time.

It will hardly be worthwhile reprinting pp. 53-54, a note in errata will be amply sufficient. I have boggled awfully about that blessed line and am not yet satisfied with it.

As regards the etching I hardly think that you can do better than accept the £7.10. Your printer is certainly slow and I do not usually trust to printers' promises. However as his delays suit your over-occupation, we must not grumble.

Dr. Baker has filled up the paper of queries which you have been kind enough to draw up. As it is his first book, he naturally wants to see the minimum it will cost to print.

Two days ago, I finished "final copy" of Catullus and have begun to polish it up—which will take some time. I will then copy it myself again, re-correct and give it to my copyist at Trieste, so that you may be spared the bother of decyphering me. Before sending it, however, I want to see your prose version. From Trieste you shall receive the text I have chosen—Lucian Mueller, Leipzig, Teubner '85. Of course, you will not confine yourself to it, but take what appears to you best from all editions. It will be better not to print the Latin; but to give a reference when an unusual reading is chosen. What do you think of Postgate?[1] Everything shows me that there is room for a new version.

We return to Algiers next week & leave for Marseilles early in March.

Ev yrs sincy
R. F. Burton

Cl[2]

---

[1] John Percival Postgate (1853-1926) *Gai Valeri Catulli Carmina* (Londini, 1889). This was an edition of the Latin text of Catullus, left untranslated.

[2] *Catullus* (1893). Compare with the final published translation

Faring thro' many a folk & plowing many a sea-plain
These thy sad funeral-rites seek I, O brother of me,
So wi' the latest boons to the dead bestowed I pay not thee
And I address in vain ashes a-silent for age,
Sithence of thee (very thee) to bereave me Fortune was hindered,
Woe for thee, Brother forlore, cruelly torn from my love.
Yet in the meanwhile now what olden usage of forbears
Brings as the boons that befit mournfullest funeral rites,
Taken these gifts that flow with tear-floods shed by thy brother,
And to perpetual time, Brother all hail and farewell.

62. 1890/03/05. Richard Burton to Leonard Smithers.[1]

Algiers March 5 '90

My dear Mr. Smithers

Yours of Feb 25 has just reached me—needless to say it has wandered long and far. Sheet 8 also received. As regards the list I have looked over it and find that most of it must be revised: it dates from '84-89. I cannot correct it before returning to Trieste and comparing it with my other papers. Better to endure delay or a week or 10 days than to post many circulars to the dead & the disappeared. I return Ep. 95 of the Priapeia with a few pencillings: have no Latin copy here, but it appears to me that you follow the Latin inversions too faithfully. The first point is to make pleasant reading. I keep Juv. ii till you want it back.

My holidays are nearly over (March 15) and we embark as soon as we can get a good steamer. Don't write to me or send anything till I let you know my direction—it will probably be Trieste. Enclosed is a cutting which please return: has Mr. Bridger been making a fool of himself? Men like Mr. Thompson deserve to be run in on account of their extreme carelessness.[2]

I have not been lucky with the Scented Garden: no native has been

---

Faring thro' many a folk and plowing many a sea-plain
These sad funeral-rites (Brother!) to deal thee I come,
So wi' the latest boons to the dead bestowed I may gift thee,
And I may vainly address ashes that answer have none,
Sithence of thee, very thee, to deprive me Fortune behested,
Woe for thee, Brother forlore! Cruelly severed fro' me.
Yet in the meanwhile now what olden usage of forbears
Brings as the boons that befit mournfullest funeral rites,
Thine be these gifts which flow with tear-flood shed by thy brother,
And, for ever and aye (Brother!) all hail and farewell.

[1] Huntington Library. ALS MS. Burton-Smithers Papers, Box 2.
[2] Possibly George Thompson, noticed by H. S. Ashbee in *Catena Librorum Tacendorum*, pp. 218-9, for *The Bridal Chamber* (New York, 1856). Ashbee describes his prolific output as "cheap, racy literature."

found to assist me. So I have to work entirely alone upon a single MS. all full of errors. This hurts my workman's conscience but needs must when the Devil drives. Catullus is being carefully revised, polished up etc., and a very troublesome operation is that same. I must end by copying it out myself and then have it copied by my scribes. Don't send me your prose of Catullus until you receive Müller's text—that which I have used for the verse. We can then either stick to it or change, as the spirit moves. But we will certainly omit the text, while recording only the most important var.[1] text. In this way, we shall produce a scholarlike book of use to Latinists and not a mere translation like Elton and Lamb.[2]

What do you think of this? I presume we shall have to print privately for subscribers and to put on a fancy price.

By the bye we must not forget sending programme of Priapeia to the Universities, Colleges & Professors in the United States. Of course, you have kept the list.

And in annotating Catullus, we must avoid repeating the notes of the Priapeia. This difficulty will be got over only by full reading. Adieu till next time.

Ev yrs sincy
R. F. B.

63. 1890/03/26. Richard Burton to A. B. Ellis.[3]

Trieste Austria
March 26 / 90

My dear Mr. Ellis

It was very kind and friendly of you to write about the Scented G. Mss. Yours is dated Feb. 26 and has just reached me on return from a 4 mths trip to Brindisi—Malta—Tunis—Algeria—Marseille etc. I really rejoice to hear that you and Mr. Bendall have escaped alive from those ground floor abominations stinking of half-rotten leather.[4]

Mrs. (Miss?) F. Groff[5] has I suppose printed the Zotenburg[6] Ms. of "Zayn". I shall get details from my friend.

I think you may rely upon the Damascus tradition: the grey beards

---

[1] variant.
[2] Charles Abraham Elton *Specimens of the classic poets* (London: Baldwin, 1814). George Lamb *The poems of Caius Valerius Catullus* (London: John Murray, 1824)
[3] Royal Asiatic Society. RB 1/1/7.
[4] From the book binding department of the British Museum.
[5] Florence Groff. *Zein El-Asnam. Conte des Mille et une Nuits ... Texte arabe entièrement vocalisé et vocabulaire arabe, anglais et français des mots contenus dans le texte par F. Groff.* pp. 41, 49, lith. (Paris, 1889).
[6] Hermann Zotenberg.

declare that it dates from old days. Taymúr[1] hated the Shi'ahs and the Shámis (Syrians) who fled before him and since his day no "Damascus" blade has ever been made at Dam.

I know the two Paris Mss. (one with its blundering name): they are the merest abridgements both compressing chapter xxi of 500 pages (Arabic) into a few lines.[2] I must now write to Gotha and Copenhagen in order to find out if the copies there be in full. Can you tell me what no. of pp. they contain.

Salaam (or rather namaskára) to Mr. Bendall and best wishes to you both. You will see me in England sometime after March 19/90.[3]

Ever yours sincy
R.F. Burton

64. 1890/05/10. Richard Burton to Leonard Smithers.[4]

Trieste May 10 / 90

My dear Mr. Smithers

Yours of May 6 reached me today and I reply at once.

1) It will never do to withdraw the book after 41 names have applied for copies.

2) I must not take too active a part whilst my direction is "Consulate Trieste": my service ends on March 19 / 91 after which I am free.

3) I propose my agent Mr. O. Notcutt[5] to forward the letters to you and have written to him thereanent. Of course, he must not be put to any expense. His direction is Lyndhurst, Cypress Road, Finchley N. London.

As you are sure that Mr. Norris cannot be trusted, I think that you had better take in all the letters sent to his address and then no others need be directed to him.

Of course, some one has played spy. But how can that affect you?
In haste
yours sincerely
R. F. Burton

PS. The first thing I should advise is to clear your house of copies, correspondence etc.

---

[1] Tamerlane.
[2] The *Scented Garden* manuscripts.
[3] Burton means March 19/91, the date of his scheduled retirement from the Consular service.
[4] Huntington Library. ALS MS. Burton-Smithers Papers, Box 2.
[5] Oliver Notcutt, see Register.

65. 1890/05/11. Richard Burton to Leonard Smithers.[1]

Trieste
May 11 / 90

I wrote to you yesterday through Mr. Nott.[2]—he may be absent and not forward the note at once. You must be fully prepared for a search-warrant and we must avoid any chance of questions being asked in the House of C.[3] More at some future time.

66. 1890/05/12. Richard Burton to Leonard Smithers.[4]

Trieste May 12 / 90

My dear Mr. Smithers

Put off Rob. & Kers.[5] with some pretext: the rascals want to reprint. Also one copy for:

> George Louis Faber Esq.
> H. M.'s Consul
> Fiume
> Hungary.

I have told you more than once that my Foreword will be sent you as soon as your Introduction reaches me. If I were you, I would certainly announce Catullus. Why draft roughly? We have plenty of time especially as this interruption has occurred. The subscribers will keep for 6 mths and by that time the House of Commons (I funk questions) will not be sitting and the excitement about Priapeia will have cooled down.

You must do your best to find out if the house is watched. That can easily be done. You are the best dodge about the probability of a search-warrant: but you should be perfectly prepared.[6] The detective's blind is easily seen through. I suppose Vigil. Soc. of London who already had scent of the book some time ago. Tell me when Mr. Notcutt answers you. As I told you, impossible for me to appear openly so long as I hold the Consulate.

Don't forget to hunt me out Ausonius.[7] I am again working at Catullus. Pity we can't bring him out before Priapeia—no one could have said a word.

---

[1] Huntington Library. ALS MS. Burton-Smithers Papers, Box 2.
[2] Oliver Notcutt, see Register.
[3] House of Commons.
[4] Huntington Library. ALS MS. Burton-Smithers Papers, Box 2.
[5] Robson and Kerslake.
[6] Burton may mean that Smithers' status as a solicitor would serve as initial protection.
[7] See 1889/05/13 above.

ev yrs try
R. F. B.

67. 1890/05/15. Richard Burton to Leonard Smithers.[1]

May 15

Your two of May 9 received. The thing is a misfortune and nobody's fault. But there is one precaution absolutely necessary. All the copies at the printer's should be packed up and warehoused. We must then have patience and delay till times are quiet.

Of course, no one can complain of a translation from the classics. But the notes and excursus will bring us under the act.

As for Ausonious, I intend to translate the whole and I will at once send for the French and German translations.

I hope this next mail will bring me better news. Meanwhile […]![2]

68. 1890/05/—. Richard Burton to John Payne.[3]

Trieste May[4]

My dear Payne

At last! Arbuthnot has brought the Vol and the MS. I have kicked up an awful shindy with Athenaeum Club and the Post Office here, which can offer no explanation. However all that is over now.

I am delighted with the volume and especially with the ascription so grateful in its friendly tone. I have read every word with the utmost pleasure. We might agree to differ about Cazotte. I think you are applying to 1750 the moralities of 1890.

Arbuthnot's visit has quite set me up, like a whiff of London in the Pontine Marshes of Trieste. He goes today—damn the luck—but leaves us hopes of meeting during the summer in Switzerland or thereabouts. He is looking the picture of health and we shall return him [store][5] undamaged.

Best of good fortune to Bandello. My wife joins in all manner of good wishes. Ever yrs sincy

R. F. Burton

---

[1] Huntington Library. ALS MS. Burton-Smithers Papers, Box 2.

[2] *bal.'*

[3] Huntington Library, Box 26, RFB 313. Postcard. Handwritten copy of MS by Thomas Wright. The location of the original MS is not known.

[4] Annotation: 1890.

[5] Wright gives this as "to town" in *Life* Vol. 2 (1906) p. 219, but his transcription/copy definitely does not record that.

69. 1890/05/19. Richard Burton to Leonard Smithers.[1]

May 19

Sheet 21 rec^d. News (May 14) bad. Pity that the house-people could not wait a few days. Subscribers hate return of letters thro' the Post. However, it is done now. Mr. Not.[2] wrote to me the day before yesterday and seems not to have communicated with you or matters might have been arranged better.

Mr. Arbuthnot will see you early in June. Till then do not send out any copies.

This venture has come to grief and we must get rid of it as we best can. If I were you, I should see Quar.[3] and the others and find out what they will pay for the 500 copies en bloc.

We then can undertake Catullus and be more careful about wording the prospectus. Here is the difficulty: no one will pay three guineas unless the book is appetising enough.

Don't be too sanguine about the search-warrant or concealment of the printer. Those purity-fellows are great at bribing and you never know when an underling may sell you.

Arbuthnot has been here for several days. I have shown him the book and talked over matters with him. He can after a fashion assist you with Quaritch Rob. & Kers.[4] etc.

Ev yrs sincy[5]

70. 1880/05/20. Richard Burton to Leonard Smithers.[6]

May 20 / 90

Yesterday received yours & portrait of Mr. P. Can't say I like him. His characteristic is miserable, a childish development: it ought to be proportioned so as to serve for a club. What are we to do? Can this part be changed in any way? As regards the crudeness of the art, that might perhaps be corrected by printing on toned paper—a somewhat dark yellow to give look of age.

No news—good news: I therefore hope that nothing fashious[7] has happened. Here we are in summer weather and I [purity list] summer,

---

[1] Huntington Library. ALS MS. Burton-Smithers Papers, Box 2.
[2] Oliver Notcutt, see Register.
[3] Bernard Quaritch.
[4] Robson and Kerslake.
[5] Unsigned.
[6] Huntington Library. ALS MS. Burton-Smithers Papers, Box 2.
[7] bothersome.

56   1887–1890

as during the last two years [prior] [antisummer][1]—raw and wet.

I am working pretty hard at Catullus and have sent for 2 translations of Ausonius. I think we ought to translate the whole. Ev yrs

?[2]

P.S. By this time you will have heard from Mr. No.[3] and you will see my friend Ar.[4] during (or soon after) first week in June.

71. 1890/05/28. Richard Burton to Leonard Smithers.[5]

Trieste May 28 / 90

My dear Mr. Smithers

Yours of May 23^d rec^d with enclosure which I have corrected and return. Today (Wednesday is [un dis non] for posts at Trieste) did not bring me the proofs and I shall keep this open till they come. Ought we not to hurry up the printers and finish the Vol. without delay?

By this time you have received my letter and I repeat its chief object, viz. that I leave the matter wholly in your hands as advice from this distance is a farce. You will manage all in case of search-warrants, the printers etc.

Mr. N.[6] has manifestly made his pit and sees no chance of more, ergò he won't serve us. You are lucky to have found a friend in Chambers, as the subscribers <u>must</u> have some address.

Don't forget that when we make up accounts, I want you to show Not. all such minor expenses as postage, cab-bage (as someone said) etc. Of course movement implies expenditure.

It would be valuable to know what German Law could do in this case. Pr. is a cento of verses by Catullus, etc. Catullus is openly published and never prosecuted. A private vol. cannot injure the "morals of the people" nor in our case is it issued or published.

My friend Ar.[7] has written from Paris and will see you about 1st week of June.

Quar.[8] should be our last resource. It appears to me that your idea of sending circulars to safe names is very good & Mr. N. can give them,

---

[1] *antisummer*

[2] Perhaps Burton is trying to conceal his identity here in case the letter is intercepted.

[3] Oliver Notcutt, see Register.

[4] F. F. Arbuthnot, see Register.

[5] Huntington Library. ALS MS. Burton-Smithers Papers, Box 2.

[6] Presumably Harry Sidney Nichols, see Register.

[7] F. F. Arbuthnot, see Register.

[8] Bernard Quaritch.

especially M.P.s who would be interested in the affair.

Here I stop & await proofs.

May 31

Yours reached me last night too late for post: I send Introduc. this morn. One ought to have revises but I leave this to you. By the bye when the detective showed warrant from Scot. Yard could you gather if he had been directed to look after a swindler hunting for subscriptions, or was he sent about the Pr. in particular?

Ev yrs
R. F. B.

72. 1890/06/18. Richard Burton to Leonard Smithers.[1]

Trieste June 18 / 90

My dear Mr. Smithers

I did not answer yours of 5th and 8th inst. expecting every day the proofs promised on June 5. Hope there is nothing wrong, but with me no news is always good news.

Arbuthnot wrote to me a few days ago giving an account of his visit and decidedly objecting to my issuing anything before taking my pension.

I have asked him if he would object to our sending out 20 (no more) copies to perfectly safe men, so as to cover printer's bill and he doubtless will answer me at once.

By the bye how much would it cost to cancel all the pages where my name appears? I should be most unwilling to do this but it might be found necessary.

Meanwhile, I am most anxious to finish off Pr., so as to take wholly to Catullus. Our transl. will give us a fine opportunity of advertising Pr.

Have you not been able to hear anything about Ausonius? Old Quar. has promised to look out, but he will take his time.

I shall keep this open till post comes in and send it on if no proofs come from you.

3 P.M.

No proofs, so I send this off.

Ev yrs sincy
R. F. B.

---

[1] Huntington Library. ALS MS. Burton-Smithers Papers, Box 2.

73. 1890/06/26. James Augustus Grant to Sir Samuel Baker.[1]

19 Up: Gros^r St London
Midnight 26 June 90

My dear Baker

I have many apologies to make for not writing you sooner but I really did not know what to say about when we could accept your & Lady Baker's kind invitation. Our boy has not been right and we could not fix on a date—there were other things besides connected with our going North and as Mrs. Grant makes all our appointments I asked her if she c^d write definitely to Lady Baker as I did not know what to say to you!

In consequence I was not at the club for a fortnight I believe & today I got then the circular signed Fyfe which you received—I am not to give a farthing for a steamer as I already told you—the Africans have not been straight in the matter with me. Sub^s do not appear to flow and I doubt their getting enough to send out a respectable steamer—for even with £5,000 if they collect their sum it is not half enough to support a steamer.

I went and asked Stanley today about his book—it comes out on the 28th for the "Press" and later for the public so as to be simultaneous with America I think he said.

We have rcv^d no invitation for his marriage tho' he left the names of 200 before he went on his tour to Scotland—he was surprised because your names & ours were placed by his own hand after the invitations to his officers—but he is to see at once where the hitch is. I believe myself that no one has received their cards of invitation as yet. I wonder whether you ever heard a diabolical story told me by Nineveh Layard[2] the other day. It seems that when he was on the Council of the Geog^l Society about 1862[3] a letter from Speke was read reporting that Burton had made an attempt to poison Speke—the poison was to be put or, was put, in Speke's medicine—but the native—called an "Arab"—never administered the poison because he was too much attached to Speke.

I have hunted up the records of the Geog^l Society for Speke's report and, as yet, I have failed to find it. But I have it from lips of his sister that this is a fact & that it caused her brother great distress for some time—I have a bad memory & do not remember the circumstance but I have always felt bitterly towards Burton & declined to be introduced to him when asked by Mrs. Burton. It is probably for the reason that I must

---

[1] Smithsonian. M063d. ALS MS.
[2] Austen Henry Layard (1817-1894) who was given the Gold Medal of the RGS in 1849 for his excavations of Nineveh.
[3] According to Clements Markham *The Fifty Years' Work of the Royal Geographical Society* (London: John Murray, 1881) Layard was on the Council in 1860 and 1861, then resigned from the Council.

have known of this poisoning case. I shall find out when it took place—my own idea is that Burton felt so sore at S.'s discovery of the Vic. Nyanza that he tried to get rid of him by poison and claim the discovery himself.

It is quite possible that S. did not hear of it till the journey he & I made together when "Bombay" may have told him. The consequences of this plot if it had succeeded would have been curious. I sh^d never have entered Africa neither would you have discovered the Albert—neither would Stanley have been known except as the discoverer of Livingstone—a pinch of poison makes a vast difference in our careers—but thank God, the villain failed in his object. I believe all the Council of 1862 are dead except Galton and Layard—I asked Galton twice about it—but he would not say yes or no—& I think he must know it. Layard has a perfect horror of Burton and spoke quite openly of him in the presence of two [or] three others—I have written Kenneth Murchison to search for any clue to this tragic affair.

I hear Burton has softening of the brain—I rather hope he may get his punishment—cruel though it is to think of such a thing—but we will talk over everything when we meet—with our kindest regards to Lady Baker & yourself ever believe me

yours sincerely
J. A. Grant

74. 1890/06/26. Richard Burton to Leonard Smithers.[1]

Trieste June 26 / 90

Excuse hurry and pencil (I want to write by return of post). I had written you a long letter but yours of June 22 has quite changed matters. Thanks for Ausonius. I hope to receive him as soon as possible.

Remains only to accept your proposal and wholly to efface my name. The title should be:

Priapeia
by Nemo & Juvenis.

In your introduction I have modified p. xi so as not to dislocate whole affair.

I forward corrected proof of my ~~Foreword~~ Word to the Reader, with a few unimportant changes which can be easily made.

Also I send £25 for print expenses. The list of errata (marked X) will be quite sufficient. No revises of errata or Index wanted. I should like to revise your and my Introduction.

Notice to future subscribers will do very well.

The Frontispiece will now do well enough.

---

[1] Huntington Library. ALS MS. Burton-Smithers Papers, Box 2.

I am much vexed at leaving you after this fashion; but I must regard the advice of friends. Henceforward you will act as you please taking every precaution for your own safety and keeping me au courant.

Please send presentation copy to:

>Ralph Leslie Esq.
>St. George's Club,
>Hanover Square,
>London.[1]

If you see that things are safe you had better push the work as much as possible. After their failure at Sheffield the Vigilances will probably hold their tempers out of shame.

Don't trouble yourself about sending original accounts. I am quite satisfied to leave everything in your hands.

On July 1 [we] start for our summer holiday returning in early September. Write to me care of Consulate Trieste and the letters will be forwarded. From time to time I shall send fresh directions. And my last word to you is

Caution.

Ev yrs

R. F. B.

75. 1890/07/15. Richard Burton to Leonard Smithers.[2]

July 15[3]

My dear Mr. Smithers

Yours of July 1-6 reached me only this morn. I return the three pages you want but I regret that the errata sheet has remained at Trieste and cannot be found till my return in Sept. You will probably have kept notes of the important corrigenda and none of the others are required. Sorry to give you this trouble. Ausonius of Corpet[4] (French translation) has at last come to hand and it appears complete. I am still looking out for German translations.

We shall have a fine field and virgin in England. I am now copying out Catullus; but you had probably better finish off all your work with the Pr. before sending on Ms.

The disclaimer (p. xi) is as you say strong; but everyone will see my hand in the book, not to speak of the first Prospectus which we sent out. In those to follow, you should send just one, not mentioning any names

---

[1] Burton's physician at one time, Dr. Frank Leslie.
[2] Huntington Library. ALS MS. Burton-Smithers Papers, Box 2.
[3] Pencil annotation: "/90".
[4] Etienne Francois Corpet (1804-1857) translated Ausonius into French in 1842, republished in 1887.

but Outidanos & Neaniskos. Arbuthnot will do his best & so will Dr. Leslie to whom I suggested a copy being sent. I don't want to write anything in any of the copies until I return home pensioned. Catullus will serve to advertise the remaining copies.

As regards J. Payne, I don't think there is any risk of damaging him and if he disclaims the volume, he will only advertise it.

I congratulate you on the baby's improvement and only hope that you will soon find time for your annual holiday. What a bother those printers seem to be!

Thanks for your offer to furnish me with accounts & vouchers. Of course in cases of business this is the better plan. Kindly enter all first names of subscribers upon my old list and don't forget a prospectus to the Savage Club.

Yesterday was our first summer day: till that, all was winter and we suffered accordingly. However the air here and the excellent Hotel will soon set us up again.

Please write as often as you find time and let me know all the news.
Ev yrs sincy
Outi.[1]

76. 1890/08/03. Richard Burton to A. W. Thayer.[2]

Hotel Baur au Bar, Zurich[3]
August 3/90

The coterie was rejoiced to receive your budget of July 19 and to hear news of you which had long been expected. You have had a most interesting and exciting time—of course all [recompensed] your most efficient services to the cause and fêted you to the top of your bent, that was only to be expected and had it not been done your friends would have had reasons to grumble and complain. [Brun] was especially generous to you and [Brun] is not given to that kind of thing without all-sufficient reasons. I am delighted to hear that vol. 1 is to be reprinted, and now for the finishing of your magnum opus,[4] which you must press

---

[1] Outidanos.
[2] Boston Athenaeum. Mss. L168.
[3] Letterhead.
[4] Thayer's biography of Beethoven, originally published in German, and posthumously in English, and apparently still considered definitive: *Chronologisches verzeichniss der werke Ludwig van Beethoven's* (Berlin: F. Schneider, 1865). Although Thayer published three volumes in his lifetime, the first in 1865, the fourth and final volume of the work was only completed, from his notes, after his death. Thayer complained that he could not face the task of finishing it, due to his "head". Burton is referring above to Thayer's invitation to Bonn in June 1890 to attend the Beethoven

on for as soon as you have had a fair portion of rest after so much excitement. What you will want is collaboration or rather assistance in ordering and digesting your notes. Amongst your many admirers surely there will be found one ready to take the place of secretary or to find some young literati who is ready & willing to assist you in the rough work. This will at first be probably "antipathetic" to you after labouring so many years alone & single handed; and it will require a mental effort on your part to accept the inevitable—but I believe it is the inevitable and that it must be accepted if the work is to be finished. I hope I have not said too much but as a friend I feel myself bound to say it.

We have been at Zürich since July 14 and we start tomorrow en route for the Engadine. The weather, up to yesterday was unusually hot, has now broken into rain and mist, exactly what we don't want. However in early August it is not likely to last. Mr. Cautley knows where to forward our letters.[1]

Here we have made acquaintance with a very pleasant fellow George Catlin[2] (nephew to the Old Redskin[3]) Consul for U.S. He knows Montgomery & a host of other people and is well acquainted with your name. We shall have much to talk of when we meet—including the "unlucky Hebrews".

About end of Augt we go to [Basle] and later sleeping car to Milan; after that Venice and Trieste.

I have distributed all your greetings & good wishes and the recipients order me to re-ci-pro-cate.[4] And now nothing remains but to say au revoir

Ever yrs sincy
R. F. B.

77. 1890/08/08. Henry Morton Stanley.[5]

On the 8th August, after nearly a month at Melchet, we went to Maloja in the Engadine,[6] where we spent a few quiet, happy weeks. Sir Richard Burton and his wife were there. Stanley had last seen him in

---

Association's celebration. Thayer also wrote books on *The Hebrews and the Red Sea* (Andover : W. F. Draper, 1883) and *The Hebrews in Egypt and their exodus* (Trieste: Morterra & Co., 1892).

[1] Burton's Vice Consul in Trieste, see Register.
[2] George Lynde Catlin (1840-1896) a Yale graduate who had served in the Civil War and was a journalist before entering the US Consular service. Author of *Over the hills to the poor house* (1874) and other works.
[3] Catlin depicted 'Red Indians' in the US.
[4] The syllables reciprocate.
[5] Henry Morton Stanley and Dorothy Stanley *The Autobiography of Sir Henry Morton Stanley* (New York: Houghton Mifflin, 1909) pp. 423-4.
[6] Switzerland.

1886. Had a visit from Sir Richard F. Burton, one of the discoverers of Lake Tanganyika. He seems much broken in health. Lady Burton, who copies Mary, Queen of Scotland, in her dress, was with him. In the evening, we met again. I proposed he should write his reminiscences. He said he could not do so, because he should have to write of so many people. 'Be charitable to them, and write only of their best qualities,' I said.—'I don't care a fig for charity; if I write at all, I must write truthfully, all I know,' he replied.

He is now engaged in writing a book called 'Anthropology of Men and Women,' a title, he said, that does not describe its contents, but will suffice to induce me to read it. What a grand man! One of the real great ones of England he might have been, if he had not been cursed with cynicism. I have no idea to what his Anthropology refers, but I would lay great odds that it is only another means of relieving himself of a surcharge of spleen against the section of humanity who have excited his envy, dislike, or scorn. If he had a broad mind, he would curb these tendencies, and thus allow men to see more clearly his grander qualities.

78. 1890/08/08. Squire Bancroft..[1]

The two great explorers, SIR RICHARD BURTON and SIR HENRY M. STANLEY, were both friends of ours, and often dined with us. I couple their names because we were once together, with Lady Burton and Lady Stanley, at an hotel in the Engadine, and afterwards on the Lake of Como. My wife grouped them for a photograph, with Captain Mounteney Jephson, Stanley's friend and companion on his last great enterprise in "Darkest Africa," and a faithful black servant, Sali, who suffered terribly from the Engadine climate. One glorious morning I remarked to Sali that at any rate that day, with such a splendid hot sun, must be all right; but he only whined, "No, no, no, sar; ice make him cold!"

Burton was full of talk and anecdote; Stanley was silent and reserved. But my wife could always succeed in thawing him, and we remember well the dramatic force with which he told us interesting stories of his conversations with the King of Uganda.[2]

79. 1890/08/15. J. A. Symonds to Richard F. Burton.

August 15 1890

Dear Sir Richard

As I mentioned to you that I had written an essay on paederastia

---

[1] Marie Bancroft and Squire Bancroft *The Bancrofts: Recollections of Sixty Years* (London: Murray, 1909), p. 414.
[2] Stanley's conversations, that is.

among the Greeks, I am going so far upon the path of impudence as to send you a copy of it. It was composed some while ago, before I had seen either Meier's article in the *Leipzig Encyclopaedie* or your own Terminal Essay. If you look at it, you will see that I have treated the subject from a literary & historical point of view, without attending to the psychology & physiology of the phenomenon. Since I wrote this essay I have been able to add a great deal to it, which, if I ever dared to publish it, would go to confirm my theory about the Dorians (p:23), & to make the discussion more interesting. If you do not care to read, or to keep, the opuscle, please send it back, as I have not many copies. Otherwise take it as a very little sign of my respect for you; & anyhow believe me sincerely yours

John Addington Symonds

80. 1890/08/18. Richard F. Burton to J. A. Symonds.

Maloja
Upper Engadine
August 18/90

Dear Mr. Symonds

On the evening after I had the pleasure of meeting you, the "Problem" found its way to me. I have still two up which accounts for blunders.[1]

Gout is stubborn for too immediate action, I was to start early next morning, I was funky[2] about the weather — quid plura?[3] all this circumbendibus[4] to usher in an apology for not answering yours of Augt. 15. However two days of exceedingly pleasant driving (including one break-down welcome for its novelty) landed me at Maloggia the ill-omened term evidently a congener of Madora, euphemistically and [Hispanico] written Maloja.[5]

And now for the "Problem." Had you not told me that Meier was then unknown to you I should simply have referred your treatment of the question to his inspiration.[6] Specially in the case of the Dorians the consensus is wonderful. I am so glad that you are holding to the opuscle and hope that you will see fit soon to print if not to publish it.[7] Especially

---

[1] Two feet up, due to gout.
[2] Nervous or timid.
[3] What is still to come?
[4] Not getting to the point.
[5] Maloggia is the Italian name for Majola.
[6] M. H. E. Meier on `Paederastie' in Ersch and Gruber's {\em Allgemeine Encyklopädie}, (Leipzig, Brockhaus, 1837).
[7] `As I mentioned to you that I had written an essay on paederastia among the Greeks...' See Symonds to Burton 1890/08/15.

interesting it would be to trace the gradual degradation of the Achilles–Patroclus ideality through the Latin writing and down to Shakespeare.

Will you kindly give me the name of the French (? German ?) physicist who explains Le Vice by a third sex.[1] It would correspond with my masculo-feminine temperament. I feel most flattered by your sending me no. 6. It will be most useful to me if I ever carry out my design of producing a detailed study of παιδερᾰστίᾱ[2] ancient & modern.

We are expecting Mr. & Mrs. Stanley[3] today and I look forward to meeting him after some 6 or 7 years. Prof. Oscar Browning is here and lastly her Grace of Leinster[4] who is the Yankeeist article I ever saw out of Boston.

Dr. Baker[5] asks me to thank you most cordially for the interest you [...] in his History and to regret thus circumstance the miscreator preventing him passing the evening with you.[6] Believe me ever
Sincerely yours
R. F. Burton

81. 1890/08/27. Richard Burton to Leonard Smithers.[7]

[Kunsaal] Maloja
Engadine
Augt. 27

My dear Mr. Smithers

---

[1] 'Burton's acquaintance with what he called "le Vice" was principally confined to Oriental nations. He started on his enquiries, imbued with vulgar errors; and he never weighed the psychical theories examined by me in the foregoing section of this Essay. Nevertheless, he was led to surmise a crasis of the two sexes in persons subject to sexual inversion. Thus he came to speak of "the third sex." During conversations I had with him less than three months before his death, he told me that he had begun a general history of "le Vice"; and at my suggestion he studied Ulrichs and Krafft-Ebing. It is to be lamented that life failed before he could apply his virile and candid criticism to those theories, and compare them with the facts and observations he had independently collected.' Symonds, *A Problem in Modern Ethics* (1896), 78.

[2] Pederasty.

[3] Henry Morton Stanley, the explorer and journalist.

[4] Hermione Duncombe (1864-1895), married to Gerald FitzGerald, Duke of Leinster.

[5] Frederick Grenfell Baker.

[6] 'Circumstance, that unspiritual God and miscreator'---Byron. Baker wrote a history of Switzerland, *The Model Republic* (1895).

[7] Huntington Library. ALS MS. Burton-Smithers Papers, Box 2. Incorrectly annotated in pencil '1889' and therefore wrongly sequenced with the 1889 letters. A garbled version appeared in Young 1979 with transpositions from another letter.

Before answering yours of 21st I awaited the dates in motion of our movements and now they are determined. We leave this for Trieste on Sept. 1 and shall be about a week on the road, so you will know where to write.

Much pleased to hear that you have managed an agent pro tem. It was my blunder confounding sheets b & d.

Which is the right phrase Nunc Plaudite or [Vos]? For the life of me I can't remember and yet I could not have changed [Vos] to Nunc without reason.[1]

In Sept.-Oct. you must send out ample stave of adv^{ts} & rush the book as hard as you can. Parliament will not meet till later on.

Ausonius is desperately dull & will absolutely require the support of Juvenal. Meanwhile I am carefully supervising Catullus so […]

82. 1890/09/03. Isabel Burton to the Morning Post.[2]

SIR RICHARD BURTON and MR. STANLEY.

Sir,—Amongst other good things which our Swiss journey has brought us this summer, the chief has been an accidental meeting with Sir and Mrs. Stanley and Mr. Mounteney Jephson, for a fortnight, at the Hotel Kursaal Maloja, in the Upper Engadine. The colossal hotel stands on a small plateau, the frontage to the east looking on the picturesque Sils lake, surrounded by mountains; the back of the hotel west, looking on other mountain scenery, and the precipitous descent into Italy *viâ* Chiavenna. On Sunday night, the 25th ult., we had a grand storm. The lake was black and green. Dense, black fearful looking clouds enveloped the mountains, the whole lit up by red lurid lightning, accompanied by a glorious artillery of thunder, it turned night into day and lasted some 15 hours. This was attended by hurricanes of wind, rain, sleet, and finally snow, a perfect Dante's "Inferno," which left us on the 26th with snow-covered mountains, blue sky, warm sun, and an atmosphere which makes it a pleasure to live. But this is not what I sat down to write. We had often seen Mr. Stanley in a casual way, but we had never lived in the same house, we had never got to know him. I have had amongst my treasures for many years a note from Mr. Stanley, telling me how much he thought of my husband; and Sir Richard has always had and always testified his great admiration for the "Prince of Travellers." But now that they are always together, exchanging their mutual experiences and ideas, this admiration has developed into a sincere liking and friendship on both—on all sides—that will will last our lives. I can remember being

---

[1] 'Nunc Plaudite' appeared in the published version of *Priapeia*: "the ingenuous ancient imperative, Nunc plaudite!".

[2] *Morning Post* Wednesday 03 September 1890 p. 5.

prepared, from newspaper reports, to see a blustering, noisy, swaggering American, who would want to knock down and kill everything, and would be rude if one spoke to him. When I went forward to welcome him, I told him that I congratulated him on all his achievements, especially the last (his marriage), and that in my opinion he had got quite too much for one man. He stood quite still and stared at me with eyes that seemed of glass or stone, as if he did not see me for at least two minutes. I also stood quite still, and felt by instinct that this peculiarity is the effect of absolute shyness, and not from *hauteur*, and I have often remarked it in travellers fresh from the desert. We then all sat down, and Sir Richard and I had a hundred thousand things to ask him about, and were both charmed. We think we never met a man so modest, so unwilling to talk of himself and achievements, and yet so simple in narrating clearly any fact you may want to hear and understand. In a soft, quiet voice he will relate the most interesting things, and unconsciously changing his voice and manner, he acts the scene till you seem to see it. We are a party of six, Mr. Jephson being with them and Dr. Grenfell Baker with us, and it is just in our own little circle that his most attractive qualities come out. Without any affectation, he seems to shun all lionising, and to court perfect repose and privacy. He seems to us to be a man of the kindest heart and consideration, and it is only too evident that his followers perfectly idolise him, and would give their lives for him. I know this from Mr. Jephson, whom I knew before he went to Africa. He has also with him his black boy, Saleh, who looks contentment itself. You may see him playing dominoes with English boys (gentlemen's sons) at the next table to his master, in perfect security and happiness. Mr. Stanley is also possessed in the highest degree of another quality of the desert, which is given to a few only, and which also distinguishes my husband far from other men; a sixth sense, an intuitive perception which unveils all that surrounds you, however hidden, hence to mention one small item—lying or intriguing, it is like the gambol of an elephant, and one can scarcely help laughing in the face of any one who attempts it.

Mrs. Stanley, as all the world can tell who have the privilege of knowing her, is a sweet, sympathetic womanly woman, gifted with the highest and most refined intelligence. She seems to understand the great man thoroughly, an achievement in married life seldom accomplished under a year. I could not help remarking to her, after the first greetings were over, what an interesting and romantic meeting is ours. I said, "Thirty years ago my husband was the pioneer of all these travels, and I was the bride. Many travellers have intervened since then, and now (though our fate and yours are very different), after 30 years your husband has crowned these explorations. He is the hero, you are the bride, and we meet in this remote part of Switzerland." I know that these few facts will interest the public, and it is a pleasure to me that my husband, Richard Burton, and I, should testify our sentiments concerning Mr. and Mrs. Stanley. — Yours, &c.

Maloja, August 28. ISABEL BURTON.

83. 1890/09/08. Richard Burton to Leonard Smithers.[1]

Trieste Monday Sept. 8 / 90

No need to enclose (in other envelope) or register letters.

My dear Mr. Smithers

I returned home yesterday night & found two letters—Augt 27 & 30. We can now correspond regularly till mid-November.

The new prospectus, the title-page and the circular of Ovid will do very well (no objection whatever to sending it out with Priapeia.)

I have read reprint of the cancel sheet and deeply regret the necessity of change. But you will see that to oppose the general voice of friends & well-wishers would be impossible.

I return your three trans. of Cat. with pencil scribblings jotted down on the spur of the moment. You are by no means bound to adopt them but you will see what I aim at. Before translating you should read all the versions hitherto made and note their defects. Mostly they are not literal enough & they skirt the manifold difficulties & delicacies of one author's style. Above all things no hurry, we have plenty of time. My part of the work is finished for last copy and I have done half Ausonius.

Augt 30. The index is very good & by no means too detailed: it must have given you no end of trouble.

As regards Catullus we will certainly not insert the Latin. Take Müller's text as our main stand-by with variations where we find something better.[2] The title page will do very well only I would add

    by the Tr. &c &c
    Outidanos & Neaniskos

so as to emphasize our individualities. We must avoid all trite notes and dwell at full length upon the erotics which must be our main raison d'etre in view of the host of predecessors.

Maloja (Maloggia) in the Engadin did us both a power of good; also meeting Stanley & his wife—I liked her very much.[3] Also the Bancrofts (Mr. Mrs. and Master) were there and the first as usual kept us all astir.[4] There was my old acquaintance Lord Dunraven, as pleasant as ever &

---

[1] Huntington Library. ALS MS. Burton-Smithers Papers, Box 2.
[2] *Q. Valerii Catulli carmina, recens. Lucianus Mueller* (Lipsiae, 1877).
[3] Henry Morton Stanley. See Stanley's reminiscence of this meeting above.
[4] Squire Bancroft, see Register and the reminiscence above.

his very charming Duchess of Leinster.¹ Altogether we had a very good time, and we are resolved to pass next summer there before returning to England for good—or bad.

Tell me what you are doing and believe me ev yrs sincy
R. F. B.

The
Car.
of
C. V. Cat.
now Englished for the first time
literally & realistically
into Verse & Prose etc.

84. 1890/09/09. Richard Burton to Colonel Chaillé-Long.[2]

Consulate Trieste
September 9th, 1890

My dear Chaillé-Long

Very glad to see your fist once more and pleased to read your papers. You have indeed hit the nail on the head. Lately I met H. M. S. and his wife at Maloja, Engadine, and like her very much. He was still in poor health, and I thought somewhat depressed preparing for his lectures in the States. He is to give 50 and if possible 100, Major Pond being the impresario. What the deuce have you been doing in Corea? Making money, I hope. When you are settled in Egypt, please send me a line. I was choked off the mines of Midian by the idiot who made over the country to the Turks, and I know the Turks too well ever to do biz with them. You will find Nile Valley, wonderfully altered and the keeper in full possession. My wife joins in kindest remembrances.

Ever yours sincerely
R. F. Burton.

P.S.—Can't you pass through Trieste en route for Egypt? There is a bedroom for you. I want to talk over your Stanley article in The Republic.[3] Nothing like a U.S.-er to pitch into another. Vive

---

[1] See Register.
[2] Colonel Chaillé Long *My Life in Four Continents* Volume 2 (London: Hutchinson, 1912) pp. 414-31.
[3] [Footnote by Chaillé Long] The article in question was published in The Republic Magazine in May, 1890, and was entitled "The Burlesque Rescue of Emin," for it was generally conceded that the pretended rescue was burlesque. Emin had followed Stanley to the coast to encaisser la forte homme [collect the strong man], but failing to get it he scuttled back to his

Valeque.

85. 1890/09/20. Colonel Chaillé-Long.[1]

In Paris I received a letter from Sir Richard Burton, known to me familiarly as "Dick Burton." The letter, dated September 20th, begged me to come to Trieste and go thence to Egypt, that it was little, if at all, out of the way, and that he, as well as 'Isabel' (Lady Burton), was anxious to make the acquaintance of my wife. I was seriously considering the proposition to join him and Lady Burton, when a despatch from Trieste, October 20th, announced Burton's sudden death.

Burton was the prince of African explorers, a noble soul for whom I had a special attachment. His death caused me inexpressible pain. ...

The fact is, Burton had been badly treated by Speke and Grant, and hence his *mésintelligence* with them. Burton always claimed that Speke, his subordinate, had acted without his authority and had taken advantage of his illness to leave him, and take from him the honour of the discovery of the Lake Tanganyika, which belonged to Burton as chief of the expedition.[2] Burton's characteristic was loyalty, sincerity, with a horror of hypocrisy and cant. The Royal Geographical Society held him in little favour because of his independent and critical speech. Like Gordon and Baker, Burton was not liked by the cronies of the R.G.S.

Burton at twenty-one was a lieutenant in the 18th Infantry in Bombay. There it was he laid the foundation of his future fame in Oriental letters, by the acquisition of Hindustani, Guzerati, Persian, Marathi, Sindhi, Telugu, Afghan, Armenian, Turkish, Arabic. To these should be added a number of African idioms. He not only spoke the foregoing languages and several European tongues, but understood their literature.

Returned from his celebrated journey to Mecca, Burton found his vocation gone and himself without means. He was a splendid swordsman and a perfect master of bayonet fencing, then unknown in the British Army. With the idea of improving his circumstances, he wrote and published a manual of bayonet-fighting. A few years afterward it became the text-book of the Army, and he was authorized to draw upon the War Office for the sum of one shilling. The story sounds

---

provinces. The remark "Nothing like a U.S.-er (United States-er) to pitch into another" is made by Burton, who delighted to tease the author with the Americanism "pitch into," which amused him. Stanley was still paraded at that time as an "American," the R.G.S. not being quite decided to accept him as British subject.

[1] Colonel Chaillé Long *My Life in Four Continents* Volume 2 (London: Hutchinson, 1912) pp. 414-31.

[2] Speke did not claim or receive credit for discovering Tanganyika.

like a bad joke, but it is a fact. Sir Richard drew the shilling, and, instead of wearing it at his watch-chain as a memorial of the gratitude of his Government, gave it to a beggar. In spite of the conies of the R.G.S., who despised him, he was finally appointed H. B. M.'s Consul at Trieste, the salary of which enabled him to live modestly.

86. 1890/09/24. Richard Burton to Leonard Smithers.[1]

Trieste Sept. 24 / 90

My dear Mr. Smithers

I return Arbuth. who, as usual, is very nice and I join him in congratulating you upon the end of Labour No. i. My copy is not yet come: can there be any foul play in the matter? I delayed writing to you until your well deserved holiday comes to a close.

We must begin Cat. in real earnest about beginning of Oct. Never be deterred because someone has used the right word. Annex it impudently & glory in the theft unless it pay better to acknowledge it as a loan—this can occur only occasionally. Don't begin notes till we have both finished our transl. I shall have a small selection but they should go under Neaniskos.

As soon as you re-coup, please write personally to my wife and repay advances; with many thanks, saying nothing more except private chat & about the baby. I do not wish her to know that we make coin by it & I wholly ignore Catullus. Let me have accounts as regularly as you please when there is anything to account for. Also direct all letters to me, not to Lady B. because accidental openings often occur. I am very hopeful about Cat. & I think that Outid. and Neanis. will make names for themselves.

I am working too hard at Scented Garden for other disport and keep Ausonius for the winter which will easily see him finished. But he is flat and will want a blend of the sparkling & spicy. I am thinking of going at the (Greek) Anthology next. What do you say to it?

Write soon, ev yrs

R. F. B.

1 Copy (no engraving)
    Henry R. Tedder Esq.
    Librarian Athenaeum Club
    Pall Mall

1 Copy (no illustrations)
    Monsieur Hermann Gotenberg
    Bibliotheque Nationale

---

[1] Huntington Library. ALS MS. Burton-Smithers Papers, Box 2.

Rue Richelieu
Paris

I think you had better have two sets (bound only when wanted).
The greater part with the Frontispiece.
A few (specials) without it.

87. 1890/10/04. Richard Burton to Leonard Smithers.[1]

Trieste Oct. 4

My dear Mr. Smithers

You have had a sad tale of disaster to tell me and I deeply regret your disasters. Don't keep silence, as croaking and cursing are good for the spirit; continue to tell me all & let me hope that misfortune is in the descendant. As regards your difficulty about agent you should consult Arbuthnot: I will do the same. But why not confine yourself to sending out only the copies applied for by safe people & keep the rest till we can advertise in Catullus.

Do I rightly understand that you have already 240 subscribers?

I wrote that post-card to show innocence and to see whether it would arrive safely. No sign of your letter having been opened.

I am now upon a new lay. Read "Memoirs" and return. The little vol. (200 pp.) is being translated into English and will be ready for printing by early spring. It is most interesting & I shall add notes. The subject (natural hermaphroditism) has strongly affected Germany. All you will have to do is to collect biological details about Chevalier d'Eon & other men-women. This should follow Catullus and there should be no row about printing it privately.

I rejoice to see that you are not ceding to evils but [contra fortia]. The enemy is acting like a ruffian and so roughly that we can finesse him. ev yrs sincy

    Outidanos
    (who still expects to be famous)

Presentation copies to Dr. Leslie ("to be forwarded to Canada") and John Payne.

None to Cotton[2] (Academy).

Send Prospectus (in my name) to Lord Dunraven (who is quite safe) 27 Norfolk St Park Lane London W.

You should keep some of the old Prospectuses and Advts <u>for safe</u>

---

[1] Huntington Library. ALS MS. Burton-Smithers Papers, Box 2. Incorrectly dated in the box. A sheet from this letter is apparently out-of-sequence in the box and has been inserted based on content.

[2] James Sutherland Cotton, editor of the *Academy*.

people only.

Presentation copies to Tedder[1] and Zotenberg (not Gotenburg), the illustration (etching) cut out. "Copying clean" will be merely mechanical. Shall not be sorry to return to Arabic.

We had the usual burst of fine weather in the last third of August ending with a violent storm and a great fall of snow. Now the world is still somewhat white, but the weather is all perfection. The season however is ending and people are all on the flit.

When do you take your holiday?

We shall stay at Trieste till mid-November after which I intend proceeding to Corfu & Athens.

With many good wishes ev yrs sincerely.

R.F.B.

88. 1890/10/19. Richard Burton to Leonard Smithers.[2]

Trieste Oct. 19[3]

My dear Mr. Smithers

I have received a fine breezy note from you (Oct. 12): much pleased that you stick to Darwin's favorite "It's dogged as does it."[4] Our long lane must have a turning soon. Let me know your other address and see specimens of new Circulars. Don't trouble about money or accounts till press of business is over. Certainly no change of binding—you have explained the cause of its lightness. How many presentations have you sent for me? And could you kindly send my name to each and every in the shape of a card. That will save me the bother of writing. You should keep seventy prospectuses (the old ones) with "Translator of the A. Nights" in it. If I have not spoken of it before send Prospectus to

George L. Faber Esq.,
H.B.M.'s Consul, Fiume
Hungary

Glad to hear that Catullus progresses. I shall expect him in a week and that will give me some 20 days to look over and copy my own work. You ought not to delay beyond that as I start for Greece about Nov. 15.

---

[1] H. R. Tedder, the librarian at the Athenaeum Club in London.
[2] Huntington Library. ALS MS. Burton-Smithers Papers, Box 2. Incorrectly dated there as 1889/10/19.
[3] Pencil annotation "/89". However the content makes it clear that this is 1890. Burton died the very next day, October 20th 1890.
[4] Anthony Trollope *The Last Chronicle of Barset*. See for example the letter from Charles Darwin to George Romanes dated 1877 *More Letters of Charles Darwin* Vol 1 ed. Francis Darwin (John Murray, 1903) p. 370.

Thanks for kind offer about Chev. D'Eon & those of same kind.[1] I am preparing the book very carefully and want it to be a joint venture—it seems to be certain of taking. The subject is most interesting and quite new as a thing. I shall have hard work but no matter. Glad to hear that you have shaken off the cough and have recovered from "holiday", we have had a succession of violent storms here.

ev yrs
Outi[2]

---

[1] Chevalier D'Eon de Beaumont (1728-1810), a notorious cross-dresser.
[2] Outidanos, the pseudonym Burton was to use for the *Pripaeia*.

1890-1924 Posthumous

89. 1890/10/25. James Augustus Grant to *The Times*.[1]

Sir,—In *The Times* of the 21st inst. there is a notice of the death of Sir Richard Burton, an extract from which I give here :— "To the unhappy dispute between Burton and Speke, which gave rise to such bitter feeling, it is not necessary to do more than allude." I do not myself see why your readers should have any doubt as to which of the two travellers was to blame for this "unhappy dispute," neither why a slur should rest on the memory of Speke, one of the most upright men I ever knew—brave, noble, and true.

Burton's instructions from the Royal Geographical Society were :—

"The great object of the expedition is to penetrate from Kilwa, &c., and to make the best of your way to the Lake of Nyassa, &c. Having obtained all the information you require here, you are to proceed northward, &c., towards the source of the Bahr-el-Abiad (White Nile), which it will be your next great object to discover. You will be at liberty to return to England by descending the Nile, or you may return by the route you advanced."

On his return from Unyanyembe after discovering Lake Tanganyika, his companion, Speke, wished him to follow up the above instructions, but Burton, using strong language, declared "he was not going to see any more lakes." Hence Speke went north alone and discovered the Victoria Nyanza, returning to Unyanyembe with his 20 followers. The discovery of this lake seems to have been galling to Burton; it created a "bitter feeling" and few words were exchanged by them during the remaining part of the journey to the East Coast. Things went from bad to worse. Speke was too generous to publish what occurred at this time, but he communicated grave charges against Burton to his relatives and to the Geographical Society, and the judgement of the Society was shown in the fact of their selecting Speke, and not Burton, to complete his discoveries.

The two travellers had no sympathies, their natures entirely differed. Speke observed and mapped and collected the specimens of natural history. He was the geographer and sportsman of the expedition. Burton knew little of these matters. He excelled in his own line, made copious notes by day and by night of all he saw and heard; he had the gift of languages; while surrounded by natives he amused them, won their confidence, and so obtained those stores of information which have been since transferred to something like 80 volumes. He travelled with three

---

[1] *Times* 1890/10/28, p. 11.

heavy cases of books for consultation. These included a work on the Upper Nile, which would have been of important service to Speke-had he ever seen it!

A sore subject of "quarrel" was the non-payment of the Wanyamwezi porters who had accompanied them to their own "Land of the Moon." These men did not receive their just wages, in consequence of which upwards of 100 of the same race deserted the next expedition, which was in command of Captain Speke and me.

Under the above circumstances, and many more I could name, no one will feel surprised that "unhappy disputes" and "bitter feeling" existed between the two travellers, and I cannot see how it can be said of Sir Richard Burton that "no man ever succeeded better with the natives of Africa and Asia." Neither do I agree with the writer of the article that he was "a man of real humanity," when I consider his treatment of his companion and his native followers.

My long dead friend's honour is to dear to me to allow a shade of doubt to rest on his honoured name; therefore, with all respect for those who mourn the more recently dead, I ask your insertion of this in your valued paper.

I have the honour to be your obedient servant,

J. A. Grant, Lieut.-Col.

Househill, Nairn, Oct. 25.

90. 1890/11/01. Sporting Truth.[1]

I had the pleasure of a slight acquaintance with the late Sir Richard Burton, familiarly known to his friends as "Ruffian Dick." Not that there was anything offensive meant by that epithet. Indeed, in his case it had a playfully complimentary significance. There were in the old days, as many readers of SPORTING TRUTH will recollect, two famous pugilists who went by the nicknames respectively of the Old and Young Ruffian—the term referred purely to their style of fighting, and was not intended to convey the idea that they were any less decent or civilised members of society than their neighbours. For much the same reason was Sir Richard Burton dubbed "Ruffian Dick" by his pals. He was, without doubt, a terrible fighter, and sent to their last account in single combat more enemies than perhaps any man of his time. A man of peculiar temper, too, and strong individuality, with a wholesome contempt for Mrs. Grundy and all her ways. But his great distinguishing feature was his courage. No braver man than "Ruffian Dick" ever lived. His daring was of that romantic order which revels in danger for danger's

---

[1] Anonymous. *Sporting Truth*. Saturday November 1, 1890. Page 2. A small portion of this piece was reproduced by Isabel Burton in her *Life* (1893), Vol. 1, p. 181.

sake. No crisis, however appalling, could shake his splendid nerve. He was as cool when his life hung on a hair's breadth, as when he sat smoking in his own snuggery.

I know of nothing in the annals of adventure to surpass his memorable journey to Mecca with the Mahommedan pilgrims. None but a follower of the True Prophet had ever penetrated the shrine where the coffin of Mohammed swings between earth and heaven. No eyes but those of the Faithful were permitted to gaze upon that Holy of Holies. Certain and speedy death awaited any infidel who should profane with his footsteps those sacred precincts or seek to pry into those hidden mysteries. There were secret pass-words among the pilgrims by which they could detect at once any one who was not of the True Faith, and detection meant instant death at the hands of enraged fanatics. Yet all these difficulties and dangers—apparently insurmountable—did not deter Ruffian Dick from undertaking the perilous enterprise. He went through a long course of preparation—studied all the minute ways of the Arabs—he already spoke their language like a native—professed the Mohammedan religion, acquired the secret pass words, and then boldly joined the great annual procession of pilgrims to the shrine of the Prophet.

Careful and well-coached as he was, he forgot himself once, and was within an ace of betrayal and death. There are certain natural functions which the Mohammedans perform in a different attitude from that in vogue among Europeans. One night Ruffian Dick forgot this, and on returning to the tent noticed one dark pair of eyes fixed on him suspiciously. The rest were all asleep but Burton felt that he was suspected by the watchful owner of that one pair of eyes. The next morning that too-vigilant pilgrim was found dead—stabbed to the heart. "It was a case of his life or mine," said Ruffian Dick calmly when telling the tale. From that pilgrimage he came back safe, but there was not a single hour of the months it occupied that his life was not in his hands. The slightest slip would have betrayal him. But his coolness and nerve never deserted him, and he lived to be able to say that he was the first "infidel" that ever gazed upon the mysteries of Mecca.

How perfect his disguise was, the following anecdote will show. On his return from the pilgrimage to Mecca, his leave had expired and he had to return to India at once without time to rig himself out with a fresh outfit. One evening a party of officers were lounging outside Shepheard's Hotel at Cairo; as they sat talking and smoking, there passed repeatedly in front of them an Arab in his loose slowing robes, with head proudly erect, and the peculiar swinging stride of those sons of the desert. As he strode backwards and forwards he drew nearer and nearer to the little knot of officers, till at last, as he swept by; the flying folds of his burnous brushed against one of the officers. "Damn that nigger's impudence," said the officer. "If he does that again I'll kick him." To his surprise the dignified Arab suddenly halted, wheeled round, and exclaimed, "Well, damn it, Hawkins, that's a nice way to welcome a fellow after two year's absence." "By G—d, it's Ruffian Dick," cried Hawkins. And Ruffian Dick it was, but utterly transformed out of all resemblance to a European. His complexion was burned by the sun to a deep umber tint, and his cast of features was more Oriental than English, so that in the robes of an Arab he might well pass for one of that nomad race.

I remember on one occasion meeting him on his return from one of his many daring expeditions when he had brought back with him an ugly scar across the face. He frankly told us that he had received it from the husband of an Oriental lady with whom he had had an intrigue. "Ruffian Dick" had been caught red-handed, and in the brawl which followed, had received that nasty cut across the face from a yataghan. "And is that man living now, Ruffian Dick" asked one of his auditors. "I think not" said Burton, coolly.

"Ruffian Dick" had a stern, fierce, almost forbidding face, and not of remarkable power and character, and I remember an excellent portrait of him, I think by Oules, in the Academy a few years back, which attracted much attention. His wife, a tall and handsome lady, was almost as intrepid as her husband, and followed him in many of his adventurous journeys. She was devoted to him and so far from being jealous of his attentions to other women, took quite a frank delight in telling the stories of his amours. But "Ruffian Dick" was not only a great traveller and explorer, he was a scholar and a man of letters. I daresay some readers of SPORTING TRUTH have seen, or at any rate heard of his unexpurgated edition of the "Arabian Nights," which is hardly the sort of book a man would care to leave lying about on his drawing room table. He spoke and wrote fluently I am afraid to say how many languages, translated the poem of Camoens from Portuguese into spirited and graceful English verse, wrote an elaborate history of the Sword, besides narratives of his own adventures- But if his widow ever chooses to write the story of his life, the public will have some much racier details than it has ever had yet of the extraordinary career of "Ruffian Dick."

91. 1890/11/02. G. W. Smalley.[1]

SIR RICHARD BURTON: SOME PERSONAL RECOLLECTIONS OF AN EXTRAORDINARY MAN

   G W S
   London, October 22.

---

[1] *New York Tribune* (1866-1899); Nov 2, 1890, p. 16.

I believe I first met Richard Burton at a dinner given by Mr. Bateman, at that time manager of the Lyceum Theatre, some twenty years ago. He was then about fifty; in the prime of a strength and vigor which it seemed as if nothing could shake. His fame had been established since 1850, when he returned to England after his discovery of Lake Tanganyika. In every way he was a notable figure; a man at whom you would look more than once whether you knew who he was or not. He looked like what he was—a traveller who had seen many men and many climes. An Eastern sun had tanned him brown; a yellowish, muddy, freckled brown; a complexion a man may be born with, but seldom attains to later in life. From the mere hue of his skin you would set him down as a native of the tropics, born somewhere in Asia or Polynesia. If such a notion came into your head, it was dispelled at once by the features and bearing of the man. There was about him such an air of energy and force and masterfulness as we do not readily associate with Orientals. Those rugged features and the burning light of his blue eyes, deep-sunk, with a certain fierceness about them and him, the stature, the broad shoulders, the muscular frame, the air of alertness and cool readiness for whatever might be coming—in none of these traits was there any likeness to the languor and leisurely indolence of the softer races. He had, indeed, something of the Arab about him, and still more of the Malay, for whatever the Westerner may think, there are plenty of Oriental peoples with all the vital force of the European; or of the tigers In their own jungles. He had points of resemblance with Mr. Stanley, I afterward thought; the mouth and especially the singular smile were in each of the two men very much the same. The muscles of the mouth seemed trained to other uses than the expression of pleasurable emotion.

This dinner lasted, or the talk lasted, from eight in the evening till four next morning. There were other interesting persons, but it was Burton who kept us till this unreasonable hour. His talk had the kind of fascination which Robinson Crusoe's might have on his return from his island in the Pacific; or which Othello's had; or which Mr. Stanley's has when he unbosoms himself frankly, as he sometimes does when the company is to his mind; or when most of the company have departed. It had a dramatic power which was remarkable, and a use of pantomime which both men evidently learned from long intercourse with African tribes, on whom any other language than that of pantomime was thrown away, unless you happened to know their own. But there I drop the comparison. Burton's conversation, with all its merits and its quite irresistible attractiveness, had other qualities which were altogether his own. Some of them have since come out in his translation of the Arabian Nights, and still more in his notes to the translation. It is better to indicate them and pass on. But whatever his faults were, it might be hard to name another man who could and would have kept about him for eight or nine hours a group mostly composed of hardened men of the world, of journalists, of men who had to go far in search of novelty, and who, moreover, had to be up early next morning for work; or most of them had. A biography of Burton made up of the materials which he himself supplied on that occasion, would be something of which there is no present example in literature.

He was at this time, I think, consul in Damascus. Some years after there was a smoking party given by a well-known Londoner. I went late, and on my way upstairs stumbled against a man sitting on the steps, with a book and pencil in his band, absorbed in his reading and the notes he was making. It was Burton When I spoke to him he woke up as if from a dream, with the dazed air of one not quite sure where he is. I asked him what he was reading. It proved to be Camoens, and he told me he was translating the Portuguese poet. It seemed an odd place for such work, and I said as much. "Oh," answered Burton, "I can read anywhere or write anywhere. And I always carry Camoens about with me. You see, he is a little book, and I have done most of my translating in these odd moments,—or, as you say, in this odd fashion." And he added, with a kind of cynical grin on his face, "You will find plenty of dull people in the rooms above." He had been bored, and this was his refuge.

"Besides," he said, "I have been up all last night, and I can't waste time." I looked at him with that sort of curiosity one has in the presence of a perfectly unique, or, at any rate, original person, whose character and capacities are both evidently beyond the common. And I asked, "Are you never tired?" he answered "Never." Indeed, now that he had fairly withdrawn his attention from his book, he seemed wide awake and fresh. As he did not seem to mind, I pursued him with questions.

"What do you mean by 'never'?"

"I mean that I cannot remember that I ever knew what it was to feel tired or to be unable to go on with any work I wanted to do."

"Do you know Portuguese well?"

"Yes, it is no effort to master a language or a dialect."

"How many do you know?"

"Twenty-seven!"

I forbore to ask him what they were. He added, however: "I include different dialects of the same language in the twenty-seven." Bayard Taylor had a similar gift of tongues and power of mastering local peculiarities of speech. "I know," said Taylor once, "all the various patois and dialects of South Germany as well as any peasant knows any one of them which he speaks."

There came from the drawing-room on the floor above a great noise of talk; you might call it a roar of human voices. There were clouds of smoke drifting and eddying about Guests and servants were passing and repassing. And there in the centre of this stream and amid all the social hurly-burly sat Burton, indifferent to every thing around him, forgetful of it, hearing nothing but the music of Portuguese verse, living over again the miserable yet heroic life of a poor poet who had been dead three hundred years. There you saw one side of Burton which not everybody has seen; or had then seen. He was known, of course, as a writer of books. He had written many books, too many; some of them good, but the Burton the world knew was the daring adventurer, the explorer, the great traveller, the man who delighted to put his life at the mercy of a multitude of Moslem fanatics at Mecca, or of black savages in Central Africa.

He had already done most of the exploring work on which his fame, or that part of his fame, will rest permanently. He had made his expedition to Somaliland, a perilous endeavor. He had entered the sacred city of Harrar as he had entered Mecca, a thousand deaths encompassing him. He had plunged into Africa and had to plunge out again, he and Speke just escaping with their lives. He had tried again and journeyed to Ujiji, he and Speke the first white men to do it, and found his great lake, Speke finding also the Victoria Nyanza. He had gone on a mission to the King of Dahomey. He had gone to South America and crossed that continent; parts of it then not much better known than Africa itself. The world knew him, in short, as a restless spirit with a passion for travel, for penetrating into the least known recesses of the globe; careless of health, of danger. Impelled by a spirit which seemed to belong rather more to the Elizabethan than the Victorian era. He had not travelled to write books, he had written books because he travelled. And here he was on a thronged London staircase in Belgravia at midnight deep buried in the stanzas of the Lusiad; his soul engrossed in pure literature. He had in him, in truth, the soul of a scholar as well as of the crusader or the buccaneer. "His translation of Camoens," says a competent critic, "is in itself a masterly performance, abounding with the most recondite and learned annotations." And many of his books of travel are full of exact and curious learning.

The one piece of literature with which Burton's name is likely to be most closely connected is his translation of the Arabian Nights. That, too, is a masterly performance, yet it cannot be discussed merely, or perhaps mainly, as literature. The book is a kind of Encyclopaedia of Eastern life, and Burton has dealt with it as a man of action might deal with a series of physiological problems, of which many are entirely outside either literature or the ordinary range of human interests or social interests.

He has handled some of the most repulsive questions that can be raised with the most complete unreserve. "The sense of decency," said a European traveller, "does not exist in the East." Burton was in many points more Oriental than European and this elaborate work proves it over and over again. It will remain a monument of knowledge and of audacity.

A portrait of Burton was painted some years ago by Sir Frederick Leighton; probably the strongest and most masculine of all the portraits which have come from the hand of the accomplished President of the Royal Academy. He has drawn Burton as he was, extenuating nothing, and the force and fidelity of the painting leave nothing to be desired. Where this picture now is I know not, but it ought to be, if it is not, in the National Portrait Gallery. For Burton will always have a place, and a high one, on any list that can be drawn up of the extraordinary men of his own time, a man whom few surpassed in courage, in versatility, in actual exploits, or in some of the qualities which are most essential to the heroic character. He died Consul at Trieste, almost unknown to the people among whom his last years were spent, and half forgotten in England. That is all the British Government thought itself able to do for Burton except to confer on him a Knight Commandership of the Order of St. Michael and St. George, an honor which he shares with some two hundred others, many of them successful colonial politicians. G. W. S.

92. 1890/11/29. John James Aubertin.[1]

[…] on the 29th, in a very fine morning, I was again shaking hands with Mr. and Mrs. Lay at Hankow.[2] It was here that, on looking through some newspapers, I came upon a telegraphic paragraph from London, headed, "Death of a Man of Note." My friend of many years, and my colleague, not competitor, in translation, Captain Sir Richard Burton, had gone. Linked with some foes and with a thousand friends, this indefatigable author and explorer was, perhaps, too independent of public opinion to be conventionally popular and to be fairly recognized and rewarded. His papers showed that he was on the point of writing to me in answer to my letter on the subject of my visit to Macao; but the letter was never written: "Flere et meminisse relictum est."[3]

---

[1] John James Aubertin *Wanderings & Wonderings* (London: Kegan Paul, 1893), p. 361. Aubertin was travelling in China at this time. Earlier in this work he recalls, in passing, visiting Dalmatia with Burton (p. 194) and his "visit to Egypt in 1879-80 with my late friend Captain Sir Richard Burton" (p. 9).

[2] Hankou, China.

[3] "Ora Negatur/Dulcia conspicere; flere et meminisse relictum est." Petrarch. "No longer is it permitted me to see the dear countenance of my departed friend; but I may still weep and brood over the remembrance of what I have lost."

93. 1890. Francis Galton.[1]

Burton had many great and endearing qualities, with others of which perhaps the most curious was his pleasure in dressing himself, so to speak, in wolf's clothing, in order to give an idea that he was worse than he really was. I attended his funeral at the Roman Catholic Cemetery near Sheen. It had been arranged by his widow, Lady Burton, a devoted Catholic, and was crowded with her Catholic friends. I did not see more than three geographers among them, of whom Lord Northbrook, a former President of the Society, was one. From pure isolation, we two kept together the whole time. There were none of Burton's old associates. It was a ceremony quite alien to anything that I could conceive him to care for.

Anyhow, I was glad to be instrumental in procuring a Government Pension of £300 a year for Lady Burton, and in this way. At a meeting of the Council of the Royal Geographical Society, Sir Mountstuart E. Grant Duff, the then President, said that private information had reached him (of which he mentioned some details) that Government would be disposed to grant a pension to Lady Burton if a good case could be made out relating to Burton's services to science, and if the Council of the Society were to back it. Would any one undertake to carry this through? No one answered, so he addressed himself to me personally, asking if I would. I expressed a cordial desire to help, but feeling at the moment too ignorant of the views of competent authorities concerning Burton's linguistic knowledge (on which much emphasis had been laid), and of much else that might with advantage be advanced in his favour, was unable to answer off-hand, but willingly undertook to inquire and report. This I did, asking the opinions of many, with the result that Burton's knowledge of vernacular Arabic and other languages was considered to be unequalled, but not his classical knowledge of them, and that it was better to rest his claims on his wide discursiveness rather than on any one specified performance. I followed this advice, and my Report formed the basis of the proposed application, which in due course gained its end. My own acquaintance with Lady Burton was slight, and my memories of her husband refer chiefly to his unmarried days.

Several of us subscribed to have a public memorial of Speke, and obtained a plot in Kensington Gardens to place it. It now stands in the form of an obelisk, by the side of the broad gravel walk leading northwards from the Albert Memorial. There was much difficulty in selecting an inscription which should not arouse criticism, for there were still those who maintained with Burton that Speke had not discovered the true source of the Nile. Lord Houghton solved the difficulty by

---

[1] Francis Galton *Memories of my Life* (London: Methuen, 1908) pp. 171-2, 199-200, 202.

simplifying the proposed legend to "Victoria Nyanza and the Nile," which words the obelisk now bears.

Speke, Burton, Grant, Baker, Livingstone, and Stanley are all gone; I wish it could be arranged to make a joint and interesting memorial of our great African explorers in the plot where Speke's obelisk now stands in neglected solitariness. It would not require more than two or three extra yards on either side, parallel to the Grand Walk, and the same in depth, to give room for this, and to allow of the growth of a few hardy plants suggestive of tropical vegetation, with pathways between them. England has done so very much for African geography that she ought to bring the fact home to the national conscience.

94. 1890. Verney Lovett Cameron.[1]

It is a difficult thing to sit down quietly to write the description of a dear friend at any time, and when the friend is (or was, I am sorry to say) so many-sided a man as Richard Francis Burton, the task becomes a thousand times more difficult than in the case of an ordinary individual. I do not propose in any way to give the story of Burton's life—that has been done already, and doubtless will soon be done again—but rather to give to the world my own impressions of him as a man. Others may have known him longer and perchance better than I, but still I have known him intimately; I have been his companion in health and in sickness, in anticipation and disappointment, and have seen him in many and varying moods, and if I have the requisite skill may haply give a sketch of him which will represent him fairly to the world.

Burton was a man whose mental capacity was extraordinary, and whose physical powers were far above the average, whilst he also possessed a phenomenal love and power of hard work. It may be asked why a man so exceptionally gifted did not achieve a phenomenal success and die a Peer and Knight of the Garter. The answer is not far to seek; he preferred a position where he was practically independent, and where he could say and do what he liked, to one which, however splendid, would involve certain restraints. He was not a man to endure the wearing of any fetters, not even if they were golden and bejewelled. His independence he valued before all else, and this love of freedom and his unflinching, outspoken honesty prevented his ever becoming a courtier. If he could have stooped ever so little no one can calculate the heights (as judged by ordinary standards) to which he must have risen.

Many of his friends have lamented that his rare qualities and

---

[1] Verney Lovett Cameron "Burton as I knew him *Fortnightly Review* LIV (December 1890) pp. 878-884.

unequalled services in travel and to science, as well as those rendered to his country in Scinde and in the consular service, had never been properly recognised or adequately rewarded; not one word of complaint or repining was ever to be heard from his lips on this subject. He knew, and made no secret of his knowledge, the reasons why honours had not been showered upon him, and always averred that it was his own choice that it was so, for he far preferred to remain as he was to placing himself under an obligation to any than. His horror of being thought a self-seeker often caused him to say and do things which have been distorted to his disadvantage, but he never bore malice, and was more free from jealousy than any other man I have ever seen. Perhaps when one first met this tall, dark man, with his scarred face, piercing dark eyes under the overhanging brow, his mouth hidden by a long moustache, one thought the face a striking one but not attractive, and the cynical and sarcastic remarks which he often made did not tend to at first overcome this feeling. Then one came to know the man, however, one found that those eyes could beam kindly upon his friends, that advice and information would take the place of cynicism and sarcasm, and that under the rugged exterior there was concealed a heart as tender as that of any woman. Witty remarks and humoristic sayings abounded in his talk, but it was rare indeed that they were calculated to really hurt any man but himself, and it is a fact that most of the stories that have been circulated to his detriment have arisen from his way of telling anecdotes about himself, and putting his own share in the transaction in the blackest possible light. He knew his friends would understand him and recked nothing of what the rest of the world would think.

His entire freedom from jealousy was amply proved to me on the few and rare occasions when he permitted himself to say anything about his dead companion, Speke. Of Speke's work as an observer and geographer, and his industry, he ever spoke in the highest terms of praise, while of the causes of the unhappy difference between them he refused to say ever a word. Of things which had been said against himself he could give satisfactory explanations in every case, and clearly explained how easy it might be for accusations to be bandied about which had no other foundation than the delirious fancy of a fever-stricken brain. He showed, and in this my own experiences corroborate his, that often an idea is conceived during an acute attack of fever, and endures afterwards during periods of apparent convalescence, when the fever has not been really cured, but only rendered latent, sufficiently long to make as permanent and lasting an impression upon the memory as an actual occurrence, and that these fancies or ideas are often cherished for years as being actual facts. To the morbid influences of solitude or restricted companionship, and bad food (implying lack of nutrition for the brain as well as for other organs), to illnesses and demoralising surroundings he—and here again I can fully bear him out—attributed many random sayings and even writings which had been reported to the detriment of other travellers, and which both for the credit of those who first said or wrote them, and also of those who circulated them, especially of the latter, ought never to have been made known to the world at large.

Notwithstanding the allowances he made for the circumstances by which men were surrounded, as influencing their thoughts and sayings, he did not consider that they could be used as an excuse for acts of violence, and always held that it was both unjust and unlawful to force a way into or through any country in despite of the wishes of the natives.

In regard to slavery he was fully in accord with all the best feeling on the subject, and, though he did not enter into the matter actively himself, always encouraged me in my endeavours to combat this evil, and gave me good and wholesome advice, which moreover had the advantage of being practical and practicable.

In his feelings towards the negro race he held a wise position, as far removed, on the one side, from the looking upon each and every man with a dark skin as a "nigger," as from the gushing philanthropy which exalts the negro of the West Coast, debased by gin and spurious civilisation, on a pedestal of impossible virtues, on the other. Gin and gunpowder he would always have tabooed in Africa, and he was equally strong against the forcing upon the negroes a meretricious imitation of European civilisation, instead of leading them onwards and upwards to a true civilisation of their own. So averse was he to the results of this spurious culture, that those who did not know the true feelings of the man, when they have read his humorous and cynical remarks upon its unhappy victims, have often considered that he was hostile to them and not to the system of which they are the lamentable results.

His scientific, apart from his linguistic and scholarly attainments, were most wonderful, and if he had cared to make them known to the world he would have ranked high as geologist, naturalist, anthropologist, botanist, or antiquarian; in fact, he was admirably equipped in all ways as a scientific explorer, and when you add to the above qualifications his marvellous aptitude for languages and his equally marvellous accuracy, it must be allowed that no traveller of present or past ages outrivals, even if any equals or comes near him. Going over ground which he explored, with his *Lake Regions of Central Africa* in my hand, I was astonished at the acuteness of his perception and the correctness of his descriptions. One was tempted to apply the phrase of verbal photographs to his records of travel, but though equalling photographs in minuteness and faithfulness, they far excelled photographs in being permeated with a true artistic sense. As in Central Africa, so in other countries, the writings of Richard Burton on his many and varied travels, though they were not profitable to him in a pecuniary sense, being "*caviare* to the general," will hold their place with those of Bruce and a few others as standard and classical works when much of the sensational literature of so-called exploration, which is now poured out with as much rapidity and facility as three-volume novels, and of an equally sensational character, will have been entirely forgotten.

His translation of the *Lusiads of Camoens* proves both his philological and poetical powers, as does his rendering of *The Thousand Nights and a Night*; but while the latter must be locked in the closet of the scholar, the former can be read by each and all with advantage. The erotic nature of much of *The Thousand Nights and a Night* and of some other works which he had a share in preparing for the press has been brought forward by his enemies as proving that he had an impure mind, but nothing could be more unfair. As the pathologist must study pathology in order to find a cure for disease, so Burton, as a student of human nature, had to examine and analyse the impure as well as the pure, for human nature is so intimately compounded of both good and evil that he who studies one alone is apt to arrive at conclusions more erroneous than he would if he had never studied at all.

Of his religious opinions it is more difficult to speak than of anything else; his intellect recognised the fact that there must be a Creator, but it did not and could not tell him who or what that Creator was. His was a mind which required absolute proof of any system of religion before he could believe, but at the same time it was so acute that it detected flaws in any chain of reasoning by which any one endeavoured to prove to him that a religion was true. For those who faced him in theological discussion he was a difficult man to grapple with, as his retentive memory was so stocked with facts culled from Bible, Alkoran, and ancient and almost forgotten history that the brave man who entered into the lists with him found himself confronted with weapons of which he had never dreamed, his most cherished arguments confronted by others of which he was obliged to admit the cogency, in fact, his forces both outnumbered and out-generalled. Perhaps the best thing that one can say about Burton in his attitude towards religion is what he used to say about religion himself: "I cannot understand it, and therefore I know nothing." It was certainly not for want of study that he neither knew nor understood, for I do not believe any man was ever more qualified to write a critical comparison of the various religions of the world. Notwithstanding his own attitude of unbelief (or rather lack of belief) he never disputed the right of others to believe what they chose, or attempted to sap their faith. His ever affectionate and devoted attachment to his wife, who is an ardent Roman Catholic, is proof of this if proof were wanted.

Another point of superiority in Burton to most men was his power of instantly putting a stop to argument and dissension, and this whether the parties were white, black, or of both colours. Fortunately I have not seen him have cause to do this more than twice or thrice, but on each occasion his influence was magical. As he could control others so he could also control himself, and in my experience of him I have never seen him lose his temper, and the perfect submission with which during the last few years of his life he acquiesced in the regulations of his wife and his doctor, without one word of murmuring or symptom of dissatisfaction, was one of the most touching things I ever witnessed, and also a proof of how completely he had mastered what in his young days had been a fiery temper. These minute regulations were doubtless dictated by loving care and medical necessity, but none the less must have been galling to one who had always been a rule to himself, and had eaten, slept, drank, smoked, and worked as and when it best suited his own inclination.

Burton must always live in our memories as a great man who achieved much, and who might have achieved more had he not been peculiarly sensitive and afraid of the reproach being made that he was working for his own advantage. Had he lived in the Elizabethan instead of the Victorian era he would have been an epoch maker. And perhaps an age may again come in which a man of his exceptional type may find due scope for his energies and abilities. As it is, Scinde, Mecca, Harar, Somaliland, Tanganyika (to say nothing of lesser journeys), are proud names for him to have emblazoned on his escutcheon. ...

Soldier, scholar, poet, explorer, it will be long before we again see his equal, and as we feel his loss and regret never again to hear his voice, so must our sympathy be true and deep for her who has been his loyal, trusty, loving helpmate for so many years. Good-bye, Dick.

95. 1890. Edwin de Leon.[1]

A totally different type of man was shown in Richard Burton, a reversal of most of the characteristics of Gordon. Self-reliant, self-sustained, seeking no support from heaven or earth, substituting self-will for faith, and strenuous effort for Divine assistance; endowed by nature with a frame of iron and muscles of steel, he was an athlete who might

---

[1] Edwin de Leon *Thirty Years of my Life on Three Continents* Volume 2 (London: Ward and Downey, 1890) pp. 103-21.

have figured in the arena in Greek or Roman times. Audacious in speech and act, and fond of shocking the prejudices of those with whom he talked, he was the expounder of the most outrageous paradoxes possible to conceive. He was eminently a social animal; loved the pleasures of the table, and would talk with a friend all night, in preference to going to bed, and in the Chaucerian style. Yet with women I never knew him even hint an indelicacy; for the charm of his conversation was to them very great, he had so much to tell.

In his earlier days he was a strikingly handsome man; and even since his face had been scarred and furrowed by wounds and trials, there yet lingered on that expressive countenance the "faded splendour wan," which had survived his youth. Among his personal habits was that of carrying in his hand an iron walking-stick, as heavy as a gun, to keep his muscles properly exercised, and a blow from his fist was like a kick from a horse. Mind and muscle with him were equally strong propellers, and the animal nature as vigorous as the intellectual. He had the faculty of making staunch friends and bitter enemies, and many of each.

Burton had a curious characteristic, which he shared with Lord Byron: that of loving to paint himself much blacker than he really was; and to affect vices, much as most men affect virtues, and with the same insincerity.

It amused him to reverse Hamlet's advice, of assuming a virtue though he had it not, and to startle strangers with dark hints of things unmentionable to ears polite.

In some conversations with Trelawny,[1] recently published, that old and intimate friend of Byron dwells on that trait of Byron's character, laughing good-naturedly at it, when questioned as to Byron's real moral character, by his curious interlocutor, who seems to have taken Manfred as a true type of the poet, darkly hinting at haunting memories of past sins.

"Alone with me," says Trelawny, "Byron never boasted of his vices. When others were present, he tried to shock them, and blacken his own character; but he had few vices, and none of those he most affected."

This paragraph might have been as truly written of Burton as of Byron; and a propensity such as this, shared in by two men of such superior intellect, and strong hatred of cant or pretension of any kind, offers a theme most puzzling to the student of human nature. Nothing amused Burton more than to defy popular prejudices, and horrify simple-minded people by darkly hinting at imaginary sins committed by himself or comrades under stress of circumstances or the pressure of necessity, during his wanderings among savage men in remote places on the sea or on the desert.

---

[1] Edward John Trelawney (1792–1881).

He told me, among many others, one story corroborative of this, over which he chuckled most heartily, while narrating it.

Dining in England with a very strait-laced set of people in the country, who, he fancied, considered him as something little short of an ogre, he met several very young ladies, and he made up his mind to horrify them. He commenced giving a narrative of an imaginary shipwreck on the Red Sea, or the Blue Nile, remote from all human habitation or help.

After describing how they all suffered from the pangs of hunger, and the wolfish glances they began to cast on each other from time to time, as the days wore on, and no relief came; dropping his voice to a mysterious whisper, almost under his breath, he added: "The cabin-boy was young and fat, and looked very tender, and on him, more than on any other, such looks were cast, until" Here he paused, looked around at the strained and startled faces of his auditors, in which horror was depicted, and then abruptly concluded, as though dismissing a disagreeable memory "But these are not stories to be told at a cheerful dinner party, in a Christian country, and I had best say no more. Let us turn to some more cheerful subject." Of course he was pressed to continue, and complete his story, but stubbornly refused; leaving his hearers in a most unsatisfactory state of mind as to the denouement of the unfinished narrative. Burton told me he was thoroughly convinced, by the startled looks cast upon him by the younger ladies, that they believed that he and his tougher comrades in the shipwreck had roasted and eaten that cabin-boy, whose tenderness he had so eulogised. They seemed to have no doubt that he really was a cannibal, in fact as well as in intention.

It frequently is a tendency, observable in men of strong will, to scoff at the judgments and prejudices of their weaker brethren; yet there are but few men who would carry it so far as this, and never subsequently take the trouble to remove the impression thus formed.

At one time General Gordon made overtures to Burton, to join him in the Soudan, with a view to co-operation in the work to be done there; while the former was in the employ of the Egyptian Government, during the reign of Ismail Pacha. But Burton did not relish the idea. His reason was the very simple one, that there could not be two heads to one body, and that neither Gordon nor himself could play a secondary part, or obey the orders of a superior. It is a curious matter for speculation, as to what the result of such a coalition would have been, could the terms have been arranged. For nature never made two men more diametrically opposed in thought, feeling and principle, than those two celebrities. It is more than probable that such a combination would have resulted in a speedy conflict and collision between two characters as strong and stubborn as theirs.

As their characters and conduct were so totally different, so also were their methods, and their plans and purposes. For the one represented the St. Paul, after his conversion; the other, the Saul of the earlier period. The one was the apostle of persuasion, with an appointed mission; the other the apostle of force, and of worldly expediency, without fanaticism.

The cardinal mistake in Gordon's policy and treatment of the natives in the Soudan, was the attempt to deal with a set of unscrupulous savages as though they were susceptible of the finer sympathies of civilized human beings. His final effort, and the treachery through which he perished, prove this conclusively.

Richard Burton would have made no such mistake. He thoroughly knew the men he had to deal with, and had no illusions. He would have had no confidence in African sympathy or affection for the foreigner and the Christian; and might probably in his treatment of the Soudanese have been as much too harsh as Gordon was too kind.

The combination of two such systems must have proved utterly incongruous and incompatible, and the conflict of two such opposite characters inevitable. Yet could the different characteristics of the two men have been blended into one, the apparently insolvable question of the colonization and civilization of Central Africa might have found the man fitted to grapple with and settle it.

In the latest and, for the moment, most conspicuous African semi-political missionary, Mr. Stanley, the ideas of Burton, not of Gordon, seem to have prevailed. In his hand is the sword of St. Peter, not the cross of St. Paul; and the heads as well as the ears of many centurions are lopped off as his march progresses. Stanley, like Burton, attempts to make no "Pilgrim's Progress;" and seems sometimes almost ruthless, in forcing his way through reluctant or hostile communities or tribes.

As Burton's explorations were never made with strong-armed escorts, it is impossible to say whether he, under similar circumstances, would have done as Stanley has, and forced, where he could not find a path of exploration, over the bodies of resisting Savages, seeking to expel the invader from their country.

The earlier as well as the closing incidents of Gordon's career constitute a drama in which there were many acts, the last of which was the saddest and sternest tragedy of modern times.

But he was not the pioneer in this effort to conciliate the Soudanese. Years before, Said Pacha, Viceroy of Egypt, had attempted to organize the government of the Soudan, and annex it to Egypt in fact as well as in name. He visited the country, penetrating as far as Khartoum, and gave a most liberal charter, under which existing abuses were removed. He gave them a most able Governor, in the person of Arakel Bey, who, had he lived, might have rivalled the reputation of his more famous brother

Nubar Pacha. But Arakel Bey died from the fever of the climate, and the Viceroy's other representatives were unable or unwilling to carry out the promised reforms, aggravating discontents by the promise of better things.

Sai'd Pacha's policy was that of Gordon a policy of conciliation, and an appeal to an enlightened self-interest, made to the natives by one who they knew was capable of carrying it out. But it failed, for the reasons stated.

Said's successor, Ismail, resorted to force to compel the submission of the warlike Soudanese; and the successive Governorships of Gordon and Baker Pachas, created only a chronic condition of rebellion and resistance to Egyptian authority outside the range of the repeating rifles of their soldiers.

This is the moral of the story so graphically told by Sir Samuel Baker, in his narrative of the expedition made by him; the mark made by it being similar to the passage of a ship through the sea as it was opened before, closing behind, leaving no trace of its pathway.

Practically the same result has followed every effort made there, including Emin Bey's at one time regarded as too firmly established to be shaken.

Today the net result of the sacrifice of so many noble Christian lives, martyrised for duty and love of fame, has been the re-closing of that part of the African Continent to civilization, and the renewed sway of the slave-hunters, the Mahdists, and Dervishes, over a vast area, once partially redeemed.

The infant Congo settlement is the only point of light amidst the surrounding darkness, a forlorn hope a problem yet to be solved.

LADY BURTON.

Lady Burton was and is a remarkable woman, and a fitting helpmate to her husband in many respects, although in mind and character his direct opposite. A strikingly handsome and imposing-looking woman, she attracted and fixed the roving fancy of Burton in her early youth; and submitted to the spell of his personal magnetism, although at that time no two human beings could have been more utterly unlike. She was one of the old Arundel family, staunch Catholics all of them; a model of all the feminine proprieties, yet engaged herself with the free-thinking pilgrim from Mecca.

One day he came, claimed, and took her away; like the lady in the romaunt of the Sleeping Beauty.

She adopted many of her husband's ways of life and theories as to woman's sphere of duty; and used, on their expeditions in the East, and in their tent life, to do a man's work after a march, and made herself a good shot with rifle and pistol, with no hesitation in using either effectively, if necessary. Intellectually, she was quite the peer of her husband; and Burton declared seriously to me, that his wife's books sold better, and made more money, than his own.

The most striking and interesting of those books of hers is the "Inner Life of Syria," wherein she describes the Eastern woman and her ways and surroundings, with a verve and picturesqueness which recall the letters of Lady Mary Wortley Montagu; with the addition of a fund of information derived from long intercourse with the inmates of the Harem, which her gifted precursor had no means of acquiring.

Any one desirous of knowing what the Eastern woman really is, and what her actual life, can get the information better through Lady Burton's books than from any other source,

In one respect, Burton's influence over his wife was limited. He never could shake her religious faith, or the fervent practice of her religion. On this one point she was adamant.

In many passages of her book on Syria, her declaration of faith passes almost into mysticism, although veiled by the pretext of a dream.

The fervent appeal to the Queen, to do tardy justice to her husband's services, in the same book, shows how warmly the woman's heart still beats for him after so many years of wedded life; and gives "that touch of nature" which "makes the whole world kin."

Men who have not done a tithe of his work, for Queen and country, have received peerages, pensions and large money grants, for their recompense! When, however, the work done and its recompense become proportional, in any country, we shall have arrived at the millennium!

Lady Burton's latest labour of love has been to issue an expurgated edition for the use of families of her husband's literal translation of "The Thousand and One Nights;" familiar to our boyhood through the English version of Galland's French translation, from which all the crudities and indecencies of the original were carefully expunged.

Burton has given those wonderful narratives in all their naked simplicity, told, as they were, without regard to decency or morality; and it is a painful commentary on the refinement of the nineteenth century that he has made more money out of the prurient taste of the higher class of the community, to whom it was offered at exceptionally high prices, than out of his books recording his strange incidents of explorations and adventures, almost unparalleled in modern travel.

It is melancholy to have to add that the improper book sold, and paid liberally, while the proper one did not. To Burton's cynical humour this fact must have been very amusing; but it tells badly for what we pompously term "The Spirit of the Age;" for the readers must have been all English in both cases, that being the language in which both books were published.

At the present time, with broken health, and a spirit doubtless soured by the small recognition his great services have received, Richard Burton lives retired, in the nominal charge of his Consulate at Trieste, while smaller and meaner men strut conspicuously over the public stage, and fill the public eye.

To the few who know and properly appreciate him and his gifted wife, they both fill a high place in the records of our century; but it will probably be reserved for posterity to appreciate them at their true valuation.

96. 1890/—/—. Isabel Burton to A. W. Thayer.[1]

Dear Friend—

If by mistake I threw away a <u>Hakluyt</u> Society bound in pale blue, or a <u>Biblical Archeology Magazine</u> please bring them back to me & tell me if the man brought back my <u>trunk</u> or left it with you. I <u>expect you tonight</u>. Will you bring back any novels or books <u>lent</u> to you <u>if you have any</u>, as the last books are being packed up, & I cannot lend any more.

Your affect friend
Isabel Burton

97. 1891/04/11. Isabel Burton to Colonel Chaillé-Long.[2]

Langham Hotel, London,
April 11th, 1891.

Dear Mr. Chaillé-Long,

You must have thought me so ungrateful for not answering your kind, sympathetic letter of five months ago, but indeed I have felt it deeply. Losing the man who had been my earthly God for thirty-five years in two hours was like a blow on the head, and for a long time I was completely stunned, and the hundreds of kind, sympathetic letters that I received accumulated in a box.

After fourteen weeks' hard work, which was fortunately a necessity and aroused me from my stupor, I had finished all my work and arrived in England. I took to my bed, where I have been ever since, for my courage broke down. I am too weak to write except by dictation. I am going into a Convent for a short while. I shall send you a card for the funeral, in case it will be convenient for you to come.

With my grateful thanks for your kindness,

---

[1] Boston Athenaeum. Mss. L168.
[2] Colonel Chaillé Long *My Life in Four Continents* Volume 2 (London: Hutchinson, 1912) pp. 414-31. "In November I received a notice of my friend's death. I immediately addressed a letter of condolence to the bereaved Lady Burton, a reply to which found me in Egypt."

Yours very sincerely,
Isabel Burton.

98. 1891. Georgiana Stisted.[1]

Throughout life he kept up a regular correspondence with his sister, whom he tenderly loved, and who much resembles him. A fortnight seldom passed without a letter in his quaint little handwriting, which often required our joint efforts to decipher. Frequently one would contain some terse remark which became a household saying for months afterwards. "What fools think others don't," for example; or writing about people with very large self-esteem,—"People much to be envied,—pity they are such beasts;" again a-propos of those who receive kicks and cuffs from the world without resenting them, "a good plan, if you can but follow it." He always wrote fully about himself and his plans, but invariably noticed any little piece of family or society news we had told him, however insignificant it might have been. The last letter was written within a few days of his death, rejoicing in improved health, and anticipating his return in the spring.

Each time he came to England we saw him frequently. When we lived at Sydenham he often went with us to the Crystal Palace. We used to joke on these occasions, declaring he explored the palace and grounds as thoroughly as Harar or Lake Tanganyika; and generally we had to divide into two parties, one resting while the other accompanied him. Later, when we moved to Folkestone, that place received its share of attention. Caesar's Hill, the Warren, and Sandgate, &c., all were carefully reconnoitered. In short he seemed unable to rest until he had walked or driven all over a new place and its environs.

The fine bracing air of Folkestone always revived him, and he invariably left us looking and feeling better. Most devoted care was taken of his health by both wife and doctor; and if he could only have lived in really pure air, done less work, and slept more, ten years might have been added to his existence. We tried hard to persuade him to spend the winter with us instead of going on to Cannes the year of the Riviera earthquakes. Gipsy-like, he abhorred the idea of tying himself down for any length of time. So long as it was possible even to be carried in and out of trains and steamers, travel he would; and he had only just returned from the fatiguing trip to Malogia,[2] to rest a few weeks before starting for Greece, when one night he died suddenly, quite worn out. The brave heart so unmercifully tried could literally beat no longer. And no doubt

---

[1] Georgiana Stisted "Reminiscences of Sir Richard Burton", *Temple Bar* Volume 92, July 1891, pp. 335-42. Also reprinted in *Littell's Living Age* 190 (1891) p. 406.
[2] Maloja, in Switzerland.

he knew what was best for himself. Better to die in full possession of his glorious faculties, able to the last to work with those who lead the van of human progress, than to husband his remaining strength for all the horrors of old age. We

> *"Who lack the light that on earth was he,*
> *Mourn."*

But for him the quick, painless death in the zenith of his matchless genius was surely well.

99. 1892/04/06. Isabel Burton to A. W. Thayer.[1]

April 6/1892
Our Cottage
2 Worple Road
Mortlake SW
Surrey

Dear old friend

I got your kind letter <u>yesterday</u>, being down at my hermitage near my "Jemmy's" grave. I was so glad to get your splendid account of Albert Letchford's picture—I always think all he paints is perfection & I am sure that this will be a great success, & a great happiness to me too. I have written him a long letter today, & sent him the 500 florins, by order on the Credit Filiale, & begged him to forward it to me & thanked him warmly. I hope his trouble will be rewarded by the publicity & fame I hope to give it bye & bye before long.

I cried much over your letter, & all you said about my darling. No! <u>Time brings no healing</u> & I miss him more & more. I am only happy here in my cottage retirement, I pass much time in our Tent, (the mausoleum) & feel a longing to be in it for good—I was very near it, as I have had influenza since 27 Jan^y, & was so bad as to have all the last sacraments, but God snatched me back, & I am convalescent but weak, & that is what keeps me so silent. I cannot write much for my head's sake. My health & spirits are <u>gone</u> with <u>him</u>. I am so sorry for all you tell me, but you know you are a wonderful man for your age, & considering that you live in <u>Trieste</u>, which is of <u>such</u> a nervous & excitable temperature.

But I do grieve & so did Jemmy that you neglected your Beethoven for your Hebrew—God bless my dear friend now & for ever, in May we meet <u>here</u> & <u>there</u>. Why did you speak of my long loving kindness to <u>him</u>—what else could I be to the half of myself, my life, my soul, <u>as he was</u> for near thirty-six years.

Do not forget if you come to England to let me know at once that I

---

[1] Boston Athenaeum. Mss. L168. ALS MS.

may do all I can to make your stay happy & agreeable. You ask what I am doing. I am trying to get all the Life ready for the press & making arrangements. I am tackling Catullus—I have got the first & last part of his life done. But as my books have only just been unpacked & housed, I have not got on so well as I hoped but I think I shall improve now. I have been so handicapped by illness, & 4 deaths in my immediate family—& workmen in both my houses from August to February—I could never get them out. Two of my boxes of books &c have been lost altogether. There were 204 & I have had 202.

Give my love to the Thorndikes[1] & all other dear old friends & believe me ever your affect Isabel Burton.

100.   1892.   Albert Leighton Rawson.[2]

Those who have read the books of this traveler and scholar during the past forty years may be counted by millions. His writings have delighted readers in every part of the civilized world, and it may be said that his travels were as extensive, though chiefly in the uncivilized regions were they most valuable. This is to class parts of Arabia and Africa which he visited as uncivilized, and I feel sure that no one who has visited those regions will object to styling the great majority of the people barbarians.

I have heard Burton say of them: "The worst races are not necessarily the lowest in the scale as to intellect; they are those whose talents are given to vice and cruelty among themselves, neighboring peoples and strangers. Such people are in the way of true civilization, and like tigers, cobras and other hindrances to the peaceful occupation of some of the fairest portions of the earth, the sooner they are helped to disappear the better it will be for the rest of mankind."

Richard Francis Burton was born, March 19th, 1821, son of Lieutenant Colonel Burton, a retired Irish officer. He inherited his father's military talents and love of a roaming life, and his mother's wit and powers of observation and description. These he used to the very best advantage on his journeys in new fields, as every candid reader is pleased to say on reading almost any one of his many volumes. His early life was begun as a boy in Tours, France, a city of books and bookmakers, and there he made himself familiar with the language as derived from his playmates, and which was soon polished by masters,

---

[1] Charles Faunce Thorndike, Chaplain at Trieste—see Register.
[2] Albert Leighton Rawson "Personal Recollections of Sir Richard Francis Burton, K.C.M.G., F.R.S.[2], F.R.G.S" *Frank Leslie's Popular Monthly*, 1892, pp. 565-76. **This bizarre 'reminiscence' appears to be pure fantasy**. No corroboration exists for any of its unusual claims, and if Burton really had met the Pope, Isabel would hardly have suppressed the information.

willing teachers of such an apt student, at Blois, another historic French city. His recollections of those early days were amusing. "Frenchmen, and French women in particular," he was wont to say, "seemed to me to be forever in masquerade, not only in dress, but in thought and expression."

He probably never changed that opinion.

I asked him why he thought thus of his coreligionists, and he answered: "The Catholic religion redeems a Frenchman, but an Irishman ennobles the Catholic faith."

"They have some great men in France," I ventured.

"Seldom that one can be so named who was a zealous churchman. Great and good men everywhere belong to a higher order than any church."

"How did you enjoy your life at Oxford?"

"Trinity College was supplied, as usual, with boys, or 'men,' as they are proud to call each other, who cared more for physical than for mental culture; their pleasures, too, were of the same color. My studies were very little trouble to me, for the tutors never seemed to take pains to teach us anything. If we found out by ourselves, we were fortunate in gaining some degree of recognition; but if we failed through lack of method in our instructors, we were demerited, degraded, and finally plucked. I did not dare to bring such a disgrace home to my 'governor,' so I helped myself to a leave of absence."

"Your days in the private school at Richmond were more pleasant, it must be presumed."

"Indeed they were. Richmond is one of the fairest spots in beautiful England, and our school (Watson's) one of the best, and I really learned more there than at Trinity, counting the same number of days to each place. I would abolish colleges as they are now, and turn them into schools for specialties, to fit boys for some certain business or walk in life. If a boy is born to a title, let him cram history, poetry and biography; if his lot is to be a gentleman, fill him up with poetry, romance, general literature and politics; if to commerce or manufacture, stuff him with the elements of mechanics, of engineering, chemistry, and the details of some certain line of trades; and so on give each one a fair start in life."

The earnestness with which he advocated such a change in the methods and system of teaching was convincing of his sincerity. One of his arguments was (1869): "In answering your inquiry I am free to say I never liked the present academic or collegiate system, because it enables men of mediocre ability to creep into places where they may do infinite harm. Look at my case in India in 1857. I had suggested the necessity for an increase of British power, as a means of protection and prevention of certain wrongs and abuses, at Aden and its coasts and in the Red Sea, when my college-bred superiors, instead of comprehending the necessity and providing the means, reprimanded me. If they had heeded me the frightful massacre at Jiddah might have been avoided, and a check been put on the slave trade many years sooner than it was done. It is strange, but true, that human life is the price of incompetency in office."

He obtained an appointment in the Indian Army in 1842, and felt he had entered on a sure road to fame; but he soon discovered that preferment would come only with gray hair, and he was too impatient to wait when he saw so much to do. Sir Charles Napier recognized his ability, but Sir Charles was not all in all, and Lieutenant Burton was coolly ignored in favor of some more fortunate though less competent man, who happened to have a friend near the powers.

Precious time was lost, and in a letter of that period he wrote (1859): "If I can do so, you may look for me any day in the United States, on the way to Utah and the Great Salt Lake, and you may do for me a necessary and valuable service if you will compile a dictionary of local slang supplementary to Bartlett's, including of course the Western varieties, for my use. Also, if you will give me a list of articles needed or most useful on the journey across the plains."

I introduced the traveler soon after his arrival in New York to the foreman of Colt's factory, and we together examined a number of revolvers at the store. While we were debating the matter, as to which would be most useful, Mr. Colt came in and was made acquainted with Burton, and begged the favor of making him a present of two handsomely mounted and chased navy "popguns." We all adjourned to the Astor House, where the genial proprietor joined the party.

After listening to one of Burton's tales of his life in India, Colonel Stetson said he would call in a man from the office who could understand that kind of story, and he introduced Mr. Parkinson, the confectioner, and Edwin Forrest, the actor. Burton and Forrest were all in all to each other for three hours or more, the rest of us were only too happy in listening, and occasionally, when Mr. Forrest suggested, assisted at "circumventing Colonel Stetson's poison," which ceremony usually emptied a quart decanter of the best French brandy at each round.

"There's no other liquor fit for gods and men," said Forrest.

"Not every man is worthy of such ambrosial dew," said Artemus Ward (Browne), who looked in the door that had been left ajar by the ganymede.

"Oh, dew come in!" said the tragedian.

Twenty-eight years after that "glorious night" the English Consul at Trieste, writing about other things, concluded his letter in these words: "And then the memory of that night with Forrest, Ward (Browne) and the others, including yourself, is still fresh and a source of lively pleasure. The stories told by Forrest, Ward and yourself enriched my leisure hours all the way to Utah."

The consul and I were the only two remaining of that party.

My desire to travel in the Levant, Egypt, Palestine and Greece had drawn me toward sunrise as far as London; there I halted for the benefit of introductory letters to Dr. Birch, of the British Museum, and others, and I found a home in Great Russell Street, nearly opposite the British Museum. I was anxious to make the acquaintance of the artist W. H. Bartlett, who had visited the countries I wished to see, and found him through the kindness of Mr. Virtue, his publisher.

Mr. Bartlett took me to his color man, and I bought a liberal supply of materials, both oil and water, for use on a journey which was planned to take me far away from supplies, and the generous dealer invited me to dine with him at his club. There it was made known that I intended to visit the Nile land, and many remarks were made by way of suggestions for my benefit in preparation and on the road, and one of the company at the table said he had met Lieutenant Richard F. Burton, who was an officer in the service of the Honorable East India Company, and that he was then in London, and he would undertake to give me an introduction to him.

In about a week I had the pleasure of unfolding my plans for the coming year, which then extended no farther than Egypt and Palestine, to one who listened with deep interest. He said he had been to Europe on leave of absence over three years, and intended to return to India in a few months, when he hoped to meet me at Cairo, or Alexandria, as it might be.

He was a fine-looking man, English (Irish) all over, and in conversation made you feel at ease. He was not obtrusive in opinion, nor would he dispute on any topic, unless requested to do so for the sake of bringing out his great knowledge of men and things. A desire to know something about the United States led him to ask questions, or to lead the conversation in that direction, many times during our five weeks of social intercourse.

A day with him in the British Museum was full of surprises and delight for me, because of his very intimate knowledge of objects in the Oriental sections, and he was ever ready with a story or an incident in his own experience to the point. In the East India Company's rooms he was more at home, if possible, and threw a charm around every object that he noticed or I spoke about. I grew, as it were, by jumps of years when in his company. His kindly helpfulness was shown in correcting the errors in an outline grammar of the Arabic language, which I had prepared in MS for an inside pocket, and permitting me to copy his Turkish grammar, and a small one in Sanskrit.

His advice was to enter an Arab school in Cairo, and learn the dialect of the Koran, in order to get the intonation of the natives as well as the idiom, and he seemed to enjoy repeating the old adage, The traveler is wise who conceals his treasures, opinions and country; and also that other one, in which you are advised to conform to the habits and manners of the people among whom you happen to find yourself; and he was ready with many rich stories of his adventures and mishaps before he learned the true value of those wise counsels.

I had visited nearly every section of our country, from Hudson's Bay to Panama, and the Atlantic to the Mississippi, and was ready, therefore, to say something in reply to his inquiries, and sometimes to interest him to a high degree.

His accounts of life in India were always full of incident, and never prosy. He studied man, and was ever ready to compare notes with other students.

"I say, when you are in Jerusalem, just try to find any present excuse for calling the place El Kudus."

"And yet, many millions look to it as the sanctuary of their holy religion."

"And more millions turn their faces toward the Kaaba at Mecca, and would be taught to revere the North Pole if some saint should select it as his retreat."

"Or swear by the Mormon Bible."

"Tell me what that book is in origin and make-up."

I told him the story of the invalid preacher Spaulding, his fiction of the Ten Lost Tribes and supposed origin of the people who inhabited this country before the Indians, and how Joseph Smith and Rigdon reconstructed the work, and published it as a divinely inspired and miraculously preserved book. I was able to tell him that the place where Smith said he found the gold plates which, he asserted, were covered with hieroglyphics, was in a field next to the farm of my uncle, Benjamin Armington, who lived at Monticello, a few miles south of Palmyra, N.Y.

"It would not be strange," he said, "if the devotees of that book became a powerful people. Time will work wonders in obscuring the origin and in throwing a mysterious halo of sanctity around the book and the early promoters of the faith, and at length will cover up all, or nearly all, of the questionable features and sanctify every other, as has been done with the Vedas, the Shastra, the Granth, the Bible and other sacred books. The leaders recruit their ranks from able-bodied men and women who are religious, or superstitious, which is much better, and aim to teach them the faith as it is in Mormon, whether or not they know anything else beside work at their trade or occupation. This will breed a race of fanatics who will be the tools of any so-called religious teachers."

"In what does this differ from the history of all other religions of which we have any account?"

"Not in any essential word or deed. Even Joe Smith, as he is called, died in the faith, if not for the faith, and he will be canonized in due time."

"Brigham Young, his successor as the prophet of the people, is President of the Church and Governor of the Territory under the United States, uniting the Church and the State, which is contrary to the spirit of the founders of the nation, who tried to keep them apart because of the long train of evils that had followed such union in the past, in the Old World."

"When religious fanatics are left to themselves and can carry out their own sweet will they invariably attempt to control the civil power. They are impatient of any and all criticism, proud of their assumed position as the mouthpiece of God, and naturally autocratic and despotic over their fellow men, whom they consider their inferiors, poor blind lost sinners in need of salvation which is in their keeping."

I was amazed at this outburst and reminded him that the adage taught secrecy in opinions.

"Yes, I always observe that rule when among strangers; but even in these few days of our acquaintance I feel as though we had known each other many years, for we have followed out similar lines of inquiry and are interested in similar studies."

Burton seemed to me at that time to love travel as a means of adding to his stock of knowledge of men and things and of gratifying a spirit of restless and insatiate curiosity, and I had to promise him to keep up a series of notes of my travels that we might compare when we should meet again in Egypt.

His kindly interest in me was shown in many ways; for instance, in an inquiry as to how I expected to get about among Arabs and Mohammedans without an interpreter, who would be very expensive as to salary, and more so in his cheating me in every purchase. I told him of a few lessons in Arabic I had in company with the poet Longfellow at his home in the Washington Headquarters, Cambridge, when we were taught by a native from—

"Tangier?"

"How do you guess?"

"By your pronunciation of the word Arabic, which is that of the Maugrib, the west of Africa. You will do well to keep to that style, as it will help you much in passing as a native in Egypt. You cannot go about, away from the streets in which Europeans live, without being worried by all sorts of fanatics who hold it a duty they owe to Allah to persecute any stranger who wears a hat as an infidel to the true faith: that is, in the prophet Mohammed. As soon as you arrive in Egypt apply for admission to one of the schools attached to the El Azhar College, and sit on the ground with the native boys and drink in the tones of their voices. Don't stop to think they whine and yelp, for in a few days their cries will be music in your ears, when you can understand what they say, and say the same yourself so they can understand you. Then you can go about Egypt, anywhere you will, without molestation, for the Maugribs have a good reputation in Egypt as men who are skilled in all the arts that made Spain the delight of the eyes in its wonderful mosques, now in ruin or desecrated by the foot of the infidel."

"There spoke the true believer!" I exclaimed.

"Believer in art and architecture as educational. Who can look on the Alhambra, even in its copy at the Crystal Palace, without pleasure at the beautiful forms and colors, and wish there were architects in our day who loved their work as the Moors did? In Egypt you will find enough to keep you busy a lifetime if you so desire, but above all do not neglect the Coptic churches. The Copts are the remnants of the old Pharaohs—people, priests and all gathered into one fold of a few thousands under one Patriarch—and they live in villages that are walled in, or in a quarter of an Arab city, to enter into which you must have a special permit. If you wish to see the inside of the churches you must get a permit from the Patriarch in Cairo, and have a muftach (key) in your hand in the form of a coin of the realm, at least a mejidi; and be sure to remember the poor before leaving the sacred precincts."

"The traveler must be a sort of wandering cyclopedia of religion and mythology?"

"For what do you travel if it is not to gather pearls and other gems? You must consent, and strive also, to become a devotee to the great systems of worship of symbolic objects of devotion, Tree, Phallic, Serpent, Fire, Sun and Ancestral. Learn their inner meaning, and respect all who sincerely hold to any one or all of them as you respect yourself."

"I have paid some attention to comparative mythology, and to the history of religion as displayed in antiquity among the cultured nations."
"Do not overlook the so-called uncultured or barbaric or semi-civilized peoples, for they are not so skillful in hiding their true sentiments as the cultured hypocrites are. Study them if possible in their native tongue and in their homes. A Christian in Sunday dress and at church is one thing, and in a working dress or business garb, at home or in the counting house, is another and very different sort of thing; but the semi-civilized man changes his dress only at long intervals, and, like other mortals, those among them who are able to change dress oftenest have the flimsiest store of religion."

"Do you regard religion as a sign of mental health?"

"No. In its extreme developments it is an evidence of disease, spiritual immaturity, mental decay. Religion and insanity are more than cousins, for the highly excited enthusiast becomes insane in many cases. This is another reason why you should travel in disguise among Mohammedans. They have many fanatics among them who feel it a duty to keep an eye out for intruding infidels. And it is a well-known notion of theirs that an unbeliever or infidel pollutes any sanctuary he may enter. Such pollution must be done away, as we wash a floor, scour a rusty knife or polish silverware; but if water—the water of life—is polluted, what remedy can be applied less than to take the life of the infidel wretch who does the mischief? So reasons the Oriental, and you must be warned beforehand of danger."

He illustrated his remarks by relating incidents of his experience in India, and one may be repeated here, for I have not seen it in any of his writings. Notice had been given that a famous imam had returned from Mecca, and would give some account of his pilgrimage at a certain mosque at the hour of and immediately after the morning prayer. Burton wished to be present, and, dressed as a true believer, he was among the early arrivals, and spread his prayer carpet near the mimbar (pulpit) and between two very aged Moslems. He performed his devotions without attracting attention, but when the speaker enlarged on the delights enjoyed by the hadji he thought he must have showed more than the orthodox amount of emotion and interest, for the two faithful ones beside him inquired of him why he had delayed so long a visit to the Kaaba. He answered, "My going and coming has been determined by Allah, the arranger and guide of all souls;" and they were satisfied as to his integrity as a true believer.

But he said he felt safer when outside of the mosque, carrying his carpet under his arm and swinging his rosary. He could not feel at that time that he was prepared for the honors of martyrdom. A sudden introduction into paradise among a galaxy of houris without the orthodox preliminaries might have been embarrassing.

"Mohammedans make a fetich of the mosque, and Christians are not entirely free from this vice, for they require you to remove your hat in church, no matter how cold it may be, and no service going on. Some also make the sign of the cross whenever they pass in front of the altar, whether near or far off, even in the street before the church door. You have only to feel that God is in or near the altar, and the ceremony is explained. The notion that God is everywhere, and therefore nowhere, is not consoling to these enthusiasts; they must have Him bottled up where He can be found when wanted."

"The Arabs of the desert are said to have a very simple and pure religion."

"Their religion may be very pure, but it cannot be simple. The Arab's desire, first and last, is for children, and that develops fetich worship, and the web of superstition clinging about them is intricate and beyond explanation in a few words. Every breath they draw, from the cradle to the grave, is perfumed or tainted with it."

"I have heard that the Druses in Syria, who have their chief centre at

Dayr el Kamar (Convent of the Moon), in Mount Lebanon, are Phallic Worshipers."

"If you could successfully penetrate their secret you would render a great service to scholars. Many ancient texts might be cleared up if we could get hold of their ritual. Why not make that one of your objects of pilgrimage?"

So we conferred together, each speaking frankly and looking toward the future.

My Maugrib teacher had given me a very high opinion of Tangier and Algiers, so when I was in Marseilles I felt tempted to make the trip to Algiers in one of the steamers which ply between those ports, but was persuaded that my time was worth more for Egypt.

I had been favored with letters of introduction to the President of the French Republic, Louis Napoleon, and was most graciously received by him, and permitted to make a sketch for an ivory miniature. He gave me a letter to Pope Pius IX., which obtained for me an introduction to the Vicar of Christ in the Vatican, and permission to make a portrait on canvas. The sittings were very early in the morning, as soon as it was light enough, or, as his holiness put it, "When Dame Nature first opens her eyes to see what is going on."

After a sitting it was my custom to walk about the galleries, visit the Sistine Chapel, or the Vatican Library, whichever seemed desirable for the day; and one day I met a company of Englishmen and ladies, among whom was Burton. I took him to see my picture the next day, and having spoken of him to the Pope, his holiness said he would be glad to meet Mr. Burton, of whom he had heard through Mr. Manning, a new convert to the church in London.

His holiness conversed with Burton in the French language, and they got on famously together. I credited the best touches on the portrait to the animation in the sitter's face produced by Burton's replies to his inquiries about England and India. One reply announced a forthcoming book, to be entitled "Scinde; or, The Unhappy Valley," and the Pope exacted a promise from Burton that he would send him the work as soon as it was ready. When assured that he should have the books (it was to be in two volumes), the venerable Pontiff invited him to visit the library, and instructed an attendant to see that he was permitted access to any of the cases, as he might wish. This privilege had been given me some days before, and I suggested that we go together that day, and hunt for certain manuscripts that were said to be hidden away in the vast depths of that unexplored region. Our search was rewarded, for we were shown some rare works, from which we made notes.

My next meeting with Burton was in Cairo, Egypt, when he was on the way, as he supposed, to cross the Arabian peninsula, a task that was reserved for Mr. Palgrave,[1] some years later. He was in high hopes as to the value of his proposed journey across Arabia, and devoted himself to preparation, especially in language, knowledge of the Koran, the practice of the Mohammedan religion, and inquiries from Arabs who had been into the interior, or anywhere inland from the large ports on the Red Sea or the Persian Gulf. So, when he found I knew something about Arabia he was doubly pleased with my bronzed face, and when we had retired to the seclusion of his room at the hotel he inquired: "Why do you wear so large a turban?"

"My emameh is large, but the sun is hot in Egypt, and was hotter in Mecca and Medina."

"How have you that knowledge?"

"By personal experience," I replied. "I have been up the Nile, across Abyssinia to Axum and Massowah; to Aden, Mocha, Jiddah, Mecca, Medina, and Yembo or Jembo, Petra, Jerusalem, Damascus, Dayr el Kamar, Beirut, Alexandria, and am now here in El Kaheerah, victorious over many perils and privations."

"I should say so. You look and act like a born Arab. Give me the salutation of peace. Again I say I am struck dumb at your good fortune. But you must tell me about your journeys, and more particularly of how to get to the Holy City of the Prophet. How did you ever do it?"

"Do you remember the Sheik el Isherob?"

"The Lord of the Big Drink? Certainly. It was I who gave him that splendid title. He could empty a bottle of Nile water at a gulp. What of him?"

"He was my teacher at the College El Azhar."

"Then you sat among the boys of the shaven heads?"

"Yes, and recited and intoned with those who were to be made imams and doctors of the law and of medicine."

"I must address you then as hakeem?"

"As you like, only keep my secret, for I hope to make another visit at least to Mecca, to get maps, plans and views which I could not secure on this trip."

"Your secret will be safe in my keeping. Did you make any drawings or sketches?"

"Many. I was favored beyond all expectation. My teacher, guide and friend, Sheik el Isherob, or Mahammed Ion Bakee, was my faithful companion on the entire journey, and I am sure it is to his wise management my safety is due."

"Does he think you are a sincere convert?"

"I suppose he does. We never had a word about the matter. He

---

[1] W. G. Palgrave, see Register.

accepted me as a pupil on the strength of a general letter written by my teacher in Arabic at Cambridge, and always spoke of me as a Maugrib. He may have thought me a born Arab."

"The first question invariably asked of a stranger is as to his native land (*Wa ism enta bilad?*)."

"And my answer was, 'The country of the faithful,' to which he replied, 'You speak in the accent of the Maugribs of Fez.'"

"That was sharp in you. He thinks you are from Fez, or Mequinez, or some place far in the west, where the people have nearly lost their native tongue, or so changed it as to have only a distorted idiom left, with a strange and barbaric accent. How an Egyptian does pity and commiserate an unfortunate man who was born, in spite of his helpless condition, outside of Egypt!"

"Perhaps that was one reason why he was so very kind and faithful to me."

"You, of course, made him happy with backsheesh?"

"By doubling his salary at the college, supplying him with clothing, paying all expenses, giving him money and goods for presents on the way, and treating him as an equal."

"Oh, hold on now! That last is too rich."

"Well, I mean treating him respectfully and with kindly consideration. We everywhere appeared as tutor and pupil, and paraded our books whenever it was possible. We were often appealed to by disputants to settle their differences by references to the Koran or to the traditions of the prophet, and he usually referred to me as the treasury of knowledge, the casket of pearls of wisdom, the pillar of the faith, and other complimentary titles and phrases, which I humbly swallowed, as a cat gulps down cream, for in that I saw additional safety, and felt that the price could be well afforded. The books served another purpose: they were portfolios for my sketches, and I was not suspected of any evil intention, but rather commended for my great piety and devotion."

"What sketches have you?"

"I have one that might be expected to blind your eyes with its effulgence."

"Do you refer to the prophet's tomb at Medina?"

"That is it. You have guessed it. How very simple the tomb itself is! But the covering is of the richest goods, embroidered with colored silks, with threads of silver and gold. Sentences from the Koran and wreaths of flowerlike forms, in good taste and done with fine skill. Burckhardt must have seen the tombs, for he described them very accurately—Mohammed's in the middle, Omar's on the right and Abu Bakr's on the left, and all covered with richly embroidered cloths, which are in part valuable shawls, the gifts of princes of the faithful."

"The historians who mention it all differ in their descriptions."

"I have not seen any of their descriptions. I had no intention of going on the pilgrimage when we left Cairo for Philae and the Nile cataracts; but events succeeded unexpectedly, and I found myself at Aden, in a stream of pilgrims from India, and drifted along with them to Mocha, where I delayed a few days to see the coffee district; then joined another company of pilgrims as far as Jiddah, with the intent to keep on to Suez and Palestine; but being urged by several of the company and jeered at for my lack of devotion, I was forced to go to Mecca to save my reputation. Even Sheik Isherob became impatient at my hesitation, and declared he would leave me at Jiddah while he did duty for both of us. I intend to look up the various authorities, which Sheik Isherob says are many, and so be able to give a complete account of the Haram at Medina. The Kaaba is better known, and needs less particularity in its description."

"Have you sketches of that also?" he asked, with growing interest.

"Yes. Of the corner where the sacred black stone is fixed, and views of the Haram and the city."

"What is the stone like?"

"Here is a diagram of the stone as it is in its silver setting. It is irregular in outline, ovoid, nearly 7 inches high by 8½ wide in the widest part. The silver-gilt band is three-quarters of an inch across and an eighth of an inch thick, or more in places where the face of the stone sinks a little."

"Did you observe the stone itself?"

"Yes. It is nearly black, or very dark chocolate brown, streaked with yellow and dotted with reddish and gray spots and with one large group of reddish-yellow spots. I did not recognize it as an aerolite, as it has been said to be, but rather hold it to be a stratified rock with partly crystallized matter imbedded in its mass. So many millions have kissed and rubbed it, the natural color is obscured. It is shiny from hand and lip polishing, and the silver rim has lost its gold plating, except here and there a small speck where the band is turned down and so protected from touch, and the rim itself is worn thin all round and entirely wasted away in places on the lower edge."

These and many other inquiries he made, evidently from curiosity only, for he had not determined on his trip to Medina and Mecca.

He had a strong desire to see the famous serpent charmers of Cairo, and a visit to their quarter was arranged. Sheik Isherob was engaged, and an Englishman from Leeds was invited, making a party of four. The sheik of the serpent charmers lived at Fostat, Old Cairo, the city at the time the Romans ruled Egypt, and his house was near the Coptic convent or church. Every traveler knows the ways of the serpent charmer of Egypt, but the mysteries thereof are as dark and unfathomable now as ever to the ordinary eye. Burton, after seeing the sheik of the clan exhibit his power, or, rather, skill, with the snakes, said: "It is a marvelous sleight of hand backed by true courage, for they never know when the snake's poison fangs may have grown again so as to give a fatal stroke."

"But their occult power, my dear sir!"

"Come, now, we are not gathering items for a child's wonder primer. Don't talk about occult power over a brute without reason."

"Oh, then, occult power only affects those who exercise reason? I am glad to know."

"Don't rejoice in knowledge prematurely."

"But those communications from the spirit world?"

"Dead men tell no tales."

What a volume can be conveyed by a look! He looked the very embodiment of incredulity and fun.

"I have never had such a message, and until I get one by myself, or another I can trust, I must look on the whole scheme as experimental only, of course, with my most ardent hopes for success in boring a hole through the veil that separates life and death. But what has all this to do with the serpents and their charmers?"

"Nothing at all, and you have not seen the real charmers."

"No! You surprise me. Who are they?"

"The almeh—the awalim."

"Then, we have wasted precious time."

"Nothing lost. These charmers are near. The sheik, if you give him an order in the shape of a coin of the realm, or even of England or of France, will at once produce a dancing girl, and for two pieces we may see his harem in motion."

We made a joint-stock venture of it, and saw two very fair dancers—or, rather, posture makers—and four assistants, younger and much more handsome, and quite pretty as Arab girls go, and for an hour had a fine exhibit of pantomime, in which a love story was enacted, from the first shy and modest glances to the quarrel, the reconciliation, elopement and final blessing of the parents, accompanied by music and clapping of hands of the husbands and brothers and cousins of the women; and in all the exercises the serpents were kept lively, erect or crawling about between the feet of the dancers. We were unable to discover any evidence of occult power, or of any other power than that of habit. The snakes had been trained by long and patient practice, and permitted the men or the women to poke them about, usually without showing signs of rage or irritation; and when stirred up with a stick on purpose to make them angry they were half asleep and struck very lazily.

We were very much disappointed in the quest of wonderful works, and, except for the girls and their dancing, we considered the day wasted, only that it served as a means of exposing a very popular fraud.

Not long after that the then pretty young (grass) widow Blavatsky, fresh from Russia, visited the same serpent charmers with us, but with a very different result. She went into ecstasy over the entire performance—dance, snakes, music, and the noises of the attendant rabble that surrounded the actors.

"What do you think of the fair Cossack?" I asked Burton.

"A dangerous young woman—trebly so from having a husband so near the frozen Caucasus while she exposes herself to the ardent sun of Egypt."

"And of her mesmerism?"

"Biology is a new study—not a 'science' as it is erroneously called, but yet in the experimental stage. Madame is reported to have done many wonder works. If we could see some—even one!"

I arranged a meeting with Mme. Blavatsky, her Russian friend, Burton, Mr. Broadway the dentist, and two or three others whose names I have forgotten, as they were not written in my notebook with the others. They came late, after we had been in the room at Shepheard's nearly an hour. And we all noticed that they became very deeply interested at once in Madame's phenomena. Burton had been introduced as Mr. Jones, of England, and he soon made himself useful by mesmerizing a young woman. Nothing peculiar happened, except that she said several times, "I don't get any light—I see no light," which we afterward interpreted to mean as a hint for the operator or mesmerizer to give her a leading idea so she could go into an intelligent trance. Late in the evening a young English girl came into the room with her father, and out of curiosity asked to be put under the influence. While in a trance, as it was said, she told us that a number of persons were in the room who had been neighbors of the Burtons' at Richmond, where Sir Richard went to school when a lad, and who were reported dead.

"I see," said the medium, "a short, fat, French woman standing behind Mr. Burton, who says her name is Pujol, and that she knew him at Blois, in France."

Many other names she gave, some of which Burton remembered as of persons he had known, and he expressed the utmost astonishment that a stranger whom he had never met before should be able to tell so much that seemed to be real and true information.

"What surprises me most is that she told me things I did not know before; for instance, what disease my grandfather died of. I must inquire if she was correct in her statement."

It was many years after that before I had a chance to remind him of the circumstance and inquire if he had verified the report, and he said: "The young woman told me correctly as to the nature of my grandfather's last illness, and, whether it is imagination or not, I seem to feel the approach of the same insidious malady."

"How now about dead men telling no tales?"

"It was a live woman that told me, not a dead one, and there may be a subtle connection between our souls that enables certain peculiarly organized persons to read each other's minds. Or if not to know their thoughts, which seems utterly improbable, at least to be conscious of their physical construction, as, for instance, in my case. If she was able to see that I was affected by a certain disease, she might also know it was inherited, and from which line of parentage. We are literally and truly wonderfully made."

The days at Cairo passed like a crowded dream. We went about on foot or on donkeys or horses, as the mood took us, and saw much of the Arab part of the city. Every great mosque was visited in search of ancient lamps, of which there were many, and of carved screens and pulpits many.

"If life were long enough, or one were rich enough to indulge in the luxury of having a secretary who was a scholar and antiquarian, such subjects could be taken up with advantage. A book devoted to the ancient lamps of Islam—gold, silver, brass, bronze, iron and glass—would afford a rich mine of archaeology in their fine work, various patterns, some of which are unique, and in their inscriptions, which add to our information as to the history of the Caliphs. The names, titles, pedigree, and in some cases the deeds, or what works he was most noted and honored for, are engraved on the lamp. But the detested Giaour is here, and will in a few years strip Egypt of these treasures. Then the scholar will have to hunt all over the civilized world to find the precious relics of which these semi-barbarians have been robbed, by the force of arms or of money."

"If they don't have wit enough to take care of what they have, the natural outcome will be that Egypt will be stripped of its antiquities, except, perhaps, the great pyramids, and future generations will lose the pleasure of contemplating the past in the Nile land for lack of materials."

"You suggest, logically, a protectorate."

"Napoleon tried it."

"Too soon. The learned world condemned Herodotus and voted Egypt dull and stupid. Later discoveries have sustained the story of the Greek historian, and proved the high antiquity of the Coptic people."

"And confirmed the Old Testament history."

"What! did you say history? Is there history in the ever-changing summer cloud? Are the Greek myths history, and are we derived from the gods by descent? The poetical legend,

'The sons of God saw

*The daughters of men
That they were fair,'*

would, under the rule, become history. Oh, no, we must not indulge in dreams, except as dreams, and in that light the allegories of the Bible are exceedingly beautiful. But history is not made, it grows, and the spiritual life and character of Abraham like the sunrise bursts on us, not like a human history, but like a complete idea, so elaborately wrought out in St. Augustine's 'City of God.' A scheme, not a growth nor a history. True history is not artificial, either in its plans or in its details. The poetical myths and miracles lift the whole Bible into the clouds."

He built largely on the great work of his life, a translation of the "Arabian Nights' Entertainment," which, he said, "Will introduce the people of the West to the Oriental Arab as he is in his true character—the inner man."

But Lady Burton has cut out every characteristic feature, and so has greatly reduced the value of the work, which was in ten, and is now in six, volumes. She edited his work from the conventional, artificial standpoint in morals, while her husband had assumed that true morality has its basis in human nature, in natural laws, and therefore the exact truth is the most valuable in literature, if not elsewhere.

On this topic he once said, in answer to a question: "I have no respect for what is called divine truth. 'Divine' truth, like German silver, or oroide gold, has very little of the true silver or gold in its composition."

Burton was a temperate man in all things. He ate and drank in moderation, and I never saw him smoke more than a quarter or half a cigar. He preferred the water pipe (nargileh in Arabia, or hookah in India), but he would sometimes say that tobacco was a heavy and useless drain on the system. We have often been on a trip of ten or twenty miles together, in the vicinity of Cairo, from three in the morning till eight or nine in the evening, and only refreshed ourselves with a few dates and milk, or water, as we could get it, and he sustained his activity and liveliness in conversation to the end. He had a perennial stock of good stories, every one of which illustrated some trait in human nature. He seldom indulged in a story that was merely funny, although he was very fond of wit and humor, and was himself witty in a large degree.

Lady Burton has by her prudish abridgment of her husband's work denied to millions a knowledge of the native simplicity and wonderful resources in linguistic expression of the Arab mind, that now, so far as that incomparable work is concerned, can only be felt by scholars who can read the original Arabic. But regrets are vain, now that the mischief is done. We may feel thankful that she is not able to expurgate the Arabic text. What a pity she was not among the revisers of the Old Testament!

Burton, after his visit to Salt Lake, in a letter written on board the steamer and mailed at Panama, says: "I was pleased to find the Mormons indulged in plain words about certain things, such as are used by the Arabs in similar cases, as you well know. ... This in no way reflects on their morals, for it is merely a question of taste in language, or, rather, it exhibits the growth of usages in language. Words that were in use and considered in good taste by our grandparents have now to be tabooed for having become too familiar, and we use other words, borrowed from some other language, because their meaning is obscure and therefore less offensive; and those who follow us will condemn our words and adopt others to suit themselves. It is only a question of taste."

Sir Richard was an anthropologist from personal experience and original insight, and his opinions and observations on the peoples whom he visited in various out-of-the-way sections of the world have a very great value.

As a traveler he deserves a high position. He was the pioneer of inland travels from the east coast of Africa, and when such a journey required a peculiar fitness such as he alone at that time had in an eminent degree. Captain Burton, in 1863, discovered and described minutely what are now known as the Yellala Falls, on the Lower Congo. He also ably argued that the Lualaba is the Upper Congo. He modestly neglected to urge his claim to his African discoveries after the death of his friend and companion Captain Speke in 1864, but there is in the minds of thousands of his early readers a pleasant memory of his successful trip, which was a terribly perilous journey, to Lake Tanganyika.

His books are pleasant reading. You can jump over the statistics and other dry matter, for he kindly bunches them so the cautious reader need not worry through them, and he fills his pages with clear, comprehensive and entertaining observations on men and their affairs that entertain and inform the attentive reader. He made three or four books on the negroes of West Africa, filled with the results of his travels in the neighborhood of the Gulf of Benin, the Bight of Biafra, the Cameroons, Dahomey, and the Congo and Loango. In 1864 he was sent as Consul to Santos, in Brazil, and visited Paraguay, the La Plata States, Chile and Peru, and wrote books on "The Highlands of Brazil" and "The Battlefields of Paraguay."

With what intense satisfaction and delight as an Arab scholar did he accept the assignment as Consul at Damascus in 1869! After so many years of wandering about the world in uncongenial climes, among uncanny peoples often, how pleasant to find himself in the one peculiar Arab city that encroaching Christendom has left to the descendants of the people of the immortal Haroon al Rasheed.

He wrote, "Here I am at length, *mirabile dictu*! It must have been by some unheard-of error at headquarters that I was sent here, of all places the most welcome to me. Dear me! will it last? When the manipulators of the red tape wake from their temporary dream they may hasten to undo the only good they ever did for me. A thousand thanks for your letter to Abd el Kader, prince of all Arabs, the living embodiment of my ideal of the great Haroon. I have seen him only once, but that was sufficient to make me feel the greatness of his soul. He sends greetings—the peace of Allah—by me to his brother across the sea."

The college-bred officials again blundered. His friendly acquaintance with the exiled chief, social greetings of Syrian chiefs, and simply respectful manners toward the Greek ecclesiastical dignitaries, aroused Oriental jealousy, and he was *legislated* out of office. The consulate was put on a subordinate footing, and Captain Burton returned to England.

"I felt it, I knew it was coming. I am almost a believer in prophecy. If premonitions were ever repeated frequently enough for us to arrange them into a system something practical might be made out of them. Now we never know when to believe or disbelieve their hints. If the old Hebrew prophets, the Cumaean Sibyl or the Oracle at Delphos were of no more certain sound, there is no wonder the shrines were bought and sold."

Burton visited Iceland in 1872 and made a book on the Geysers and the sulphur deposits, which is good reading. He wrote from London: "The Icelanders are full of genuine good human nature, but the terrible frost grinds and pulverizes men and women into mere paving stones. They live too close to each other individually. No room for expansion. I should stifle physically and morally there. They are the opposites of the Arabs, who have too much room, and do not live near enough to each other. Even their hell is icy. Ugh!"

Now the clouds gather. Growing old, more anxious than ever to do some important literary work, he felt hampered and worried by the indifferent treatment he received from his superiors in office.

"My Dear Friend: I write you this from the tomb, alias Trieste, where they have buried me. I feel that this is the last move, and that I shall close my pilgrimage here in this the very dirtiest of dirty Austrian cities."

A keen regret he felt was in his failure to induce Abd el Kader to visit the Exposition at Vienna. It was like him, for he was wont to study for others their welfare, pleasures and honors.

After his second visit to Midian I wrote him, asking many questions about the country and its peoples, and sent him my itinerary from Medina to Petra. He replied patiently, but to my reference to some attempts of certain Biblical scholars to connect Midian with the place so called in the Scriptures he literally boiled over with indignation.

"These ha'penny brains imagine the Almighty has nothing better to do than to remake the world to suit their dream. The cosmos is countless myriads of cycles old. Absolutely there can have been no beginning. Six thousand years ago! Why not put it six weeks ago? But this is the sort of men the colleges send into the world as leaders of thought in the church. Leaders! Ah, I forgot myself for a moment; I am neither His Holiness the Pope at Rome nor His Grace of Canterbury, and my opinion is not called for. I feel indignant just the same when precious time and money are wasted in such high places in bringing up the old, old dream and restating the old, old myth."

Burton was a rare, fine, thoroughly human man. His books even are not a good exponent of his real character, for he always hesitated to write about himself.

101.　1892/11.　Isabel Burton in *The New Review*.[1]

Sir Richard Burton: an Explanation and a Defence.

"What part has death or has time in him,
Who rode life's lists as a god might ride?"
SWINBURNE.

Two years ago this October 20th that Glorious Soul winged its way on its last great journey. The horrible excitement of pain and anguish, of fear, the sensation of being hunted, and alone in a big grey desert, has subdued itself to desolation, has become

"The custom of the day
And the haunting of the Night,"

with a sense of hopeful "Waiting." Let me try to tell you the tale as simply as I can in such limited space.

From October, 1883, Richard suffered acutely from gout, and had three dangerous bouts that laid him up for eight months, three months, and ten weeks, which he bore with gentle patience and courage. He was attended in the two first attacks by the best doctors Trieste afforded. In all these three attacks I never left his room, day or night, and I frequently used to disobey orders as to diet. When he was free from pain he was immensely cheerful, and used to laugh like a schoolboy at his Trieste doctor, who would speak English for the sake of learning and practising it. "What him eat to-day?" "Pheasant, doctor!" He plunged his hands into his hair as if he were going to tear it all out. "What for you give him the wild?" (German, *alas wild*, meaning game.) One day after about six months he said, "You sail give him ten drops of rum in a tumbler of water for his dinner!" Peals of laughter came from the sick bed. "Ach! das ist

---

[1] Isabel Burton "Sir Richard Burton: an Explanation and a Defence *The New Review* 7 (42) November 1892, pp. 562-78. See also *The Morning Post* 19 June 1891 [reproduced in W. H. Wilkins *The Romance of Isabel Lady Burton* (New York: Dodd Mead, 1897)], and The Echo December[?] 1891 [reproduced in Isabel Burton *The Life of Sir Richard F. Burton* (London: Chapman and Hall, 1893) pp. 487ff].

gut to hear him laugh like dat? Vat for he laugh?" I answered, "Because he gets a brandy-grog fit for a sailor every night, or he would have been a dead man long ago." More tearing of the hair and real displeasure. When he got over that illness he was a veritable skeleton, his legs were like two sticks of sealing wax.

I could give a delightful sketch of our last three years, with the places visited, of the interesting people we saw, and the things we did—but it would fill up a number of the NEW REVIEW, and must wait for my book.

Everyone remembers the awful shocks of earthquake that took place in the Riviera on Ash Wednesday in 1887. A little before six there was a sound like a monster express train hissing and rumbling by. I said to Richard, "Why! what sort of express train have they got on today?" It broke on us, upheaving, and making the floor undulate, and as it came Richard said, "By Jove! that's a good earthquake." I said, "All the people are rushing out in the garden undressed; shall we go too?" He said, "No, my girl; you and I have been in too many earthquakes to show the white feather at our age." "All right," I said, and he turned round and went to sleep again; so I did my toilette, as I had intended, and went off to Mass and Communion for Ash Wednesday as I was obliged to do. There were seventeen hundred scared people, who had neglected their religion, trying to get into the Confessionals. As soon as I got back I went to take my coffee, and while so doing another great shock came. I ran in to my husband, but still he would not get up. About nine o'clock there was another bad shock. I again begged him to get up. He said, "Well, I think I will this time; it is getting too shaky." He slowly got up and dressed, and we went about our usual business, writing, calling, driving, and watching the trains fill up with terrified people, which was rather an amusement, as some of them were very scantily dressed, and had not even waited for their baggage. He enjoyed it as much as a schoolboy, took notes, and caricatured them in their light costumes. On the 25th I got very uneasy about Richard. I saw him dipping his pen anywhere except into the ink. When he tried to say something he did not find his words, when he walked he knocked up against furniture. He would not take any medicine, because we were to leave next day to go over to Nice to inspect the ruins, from thence to Mentone ditto, and then make our way straight back to Trieste; but I took him to Dr. Frank, who was a very old friend of ours, and whose wife, Lady Agnes, had made our visit to Cannes thoroughly happy. Dr. Frank examined him, found him as sound as a bell, prescribed rest, and thought I was nervous. On the 26th the same symptoms returned, and though we had packed up I absolutely refused to move, and Richard said, "Do you know, I think that that earthquake must have shaken me more than I was aware of." Now it was not only the shocks of earthquake, but that the earth for several weeks kept palpitating in a manner very nauseating to sensitive people, and he was intensely so. He forbade me to send for Dr. Frank, saying it would pass; but I disobeyed. Dr. Frank, thinking I had got a "fad," did not hurry, but passing by on his rounds thought he would look in and say good-bye. He stayed with us half an hour, assured us that Richard was all right, and as sound as a bell, and was just feeling his pulse once more preparatory to saying good-bye. While his pulse was being held, poor Richard had one of the most awful fits of epileptiform convulsions (the only one he ever had in all his life), an explosion of gout. It lasted about half an hour, and I never saw anything so dreadful, though Dr. Frank assured me he did not suffer, but seemed doubtful as to whether he would recover. Soon the blackness disappeared, the limbs relaxed, he opened his eyes, and said, "Hallo! there's the luncheon bell; I want my luncheon." Dr. Frank said, "No, Burton, not to-day; you have been a little faint." "Have I?" he said; "how funny, I never felt anything." To make a long story short, that was the beginning of his being a real invalid. Dr. Frank found that it was impossible for me to move without a travelling doctor. Richard strenuously resisted it for several days, saying "he should hate to have a stranger in the house, that we should never be by ourselves, that we should have an outsider always spying upon us, who would probably quarrel with us, or hate one or both of us, and make mischief, and confide all our little domestic affairs to the world in general—that a third was always in a nondescript position." Now, this was a risk we had to run; but I argued that if we put by £2,000, and gave ourselves four years of doctor, till 1891, unless he *previously* got quite strong, that it would tide him over the worst crisis of his life into a strong old age, and that as soon as he was free from Government, and we settled down at home, we should be in the land of doctors and free to live by ourselves again, and to do what he liked, which had already been arranged for 1891. He then consented. I telegraphed to England and Dr. Ralph Leslie was sent to us. As soon as the case was handed over to him we commenced our Via Crucis to Trieste.

It was astonishing, in spite of malady, what wonderful cool nerve he had in any accident or emergency.

On June 19th we began a three days' feasting in honour of the Queen's Jubilee. First there was a special service in the Protestant Church. Then on the 20th we had a banquet and a ball in its honour. He was brought down to dinner, where he made a most loyal and original speech, immediately after which he was taken upstairs again. It was the *only* occasion on which he would ever consent to wear his Order of S. Michael and S. George.

After seven months, on October 15th, 1887, Dr. Baker came to relieve Dr. Leslie, who had had an offer of an appointment for China, Siam, &c. We were very sorry to lose him, he was so genial and good-humoured, one of the best-hearted men that ever lived; I may say a man who would go twenty miles out of his way to do you a service, and—

great praise—he never said a word against anybody; above all, he had a true reverence for Richard. Dr. Baker had met us in Cannes in our trouble, and had been so kind that I urged him to accept our offer.

On March 19th, 1888, our birthday, Richard finished his last volume of the *Supplemental Nights* (the sixteenth volume). We were exceedingly relieved, because he had always had such a fear of not living to keep his engagements, and we had received money for it.

On April 2nd we began a second "Reviewers Reviewed" on the *Arabian Nights*' critics. (The first one was on the *Lusiads*. The rough handling Richard had received having raised our ire.)

Our days at Trieste after Richard got ill were passed in the following way:—Instead of getting up, as we used to do, at any time from three to half past five, we rose at seven, had a breakfast of tea, bread and butter and fruit on a little table near a window, where he used to feed the sparrows and other garden birds on the window-sill, so that an almond tree which brushed up to the window was covered with them waiting, and, as he remarked, "they were quite imperious in their manners if he did not attend to them at once." He then wrote his journals—two sets, one private, which was kept in a drawer in my room; and one public ephemeris of notes, quotations, remarks, news, and weather memoranda; then he would fall to his literature. If it was Thursday we answered all the correspondence. At nine o'clock the doctor would come in, and as I, being ill, could no longer stoop to help with his bath and toilette, Dr. Leslie, and afterwards Dr. Baker, superintended the bath and the electric foot-bath; but he shaved himself and dressed himself. During the bath he would frequently read out passages from what he was writing to them. The toilette finished, he resumed his literature till half past ten, when, if the weather permitted, he would go out for a good walk with the doctor. At twelve o'clock we had breakfast, which was really luncheon, after which he smoked (always the tobacco of the country—those long, thin black cigars with a straw down the middle), and played with the kitten, and talked. He was very cheerful and enjoyed his meals; he would then lie on his bed with a book, and sleep perhaps for an hour, and then get up and do more literature. A little after three, if it was winter, he would go for another walk in the garden, or, if bad weather, into the hall, or in summer time, at about five o'clock, for a good long drive, or very often an excursion in the neighbourhood, and was always accompanied by the doctor or me, or both of us. Tea was at four, a sit-down tea, which was purposely made into a meal of all sorts of fruits, cake, sweets, and jam; because it was the hour for our intimates to pour in, and he enjoyed it. If any friends, English or other, were passing through Trieste, they lunched and dined with us. He liked company, and it did him a great deal of good; and he always used to say "that he liked to see his fellow creatures, at hotels and public places, for instance, even if he did not want to mix with them," but generally all the nice men in the hotel collected round him, smoking and listening to his conversation. After tea and talk and walk were over, he went to his room and worked steadily till seven, or half-past, when we had dinner. He enjoyed his dinner, after which he sat in an armchair and smoked and talked. Glorious talk and sweet musical voice that we shall never hear again on earth—a perfect education to those who had the boon of hearing him! Sometimes, if the nights were fine, we used to sit on our verandah overlooking the sea and mountains, and watching the moon and stars through a telescope planted there for the purpose. At nine o'clock at night he retired, the doctor again helped him to undress, and then left for the night; and I said night prayers with him; and we talked awhile. He would ask me for a novel—he always said "he cooled his head with a novel when the day's work was done"—and we went to bed, he reading himself to sleep. Sometimes he did not sleep well and was restless, and sometimes very well, but in all cases far better than he had ever done before he was an invalid.

After the cessation of his work for the *Arabian Nights*—the last appeared November 8th, 1888—he passed some months between the *Supplemental Nights* and the *Scented Garden*, that is the famous burnt manuscript, in writing what he called "chow-chow," odds and ends that he had been waiting to finish up.

I may as well mention this, because it is represented to the world that my poor husband had been engaged on a most beautiful and scientific work for thirty years, that he had finished it all but the last page, that it contained gems of science, that it was full of transcendental Oriental poetry, and that I brutally burnt it, the day after he was dead, in either wanton ignorance or bigotry, Now, the truth is this. Ever since 1842, whenever my husband came across any information on any subject, he collected it and pigeon-holed it, and at this particular time the accumulations of twenty-seven years (since Grindlay's fire, which lost all preceding ones) were pigeon-holed in different compartments, on as many as twenty different subjects. As fast as he had finished one book, he opened a compartment to produce another, and sometimes had several books on the stocks at the same time, on as many different large plain deal tables. It was towards the end of 1888 that he pulled out of its nook the material which would go towards the *Scented Garden*, and he translated it from an Arabic manuscript called the *Perfumed Garden*, by the Shaykh El Nefzawih, a Kabyle Arab of the early sixteenth century (925 Hegira), the French translations of which are as poor, as translations of the original, as all the translations of the *Arabian Nights* were (except Mr. John Payne's) until Richard's came out, which was the perfect one. The only value in the book at all consisted in his annotations, and there was no poetry. I have often bewailed my own folly in considering that I was in any way responsible to or owed any explanation to the public, respecting my husband's writings, and the only object of my letter was to deliver myself from the bother of the letters and visits of a very large number of would-be purchasers. I never supposed for an instant that my action would excite any comment, one way or the other, much less did I suppose that anyone would attach any kind of blame to my husband, any more than to the printing of the *Arabian Nights*, which gave him great *kudos* and plenty of money. I know that no one would have *dared* to blame him had he been alive, nor to have represented me as throwing a blight on his reputation for whom I would at any moment, during a period of forty years, have cheerfully given my life. I knew that this book, being the outcome of sickness during the last two years of his life, was not up to the standard of his former works. Turner's executors burnt a few of his last pictures under similar circumstances to leave his reputation as a painter at its zenith. I acted from the same motive. I should not have dared to burn any autobiography, and every word that he wrote about himself to be given to the public will be given. People must not tell me that I am no judge because I wrote with him, and for him, and also copied everything for him, for the first twenty-six of our thirty years' married life till I broke down myself, and the *Arabian Nights* was then handed over to another copyist, I doing all the rest. He laid no stress on bringing it out, except for money's sake. When he had done the Arabian Nights, he said, in his joking honest way, "I have struggled for forty-seven years, distinguishing myself honourably in every way that I possibly could, I never had a compliment, nor a 'thank you,' nor a single farthing. I translate a doubtful book in my old age, and I immediately make 16,000 guineas. Now that I know the tastes of England, we need never be without money." Had we lived to come home together, I should have talked him off printing it, as I did another manuscript, quite on a different subject, and he knew that if I had my will I would burn it. This did not prevent him, about eight weeks before he died, leaving me sole executrix of all he possessed, with instructions "to sift thoroughly, and publish anything that I thought would not misrepresent him to the public," adding, "having been my sole helper for thirty years, I wish you to act solely on your own judgment and discretion." Now, I judged, after long thinking, that the subject would be unpopular, that had he lived to explain it, to talk about it in the clubs amongst his men friends, it would have been different, that I probably should have worked the financial part of it, as I did that of the *Arabian Nights*, because I should not have read it, and large sums would doubtless have accrued from it. He always wrote over the heads of his public, and sixty years in advance of his time: I think that about fifteen people would possibly have understood it and his motives (which were always noble) if the germ was big enough to produce the good intended.

Given fifteen people to read and understand, given a dead hero who could no longer profit from the money, who could not explain or defend himself if he were attacked by the Press, who could not enjoy the praise of a small section of his fellow men; given two thousand or more other men who could buy the book and in course of time would tire of it and sell it. It would be bought by rich Tom, Dick, and Harry. It would by degrees descend amongst the populace out of Holywell-street, the very opposite result to what the upright, manly translator would have desired, and the whole contents might be so misunderstood by the uneducated that the good, noble, glorious life of Richard Burton, of which I and thousands of others are most proud, and delight to honour might sixty years hence receive a very different colouring from the truth, and be handed down to posterity in a false light.

Many people will regret that Richard did not leave his manuscripts in the hands of a literary man, a lawyer, or a so-called friend. If he had, little men without a name would have profited by it, by tacking on theirs to his big name, money would have been made, and everybody, without distinction, who could have paid would have been pandered to, but nobody would have thought of the dead man, the soldier, the chivalrous gentleman in his tomb—he knew this. I alone stand here, and I think it an honour, for his sake, to bear with the epithets of scorn that the brutality of the athlete, and the dyspepsia of the effete—mostly anonymous Braves—have showered upon me. All that he has left will be given to the public by degrees, if it is more than a mere sketch, but it is cruel to the dead to give their sketches to the world and pretend that they are their best work, simply because they fetch money.[1]

---

[1] [Note by Isabel Burton] I was told yesterday that a *Scented Garden*, from one of the numerous mild French translations, is being sold and passed off to the uneducated, not to scholars, as Burton's Scented Garden, under the false plea that I carried away with me from Trieste a copy of it. I now state upon my oath, that there were but two copies of Richard Burton's *Scented Garden*, one was his own original, and one a clean copy, that I burnt them both, and that no other copy was made from them, and I warn the world against buying a spurious article. I also was told that people talk about bringing out works in collaboration with my husband. There is only one genuine collaboration, and that will appear in time; that is *Catullus*; Richard Burton's poetry, Mr. Leonard Smithers' prose. Richard, to save me, used to pretend to his men friends that I knew nothing of these works, and people who want notoriety pretend that they were collaborating with him, thinking they can do so now with impunity. Richard did tell me everything, although he did not allow me to read the works; but now that he has left me his literary executrix I find it necessary to say that I do know my own business, that I warn people from taking liberties with my husband's name and my property to sell spurious literature. About six weeks before Richard died (not because he contemplated his death, but because we were going away for four months to Greece and Constantinople, which would leave us very little time on our return for the actual exodus on the following July 1st) we took, a week together, in the early morning, a list of all the manuscripts, published and unpublished, and their destinations when packed up for England. Hence, when I was offered assistance in the sorting and arrangements from numbers

On July 19th, 1888, we arrived at the St. James's Hotel, in London. We had not been in London for two years, and we had naturally an immense quantity of people to see, and business to transact. About ten days after Richard got rather ill, and kept us in a great fright, but it lasted a very short time, as he was at his club next day. One could imagine what a delight it was to him to return to the club. He used to like to be dropped there at about half past eleven or twelve, he would lunch there, take a siesta after, and read and write, and see his men friends, and then either Dr. Baker or I used to call for him at six. It was the only free time he used to get from our surveillance, the whole three and a half years of his illness, and it was an immense relief to him. I do not mean to say that he could not be alone in his rooms as much as ever he liked, but we never let him walk out or drive out by himself, lest a return of the attack should occur when there was no assistance at hand, and we always carried restoratives in our pockets.

The St. James's was too noisy, although Richard thought the situation quite perfect. His central point of the world was Apsley House, and he despised everything between that and the desert: just as in religion he always declared there were only two points, Agnosticism and Catholicism. Dr. Baker here took a holiday, Dr. Leslie came back to us, and after the former came back we returned to the Langham Hotel.

It would seem as if we were always changing our abode, and so it was. His magnetism was so immense, his brain travelled so fast, absorbed so quickly, that he sucked dry all his surroundings, whether place, scenery, people, or facts, before the rest of us had settled down to realise whether we liked a place or not. When he arrived at this stage everything was flat to him, and he would anxiously say, "Do you think I shall live to get out of this, and to see another place?" and I used regularly to say, "Of course you will; let us go today if you feel like that," and that would quiet him so far that he would say, "Oh, no! say next Monday or

---

of people after his death, I replied, That I did not want help, because I knew them as a shepherd knows his sheep—hence a few bitter enemies. Now, there is nothing missing of the manuscripts, and the so-called collaborations are all in my husband's handwriting, and I have them, or rather I keep all my literary treasures in a bank for safety, and take them out piece-meal as I need them. Three of his diaries have indeed been abstracted since his death, 1859, 1860, and 1861, but fortunately they are not the private ones, which were always kept under lock and key, but those containing public remarks, memoranda, and so on, which were left about. Numbers of our best books here also disappeared, notably an old Shakespeare of twelve vols., which he charged me never to part with. Of course it is impossible to say where they may have been lost during a period of seventeen months; I only got them housed last March; only after I am dead let no one exhibit theirs as "gifts from my intimate friend and fellow-worker, Richard Burton." *But there are no manuscripts missing.*

Tuesday," and then we went. During the latter days of his life this restlessness became absolutely part of his complaint, and we used to seem to be moving on every week.

On October 15th, 1888, Richard left London. Little did we think he would never more return to it alive. We stayed at Folkestone ten days to be near his sister and niece, and had some charming country drives. We crossed on October 26th, his last sight of Old England. Two years later he was gone.

Since Richard had been ill he was quite a different man to what he had been previously, in tastes and feelings. Whereas before he was always cold, and would have fires in the height of summer, now in the bitterest weather a fire in his room made him sick. He would now eat sweet things and drink milk, which in his stronger days he could not look at. He slept, instead of whole nights of insomnia, though often not as well as one could wish. He liked the world and company, whereas before he had shunned the general run of society, and in many other ways was different.

When one writes with curtailed time and space it is not easy to say what one wants, and what I am going to say (being no longer tongue-tied as I have been by a promise till now) should have gone with me as a secret to the grave, if I had not been "badgered and run to earth" by Agnostics in anonymous letters and scurrilous paragraphs.

Richard had English, Irish, Scotch, and French blood in his veins, and it has often been suggested (though never proved) a drop of Oriental, or gipsy, blood from some far-off ancestor. His Scottish, North England, and Border blood came out in all posts of trust and responsibility, in steadiness and coolness in the hour of danger, in uprightness and integrity, and the honour of a gentleman. Of Irish blood he showed nothing excepting fight, but the two foreign strains were strong. From Arab or gipsy he got his fluency of languages, his wild and daring spirit, his Agnosticism, his melancholy pathos, his mysticism, his superstition (I am superstitious enough, God knows, but he was far more so), his divination, his magician-like foresight into events, his insight, or reading men through like a pane of glass, his restless wandering, his poetry. From a very strong strain of Bourbon blood (Richard showed "race" from the top of his head to the sole of his feet), which the Burtons inherit, that is, *my* Burtons, he got his fencing, knowledge of arms, his ready wit and repartee, his boyish gaiety of character as alternately opposed to his melancholy, and, lastly, but not least, his Catholicism as opposed to the Agnosticism of the East, which is not in the least like the Agnosticism of the West. But it was not a fixed thing like my Catholicism; it ran silently threaded through his life, alternately with his Agnosticism, like the refrain of an opera.

He always had such ready, sparkling wit, and it was never offensive nor hurtful. One day as we were on board a ship, at the other side of the world, going to a rather uncivilised place, a Catholic Archbishop stepped on board. My husband whispered, "Introduce me." I did so and they became very friendly, and sat down to chat. The Archbishop was a very clever man, but no match for Richard. My husband began to chaff, and said, "My wife is the Jesuit of the family." "What a capital thing for you," answered the Archbishop. Presently some apes were jumping about the rigging, so the Archbishop looked up and said, playfully, "Well! Captain Burton, there are some of your ancestors." Richard was delighted, he pulled his moustache quietly, looking very amused and a little shy and apologetic, and said with that cool drawl of his, "Well, my lord, I, at least, have made a little progress, but what about your lordship, who is descended from the angels?" The Archbishop roared; he was delighted with the retort, and treasures it up as a good story till this day.

Heredity is a strong thing, and cannot always be shaken off. It breeds alike forms of body, forms of soul, disease to this, good teeth or scanty hair to that, or colour, or talents, or creed. My Burtons mostly have Catholic-phobia; they hate it without knowing what it is, because their ancestors seceded from it at the time of the Reformation; but one of the most anti-Catholic of them, at the age of seventeen, wrote me more than one beautiful letter imploring me to take her, and get her baptised and received into the Catholic Church, I have them amongst my treasures now, but I did not do so, because it would have been an act of treachery to her mother, and dishonourable to take advantage of a girl, and she has since been very grateful for it. Another Burton, whilst labouring from the effects of an Indian sunstroke, used always to turn his face alternately towards Mecca (evidently thinking of my husband), and then turn the other way and say his rosary, something Catholic having come into his unbiassed, unconscious brain. Richard, when he was out in India, had no one to keep him in order; so, as soon as he was well emancipated and untrammeled, he answered the call of blood, and transferred himself to the Catholic Church, and this is the way he describes it to the public— he always spoke lightly of the things he felt the most: "What added not a little to the general astonishment was, that I left off 'sitting under' the garrison chaplain, and betook myself to the chapel of the chocolate-coloured Goanese priest who adhibited spiritual consolation to the buttrels, butlers, and head servants, and other servants of the camp." He frequently spoke in after writings of "the Portuguese priest who had charge of my soul," who, when Richard committed some escapade, "was like a hen who had hatched a duckling." These writings were lent by Richard to Mr. Hitchman, with other notes, in 1887, but he did not understand the importance of it, nor what it pointed to, and left it amongst the parts he did not use.[1] When I asked Richard how it was that it escaped

---

[1] [Note by Isabel Burton] Mr. Hitchman returned all these writings, to Richard,

public comment he said, "Because, when I mention that I went to the chocolate-coloured priest of the Goanese Church, the English only think it is some black tribe, where I have been probably tarred and feathered, whilst I was very much in earnest; but since it is no use annoying my people, and as it has escaped Mr. Hitchman, and as it only concerns you and me, and is no business of any outsider, I do not wish you to say anything about it till my death or some time after my death, and that only if you are put in any difficulty." Cardinal Wiseman knew it, for he passed Richard through all the missions in wild places all over the world as a Catholic officer, and was willing to patronise my marriage. But Richard never let me know anything about it until some time after we were married, and I have kept it all my life a secret. I have always steadily said that "*I did not know*," because I never meant to tell it to anyone but those who had a right to ask, as I did not see how it concerned the public.

The public have allowed me to think it unworthy of having anything but public events related to it by the result of my stupid confidence about the burnt MSS; one almost begrudges it the truth. Look at Grant Allen, a strong and clever man, who stated a while ago in the *Athenaeum* in a paragraph, "The worm will turn," that he had been asked to write something personal, that he threw his whole soul and religion into a book, and that when he gave it to his publisher he besought him to destroy it, or "no one would ever read one of his books again." It is the same with me; but I have one advantage: I want nothing of the public, except what it accords to me freely and out of its own courteous sympathy, unless I ask it to suspend all judgment till it has had my book, because an article is necessarily limited in length; and I am conscious of being in possession of such a subject, and such material, that if they do not read me the loss will be theirs and not mine.

In the *Nineteenth Century* of March, 1892, Mrs. Lynn Linton, who had visited me as a friend, kissed me, and assured me of her friendship (other people being in the room), wrote, as follows :-

> "Women would confine the area of men's excursions to the limits of their own; and such conditions of the masculine life as they did not care to adopt, they would forbid men to practise. We have had a notable instance of this absolutism of late, at the death of one of our own most learned scholars and frank agnostics. He was no sooner dead than his widow surrounded him with the emblems and rites of her own faith, which was not his. She did not shrink from inflicting this dishonour on the memory of the man who had systematically preached a doctrine so adverse to her own. She

---

who wanted to use them for his own autobiography, which he was to begin in 1891, and I have them now for his biography.

cared nothing for the integrity of the life she thus stultified—nothing for the grandeur of the intellect she thus belittled, what she thought right, that she determined he should be made to share, now that she was absolute and he was only one of the strengthless dead; and she would not see the pitiful discredit she thus cast on the name and memory of the man she professed to love."

This lady's knowledge of my husband is limited to seeing him at a dinner-table—perhaps six times in her life—and hearing his dinner-table conversation.

But Swinburne, who travelled with us for a month in Auvergne, and is a very old friend for whom we had a great regard, brought out his glorious Elegy of my beloved husband in July, glorious enough to be printed in letters of gold, and defiled it by the following lines :–

Priests and the soulless serfs of priests may swarm
With vulturous acclamation, loud in lies,
About his dust while yet his dust is warm
Who mocked as sunlight mocks their base blind eyes
Their godless ghost of godhead, false and foul
As fear his dam or hell his throne: but we,
Scarce hearing, heed no carrion church-kite's howl
The corpse be theirs to mock; the soul is free.

(But, my dear Algernon, how could you speak of "The imperious soul's indomitable ascent"? Imperious souls do not rise; it was the humility of that soul that did not know its own worth, its own greatness, that made it soar; but I thank you for "The crested head, The royal heart." He always said that you were the greatest poet we have had since Shakespeare.)

Then, some time in spring, some vulgar little person wrote to a vulgar little paper twenty-eight lines of absolute untruths, saying that I "had written to the English Catholic papers that Sir Richard Burton had died a Catholic." This is absolutely my first statement, public or private, except to the head of my Church. He also said that I was married by Protestants, and concluded: "If you, Mr. Editor, knew more of the circumstances, you would not think the language of Mrs. Lynn Linton unwarranted by the facts. I know them, perhaps better than Mrs. Lynn Linton, and had it devolved on one to write the article in the *Nineteenth Century*, I should have been less sparing of censure than she thought it fitting to be." This is rather an imprudent statement, as the circumstances lie in a nut-shell, and are all stated here in brief. I am nothing if not fair, and the Agnostics shall have their fill, in the book, of their own side of the question. I think that the world, if a man speaks its own shibboleth, if he wears its last new-fashioned coat in the Park, has no right to complain if he does not show it the colour of the ringlet that he wears next to his skin, or the talisman that he wears round his neck, which his wife happens to see, because she helps him to dress and undress.

I feel with Walt Whitman:—

I think I could turn and live with animals, they are so placid and self-contained.
I stand and look at them long and long.
They do not sweat and whine about their condition;
They do not lie awake in the dark and weep for their sins;
They do not make me sick discussing their duty to God;
Not one is dissatisfied, not one is demented with the mania of owning things.

I am by no means going to tell you that his Catholicity was a lifelong, fixed, and steady thing, like mine. It was not. He had long and wild fits of Eastern Agnosticism, but not the Agnosticism that I have seen in England since my widowhood. It was the mysticism of the East. Periodically he had equal Catholic fits, and practised it, hiding it sometimes even from me, though I knew it. In every place we lived in, except Trieste, he had a priest from whom he took lessons, but even this stopped after he had resident doctors and could not go out by himself. From Trieste he used formerly to go to Gorizia, two hours express inland, and other towns. He was worse than ever in talk the three last years, but the things that he said were so innocent and so witty that I was often compelled to laugh or to go away and laugh. Still, as I saw his health declining, I grew frightfully anxious, nay agonised, and in 1888, two years before he died, I made a general appeal for prayers in our Church, which he saw and kept a copy of in a drawer. From our earliest married days, one of his peculiarities (used, rather, I suspect, for training me to observe him, and to understand his wants) would be that he would not tell me directly to do a thing, but I used to find in a book I was reading, or some drawer that I opened every day, or in his own room, marked by a weight, a few words of what he wanted, conveying no direct order, and yet I knew that it was one. I grew quite accustomed to this, and used regularly to visit the places where I was likely to find them, and if I missed there was a sort of "Go seek" expression on his face, that told me that I had not hunted properly, and I knew (by another expression) when I had succeeded. I used to call these "African spoors."

On the same principle he used to teach me to swim without my arms, and afterwards to swim without my legs, using either one or the other, but not both, in case of falling out of a steamer and being entangled.

We hold that "once a Catholic is always a Catholic," except by recantation, and I have two papers signed by him, one of which was put in my prayer-book, and one in a drawer, and they contained the following words: "I desire to die as a Catholic, and to receive the Sacraments of Penance, of Communion, and Extreme Unction. In case it should ever occur to me to revoke it, I now hereby declare that such revocation is to be held null and void," and another paper to the same effect, but in different words, was put in his own drawer four days before he died, so that the moment the doctor told me that he was in danger I immediately sent for the priest. He said once to me, a few weeks before he died, after an unusual burst of agnostic talk at tea, which had made me sad, "Do I hurt you when I talk like that?" and I smiled, and said rather sadly, "well, yes! It always appears to me like speaking against our very best friend." He got a little pale, and said, "Well, I promise you that after I am free from our present surroundings I won't talk like that any more"; and I said, "How I long for the time to come when we shall be living quietly together in private life," and he answered, "So do I."

His last days will be fully described later on. It was at midnight on the 19th of October, 1890, that he suddenly became uneasy with gout. I was with him all night, and between whiles he laughed and talked and spoke of our future plans. At four a.m. he got more uneasy, and I fetched the doctor, who found his heart and pulse all right, gave him some medicine, and went away; but, being called up a second time, later on, soon pronounced him in danger. I at once called up all the servants, and sent in five directions for a priest, whilst the doctor and I and Lisa, a sort of maid and companion, under his directions, tried every remedy and restorative in vain. The doctor, who was kindness itself, and in despair at his danger, applied the electric battery to the heart the whole time, and I knelt at his left side holding his hand and pulse. It was a country Slav priest (lately promoted to be our parish priest) who came. He called me aside and told me he could not give Extreme Unction to my husband, because he had not declared himself; but I besought him not to lose a moment in giving the Sacrament, for he was insensible and the soul was passing away, and that I had the means of satisfying him. He looked at us all three and asked us if he was dead, and we said no. Had he had to go back for the holy materials it would have been too late; but he had them with him, and immediately administered Extreme Unction—"Si vivis," or "Sies capax"—"If thou art alive"—and said the prayers for the departing soul. The doctor kept the battery to the heart all the time, and by Richard's clasp of my hand and a little trickle of blood under the finger, I think there was a slight thread of life until seven. Father Randal Lythegoe, a well-known theologian and Jesuit, once gave me Extreme Unction after I had been certified dead for several hours by two clever doctors; but I came to; so I sat all day by him watching and praying, expecting him to do the same. I thought the mouth and left eye moved, but the doctor said that it must have been my imagination. But what was no imagination was that the brain lived after the heart and pulse were still (I do not expect science, to agree, but theology may), for on lifting up the eyelids the eyes were bright and intelligent as in life, like those of a man who saw something unexpected and wonderful and happy, and that light remained in them till towards sunset. I think that the soul went forth with the setting sun. It had set for me forever, turning this beautiful world into a big grey desert.

Everybody in the house and of my husband's staff, except Lisa, who was a great deal in our private rooms, was doubtless surprised and perhaps wondered at my sending for the priest. Richard was so beautifully reserved, such a past master in concealing his real thoughts and feelings, whilst talking most freely, so as never to hurt his surroundings by letting them imagine that he did not trust them with everything. I used to tell him that he was like the "Man with the Iron Mask." He did not see what right anyone had to know anything, except what he just absolutely chose them to know. I cannot in a few pages describe so immense a character, but I trust that the public will understand its grandeur and its peculiarity still more when they have read my book.

There is one more charge against me, which I should like to be allowed to refute. Some people are under the impression that I hindered his being buried in Westminster Abbey. I took particular care to get a friend to go to, or to write to, the Dean to know what the intentions were, and the Dean replied that it was impossible to bury any more people at Westminster Abbey. I had no idea of accepting a second class funeral at modern St. Paul's (which, however, was not offered), so I saved our dignity by taking the initiative, following a line of our own, and refused before I was asked. In earlier days I had asked my husband, in case I survived him, what sort of burial he would like, having told him what I wanted for myself. He said: "I don't like being shut up in a vault, nor in the ground, nor cremation. I should like you to take my body out to sea, and throw it in." I said, "Oh! I could never do that; is there nothing else?" "Yes!" he said, "I should like us both to lie in a tent side by side," and we went off to the Catholic Cemetery, Mortlake, where fifteen of my people lie, and chose a bit of ground, but when we got back we reflected that it would be very stupid to send the money for it then, as we were not very well off, and that we might possibly die in Timbuctoo. He has now got the very thing he wanted, only of stone and marble instead of canvas. It is the only one in the world, and it is by far the most beautiful, most romantic, most un-death-like resting place in the wide world.

In Westminster Abbey, a wave of the arm would point out to the "trippers" the cold slab, and general corner of many men who were not fit to tie the latchet of his shoe—his name with a common list of theirs.

It makes me sad to see that there actually are people who think that the only honour that England should accord to Richard Burton, having failed to do him justice in this life, should be to bespatter his wife with mud after he is dead and can no longer defend her? Peace! I am not meddling with your concerns; let me listen without these jars for the only sound I wait to hear—and depart.

102. 1893/06/05. Isabel Burton to A. W. Thayer.[1]

Pier View
Sea Road
Boscombe
Hants.
June 5th/93

This address is only temporary, I return to
67 Baker Street, Portman Sq.
London, W. 1st July.

Dear Mr. Thayer,

It is so very long since I have heard from you, or written to you, but I never forget you, and hope you will not forget me. I am settled down in England in two little places one 9 rooms and a kitchen in Baker Street, where my sister Mrs. Gerald Fitz Gerald lives with me, like myself she is a widow and has no children, but my favourite place, and where I live most, is a very small cottage close [to] my darling husband's grave, where I am by myself. Since I left Trieste, I have lost 8 near relations, and each winter have been several weeks very ill in bed. For the last 10 ½ months I have stuck steadily ill or well, for about 7 hours a day writing Richard's Life, and a week ago it was out of my hands, and will be before the public in about a fortnight, it is two large fat volumes, and I hope you will like it, although you may perhaps not quite agree with everything. My endeavour is to make the public know my husband as I knew him myself. I am very jaded, and tired, and my sister has brought me down to the sea for a rest, where I am answering my letters, and pottering about, and I shall go back to work in early July. You will be glad to know that the dream of my life is now in my power, to bring out "a Uniform Library" of all my husband's hitherto published works "for the people," and adding to it gradually all that is not published.* I am likewise preparing two further vols. on his public work. Since last July, I seem to have recovered my power of brain and eyesight.

I make the most of my time, as my internal malady increases every day, but I am not only <u>willing</u> and <u>resigned</u>, but looking forward to <u>our happy meeting</u>. I am very anxious to know about your own health, what a happy remembrance to me are the days when Richard and you and I used to dine together every week, and when you used to read to us in the evening. I am sure you miss <u>him</u>, I venture to hope you miss <u>me</u>. I want you to tell me about your own work, and whether Beethoven makes any progress, or whether the fiend Exodus still puts a spoke in your wheel. Will you tell me <u>confidentially</u> what is the truth about Cautley[2] and his

---

[1] Boston Athenaeum. Mss. L168. Typescript with annotations and corrections.
[2] See Register.

wife, I have only heard his side. I was always sure that he would have to suffer, because he was always so discontented, even with my Richard's treatment who behaved Royally to him, but I did not think he would come to such awful grief, as he appears to have done. Was the present Mrs. Haggard a Miss Hancox, if so she is the daughter of one of my best friends. Always dear Mr. Thayer your affectionate old friend

Isabel Burton.

* The first Mecca & Medinah will be out this month.

103. 1893/12/30. Isabel Burton to Lady Paget.[1]

I will here give an interesting letter from Lady Burton:

67, BAKER STREET, PORTMAN SQUARE, W,
December 30th, '93.

DEAREST LADY PAGET,

I always picture you to myself in a beautiful Italian villa surrounded with groves, nightingales, and roses, beautifying and making it lovely, helped by Lord and Lady Windsor, with all your united taste, and Sir Augustus inwardly rejoicing, outwardly grumbling at not being in London for Christmas, with its delicious black, yellow, pea-soup fog, which is at this moment choking me and making me feel quite faint. I wish you, dearest Lady Paget, a happy and blessed New Year, and you may wish me, as a clever friend of mine did the other day, "a painless Christmas and New Year;" which I thought so appropriate. I send you my little Christmas-card as a token of affection, which displeases me in one sense, because it is meaningless and the custom. Since I last wrote to you, I stayed at Mortlake till 27th of October, and then it became so damp, so dark, so lonely and depressing near the river that I came up to town, to my Baker Street home, for the winter, and am doing my best to keep dry and warm, in order to finish my work. On the whole I have been better, but I get bad attacks from time to time, and my friends and relatives are dying like sheep. I hope you got *The Modern Review* I sent you the other day. I had half a mind to send one to Ouida, but thought it more dignified not to. I never stop working from morning till night, and I do hope I shall live to finish it. I have had a great vexation in one sense—the *Pentamerone* came out, the publisher had contracted with me that I was to erase all the vulgar words; he broke his contract, and took no notice of the erasures, but published it all quite raw,

---

[1] Lady Walburga Paget *In My Tower* (London: Hutchinson, 1923) pp. 18-23, 30-3, 182-3.

and of course omitted my preface. Now, as I know you are very fond of experiences of the other world, I want to tell you of a little consolation I had last September. I wrote, as you know, a great deal in my book about Richard and I being duals or counterparts. One day, l had washed my hands and done my toilette, and came down to tea, afterwards returning to my work sitting in an easy-chair and dictating to my secretary. I felt a sort of pricking in my band, and opening it to see what was the cause of it, there was written in Richard's handwriting, like the colour produced by little bruised veins, "duals," quite large and distinct, and underneath it, in Arabic characters "El minnat ulilleh", which means "my obligation is to God." There was more writing in Arabic, but it was too indistinct for me to be able to read it or to copy it. I am hoping for more. I should not like you to tell this except to people who think as you and I do.

(Note.—As this is not now a very uncommon experience and most intelligent and spiritually minded people believe in these communications, I give these to the world.)

I can tell you also of three wonderful instances of the other world that have happened within this last month from people I know, but I must not mention names except my sister's. (1) One of my sisters has taken a haunted house at Ascot. She is left a widow with children and is not very rich, and she got it cheap, because it had such a bad name. The noises are terrible, dragging of furniture across rooms, chains, etc., and knocking at her door, to which she always says "Come in." For a long time she thought it was a soul in Purgatory wanting prayers, and said them, and things seemed to be quieter; but eventually something seemed to come into her room, and one night pulled the counterpane off the bed. She tugged one way, and the something at the other. She got frightened and went to a monastery close by, and asked them to come. The whole community came "with bell and book and candle" and solemnly exorcised, with all due ceremony, the whole house, from roof to cellar, and she has not been troubled since. It is now proved that when the last woman lived there the thing came and lay down on her bed by her, and she shrieked and fainted, and paid £50 the next morning to be allowed to leave the house. My sister wants me to go and stay with her, and sleep in the haunted room, which I have cordially declined. (2) A priest lately died and appeared to another priest (this is amongst our acquaintances). He thought he had a delusion, so he got up, lit the gas, and opened the window. The other in his usual everyday dress sat down by his bed, and talked to him for an hour, telling him all the cause of the trouble, and said, "I have had leave to come to you and also to another priest," whom he named. The next day the priest, on waking as usual, found his gas lit, and his window open, and he went off to the other priest, and found he had had exactly the same visitation; so they carried out the wishes of their departed friend. (3) A relation of mine went last month to stay in a country house, of which the master was a very holy man. My relation, who is about twenty, went to bed with a novel, when suddenly a deceased member of the household whom he had not known and therefore did not recognise walked into the room. Supposing he had come into the room to fetch something out of a cupboard or dresser he said: "Oh, how do you do? do not mind me," and was going on reading but he saw him walk across to the table at the other end of the room, put his (my relation's) clothes off the chair on to a large table over which hung a lamp on a hook. He had a towel round his neck. He went over to the large bow window and with a knife he cut all the sashlines off the window and tied them together in a noose, stepped on to the chair, having put aside the lamp and the table, hung one end on the hook and the other round his neck, kicked away the chair, and hanged himself. My relation, transfixed with horror, unable to call out, saw the whole process of hanging and gurgling until he was dead. After this the whole thing vanished. Early in the morning he went to the master of the house and said that he had had a telegram from London obliging him to go. His host fixed him and said: "Now I insist upon knowing why, a young man did the same thing last week." My relation made some polite excuse, came to me and told me the story and asked what he should do. I said: "You must sit down and write a letter to the master of the house directly; you must tell him everything, ask him to have prayers said, and not put anybody else in that room." A week passed without an answer, and then the following came. It was as follows: "I cannot thank you sufficiently; I slept there myself the night I got your letter, I saw it all, and thought I should have died of fright; I could not sleep. I went again the next night fortified by prayer, saw it again, managed to stammer something out, and got no answer. Again I passed the day in prayer, I went there the third night, saw it again, and was able to implore the apparition in the name of Jesus to tell me what was the matter, and what I could do for it." (I must here stop to tell you that it was a man who was supposed to have hung himself nine years ago, perhaps of unsound mind, or perhaps from some mental distress.) He answered that his hanging was an accident; that he had never meant to hang himself, but he was quite mad on experimenting; that he had simply meant to try what hanging was like; he had made the rope long enough to put his feet down, he had tied a towel round his neck to prevent actual suffocation, but the rope was too tight for him, he could not undo it, and he died. For nine years he had been suffering in what we call "Purgatory," for something which he had omitted to do, and he said, "It is the only thing that keeps me out of heaven, and if you do such and such for me, I shall be free." It was done, and the soul is happy.

You must keep this to yourself, because if it is told, everybody would know who it is, and I would be censured for my indiscretion in telling it.

Your ever loving and faithful friend,
ISABEL BURTON.

(Note.—Thirty years have elapsed and I now feel at liberty to publish this letter. W. P.)

...

[Letter from a correspondent of Paget]

... Gay says Sanderson has been with her, and that she asked him why Burton (Sir Richard) had been so ill-treated by the F. O., and he says it isn't true. He says he was a perfectly impossible man to deal with and never was at his post, and always wished to govern every country he was sent to. S. says he was rather a friend of his personally, and also Lady B., and always stood up for them. ...

104.   1894/01/05. Isabel Burton to A. W. Thayer.[1]

67 Baker Street
Port man Square. W.
Jan 5th /94

My dear old Friend,

The reason I have not written is that my dear husband's "Life" has occupied me the exclusion of all things, but I am very contented now. It has been out 6 months, come the 12th, it swamped me with visits and letters, it has had a most wonderful success, three leaders, and over a thousand reviews, out of which only about 100 were spiteful. Most of the reviews have given me the meed I worked for, "that they will now know the man inside and out, that I have lifted every shadow of blame from his memory, and that his fame will shine as a clear beacon to all ages," and I am comforted. I have constant fights on, in the press, which keep me alive, I have brought out 5 vols. of his published works, Mecca, Dahome, and Vikram, and have 9 others in hand. This with about 30 letters a day and dreadful bad health will make you forgive me for my

---

[1] Boston Athenaeum. Mss. L168. Typescript with annotations and corrections.

long silence. If you are able, I want you to write to me, or dictate to somebody about your health, and tell me if having put yourself in the hands of Dr. Merli the catarrh of the stomach has ceded to its treatment. You have such a good constitution and courage, that I have great hopes for you, and the great thing I hope for you is to be able <u>to work</u>, as I know by myself what I should suffer if I could not. I cannot walk, I can go in a bath chair, or a carriage, but I can only eat enough to keep body and soul together, and walking up stairs, or standing is very painful to me, from the size and weight of the tumour, I am so glad that you had your niece with you. I am <u>so grieved</u> to hear also about your pecuniary circumstances, surely the American Government, and the Beethoven Societies would do something if asked. I remember quite well the state you were in after Bonn, and the story of the Beethoven book, and the Exodus, and Richard's advice. Do not be afraid of boring me, dear friend; <u>everything</u> about you interests me, and will always be a link between me and my old happy life. Aye' I wish we could have for once another of those dinners and intellectual feasts, that we used to have, but we <u>shall have them</u> dear friend, though you do not believe it, in the beautiful by-and-bye. I do not in any way get over my husband's death, Time has made me calmer, but he is as ever present to me to-day, as he was the last Sunday he lived, and I often grieve for you as well as for myself in his loss. To me the world is still a big grey desert, and my homes would be an empty shell, if I did not feel his presence always there, and if I did not occasionally get spiritual messages and signs from him, which I have had about 10 times. I think I told you I have two little homes, a small dry warm house in Baker Street for the winter, where a sister and I live, she is also a widow, and a little cottage by my husband's grave, which I have bought and inhabit from May to October. On the 22nd of January, my 33rd Wedding day, I am going down to pass it in the mausoleum. Do you remember the day you always dined with us, and we used to have a whole sucking pig, Richard's favourite dish. If you should ever come back to England, come in the summer, and come and see me at the cottage (stay with me). I should like so much to see you again. It is my belief that you will get better, and that you will work again. I only wish we were living nearer, that I might be of some comfort and use to you.

    I am, my dear old friend
    Yours always truly affectionate
    Isabel Burton.

105. 1894/05. John Theodore Tussaud.[1]

A great name with the past generation was that of Sir Richard

---

[1] John Theodore Tussaud *The Romance of Madame Tussaud's* (Doran: New

Burton, who, sixty-six years ago, in fulfillment of a lifelong dream, made a pilgrimage to the shrine of the prophet Mahomet at Mecca when it was believed that no Christian could go there. Besides being a great explorer he was a man of scholarly attainments, and his translation of the Arabian Nights bears the stamp of an intimate familiarity with the Orient.

When Sir Richard died his remarkable career became so much a subject of general comment in the Press that the British public awakened to the fact that a great Englishman had just passed away. Apart from his literary achievements, the account of his exploits revealed so great a love of adventure and so much disregard for narrowing conventionalities as to leaven, the story of his life with a very strong tincture of romance.

When modelling his figure I saw a great deal of his handsome and stately widow, and I am sure no woman could have taken a greater pleasure or more pains in assisting an artist with such an undertaking. Every thought, every action, she bestowed upon the work showed how deeply she cherished her husband's memory and how vividly the portrait stirred her imagination. She clothed the model with perhaps the greatest personal treasure of his she possessed—that is to say, the actual garments her husband wore when he went on his famous pilgrimage to Mecca. She tarried long over the finishing touches that should make his presentment look its best before the critical eyes of the public should scan it. Ornaments, beads, trappings, had each her full consideration, and the very weapons of defence stuck angle wise in his belt were subjected to her most careful arrangement.

Of the capacity for taking pains there was no limit in Isabel Lady Burton's nature; but the labour in producing the figure, after many trying weeks, at last came to an end; and there readily springs to my mind the pathetic picture of her bestowing upon the figure the few final touches, her fingers lingering over the pleats and folds of his robe ere she could declare herself satisfied that the task she had undertaken in helping with the model had been done at her very best. There was one little difficulty, however, that she could not quite surmount. The costume was complete in every respect except one—the sandals he had worn on his hazardous journey to Mecca had become, owing to the wet and heat and the passage of time, mere tinder, and could not be placed upon the figure. The following brief but interesting letter explains how this difficulty was overcome:

67, Baker Street
Portman Square, W,
May 22nd, 1894.

Dear Mr. Tussaud,
    I sent you a pair of sandals yesterday belonging to me, but

---

York, 1920) pp. 206-7.

to-day I have had the promise of a pair from the Prior of the Franciscans which would suit much better. I shall send them directly I receive them.

Yours sincerely,
Isabel Burton.

The monument at Mortlake, on the Thames, within which now repose the remains of Sir Richard and his wife, consists of a white marble mausoleum, sculptured in the form of an Arab tent, its cost having been partly defrayed by public subscription.

106. 1895/09/27. Isabel Burton to A. W. Thayer.[1]

Holywell Lodge
Meads
Eastbourne
Sep 27th /95

My dear old Friend,

It is exactly a year to-day since I got your dear letter, and I must tell you what I have been doing since then, and then answering[2] yours paragraph by paragraph. I was down at Mortlake nursing a nephew with obstruction of the bowels, but I got ill myself, and putting him in the hands of his sister, I went to London, where I had three weeks of nervous exhaustion. I then went up to Carlisle, 6 ½ hours train on a visit to my cousin Canon Waterton who had just built a new Church and Rectory, and I stayed with him 6 weeks, which did me a great deal of good. I then came down in a 60 mile-an-hour-train, my carriage next to the engine, which buck-jumped pretty well over the fells, and arrived in London in rather a smashed up condition. My Doctor forbid me to go out of the house during the winter, hoping to keep me from the prevalent coughs and colds and Influenza, in spite of which I caught a most virulent Influenza on the 6th of March, which has about done for me. All March and April, I lay with congestion of the bowels, howling with pain night and day, and begging God to put me out of my misery. In May and June I got a trifle better but was confined to my bed in the hot stifling and exhausted air of London. On the 1st of July I got moved to Mortlake, only 8 miles off and yet a matter of difficulty. At first I thought I got a little better, but the only rain of the year took place during my stay there, and the hot steaming malarious Thames Valley is very trying to an invalid. At the end of August I had to be taken back again. There I saw a Specialist, and I engaged a first rate Medical and Surgical nurse, and got myself moved to Eastbourne. This is the finest air in England, and I

---

[1] Boston Athenaeum. Mss. L168. Typescript with annotations and corrections.
[2] sic.

have been here a month. I have got a nice large Cottage facing the sea, in its own grounds, a little away from the town and sheltered by Beachy Head hill, and I brought all my household with me. Sometimes I think I am getting a little better, but I have relapses, and am terribly weak, and except my face am so thin that I am nothing but bones with a bit of skin over that. Whether I shall recover or not is doubtful, but you know my views, and how glad I shall be to see Jem again (Richard). It has been a terrible blow to my work, though I never lose an hour, that I am free from pain, but it is not every day that I can boast of that. Now I think enough about me.

You are just as much to be condoled with as I am, in point of health, and I would give much to hear that you have some change for the better. I envy you being able to walk, I can only get about 10 yards with assistance. I do detest meat like you, and mostly heave at the sight of any food. You must not attempt meat. You must have got very thin, I should say. I hope you are able to read. I think you and I are very much in the same condition, I do not know how old you are, but I am 64 (last March). God be praised that your Income is all right. We only want comforts, do we? My head is quite strong and clear. I can dictate from my bed, but sitting up to write exhausts me very much. You see I have got two tumours now, one a large fibroid, and one an equally large ovarian, so that I am quite choked up. Yes, you are right, we used to have delightful evenings and God has pleased to take them away from us, but dear Friend, we shall soon have them again, and much better, when our martyrdom here is over. I shall keep your letter in order to put forward to the world your remarks on my husband in the work which I still hope to finish before the end. If ever you should come to England, you must come and give me plenty of your society. I am getting rather weak now, so must close my letter. Your sincere and affectionate old friend

Isabel Burton.

107.   1890-1896. Edward Clodd.[1]

Dr. George Bird (1817-1900).

Few have heard of, fewer still survive who knew, Dr. Bird, truly the "beloved physician" of Sir Richard Burton, Leigh Hunt, Swinburne and others less distinguished. What wealth of gossip he poured forth about these men—gossip unrecorded. Only a story or two does memory hold. One is of Swinburne, unsteady of gait through drink, grumbling, as he was helped into a hansom, that the step was made so high! Another is of Burton who, complimenting a young lady on her beauty as that of Helen of Troy, was asked by her "where Helen lived?" She was not as versed

---

[1] Edward Clodd *Memories* (New York: GP Putnam, 1916) pp. 270-1.

in classic lore as the very stout lady who, after much thought as to what character she should represent at a fancy-dress ball, told her husband that she had decided to go as Helen of Troy, whereupon the ungallant spouse suggested that she should go as Helen of Avoir-du-pois.

Sitting "under the spreading chestnut-tree," *Punch* recently illustrated a story which Bird told me about Burton, apropos of his pilgrimage in disguise to the sacred shrine at Mecca. Detected, through some blunder in ritual, he would have been killed by a fanatical Moslem, but "getting there first," killed him. "And how did you feel when you had killed a fellow creature?" asked Bird. "All right—and you?" retorted Burton.

It was from Dr. Bird's house, 49, Welbeck Street, that Richard Burton and Isabel Arundell took their nuptial flight.[1] I met Burton (then Sir Richard) at meetings of the Anthropological and Folk Lore Societies, but had no talks worth recording with him, because these bore on the papers read at those gatherings. But his amazing, dare-devil career has had more than one narrator. I saw more of his voluble, excitable widow at the time when she was living in apartments in Baker Street. To a fanaticism unusual even among Catholics she added what that Church bans—belief in spiritualism. One afternoon, after general talk, she suddenly exclaimed, "Richard has heard all we've been saying," which brought the blood to my cheeks, only to recede when I recalled that nothing had passed in the conversation to bring a blush to the cheek of a bishop.

108.   1890-1896. Augustus John Cuthbert Hare.[2]

'Just before her marriage, H. went to see Lady Burton at Mortlake, and was taken to Burton's mausoleum as a natural part of her visit. Afterwards Lady Burton wrote to her saying that she wanted to ask a very great favour. It was that she would never wear again the hat in which she had come down to Mortlake. H. liked her hat very much—a pretty Paris hat in which she fancied herself particularly, but she said she would do as an old friend of her future husband wished, though utterly mystified. Afterwards Lady Burton wrote that when H. had come into the room on her visit, she was horrified to see three black roses in her hat; that they were the mark of a most terrible secret sect in Arabia, mixed up in every possible atrocity, and that—especially as worn by a girl about to be married—they were a presage of every kind of misfortune; that, in another case of the same kind, she had given the same warning, and the girl, who disregarded it, died on the day before her

---

[1] Incorrect. The Birds only moved to 49 Welbeck street later.
[2] Augustus Hare *Story of my Life* Volume 6 (London: George Allen, 1900) pp. 357-8, 460-1.

wedding. H. wore her hat again, but took out the black roses.'

'Sir Richard Burton died of syncope of the heart—died twenty minutes before Lady Burton's priest could arrive; so her report of his having been received into the Roman Catholic Church was a complete delusion.'

109.   1896/01/08. Isabel Burton to Lady Paget.[1]

HOLYWELL LODGE, MEADS, EASTBOURNE,
January 8th, 1896.

DEAREST LADY PAGET,

I was so glad to get your little letter. I am sorry to say that I am never without pain, except for two or three hours now and then, and I am terribly thrown back. I have great consolation, too, which perhaps you will hardly understand. I have lately got a rescript from Rome allowing me a private oratory, Mass and Communion in the house for the remainder of my life. My communications with my husband also make me very happy, and I have such positive proof of their being real. Certainly the misery, the oppressions, and the cruelties are terrible to bear, more lying still and feeling that one is doing nothing, except in prayer. I think it will be so lovely when it is all over; I hope it will. I am under very great advantages here, but of course I have to pay the penalty of isolation and its depression, though I really had a very happy Christmas, so many kind people came down to see me, and I have had such cards, letters and presents—about a hundred and thirty. I had a dinner-party and was carried down to it, and best of all, in the morning there was my first Mass and Communion in the house. It is very cold here, and threatens snow. I quite envy you your climate, but I do not envy you your earthquakes. I forget if Bellosguardo is sufficiently far away from Florence to do away with any danger, or what safety valves you may have about you. But if you get nervous do go somewhere else for a time till they have passed over. I hope you will have every blessing in 1896, with health and happiness, and Sir Augustus, too. Will you tell him, with my kind regards?

---

[1] Lady Walburga Paget In My Tower (London: Hutchinson, 1923) pp. 18-23, 30-3, 182-3. "Lady Burton belonged to the family of Lord Arundell of Wardour. She had been very handsome, with bright blue eyes and golden hair. Very tall, but latterly she had become heavy and large. She was a great-hearted woman, and very impetuous and romantic, and had warm friends and fierce enemies. Her remarks about the earthquake show what stupid things clever people can say. Lady Burton was one of those who sympathised most with me on vivisection, and she had once headed an English R. C. petition to the Holy Father imploring him to use his power to alleviate the sufferings of God's dumb creatures. I need not say that it had no effect whatever."

Always, dear Lady Paget, with much love,
Your affectionate,
ISABEL BURTON.

Next time you write tell me if there is anything fresh about Ouida. I forget if you said you had read *The Sorrows of Satan*, by Corelli. I was fascinated to a degree, awed and repulsed, but I read every word and think it immensely clever. I have often longed for a friend and protector like that, only from God, not from the Devil.
I. B.

110.   1896/05. Raymond Blathwayt.[1]

A Conversation with Lady Burton.

It was a lovely autumn day; great white clouds were piling themselves up in the deep blue sky; a soft wind conveyed alternate waves of light and shadow over the land; the trees were one blaze of scarlet and of gold, as my companion and I passed within the cemetery gates. Away in one corner stands what at first appears to be a white tent, but this, indeed, is the mausoleum in which Sir Richard Burton, the great explorer, soldier, scholar, and gentleman, lies buried in his last sleep. The tent is sculptured in stone from the Forest of Dean, and in white Carrara marble. It is an Arab tent, over the flap-door of which is a white marble crucifix. Upon this flap door is carved an open book of white marble, on which are inscribed Sir Richard's name and the dates of his birth and death. A blank page is left for "Isabel, his wife." Underneath is a ribbon with the words, "This monument is erected to his memory by his loving countrymen."

Unlocking the door, pushing aside, as it were, the flap of the Arab tent, the widow of the sleeping soldier led me into the silent interior. Here in a coffin of gilt and steel, here before a consecrated altar, beneath the cross which is graved upon his coffin lid, lies all that is left of Sir Richard Burton.

"There," said his lifelong companion, "there lies the best husband that ever lived, the best son, the best brother, and the truest, staunchest friend. That is what I have written of him, that is what I say to you to-day. Isn't this a beautiful place for him to sleep in? Just what he would have chosen : a tent in the desert, with the gun and air and flowers all about him." Then we went into the house and left the dead alone. The first thing that attracted me as I entered the little sitting-room—and Lady Burton's house is outside the cemetery—was a strikingly lifelike portrait of her husband, a dark, noble face, with the eyes steadfastly regarding the spectator. "Ah! there he is," I said; "you don't often see such men

---

[1] Raymond Blathwayt. *The Bookman* X (May, 1896) p. 43.

now-a-days. He and Gordon, one almost thinks, are the last of their race." "Yes, indeed," replied my hostess, "he and Gordon were simply pendants. They were men who stood out apart from the rest of the world. And yet even they differed from each other. Gordon wore his heart on his sleeve, Richard was always trying to conceal his feelings, he was always putting on a mask; but as far as religious feeling was concerned, as far as the leading of men was concerned, both had the same ideas. Gordon used to come and sit down on the hearthrug before the fire in the winter evenings, and I would sit by and listen to their talk. Gordon would say, 'There are only two men in the world who could do that; I am one and you are the other.' I have told in my book how when Gordon became Governor of the Soudan he wrote and asked my husband to come and share the work with him. 'You and I,' he said, 'are the only two men fit to govern the Soudan; if one dies the other will be left.' But Richard would not go. 'No,' he wrote back, 'you and I are too much alike. I could not serve under you nor you under me. I do not look upon the Soudan as a lasting thing. I have nothing to depend upon but my salary, and I have a wife, and you have not.'" "I am glad you like that portrait of him," continued Lady Burton, as she seated herself by a little window through which the autumn sunshine poured in a blaze of golden glory; "it was painted in 1863 by Mr. Joy, the artist, the father of Mrs. H. R. Haweis."

"There is Renan's portrait," she continued, pointing to a sketch of the great French writer, beneath which he appended his autograph; "he gave that to my husband, who, however, had but little in common with him. The photograph close beside you represents my old convent, the Convent of the Canonesses of the Holy Sepulchre, at Chelmsford, where I was brought up and where I lived for six very happy years. You know I come of old Catholic families both on my father's and my mother's side. My father was the nephew of the ninth Lord Arundell of Wardour, and my mother was the sister of Lord Gerard, of Garswood, in Lancashire. My father was a country gentleman pure and simple—and devoted to all forms of sport. He brought me up like a boy, teaching me to ride and shoot, everything, in fact, that would suit me for my after life of adventure and peril. My mother was always trying to marry me to a wealthy peer. As far as books were concerned, I brought myself up. I was simply mad on the very life was afterwards to lead in real earnest, a life of adventure. I read everything that told me about Arabs, gipsies, and nomads in general. My rooms were covered with anything that spoke to me of the Bedouins or of the gipsies. Then came my husband, my *beau ideal* of what a man should be, and I stuck to him like grim death, and would listen to no one. My parents used to pat my head and hope for better things, but I won him in the end. How old should you put me at?" she suddenly asked me, with a smile. "It is impossible to say," I replied. "Well," was Lady Burton's answer, "I am an old woman: I am sixty-three years of age. I am getting now just like my husband. I am getting into the very condition in which he was before he died, and so," she went on, speaking in a perfectly natural and unaffected way, quite calmly and without any emotion whatever, "and so I know that my end is near. I feel that I have done with the world. I want to live eighteen months longer that I may finish the work that *He*"—always *He*—"would have wished me to do. And then I shall join him once more. But there is a great deal to be done yet. I am working all day long; from ten in the morning to seven at night, I and my secretary are at it." "And what is the work you wish so much to complete?" "Well, first of all," she replied, "I am correcting his 'Catullus'; that is very hard work. Then there is his 'Pentamerone.' Then I am writing all the prefaces for the Memorial Edition of his works, published and unpublished. I am also writing his genealogy, and my own autobiography to be published after my death. I am also throwing together all the materials for his 'Labours and Wisdom,' two volumes which will be published early next year. That will contain his essays, pamphlets, press correspondence, his best letters, and a *resume,* or the pith, of all the work he tried to do for humanity at large. In short, it will be a complete book of reference for specialists on almost every variety of subject. Will you come up into my bedroom, where I usually work? There are several things I would like to show you," continued his devoted wife, as she slowly walked across the room, and led the way up the narrow little staircase, hung with pictures and photographs, all of which dealt with the romantic past of her and her husband.

On this staircase, as in the room below, as in every room in the house, as in the silent mausoleum in the cemetery, hung a card upon which were printed the words addressed by the two disciples to our Saviour, "Stay with us, because it is evening, and the day is now far spent." I commented upon it, adding, "But don't you prefer the old rendering, 'Abide with us, for it is toward evening'?" "No," she replied; "I like 'stay' best. It is more natural and more homely, I think. And now," she went on, as we entered the little bedroom, "here is everything that tells me of him. Here are innumerable photos of him. Do you not like that one?" she asked, pointing to a large and beautiful portrait of Sir Richard, which represented him with a bamboo spear in his hand, a half-burnt cigar in his mouth, seated in his shirt sleeves in his tent in Africa. It was very characteristic and full of interest. When we reached the sitting room again, Lady Burton pointed out to me Landseer's pathetic picture, "The Shepherd's Grave," in which he has depicted the sorrowing collie-dog standing wistfully over his master's last resting-place. "Isn't it beautiful?" said my hostess. "I have had that picture engraved on the cover of my book, and Richard's name is on the tombstone, and I am the dog." Portraits of old friends hung round the wall—Carlyle, "whom I respected, but did not much like," Lord Beaconsfield, Lord Iddesleigh, "who was very kind to my dear one," Cardinal Manning, Lord

Wolseley—they all were there. A picture of Sir Thomas Arundell, Lady Burton's ancestor in the tower, formed a suitable pendant to the unfortunate Mary Queen of Scots, to some of whose portraits my hostess appeared to me to bear a very considerable likeness. I looked at the book-shelves—a curious medley; science, fiction, Lyell's "Principles of Geology" side by side with some book of devotion or quaint "Lives of the Saints." "I read all sorts of things," explained Lady Burton to me. "I am very desultory, but books of travel and on the East interest me most, and I am very fond of poetry. I read novels sometimes to cool my head at night. I love weird, supernatural things. I like detective stories. I like Rudyard Kipling. He writes just as my husband used to talk, so I know it's all true; he has that downright way of going straight at things."

I expressed great admiration of Lady Burton's life of her husband, for indeed it appeared to me to be well-worthy of such praise, presenting as it does an absolute photograph of a most remarkable man, telling as it does the story of a very wonderful life. "Well," she replied, "its chief merit is that it is perfectly truthful. When he used to dictate to me bits of autobiography, I would sometimes say, 'Oh, do you think it would be well to write this?' and the answer always was, 'Yes; I do not see the use of writing a biography at all unless it is the exact truth, a very photograph of the man or woman in question.' This I have stated in the preface, or 'foreword' to my book. And it is on this principle that I have written. I have had no leisure to think of style, or polish, or to select the best language, the best English, no time to shine as an authoress. I have just thought aloud, and put down my thoughts exactly. I cannot do justice to his scientific life—I may have missed other things that would have been more brilliantly treated by a skilled and clever writer. But there is one thing I *have* been able to do—and that only I, his wife, could have done—I have lifted the veil that hid the *inner* man. He was misunderstood and unappreciated by the world, for no one ever thought of looking for the real man beneath the cultivated mask that hid all feelings and belief. I have lifted the veil, and now the world is beginning to know what it has lost."

111. 1896. Bernard Quaritch.[1]

During the absences of her husband, Mrs. Burton used to visit me for consolatory gossip, and she and I became very friendly. This feeling was maintained throughout the whole course of our relations, and she was always eager to tell me what "Richard" was doing or contemplating. After his death this intimacy continued until she became too weakly to

---

[1] Bernard Quaritch "Richard Burton" in *Contributions Towards a Dictionary of English Book Collectors* ed. Bernard Quaritch (London: Bernard Quaritch, 1898).

venture out as far as Piccadilly. Then the end came, and left me grieving for the loss of two friends with whom I enjoyed the fullest sympathy.

112.   1896/12/09. W. J. Eames to the Editor of The Standard.[1]

Sir,—Having spent months in the late Sir Richard Burton's company, both on shore and afloat, during the time he held the appointment of her Majesty's Consul at Fernando Po, I can confirm the opinion of him expressed by Captain Bushe in *The Standard* of to-day. He was, indeed, a man of iron will, and had a forcible manner of showing it. I have been often surprised at the mistaken estimate many seen to have formed of his character, and no one would recognize the man from the description given of him by Lady Burton: but, of course, she saw him as her idol. I have only seen your review of the book just published by his niece,[2] but I should be inclined to think it presented the true state of Sir Richard's mind as regards the Roman Catholic faith.

I am, Sir, your obedient servant,
W. J. EAMES, Inspector General R.N.
Culmore, Harlesden-road, N.W., December 9.

113.   1897. Eliza Lynn Linton to Georgiana Stisted.[3]

... I am very glad indeed to hear that there is to be a truthful and rational life of dear Sir Richard Burton. I have always resented Lady Burton's false and affected endeavour to claim for her husband the profession of a faith which, if he did hold, proved him the falsest and most cowardly of men. She and I crossed swords on that point, and I said to her roundly that Sir Richard belonged to the world, not only to her, and that she had degraded his memory by her assumptions of this and that principle we all know he did not hold. I said, and have ever said, a man must stand or fall by his own life, and that the greatest indignity that can be done to his memory is to interfere with the integrity of his principles expressed and acknowledged during his lifetime. It was only her intense vanity that made Lady Burton take the attitude she did. Had she really loved and respected her husband as she professed, she would have been content to leave him to himself, and not have placed herself on the throne of the superior and on the seat of the judge. She would have somehow reconciled it to herself that he was an 'infidel' yet 'saved.' Love has no better toga than this of divine partiality. 'God will save him (or her) for his goodness, for all his want of faith.' So Lady Burton would

---

[1] *Evening Standard*, Dec 10, 1896.
[2] Georgiana Stisted (1896).
[3] George Somes Layard *Mrs. Lynn Linton: her life, letters, and opinions* (London: Methuen, 1901) p. 331.

have said, and would have carried out to the letter every wish of her dead husband, and would have respected his integrity.

114. 1898. Herbert Jones.[1]

Richard Burton was not a book collector in the sense in which that term is generally understood, and the collection with which the present writer is dealing was not one to which that name would be applied by authorities on the subject. Yet it is possible that many more ambitious Libraries are less deserving of description, and it is certain that few collections of books have served a higher purpose than that which was the literary armory of one of the most brilliant, original and accomplished men of thought and action that this, or any age, has produced.

The true collector collects for the sake of the books themselves, whether it be for interest of subject, condition, editions, period of time, or other cognate reason. He may read, understand and use them, or he may not. Such points are not vital. The books themselves are of the first consideration. This was not the case with Burton. True, he collected, but he had little, if any, interest in the book for its outward and visible points, whether of value, rarity, beauty, or condition. Its contents and its contents only, in so far as they were important to the thousand and one subjects of thought and action, that his many-sided and accomplished mind was ever concerned with were the sole credentials that secured a book a place on his shelves. The most sumptuous book was little or nothing to him if it yielded no new facts or fancies. The most unpretentious volume was given the minutest attention if it held something either new or true, that would in due course be serviceable. In short, books were Burton's tools, and he gathered them and used, them, not with the curious zeal of the collector, but with the unimpassioned care which the skilled workman bestows on the selection of the implements which his skill directs; or as the soldier would choose the weapons on which his life as well as fame may depend.

This is not the spirit of the collector; the objects of whose care, or learning, or infatuation, or wealth, are perpetually being drawn from, and again dispersed in, the sale-rooms of Christie and Sotheby and Puttick. Why then treat of Burton as a collector? Because a catholic interpretation of the scope of the work entitles one to believe that a description of some of the books of a great traveller, a great orientalist, and an accomplished scholar must prove worthy of attention.

Richard Francis Burton was born March 19th, 1821, in Barham

---

[1] Herbert Jones "Richard Burton" in *Contributions Towards a Dictionary of English Book Collectors* ed. Bernard Quaritch (London: Bernard Quaritch, 1898).

House, Hertfordshire.[1] His father, Colonel Burton of the 36th Regiment, had three children in all. He retired early in life on half-pay, and lived, with his family, much abroad. Young Burton's education was of course peculiar and irregular, both while the family were abroad and in England, up to the time that he was sent to Oxford. But if irregular it was not inefficient for the future which was to be his. He studied, or rather picked up, many languages and dialects.

Oxford was not to have Burton long. It did not suit him, and certainly he did not make any effort to adapt himself to the life required in a University. He had to quit his Alma Mater and was not invited to return. The particular point on which he had to go, involved no moral or in any way dishonourable conduct whatever, and so the world was wide before him where to choose. He naturally and inevitably chose the Army, the Indian Army, and in 1842 he left England for Bombay.

In India he set himself to study the languages of the country with zeal and thoroughness. He had taken a number of books on the languages and dialects of the East with him, most of them supplied by the publisher of this work, whose long and close intimacy with the young Lieutenant began about that time. Their friendship was kept up to the end, and most of the books required by Burton during his varied career were provided by, and on the advice of Mr. Quaritch. Wherever Burton went, his books accompanied him. In the East African Expedition, Speke complains of Burton's boxes of books as an encumbrance. Reading, fencing, of which he was a past-master, and sport took up much of his time, and the materials of some of his future books were then collected. Few more accomplished young men were to be found in the Indian Army than Burton was now, but he was not favoured by the powers that be, and in 1848 we find him returning on leave to England, ill and disappointed.

Four years in England were quickly and brightly spent, and in 1852 we find Burton preparing for his famous and unique pilgrimage to Meccah. The full record of this adventure is too well known [Pilgrimage to Meccah and El-Medinah, 3 vols., 1855] to be more than alluded to here. It was full of danger through every hour of its progress, but it was as successful as it was daring. Two friends only, Mr. Larking and Mr. Quaritch, knew the particulars of Burton's scheme, and of his disguise. The latter providing a copy of Freytag's Arabic Dictionary "faked" up as an oriental volume for the use of the traveller, who would thus have a key to linguistic difficulties and a useful study, while apparently intent on his Moslem devotions. A portrait of Burton in this disguise was painted by Borgo Caratti and is now in the Clerkenwell Museum. A copy of the same is in the Kensington Library.

Though from his youth a wanderer, this was Burton's first great

---

[1] Burton as born at Torquay, according to his baptism certificate.

success as an exploring traveller. His next venture was the East African Expedition to Harar, the almost unknown capital of Somaliland. For accounts of this remarkable exploration, see Burton's "First Footsteps in East Africa, or an Exploration of Harar, 1856." His companions in this exploration, some, however, going by different routes, were Lieutenant Herne, Speke, and Strogan[1]. Of the four, Strogan was killed by the savages and Burton and Spoke dangerously wounded, Burton's wound being a lance thrust through the upper jaw.

On his return to England, the Crimean war being in full swing, Burton was not long in volunteering for the front. He got an appointment under General Beatson, in an irregular corps of our then Turkish Allies, but though brilliant and successful in what he had to do, ill-luck seemed here as always to follow all he did officially, and he soon was back in search of a wider field for his now sole passion, travelling and adventure. Two years' leave was given, and accompanied by Speke, Burton set out on the greatest and most important of African Expeditions, which resulted in the discovery of Lake Tanganyika and Victoria Nyanza (see "The Lake Regions of Central Africa," 1860).

After a short stay in Europe, Burton's next adventure was to visit the American Mormons in Utah and the Happy Valley of the Great Salt Lake. This he accomplished in 1860 (see "The City of the Saints," 1862).

Back in England in 1861, Burton married Isabel Arundel, a lady ten years younger than himself, of an old Roman Catholic family, handsome, enthusiastic, and romantically attached to him. No one can doubt but that his life was influenced deeply and lastingly by his wife's remarkable personality.

Much discussion centres round all connected with Lady Burton and her husband. Nothing need be said of these matters here. With the results of Burton's life the public have much to do, with the religious or other details of his or his wife's private life, nothing. One thing is certain, no man could have had a more devoted or a more painstaking wife, and surely errors of judgment are of small moment when balanced by a great love. There were no children of the marriage.

After his marriage, Burton was appointed to the unimportant post of Consul of Fernando Po, but in getting this, lost his appointment in the Army. One of the results of his stay there was the book "Gorilla Land, or the Cataracts of the Congo, 1875." From here also be was sent by the Government on the famous mission to the savage King of Dahomy, which was successfully carried out and rewarded by promotion to the Consulate at Santos, Brazil. In 1869 he was gazetted to the Consulate at Damascus,

All through this official life, which Burton never loved, he was

---

[1] Stroyan.

constantly engaged in study, and the acquisition of all sorts of knowledge and the mastering of endless languages and dialects. The scholar and the man of action overpowered the little of the official that was in his nature. The post at Damascus was soon lost through certain errors of judgment; want of tact on the one side, and lack of sympathy on the part of the Government with a man who was much of a soldier and little of a diplomatist. Burton was recalled, and a gloomy time followed, broken only by his visit to Iceland, resulting, as was the case with everything he undertook, work or play, in a brilliant book, "Ultima Thule, a Summer in Iceland," 1875.

Then came his appointment as Consul at Trieste, at about £700. This was his final post, here the harbour where this brilliant, wayworn, war-worn, passion-worn, heroically moulded man was to find, if not repose, at least leisure. The Exploration of Midian [*Gold Mines of Midian and the Ruined Midianite Cities.* 1878] and another West African Expedition were carried out from here, and many literary efforts brought to perfection. [Camoens. 6 vols. of 10. 1880. To the Gold Coast for Gold. 2 vols. 1883. The Book of the Sword. One volume of three. 1884.] Amongst them, the magnum opus, the translation of the Arabian Nights, the book with which Burton's name will be inseparably and forever connected. For many years the work had been his dream. Years previously he had met a Dr. Steinhaeuser, who had thought of translating the Nights, had done some of the work, and who proposed collaboration with Burton. This came to nothing, and Burton went on for years with the book alone. At length it was completed. But who would publish it? Payne, a friend of Burton, had already given his version to the world, and few believed that there was room for another that would out-Herod Herod, and in which not only would a spade be called a spade, but a damned shovel. Burton had largely assisted Payne in his translation which was such a success that it was soon out of print. Mr. Quaritch could have taken an additional 250 copies, but they were not to be had. Mr. Quaritch then urged Burton to proceed with his own translation, and it was agreed that the former should have the offer of being the publisher of the work. Lady Burton took the whole of the business arrangement of the "Nights" in her own hands and on Mr. Quaritch offering her £3000 for the work, she at once declined, saying, that she could easily get £5000 herself.

The book was then published volume by volume by the "Kama Shastra" Society, Benares. [Arabian Nights. Printed by private subscription, 1000 sets of 10 vols., followed by 1000 sets of 6 supplementary vols. 1885-1888.] This imaginary society was invented by Mr. Arbuthnot and is Sanskrit in name. The "Nights" proved a great success, over £8000 net profit being the result. But Burton's health was on the decline, £600 a year was spent on doctors for two years to prolong his life. Bat it was of no avail. His military, official and even literary life seemed to him to have failed. In work and in work alone, he found solace. Success, such as it was, came too late. His soul of iron never failed or faltered, but his iron-frame was weary and out-worn;

His real desire was to produce such scholarly work as his translations of Camoens, the Book of the Sword, Folk Lore studies, and the records of travel and exploration, but the world said to him: Produce these works and we will neither buy them nor make you famous, but give us books of the Arabian Nights, the Scented Garden, Catullus, and the like, and gold unlimited and fame unstinted shall be yours. Who shall say whether he was wise or not in following this advice? He did not stay long to follow it. He died at Trieste in 1890. His last resting place is in Mortlake. Much acrimonious and idle talk has warred around his death and his burial. Better would it be to leave that heroic soul in peace now that he has gone, "ubi seava indignatio ulterius cor lacerare nequit."[1]

[Partial listing of Burton's library, abbreviated here]

PAMPHLETS AND CONTRIBUTIONS TO PERIODICALS

My Wanderings in West Africa. *(Fraser's Mag., 1863)*
The Guide Book: Mecca and Medina. *Lond., 1865. 8vo.*
From London to Rio de Janeiro. *(Blackwood's Magazine, 1865)*
Notes on Waity's[2] Anthropology. *(Anthropological Review, 1864)*
Lands of Cazembe, trans. by R. F. B. *(Royal Geographical Society, 1873)*
Notes on Rome. *(Macmillan, 1874)*
Volcanic Eruptions of Iceland in *1874-5. n. d. 8vo.*
The Port of Trieste. *(Jour. of Soc. Arts, 1875)*
Scoperte Antropologiche in Ossero. *Trieste, 1877. 8vo.*
Notes on the Castellieri. *n. d. 8vo.*
More Castellieri. *1878. 8vo.*
Flint Flakes from Egypt. *(Reprinted from Journ. of Anthropological Inst., 1878)*
Midian and the Midianites. *(Jour. of Soc. of Arts, 1878)*
Ogham Runes and El-Mushajjar. *1879. 8vo.*
A Visit to Lissa and Pelagossa. *(From Jour. of Royal Geog. Soc., 1879)*
Stones and Bones from Egypt and Midian. *(Anthropological Institute, 1879)*
Episode of Dona Ignez de Castro (Camoens). *Lond., 1879. 8vo.*
Itineraries of the Second Khedivial Expedition. *Lond., 1880. 8vo.*
Minerals of Median. *Alexandria, 1880. 8vo.*
On the Two Expeditions to Midian. *Alexandria, 1880. 8vo.*

---

[1] "Where savage indignation can lacerate his heart no more." Jonathan Swift.
[2] Waitz's.

Correspondence with H. E. Riaz Pasha. *Alexandria, 1880. 8vo.*
Giovanni Battista Belzoni. *(Reprinted from Cornhill Mag., 1880)*
The Thermae of Monfalcone. *Lond., 1881. 8vo.*
On Stone Implements from the Gold Coast. *Lond., 1883. 8vo.*
Three months at Abbayia.[1] *(Reprinted from the Vienna Weekly News.) 1888*
Gold on the Gold Coast. *(Reprinted, Jour. of Soc. of Arts.) 1882. 8vo.*
Long Wall of Salona. *n. d. 8vo.*
Notes on the Province of Minas Geraes, *n. d. 8vo.*
Primordial Inhabitants of Minas Geraes. *n. d. 8vo.*
Proverbia Communica Syriaca. *[1870.] n. d. 8vo.*
A Ride to the Holy Land. *(Cassell's Mag., Vol. V)*
En Route to Hebron. *(Cassell's Mag., Vol. V)*
Notes on Rome. *(Macmillan, 1874)*
Supplementary Papers to the Mwata Cazembe. n. d. 8vo.
The Biography of the Book [Arabian Nights]. *s. l. et a.* 8vo.

NOTE.—The books in Burton's collection are, in nearly every instance, profusely annotated, corrected, and commented on by their owner. Most of these notes are in the smallest handwriting, and their matter, is of the most critical, practical, and illustrative nature. No subject dealt with by the authors, however important it was, but Burton seems to have had something of importance to add, and nothing was too small to escape his notice. So we find clerical and typographical errors of the most minute kind neatly corrected, dates set right, foreign names more correctly spelled, and so on. In some of the books the flyleaves, title-page, end papers, and the margins all through are completely written over. In the majority of cases also, letters, newspaper cuttings, and other relative matter are pasted in the volumes, forming personal memoranda of much interest. In Burton's copies of his own writings this is especially the case, as he apparently inserted everything he could find relating to the books. This, in some cases, is "mightily diverting," especially where the Publishers' accounts are included.

Throughout the Arabian Nights the MSS notes by Burton in his own copy are most numerous and of extraordinary interest, not inferior to those printed already. Should the work ever be reissued in extenso, this copy will be the only one in existence which can give Burton's last word on, and final revision of, his magnum opus.

---

[1] Abbazia.

115.   1898. John Payne.[1]

RICHARD FRANCIS BURTON.

>Burton, old fighter, frankest foe and friend,
>The glamour of the East it was that drew
>Our lives together, mine, that only knew
>The Orient glories by the dreams that lend
>Enchantment to the far, and yours, whose trend
>Your steps through lands untravelled, old and new,
>Still led; and this sufficed, for me and you,
>To hold our hearts unsundered to the end.
>Through stormy seas your vessel drove of life;
>Your feet were foremost in the front of strife:
>My travel in the trackless ways of thought,
>My battles in the bounds of fancy fought
>Still were. Yet oft in dreams I clasp your hand,
>Athwart the shadows of the Silent Land.

116.   1900. William Tinsley.[2]

Captain, afterwards Sir Richard Burton, as I knew him in about 1860, was a very different man from the almost maudlin sentimental hero Lady Burton made, or pictured him to be in the last years of his life. Let me say at once, that I sincerely hope that Lady Burton did win her gallant husband over to her own noble faith, but she would have obtained more credence had she not over trumpeted her victory, for there was plenty of reason for many years that he might have had some pure religious faith in his mind; for about our best religious beliefs he was often terribly plain spoken. In his younger days, in fact for many years, exceedingly clever devil-may-care Dick Burton had not an atom of religious sentiment in his mind, and he was as free in thought as Darwin on the origin of man, and was one of the firmest supporters of the old Anthropological Society, in St. Martin's Place, in about 1860. I do not imagine any man or woman is always of one mind, and especially in the matter of religious belief; and, but for the fact that, in the later years of his life, Burton was lending his name to literature by no means pure and holy, I could well believe he might have died a noble Catholic in faith, but to me, at least, it seems hard to believe that any truly noble-minded man or woman could, or would, lend their name to literature full of innuendo, if not worse matter. I refer to Burton's free translation of "The Thousand Nights and a Night," and other books even more against the taste of the pure minded reader.

---

[1] . *Carol and Cadence: New Poems* by John Payne. London: Privately Printed, 1898.
[2] William Tinsley *Random Recollections of an Old Publisher* (London: Simkin, 1900) pp. 143-149.

But the voices of Sir Richard and Lady Burton are silent, and perhaps mine should also be about them. But I had so many pleasant business dealings with Burton when he was almost a young man, and I saw so much of him, that when I read Mrs. Burton's account of the later years of his life, I almost wondered whether I had ever known the man the doubtless well-meaning wife pictured.

Perhaps it is not too much to say that Mrs. Burton did not know her husband well during their early married life, and certainly had no control over him until they were both fairly well on in years. For Burton was a rover and traveller at heart; his wife seldom travelled with him, and his best friends never knew when and where he would be likely to turn up. In fact, adventure was his pride, and surprise his delight; for he was as likely to be heard of disguised as a pilgrim off to Mecca and Medina, or exploring "The Lake Regions of Central Africa," as in the Strand with a few Bohemian friends, seeing and enjoying London life. In fact, his was a restless, almost reckless disposition, and travelling over new ground in Africa was his especial delight.

Although Burton was so fond of going almost alone to out-of-the-way places and unfrequented parts of the world, when at home, in light drawing room society, he was capital company, and an excellent talker. Those of us who knew George Sala in his best mood know what a capital talker he was, and how the ladies would flock round him. But I remember one night, at a rather large gathering of notables at my brother's house at Putney, when Master Burton eclipsed Sala, and had all the ladies round him, even to Mrs. Henry Wood and Mrs. W. H. Wills, two ladies who had no ears for foolish talk.

When Mrs. Burton came to my office with her husband, and we were talking business, she seldom ventured a suggestion of any kind, and as a matter of fact he would not allow her to do so, for if she only half uttered a word, those wonderful eyes of his were upon her, and she was silent in a moment. Burton had not at that time any belief in her business or literary qualities, and he would not let her interfere in his business, even in small matters. I am rather emphatic in this matter, because the time came when Burton was no longer lord and master of his wife, but became almost, if not quite, a slave to her will. As an example of what I mean by his control over his wife's actions, I may mention that once, when he was away from England for some few months, Mrs. Burton wrote, and we put into type, a book about "The Great Tenerife," and a set of proofs, making between three and four hundred pages in book form, were given to Burton as a surprise.[1] But Mrs. Burton was the most surprised, for he ordered every particle of the book to be destroyed, and paid the costs, which were over a hundred pounds, out of his own pocket. I do not think

---

[1] "Scenes in Tenerife" (unsigned) in *The Month: a Magazine and Review* 1867 (6): pp. 63ff.

he cared a dump about the expense, but his estimation of the book was not complimentary to the author. The above incident will sound rather strange to those who know what curiously laudatory matter Burton in after years allowed his wife to write about him and his life. I published quite a dozen books of travel for Burton, and I think most of them are quite in the front rank with any books of travel of the last half century, while not forgetting Barth, Beke, Livingstone, Du Chaillu, Speke, Grant, Baker, Stanley, and several other travellers of note.

But here is a strange fact—not one of Burton's books sold to anything like the same extent as any one of the authors' works I have mentioned. But worse than all, young Winwood Reade[1] went to the coast of Africa, thought he saw a gorilla, and came back and published a volume called "Savage Africa," which had a very good sale, in fact more than any one of Burton's books; as also did two or three volumes by "The Old Shekarry." In fact, several other travellers of the romantic school found good sales for their books.

But here is a fact worth noting—a complete set of Captain Burton's travels are at the present time, and, indeed, have been for some years, worth double the sum of all the complete sets of books of travel by all the travellers I have mentioned. I mean Barth, Beke, Livingstone, Du Chaillu, Speke, Grant, Baker, Stanley, Reade, and "The Old Shekarry." I lay stress upon this fact because I believed in Burton's books when I published them, and even though they cost me many thousands of pounds for the author and production, for which I got but a poor return, I am glad.

Of course, I am bearing in mind that the fact of there not being a large number of most of Burton's books in existence makes them more scarce, but it does not make them less notable literary works.

I think I may say that even when Burton was lord of himself he was a poor diplomatist, and when the time came that he was ruled by his wife, his reputation as a public man sadly diminished. Burton so much disliked missionaries that he dedicated the first book we published for him, called "Wanderings in West Africa," "To the true friends of Africa," "and *not Exeter Hall*." At that time Exeter Hall was the main starting point of all English missionaries who went forth on their, as a rule, praiseworthy and mostly dangerous missions. But I am afraid Burton in his, at that time, many travels, had seen some missionaries who were not exactly self-sacrificing men; in fact, he often declared in my hearing that he had seen some whose moral courage and good work in their mission was of a very poor nature. But doubtless Burton's rather one-sided or curious thoughts about religious teaching made him rather severe upon its teachers. Besides, he was no admirer of the dark races, and certainly

---

[1] See Register.

did not consider the poorest kind of black to be much beyond the dumb animal race; in fact, although he went on a kind of friendly mission to the King of Dahomey, I know he would rather have gone with an armed force strong enough to have knocked that brutal ruler and all his followers into small fragments. Many years ago Burton wanted me to publish his rendering of the "Arabian Nights," but I refused to do so, for at that time there was in the book market a beautiful revised edition, in three volumes, of the same work, by Mr. E. W. Lane, and it is a book that need not be under lock and key in any house. However, all the morbid-minded reading world knows that Burton did publish his version of the old tales, and that after his death Mrs. Burton published an expurgated edition; indeed, she took a very great interest in the production of the whole of the book with her husband. My limited understanding will not let me believe that such literary work was of a true womanly nature. As regards the great profit said to have been made out of the production of the books, the sum mentioned was as outrageous as some of the stuff in the books themselves, and the story of the destruction of the five thousand pounds manuscript was, I think, equally as outrageous; as was also the statement made by Mrs. Burton that Burton received hardly any money for his books. I paid him quite three thousand pounds. I willingly admit it was bad pay for such excellent literary work, but I could easily prove that my profits were a long way behind those of the author.

I am afraid I seem to more than throw some doubt upon some of Mrs. Burton's statements. I am truly sorry the lady is not alive to contradict me. But here let me declare that I never heard the gallant Richard Burton make a statement anyone could, or dare, contradict in his presence; he was truth itself, and hence, may I say, a bad diplomatist. He had, as I have said, peculiar opinions, to say the least of them; but they were his own, and he never threw them at anyone in an offensive way. As a matter of fact, Burton hated Consulships; but he was not a rich man, and these offices gave him good opportunity for travel, and he loved travelling. But can anyone imagine any man more unfitted for the Consulship of Damascus than Captain Burton? He had not, I repeat, at that time, any sympathy with any religion or its professors. He took Mrs. Burton to Damascus with him; she was, as I have also said, a rigid Catholic, and at Damascus Burton had little sympathy with pilgrims of any creed. His wife pandered only to those of her own faith, and had little regard for those who did not think and say as she did. Thus, Damascus only knew the Burtons for a time, and instead of rising high in the diplomatic world, as Burton's great learning and travels warranted, he was relegated to Trieste, to moulder away his latter days making literal translations of matter of no value to the literature of his own or any other country.

117. 1904. Sir Clements Robert Markham.[1]

Captain Burton was a very remarkable man, of great ability, extraordinary powers of application, imaginative and yet scholarly. Outwardly he was eccentric, often showing his rough side to bores and to people he disliked. Sir Roderick[2] never took to him. To me he was always most friendly ... He continued his friendship to me to the last.

118. 1906. Ouida.[3]

At this moment, when the name of Burton has been brought before the English public by a biography which fails lamentably to do justice to it, I venture to say a few words concerning one whom I knew well, from my own early life until his death, and who never failed to visit me on his returns to Europe. The English biographer has seldom been distinguished for skill in narrative, for terseness and lucidity in relation and representation; he generally wanders over too much ground, collects too many facts, arranges them loosely, and oscillates between too much description and too little; seems too often afraid to be morally responsible for his hero, and generally washes all colour out of his portrait.

Burton's was a life which presented innumerable difficulties to the biographer. He was a man of great reserve, of the most varied experiences, of the most complicated character; witty, sardonic, caustic, stern; who would tell you the most incredible stories with the gravest face, to amuse himself with your discomfort, and who delighted in being thought by people in general a devil incarnate. Over the greater part of his adventurous life no biographer could have any certain sight; for the chief part of its experiences it was necessary to rely upon himself; and it was an extremely difficult thing to be certain whether he was laughing at you or not in his portrayal of experiences.

But to write of him without having known him, seems to me absolutely useless. I do not think that any of the biographical articles on him have done him justice, and the recent more copious biography has the immeasurable defect of having been written by a person who was not personally acquainted with him. As well might a painter portray a lion who never had seen one! The individuality of Burton was so unique, so singular, so many-sided, so extremely startling to all commonplace people, so utterly confounding and unintelligible to all ordinary persons, that the idea of anyone presuming to know it when he was himself unknown is amazing and almost comical in its audacity. To write the

---

[1] C. R. Markham, RGS Archives CRM/47, p. 354. Note pencilled inside says 'Probably written c. 1904. New additions made up to 1912.'
[2] Murchison, see Register.
[3] Ouida 'Richard Burton' *Fortnightly Review* June 1 1906.

life of any contemporary without being acquainted with him seems a strange temerity at any time; but in the case of a biography of Burton it appears as strange as if a blind man were to try to paint a hawk in its circling flight. There must have always been but few people living contemporaneously with him who knew him well enough to be able to describe him as he was, to enter into the singularities and angularities of his temperament, and to understand his absolute unlikeness to his own generation, the virility and the independence of his nature and his character. That such a man was wasted by the British Governments of many years in the commercial squabbles of petty consulates, and the fruitless exiles of such buckram-bureaucracy as reigns there, is humiliating to those who wish to be able to feel some esteem for the intelligence of Downing Street.

Burton saw things and persons as they were; and to do so seldom results in compliments to persons and things; he had no patience with hypocrisies, formalities, or formulae, and, therefore, he should never have entered the English public service, which cannot be represented in any of its branches without them, and which is tremulously afraid of all independence of character of action and of utterance in its public servants.

It has no doubt had many great and admirable servants; but we shall never know how many it has lost by the suffocating straight waistcoats in which it has insisted on their existing, nor how many have quitted its service, early in their career, through impatience of its narrowness and harshness, and thirst for their own liberty and free-will.

I have often wondered where Burton got his Oriental physiognomy, his un-English accent, his wonderfully picturesque and Asiatic appearance, for which there was nothing in his descent and education to account. Apparently, by all inheritance, he was a commonplace Englishman of the middle classes; actually, he was a man who looked like Othello and lived like the Three Mousquetaires blended in one. Perhaps, if South Africa had been then what it is now, a more congenial field, a more sympathetic employment, might have been found for him than settling the disputes of traders and signing the papers of tourists; as it was, his genius, his force, his wonderful originality, his masterful powers, were tied up like grand dogs in narrow kennels, and became savage as the dogs become.

I do not venture to speak of the great actions and occupations of Burton's life because I can have no pretension to do so. I cannot judge of his labours as a traveller, as an explorer, as an Orientalist. I cannot say whether the jealous attempts to undervalue his achievements were or were not in any degree justified. I cannot tell whether the rabid calumnies of lesser men were or were not in any measure founded on fact, and whether or not any justice lay beneath the undoubted (and always unexplained) hostility of the Foreign Office to him. But that his great deeds were mere Munchausen tales I do not believe; he had too virile and scornful a temper to be a liar; that he had many and very malignant enemies there was no doubt; that his own sarcastic and gouailleur[1] temper made him many foes there was also no manner of doubt, and that his mere presence in a club-room made the ordinary club-man feel small, there can also be no doubt; and when we dwarf others it is inevitable that those others should throw mud behind us. Besides, to the difficulties which his character offered to any comprehension by the ordinary man there was added the delight he took in mystifying people, in terrifying them, in painting himself as the devil before the frightened eyes of timid mortals. He loved nothing better than to sit at an hotel table d'hote and paralyse his companions by diabolical frowns or gruesome rolling of his eyes. If he gained a terribly melodramatic reputation he owed it in much to this love of playing on the nerves of weaker mortals. His physiognomy lent itself to this sport, for he had a dramatic and imposing presence: the disfigurement of modern attire could not destroy the distinction, and the Oriental cast, of his appearance and his features. In the largest crowd he was noticeable.

Was it his own fault or that of his country that this man, who had in him so many elements of greatness, died, a petty consul of a mercantile seaport in the most uncongenial and unworthy atmosphere which could have been found for him by a Mother-Country which was, to him, certainly a step-mother of the most niggardly and unkindest sort? The beheading of Walter Raleigh was, I think, a kinder treatment than the imprisonment of Burton in Trieste.

I never understood why he did not leave the Consular Service, which, at its best posts, could never have been a service for him. Neither its occupations or its remunerations, its restrictions or its emoluments, were fitted for him. I never could comprehend why he kept his head in its halter a twelvemonth. He must have known that he had a bad name in it; that he was wholly unfitted for its dreary routine and tiresome obligations; that whilst he scared his chiefs, he was himself as irritated as a horse under the bearing rein.

A country which had possessed any power to ease and appreciate such a man would have given him a free rein in some vast wild land like Uganda, and not have expected from him a parish priest's morality and an old woman's scruples.

"Did you really shoot that Arab boy?" I asked him once; for the killing of the Arab boy was always being cast up against him.

"Oh, yes," he answered, "Why not? Do you suppose one can live in those countries as one lives in Pall Mall and Piccadilly?"

---

[1] Mocking.

And he laughed; with contemptuous remembrance, probably of the tolerance of his nation for the Deadly Trades which make plutocrats of those who kill men and women by the thousands before their thirtieth year in their factories and furnaces.

To shoot anybody even in self-defense sets the hair on end and the nerves on edge of the British householder; but to have capitalists manufactured out of human starvation and suffering, whilst nail-makers and pelt-cleaners and white-lead workers die for their enrichment, does not seem to the British householder any matter at all, even as to the British public the shooting of natives in Natal by batches seems a perfectly innocent and natural proceeding.

Men in the Foreign Office in his time used to hint dark horrors about Burton, and certainly, justly or unjustly, he was disliked, feared, and suspected in English political and social life, not for what he had done, but for what he was believed capable of doing, and also for that reserve of power and that unspoken sense of superiority which the dullest and the vainest could scarcely fail to feel in his presence. Beside him most other men looked poor creatures.

In the eyes of women he had the unpardonable fault: he loved his wife. He would have been a happier and a greater man if he had had no wife; but his love for her was extreme; it was a source of weakness, as most warm emotions are in the lives of strong men. Their marriage was romantic and clandestine; a love-marriage in the most absolute sense of the words, not wise on either side, but on each impassioned. She adored him, and, like most women who adore, she was not always wise. She was of great courage and intelligence, and shone in society even as she suffered solitude and met danger with fortitude. She was as happy in the great world of London as in the ruined cities of Asia, and could adapt herself to the most varying circumstance with equal spirit and patience; she was exceedingly tender and humane to animals, and of unswerving fortitude and resolution in all kinds of peril. What made the one weakness in her character was the religious superstition which is the rift in the lute of so many a female soul. Like all her family, she was a devoted Catholic; this bigotry increased with years, and after Burton's death became so great that it made her actually burn the MS of one of his most precious translations, because she deemed it of immoral tendency. This act, I confess, I could never pardon her; and I never spoke or wrote to her after the irreparable act.

Throughout the chief part of their lives he was implicitly obeyed by her, but during the close of his, ill-health made him more helpless, and compelled him to rely on her in all things, and then the religious ogre raised its head and claimed its prey; when Burton lay unconscious on his death-bed she brought a priest into the chamber, and had the comedy of religious rites gone through over a body in which life was already almost extinct, and the power of volition was already wholly dead. I know not what others may think of this act; to me it was an unpardonable treachery. I think also that it was for her sake that he remained in the Consular Service, which was so unsuited to him and so drearily wasted time, which he could have so far better employed in intellectual work or in exploration. She was naturally extravagant, and the world she lived in when in England was one which necessitated large expenditure. This occasioned many worries and frequent troubles, and caused gossip which discredited him in his chiefs' opinion. He himself, if he had not had another to maintain, could have lived on a shilling a day and a few good cigars. They had no children. He regretted it; men always do; I do not think she did so; children would have been impedimenta in the varying life which she so keenly enjoyed in the changes from Belgravia to Syria, from the Grand Hotel to the hair-tent, from the crowd of carriages in Bond Street to the solitude of Sahara under the stars.

As the passing of time increased her credulity and weakened her judgment, she became more and more possessed by religious superstition, more and more convinced that her husband was lost for all eternity; and to his acute and virile mind such fanaticism was the most harassing form that human folly could possibly take; joined to physical ills of the kind which so frequently accompany the end of a life spent in the heat and the cold of strongly contrasting climates, they lent a tormenting irritation to the pain of enfeebled strength.

"If I could only save Dick's soul!" she would cry; and I could not persuade her that his soul, if he had one, did not want her help. Women have such strange illusions as to what they believe to be their charge d'âmes!

She was a noble spirited and very humane woman; but she had the misfortune to be imbued, by hereditary and educational influences, with superstitious prejudices and persuasions which made her imagine that her supreme duty was to worry her husband until she dragged him down to her own theological level. Happily, she never succeeded; but when he was dead, there was no one who could dispute her right to dispose of his remains as she chose, and she consigned his manuscript to the flames, and his body to an English Catholic cemetery.

It was impossible to make her recognise the folly of her acts and the offence which they inspired in his friends. I think no Government could ever have more foolishly or impudently slighted two men of unique powers than the English Government slighted Burton and Matthew Arnold: to waste the energies of the one in minor Consulates, and the scholarship and intellect of the other in an inspectorship of schools, makes one long to impale Britannia on her own trident.

A man, absolutely alone, can, no doubt, do much to shape his own destiny; but he must not be married, and he must not belong to any branch of the public service. There are no more worlds to conquer, but there are still wide and wild lands to rule Burton should have been sent to rule one of these and been let alone. He would not certainly have done so with any glove over his iron hand, but he would, I believe, have governed with strict justice, with keen insight, and certainly with courage and with power.

And let us note that it was not one Government, but a series of Governments, which did this one after another. Against Burton there is the cowardly, because vague and unproven, accusation that "something wrong" was known. But in the case of Matthew Arnold no excuse or pretence of such a kind ever could be made; yet until the day of his death this brilliant and beautiful mind, the mind of a scholar and a poet, was wasted in paltry routine work. I do not believe that the native population of any provinces which Burton had ruled would have suffered under him; he had a very just mind; his sympathies were always naturally, also, with the Oriental than with the Occidental, with the native than with the invader. Downing Street never trusted him with power; and the distrust galled him bitterly.

It was impossible for those who valued his qualities, and resented his exclusion from suitable posts, ever to discover the secret of the black cross which was placed against his name in Downing Street. That there was one was never denied. That it could be placed there for any grave offence seemed impossible in view of the fact that he was retained on its active service until the day of his death. But here we are met by that mixture of injustice and tyranny which is so generally characteristic of Government offices. If he had done anything greatly incorrect he should have been dismissed for the offence, and its form declared. If he had done nothing, he should not have been subjected to the injury of whispered calumny by the hints of the department which employed him. There should be no medium between one or other of these alternatives in the measure dealt out by Government to its officials. It has been always a mystery to me why the Consular Service continued to hold him in its ranks if it had accusations or even suspicions against him, as why he continued to remain in such poorly paid and unsuitable appointments as the Governments of his day gave to him. It is incomprehensible to me why he did not leave the service which appreciated him so ill, and seek fortune on his own unshackled initiative. No man was more fitted by nature and intellect to do so.

England has many able men who are visible and famous; but I think she has many others whom she either does not recognise or does not use; and these are probably the greatest. Burton was unquestionably greater in his talents, in his powers, in his whole idiosyncrasy than any of his contemporaries who followed his own lines of thought and action: Grant or Speke or Stanley could not compare with him for an instant yet he lived and died in the inferior grades of the Consular Service: a career as fitted to him as the shafts of a tradesman's van to a racer entered for Epsom and Chantilly.

A perverse destiny dogged his steps and drove him backward from his just attainment.

But it will be replied to me that the truly great man makes his own fate, and is not to be hindered on his course.

Perhaps: who knows?

I must also leave to Arabic scholars the due appreciation (or depreciation) of the Arabian Nights and other of his translations from a language which only orientalists can appreciate. But that Burton merely used the translations of others, as his detractors venture to say is, I am certain, a cowardly calumny. He was not perhaps a scrupulous man, but he was a very clever man, a man who knew other men in all their wisdom and all their folly; and it is quite certain that such a man would never have done such an imbecile act, or given such a handle against himself to his antagonists. He was very proud of his rendering of the Nights, and held it to be the great achievement of his literary life. He constantly affirmed this.

119. 1907. Richard Patrick Boyle Davey.[1]

In the now far-off past, when Sir Richard Burton was living—"Dick Burton," as my valued old friend, Mr. Kenneth Cornish, who brought us together, used to call him—was wont to come and see me and fascinate me with his wonderful personality and the brilliant lucidity of a genius which has, I think, never received its full acknowledgment, we used to talk over these religious matters of the East with intense interest. He possessed profound learning, and a practical knowledge of Oriental mentality, with its extreme sensuousness and at the same time its intense sense of personal dignity, and he would try to make me look upon things Eastern, not through English spectacles, but through others made in Islamic lands. His version of the "Arabian Nights" is certainly not reading to be recommended to the young ladies of a convent school; but to the serious student it is the most complete revelation ever made of the inner life of the Eastern world, wherever it remains unmodified by European and Christian influences. Lady Burton, the faithful companion of Richard Burton's long married life, was another of the guides I have had through the mazes of the inner life of the Asiatic world. Even as I write these few lines of tribute to the memory of two valued friends, the tones of Sir Richard's strong voice and the flash of his wonderful eyes return to me, and I seem to hear him repeat, "No one can understand the East unless he is full of sympathy for the East, and sees the people by

---

[1] Richard Davey *The Sultan and his subjects* (London: Chatto and Windus, 1907), p. 83.

their own brilliant light, and not by the dim glimmer of a London fog. You must face your true Asiatic with no sense of your own superiority, for one soon finds that he is in many ways a bigger man than you. He is at least never a canting humbug."

120. 1908? Francis Galton.[1]

Impatient of [?] & ~~seemed to take pleasure~~ in
~~& delighted in shocking~~ making himself out to be worse than he was
& was ~~far from careful not to shock unreasonable prejudices~~
very little respect indeed for the prejudices of strangers

jealous
vain
bad speaker
a laborious student
taking notes, blind plan[?]
swordsman
power of disguise
would have been greater if he had been less
thorough bohemian & quite orientalised

~~he became familiar with~~
~~who strove to enter into~~ every aspect ~~phase~~ of life
to acquaint himself with
~~he sought to know~~
he ~~was~~ made himself at home in the most various ~~aspects~~ conditions of
life a consummate
linguist, capable of
ever eager to fascinate

a consummate linguist ~~capable~~ amusing himself with passing
~~posing successfully as~~ a ~~foreigner~~ country man of [Persian?] of more
than one nationality. Eager to live know life in all its possibilities of
life
familiarise himself with all the
Impatient of decorum showing very scant regard ~~respect~~ to the social
prejudices of strangers & disposed to shock any

What a "Bohemian" is to ordinary persons
that Burton was to a Bohemian.

---

[1] Galton Archives, University College London. 75/B. Undated, discarded, crumpled note, probably created when Galton was writing his *Memories of My Life* (1908).

121. 1919. John Payne via Thomas Wright.[1]

The marginal notes pencilled by Payne in the manuscript of my life of Burton are very numerous and illuminative. The following are a few

In chapter 29 (Vol. 2) I said in a passage, afterwards omitted, that Burton's doctrine "is that everything should be studied, everything should be talked about," etc. Payne comments: "Technical knowledge of evil things in the proper place and for the proper purposes is a very different thing from the general rubbing of noses in the sewage of depravity as Burton proposes."

By the side of a passage in which I speak of Payne's own style he pencilled: "My antique style is the result of assimilation not imitation, arrived at from the inside not the outside. The Authorized Version I feel has had more influence on my prose style than any other book, and I have so loved and studied it from boyhood that I have assimilated its processes and learned the secrets of the interior mechanism of its style. Dante also, whose *Divina Commedia* is one of the four books (the others being the Bible, Shakespeare and Heine's Poems with which I am supersaturated) has also had an immense influence on my style, both in prose and verse."

In the place where I quote Burton as saying that his scheme was "to translate literally each noun (in the long lists which so often occur) in its turn, so that the student can use the translation," Payne underscored the eight concluding words and pencilled in the margin "This formed no part of my scheme, in fact was directly opposed to the spirit of my work, which was to make the translation, whilst quite sufficiently faithful to the original, a monument of noble English prose and verse."

In Vol. 2, page 19, I put in parallel columns Payne's and Burton's translations of the poem in the Nights which commences "Renouncement, lowliness, the faker's garments be" (Payne v. 51, Burton v. 294). Payne pencilled "This piece is characteristic of the difference between the two translations. Burton says of it 'It is sad doggerel,' and so it is in his version; but I signal it as one of the finest pieces of verse in the Nights. As a piece of devotional poetry I think it worthy of Vaughan or Christina Rossetti."

Opposite my remarks on Burton's religion Payne wrote "If anything he was a Mohammedan, Islam being the only practical moral and ethical religion. Ideal religions, such as that of the Vedanta, were beyond his scope; he was like the Jews and had no ideality in his composition."

Once, in conversation with Payne, I said to him: "Your Nights stirred up a rare nest of hornets."

"Yes," he said, "and to give you an idea of their unscrupulousness

---

[1] Thomas Wright *Life of John Payne* (London: T. Fisher Unwin, 1919), pp. 71-177.

one of them—Professor Robertson Smith [Burton's comment was, "Men who have been persecuted often in their turn become persecutors."]—put it about that my translation was made not direct from the Arabic but from German translations—an amazing display of ignorance, seeing that there were no German translations with the exception of the wearisome garbled and incomplete version of Dr. Weil."

T. W. How did you deal with him?

P. I sent him the following words from the Nights, written in the Arabic character: "I and thou and the slanderer, there shall be for us an awful day and a place of standing up to judgment." After this he sheathed his sword, and the Villon Society heard no more of him. ...

In Vol. 2, p. 137, opposite my reference to the Sindbad story, Payne wrote: "Important to show this. Burton allowed that in all other respects my translation was thoroughly literal, but I could never get him to understand my objection to filth for filth's sake, altogether apart from all question of prudery. He himself had 'a romantic passion' for it. Burton's erudition, though immense as a matter of mere bulk, was, I am afraid, largely pinchbeck, it altogether lacked exactitude."

"Burton seemed to me to have, like Holofernes, been at a great feast of languages and stolen the scraps. So in every branch where I was qualified to judge. He was a man of action, not of thought or study in the true sense."

It appears that about this time Ruskin showed himself hostile to Payne's Translation of the Nights, for Burton in a letter of 15 January, 1886 [to Payne], wrote: "One line to say how much I am disgusted with the way in which Ruskin depreciated your translation. However, I suppose you will take no notice of it." ...

Seated in an easy chair, with his legs crossed and his feet on a hassock, he [Payne] was good enough to answer the many questions which in my desire to make my book as full as possible I ventured to ask him. I commenced:

You and Burton got on very well together?

P. Yes, he had a real regard for me. To look at him you would have taken him for a Chinaman.

T. W. One's looks alter as one gets older.

P. Yes. The soul moulds the features. Young men are ugly, old men handsome.

T. W. What sort of person was Lady Burton.

P (Speaking rather scornfully) Look at her face. [He referred to the portrait afterwards reproduced at p. 16 of my Life of Burton.] That will tell you. What does she look like?

T. W. She was not very diplomatic.

P. She was answerable for most of Burton's troubles. She didn't know the difference between truth and falsehood. She was able to convince herself that what she said was the right thing. She and Burton never understood each other.

T. W. No couple ever did. It would be against nature.

P. Still she had a clumsy zeal for Burton's supposed interests. Her devotion to him was a great nuisance, still it was her great redeeming feature. She told me her life would have no interest for her without him.

T. W. In writing my book I want to tell the precise truth, yet to avoid giving pain to anyone.

P. Be guided, then, by the advice of Voltaire: "To the living one owes consideration, and to the dead the truth." ...

In a letter of 8 February [1905] Payne gives his opinion of portions of my Life of Sir Richard Burton, the MS of which I had submitted to him. He says: "I am much pleased with the general style and manner of them. They are soberly and pleasantly written, interesting without strain, and will, I think, be acceptable to the (literary) just and unjust. Your condemnation of Burton's and Lady Burton's looseness of statement (to use a mild phrase) is sure to raise a storm." ...

During the months of November and December [1905] Payne read the concluding portion of the proofs of my Life of Sir Richard Burton. He wrote on 16 December, 1905:

"I send you the last portion of the proofs, and heartily congratulate you upon a most interesting and delightful work, which I think must be a great success, although, of course, there will be plenty of abuse for you (and me also) from the interested scallawags."

In one of the last chapters I had made some facetious remarks respecting Lady Burton's declaration that her husband's spirit had appeared to her. He continues "What I say about Burton's religion omit if you think well, but I should like you to reconsider those girds at the ghost. I have (perhaps an exaggerated) horror of anything like cruelty. The poor soul (Lady Burton) meant well and believed in her visions. She was, of course, a hysterian; and that explains everything. Women in all ages have mistaken *vox uteri* for *vox Dei*, and not without reason it (v. u.) being the voice of 'The will-to-be' which is the nearest approach to the concept of Deity recognized by reason." In order to please him I omitted the passage.

122.   1920.   David Scull Bispham.[1]

Sir Richard Burton is a man I am proud to have numbered among my acquaintances and a man of more striking appearance and assured

---

[1] David Scull Bispham *A Quaker singer's recollections* (New York: Macmillan, 1920) p. 152.

greatness I have never seen. He was a large man, and looked like nothing so much as an old lion—short gray hair and a bronzed skin seamed with scars, and a manner that bespoke the independence that so marked his striking career. His knowledge of Arabic and his miraculous escape from the perils of his self-imposed pilgrimage to Mecca with all the qualities of heart and mind that this bespoke, entitled him to almost any gift at the hands of Government, but his impatience of control made it impossible for him to work with others. His beautiful and almost too pious wife was a fit mate for him in personality, making them a wonderful couple merely to sit and watch.

123. 1921. Archibald Henry Sayce.[1]

It is difficult for me to realize that more than thirty years have passed since the death of my old friend Sir Richard Burton; his powerful personality and aggressive vitality seem but a thing of yesterday. Nature, in fact, had intended for him a much longer span of life; but even his iron constitution was not proof against the hardships of exploratory travel and reckless disregard of his own health. I remember his telling me that when, after parting from Speke, he arrived, wounded, starving, and deserted, at the first depot which had been provided for the explorers, he found there nothing but a few bottles of spirits of wine for a lamp, and in his desperation he swallowed the whole of the contents of one of them. He was one of the most learned men I have ever come across. Naturally it was more especially in the Oriental field that he was a sort of living encyclopedia. Here there were few questions to which he could not give more or less of an answer. But anthropology, archeology, even Etruscan inscriptions all alike interested him. It was not only Arabic or Persian that he translated with a masterly hand, one of his lesser known works is a translation of the Lusiads of Camoens. The subject, however, upon which he chiefly prided himself and considered that he possessed a special knowledge was the history of the sword; unfortunately the first volume only of the exhaustive work which he planned to write upon it was ever completed. As regards languages, Button combined linguistic facility with philological knowledge, a combination which is by no means common. In setting to work to learn a new language, he once told me, he began with "the swear-words; after that everything was easy."

For the geographer his chief claim to fame rests upon his Somali journey in 1854, when he was the first white man to enter Harar, and more particularly on his explorations and discoveries in Central Africa. But to the world in general he is best known by his pilgrimage to Mecca in 1853, in the disguise of an Indian Pathan. He was the first Englishman

---

[1] A. H. Sayce "Sir Richard Francis Burton" *Geographical Journal* 57(4) (April 1921), pp. 282-3.

to enter the holy city of the Mohammedans,[1] and the first European who has gone there with a thorough knowledge of Mohammedan history, beliefs, and ceremonies. His account of the Pilgrimage has rightly become a standard work of English literature. It was this pilgrimage that made him, next to Homer, one of Dr. Schliemann's chief heroes, as the doctor once confided to me. Schliemann's own ambition was to rival Burton's feat, and he spent a year at Alexandria with this object in view. Circumstances, however, prevented its accomplishment, and the only result was that Schliemann was able up to the end of his life to repeat the Qoran by heart. Shortly before Burton's death I was able to satisfy one of Schliemann's principal desires and bring the two together. As a *hajji* or pilgrim, Burton was free to travel wherever he chose throughout the Mohammedan world, and· we once planned an expedition together along the northern coast of Africa, beginning with Tangier and ending with Alexandria. But at the moment we were both of us occupied with our professional duties, and when the more convenient season arrived it was too late.

Burton probably inherited his restlessness, versatility, and fondness for adventure from his Irish and Highland forefathers. He passed from Oxford to the Indian army, and then into the Consular service, much as he passed from one form of study to another. He was impatient of restraint on the part of those whom he considered inferior in knowledge or experience to himself, and in one instance at all events this had an unfortunate effect. He was removed from the Consulship of Damascus just when his profound acquaintance with the Oriental and the Orient was beginning to bear fruit. 'Unexplored Syria,' which he wrote in combination with Tyrwhitt Drake, shows what he might have accomplished had he remained longer at his Syrian post. For once in a way a Consulship could have been made subservient to the advancement of scientific discovery and research.

124. 1921. Dr. Frederick Grenfell Baker.[2]

From the time, now some eighty years ago, when Richard Burton left Oxford through typical means of his own devising, down to the present period when his birth-centenary was recently celebrated, his life and characteristics have been matters of intense interest to tens of thousands of people both at home and abroad. And here I would at once like to emphasise my belief that this widespread and enduring interest in all that appertains to Burton's superstrenuous career is due less to the fame of his manifold explorations and other achievements, wonderful

---

[1] This is incorrect.
[2] F. Grenfell Baker "Sir Richard F. Burton as I knew him *Cornhill Magazine* October, 1921, pp.411-23.

and highly important though they were, or even to the unique extent and variety of his encyclopaedic knowledge, than to the atmosphere of chivalrous and single-minded romanticism that ever surrounded his exceptionally virile and human personality in all he did throughout his life.

On the other hand, it is apparent to those who have at all deeply studied his career that he, even more than the average of great men, has suffered seriously in repute from many of those writers who have attempted to portray his character or to criticise his work. To him with special relevance might be applied the dictum of the cynic who said "Post-mortem reputations are more often created, marred, or destroyed by the vagaries of biographers than by the actual life-records of their victims."

Be this as it may, the fact remains that very erroneous views concerning Burton's true personality have been widely propagated by many of those who have written about his character and his achievements.

On this account I propose in the following notes to confine myself to a brief consideration of some of his more salient characteristics such as I had opportunities of observing them during the last three and a half years of his life when I was his travelling medical adviser, his daily companion, and, I believe, his confidential friend.

No endeavour to arrive at a true conception of Burton's life and mental outlook can be expected to produce any but false conclusions unless due regard is given—amongst other essential factors—to the remarkable complexity, force, and extent of his physical and psychical organisation. And this exceptional complexity in its turn, it is as well to remember, is dependent upon the curious commingling of ethnic strains he possessed. For in himself he combined English, Scotch, Irish, French, and probably Gypsy blood, the French being derived through his descent from Louis XIV.

In the result, and although he exhibited many differing and apparently contradictory characteristics, due to the promptings of awakened echoes from far-off or nearby parental voices, certain specific features were seldom wholly absent or otherwise than indicative of his true self. Some of the more notable of these I will endeavour to describe, as I myself witnessed their presence during the long period I spent in his company.

First and foremost of Burton's characteristics I would certainly place kindness of heart and consideration for others, coupled with an old-world courtesy in manner and address seldom lacking when conversing with acquaintances or strangers. This statement is, I know, totally at variance with much that has been written about his alleged habitual abrupt and brutal manner of speech, of which I can only say that if he were abrupt or brutal there were very good reasons for so acting; but unquestionably these outbursts never formed part of his natural mode of speaking.

Burton's fathomless kindness of heart—and I think it was usually his heart rather than his head which guided him in this matter—made him always the champion of the 'bottom dog,' and that, too, whether it were a human thoroughbred or only a mere mongrel that sought his sympathies.

Till shortly before his death he remained a poor man, yet he was ever ready generously to help all those who had any kind of claim on him, and incidentally a good many who had none. It would be easy to cite examples of his efficient and unobtrusive kindness, but the limitations of space at my disposal will enable me to give but a few.

Amongst my most treasured possessions is a long and beautifully expressed letter from the late Algernon C. Swinburne, received shortly after Burton's death. In this the great poet gave me particulars of a time when he was in sore straits through illness and other troubles, and related how at the depth of his misery Burton took charge of him, and carrying him off to more congenial surroundings, tenderly nursed him back to health, happiness, and hope.

Moderation was seldom a distinguishing quality of Sir Richard's acts of kindness—or for that matter, of any of his acts; indeed, many of them were quixotic in the extreme. Of these latter the first and the last occasions on which we were together furnish conspicuous examples.

I have so often recounted the remarkable circumstances attending my introduction to Burton that I need not do more than refer to it in outline. Nevertheless, it was profoundly dramatic and charged with elements of vital import to both our lives.

In the beginning of 1887 I was convalescing at Cannes from a serious illness that had necessitated giving up my London practice and residing, for a time at least, in a more congenial climate than my own country was able, or willing, to bestow. Wholly unknown to me, Sir Richard Burton lay dying (as was believed to be the case) in a neighbouring hotel, where a consultation had just decided that a fatal termination to his illness would shortly take place. At Lady Burton's earnest entreaty it was also determined that the patient should be informed of his critical condition, and, on account of the physicians being all either friends or acquaintances of Burton's, it was thought best a stranger should undertake this unpleasant duty.

The choice fell upon me, and thus my first meeting with the man who since my boyhood's days had been my greatest living hero was brought about through my having been selected to inform him he was dying.

It will be sufficient here to say that on entering the sickroom I found the patient apparently quite conscious, and generally far better than I had been led to expect, and I at once as sympathetically as possible told him what I had been instructed to convey.

More than thirty years have elapsed since that interview and yet I can still vividly see the scene; but most of all do I see Sir Richard's wonderful eyes intensely gazing at me with that extraordinary faculty of his for appearing not only to look at, but through and over and around one. This peculiarity I found later he was able to exercise when greatly interested in a speaker or in the words he uttered, an ability possibly inherited from his Gypsy or from his Gaelic forebears.

When I had finished speaking, Burton quietly asked whether I believed he was about to die, to which I replied that personally I knew very little about his case, but felt bound to tell him the members of the consultation were amongst the leaders of their profession, and that they all agreed as to the seriousness of his illness. Ah, well, what must be, will be, he responded calmly, and with what I in after times knew to be a characteristic shrug of the shoulders, and without any further reference to his grave physical condition, he proceeded to chat quite cheerfully, and finally told me a story from the 'Arabian Nights'!

The point in the foregoing which I wish to stress is that here was a man suddenly struck down by what he believed to be a fatal illness, long ere the principal tasks he had set himself to accomplish were completed. And yet this man, in accordance with the habits of a lifetime, and as a matter of course, was able by an effort of will to abandon all concern for his own dire condition and to concentrate himself on entertaining a stranger—and a stranger, moreover, who was the bearer of such serious and fateful news.

Remembering that Burton had spent a large proportion of his life amongst Mohammedans, with whom hospitality is often of the nature of a sacred function, it is not at all surprising to find his social habits were largely tinctured with the same belief, while to this was further joined his inborn courtesy and natural kindness of heart.

I may add that at the pressing invitation of both Lady Burton and her husband, and with the willing consent of their own very distinguished physician—who was also mine—Dr. Frank, I at once took charge of the patient, and so continued till compelled by recurring ill-health to relinquish my duties into the highly skilled hands of the late Dr. R. Leslie, a Canadian physician. Later on in the year, when sufficiently well, I again took medical control, and so remained till the end came on October 20, 1890, at Trieste.

On looking back over a fairly eventful and certainly highly interesting career, it is one of my greatest joys to know that the commencement of my old friend's recovery of much of his former strength and health, and his actual recession from the gates of death, coincide with the very day of our first meeting. Largely through his indomitable spirit, he was enabled to carry on bravely and well for nearly four years of active existence, especially with respect to literary production, which latter, indeed, was almost as great as before his illness.

While yet a youth, and as part of his preparation for the life he had mapped out for himself, Burton made it a daily practice to cultivate habits of stoicism with respect to bearing physical or mental discomfort; and during the time I knew him he certainly bore his many attacks of suffering with remarkable fortitude, and without complaint.

At all crises of his life, even when the weight and friction of years, constant toil and worries innumerable had left their indelible marks, I believe Burton to have been absolutely fearless, both in a moral and physical sense. More than that, I believe he did his utmost on all occasions to help those who happened to be his companions in the midst of perils. I myself have been with him in the hour of danger, and can bear personal witness that his habitual cool-headed courage never deserted him.

It is hardly an exaggeration to say Sir Richard never performed an act nor conceived an idea quite in the same way as such acts and such thoughts would have been conceived or carried out by others. And this was specially apparent when he was defining his own concepts. Though to describe this peculiarity fully and accurately is, I fear, impossible, it was obvious to anyone who was much in his company, and may be inferred from the fact that he was largely dominated by various Eastern modes of expression and was specially susceptible to the influence of sounds. The words, phrasing, and style of the Old Testament, of Shakespeare, and of Chaucer were peculiarly sympathetic to him, as were those of other works usually regarded as archaic in their diction and construction. To Burton, as to many of us, the sound of numerous modern words caused mental distress, while certain of these even brought about a feeling closely akin to pain. I have actually known his health injuriously affected not only by such sounds but also (as is so often the case with certain animals) by various combinations of musical notes not generally regarded as either unpleasant or harmful.

In this relation I may mention that he had the Eastern's full and discriminating colour-sense, being always attracted or repelled by specific pigments, and most certainly both his health and his spirits were much influenced by the prevailing hue of his surroundings.

In like manner, of the many languages Burton knew there was one at least—German—he habitually avoided speaking, chiefly on account of its unpleasant sound. Indeed, during our many travels in Austria I do not remember one single instance when he voluntarily spoke this tongue, and that too although he daily read the local newspapers. His own explanation to me was that German always greatly irritated his brain and obscured his judgment. It has certainly greatly irritated the brains of a good many other people since those far-off peaceful days he and I together spent in Austria!

With regard to Sir Richard's extraordinary linguistic abilities, the statement has several times lately been made in print (without, however, any adequate evidence in proof of it), that he was not really so profound a scholar in certain languages, notably in Arabic and in Persian, as were some of his contemporaries.

Whether this statement be literally true or not is, of course, a matter of no moment. But what does matter, and especially distinguishes Burton's powers as a linguist from those of others who might possibly be accounted his rivals, is that while he knew very thoroughly, not only one or two or three, but some thirty or more languages and dialects, he could also speak them with the appropriate gestures, inflexions, accent, and mode of address such as would be employed by natives of the country to which each belonged, and that, too, whether those natives were educated or illiterate. As a consequence, one can be perfectly certain Burton would never do so foolish a thing as I remember a well-known university 'scholar' doing who made an oration to a large crowd of modern Greeks in ancient Greek, and employed, moreover, the then orthodox Oxford accent and our own special insular gestures!

As I myself can vouch, Sir Richard was able not only to carry on long conversations with learned Orientals—no less than with Western foreigners—in their own tongue on subjects of deep interest and profound learning, but could with equal facility speak numerous dialects, in which he would unmercifully chaff the most ignorant natives, freely employing the slang of the bazaars and the streets.

For myself, it was a wonderfully interesting experience to be near Burton when amongst Bedouins or other Mohammedans while he discussed deep topics of religion and history with their sheikhs or indulged in polite intercourse with the ordinary members of a tribe.

In this connexion the following incident may be instructive. Once while in London Burton was aboard a Thames steamer when a stranger came up to him and commenced speaking very slowly a 'language' not one sentence of which could Sir Richard understand. Seeing this, the stranger said in English 'Are you not the celebrated Oriental scholar and linguist, Richard Burton?' 'Certainly,' he replied, 'that is my name.' 'Then,' continued the stranger, 'may I ask how it is you do not understand Persian when I speak it to you?' 'Oh,' said Burton, 'was it Persian you were speaking? I really must apologise for not recognising it as such, but the fact is I only know the language as it is spoken and written in Persia by Persians!' In the result it was discovered that the stranger was a well-known retired manufacturer who had devoted his leisure to teaching himself Persian from books and without the help of a native, or, indeed, any kind of master!

Another example of Burton's wonderful and efficient knowledge of languages (and, incidentally, of his partiality for practical joking) may be given. One day at Trieste there drifted into lunch, after a preliminary visit to the Consulate, a patriarchal, white-bearded professor from one of our Irish centres of learning, who, as he told us, had passed the greater part of his life teaching Latin and Greek. Listening to the conversation on general subjects between Burton and his guest, I was somewhat surprised to hear the former leave off speaking English and substitute Latin. An astonished and not too happy expression spread over the Professor's face as he began a laboured reply. This, however, he very soon dropped and exclaimed 'If you don't mind, Sir Richard, we will continue our conversation in English!'

In the matter of dress Burton embodied the unconventional in both style and colour. He took little note of changes in the fashions, preferring always what was most comfortable and suitable to his needs. He abhorred dress-clothes and the wearing of waistcoats (he usually discarded the latter entirely), while he clung with enthusiastic loyalty to the tall, grey broad-brimmed hat of a former generation.

A great deal has been said and written concerning Burton's impulsive and violent temper, and of his alleged habit of quarrelling without reasonable cause with even his best friends. And in all probability there is a certain measure of truth in these accusations that is to say, during his tempestuous youth and up to a few years before his serious illness at Cannes. After that event, and throughout the time I knew him, he took life with philosophic calm, and was for the most part cheerful, considerate, and equable in temper.

Much even of the former mental conditions can, I consider, be explained by his lifelong obsession for assuming poses intentionally to lead others to believe he was in reality the 'Ruffian Dick' of tradition, filled with diabolical wickedness and possessed of a fiendish genius for indulging in fiery outbursts of rage and 'blazing indiscretions.'

Several of Burton's quarrels have become almost classical, of which his troubles with Speke and with Grant are perhaps the best known. Another that has been often quoted is interesting if only for the reason that at a private dinner party, and in the presence of a number of prominent people, he deliberately gave the lie to his official chief, who was one of the company, on account of some opinions which that distinguished Cabinet Minister, with his habitual volubility, had just uttered.

A less known but very typical instance of Sir Richard's lifelong fight on the side of truth and decent public and private living is seen in an incident that took place shortly after one of his returns to London. Having accepted an invitation to be present at a large reception given, as he understood, in his honour by a much-travelled and very popular peer, he arrived at the latter's house at the time appointed. Here he was cordially received by his host, who conducted him into a salon filled with the invited guests, and after a short conversation, introduced him to a distinguished-looking man with the remark, 'Allow me to present you to your fellow-lion, Mr. _____.' Burton, ignoring the outstretched hand, and putting his own hands behind his back, looked the stranger full in the face and sternly said, 'Mr. _____, when I am in Persia I may be a Persian, when I am in Arabia I may be an Arabian, but when I am in England I am an English gentleman,' and turning his back, deliberately marched out of the room and out of the house. It is needless to say the sensation that ensued was profound and led to all kinds of rumours. These, however, were quickly solved when public apologies for having sponsored 'the other lion' appeared from various quarters in the Press, where the announcement was shortly made that a warrant was out for his apprehension. The man, fortunately for himself, at once fled the country, and although an extremely scholarly and polished individual, it soon became known he was one with whom no self-respecting person would care to shake hands. Burton's encyclopaedic information included the black dossiers of many of those we in England were ready to receive with open arms, as is too often our hospitable but foolish custom.

It is not my purpose, as obviously it is not within my capacity, to discuss, or even to enumerate, Burton's works, much less to criticise his learning in the many fields—be they well-tilled or fallow—he so thoroughly traversed and enriched, nor to examine his achievements as an explorer. Had all others whose capacity was equally defective followed a like course, it would have been better for Burton's memory, and far better for the interests of truth and honesty.

Burton's general outlook on life was one of broad tolerance for the opinions and frailties of others, no matter how widely they differed from his own. To this an exception must be made in the case of one particular category in which he placed prudes, prigs, Pharisees, politicians, and publishers! Of these latter a punning acquaintance of Burton's was once pleased to observe that Sir Richard's pugnacity and impatience would always make him a foe to Peace!

So also it must be admitted that Burton invariably found it a great trial to his habitual courtesy to remain civil to that large class of our race who have been reared under the numbing restraints of a narrow conventionality, and whom he was never weary of shocking by sudden outbursts of assumed 'frightfulness' in manner and speech.

Unfortunately for his well-being, Sir Richard was markedly deficient in the commercial faculty—so far, that is, as it related to the making of money, a fault, if it be a fault, that distinguished him from some of his later contemporaries. For him it was always the object to be obtained and the means of obtaining it, rather than the reward for so doing, that attracted him, though the existence of serious obstacles in the path of an enterprise also doubtless urged him to undertake and carry it through to a successful termination. He told me that for lack of a few pounds on more than one occasion he had to abandon a promising expedition or other undertaking.

From the great majority of Burton's books (and over these he literally spent the best he could give in the matter of time, talent, and labour) he actually received little or no profit, and not till the "Thousand Nights and a Night" appeared did he derive anything at all commensurate with his work.

On the other hand, I well remember the publication of a much advertised book by one of the foremost of the new type of explorers that was simply crammed with obvious mistakes, chiefly through lack of knowledge and haste in compiling. Shortly after its appearance Sir Richard met the author, and in my presence asked him, in his usual frank way, why on earth he had brought out a work so overflowing with gross blunders. To this the sole reply was, "I made (naming a very large sum of money) out of that book." Burton simply shrugged his shoulders and contemptuously murmured, "A-h, just so."

Loyalty—that "Aristocrat of the Virtues," as dear Mrs. Lynn Linton used to call it—was another of Sir Richard's prominent characteristics. In my own experience of him—and this was doubtless true of his whole life—he ever remained faithful to a person or a cause to which he had once given his friendship or his support, though, unhappily, on many occasions he was forced to lament the perfidy of those he had generously assisted.

Many years ago, when staying in Rome, I happened to meet a very distinguished retired diplomat who had then just published his exceedingly interesting autobiography. In discussing this he mentioned he had included in it a list of those celebrated people who were born in 1821, and whose numbers made that year specially remarkable. He concluded by observing that, curiously enough, both Burton and he were born in 1821! It would, I think, be interesting, though not altogether pleasing to the people concerned, were a second list compiled showing the names of those who owed much of their fame and fortune in after life to Sir Richard's help and advice.

I have seldom met anyone who possessed in greater degree the Heaven-sent gift of winning the respect and the enthusiastic friendship of others than did Sir Richard Burton. There seemed, indeed, to be a special bond that bound him to his friends—a tested chain of gold and steel which knitted them together and symbolised Loyalty, Self-sacrifice, and Endurance.

In his dealings with women of whatever class Sir Richard was invariably courteous and considerate in his manner and kind and informative in his conversation, beneath which there ever flowed a quiet current of raillery and cynicism that, although it never intentionally hurt, very often greatly amused those to whom it was addressed. And even with them apparently he found it impossible entirely to suppress his habitual propensity for practical joking. This usually took the form of writing in ladies' albums (and he was inundated with requests of this nature) Eastern proverbs or quotations in Arabic characters which, had their fair recipients been able to translate, they would have found very far from being complimentary to their sex.

In private life, even more than in his published writings, Sir Richard never wearied of preaching against the evils of ignorance, and that too despite the abuse showered upon him for his maintaining these views by a section of the community, if not large or influential, certainly a loud-voiced, raucous, and extremely narrow-minded one. As might be expected, the chief attacks of this kind centred their violence on his works relating to the social life of the East, and more especially on the "Arabian Nights" and on the "Scented Garden."

Too much has already been published concerning the former, and with regard to the latter it will suffice to say that it would be difficult to explain upon what grounds Burton's edition of the "Scented Garden" could justifiably be abused, seeing that in fact Sir Richard, myself, and one, or possibly two others, were the only persons acquainted with its actual contents! It was this work by which Burton believed he would be best remembered after his death; it not only contained, as I know, the substance of his whole immense and unique knowledge of the Orient, but was also a perfect compendium of information relating to the outlook of the East upon the rest of the world. It was, in fact, one of the few absolutely essential books in the English language—essential, that is, to all those who are called upon to rule and govern the many millions of our fellow subjects who inhabit our vast and varied Eastern Empire. To Sir Richard it was a crime of the first magnitude that we should continue year after year to send out to posts of importance in the government of these lands men so largely unequipped with those special forms of knowledge which must be acquired if they are to appreciate the natives' points of view throughout our extraordinarily complex possessions in Asia and Africa. The grave state of things that prevails in India and Egypt is but one of the vivid, graphic, and sinister witnesses to the truth of Burton's opinions and the value of his neglected advice.

However violent Burton may have been in his earlier days, he was passionate only in temper (and very seldom even in that), being otherwise an exceptionally continent man and one who regarded sexual subjects with the level impartiality of the British scientist, strongly tinctured with the cynical humour of the Oriental. Neither was he in any sense a degenerate or a debauchee, but rather a thoroughly virile and healthy-minded, keen student of those who were, and especially of the distal and proximal causes leading to these morbid mental developments.

Out of the many interesting past events that recur to memory when writing about Burton's life as I knew it I would like further to include mention of a few, because they specially focus brightly some particular phase of his character.

During one of his many severe bouts of ill-health his wife, without informing either her husband or anyone else, impulsively wrote to the then premier, Lord Salisbury, and asked if, in the event of the death of one of our Ministers to a country in which Burton specially wanted to be appointed, and who was reported in the papers to be very seriously ill, he would give the post to her husband. She showed me Lord Salisbury's holograph reply, which so impressed me with the epigrammatic manner in which it expressed the official view of Burton's superpatriotic modes of diplomacy, that I believe I am quoting it almost word for word.

The letter ran

DEAR LADY BURTON,-

As Her Majesty's Ministers have no immediate intention of annexing _____ to the Crown of the British Empire, I would not feel justified, should a vacancy occur, in proposing your husband as Minister in that locality.

I am, &c.,

SALISBURY.

I quote this letter also because it has recently appeared in print, where its author was given as Lord Russell, a mistake that entirely does away with its real point.

I commenced these reminiscences by laying stress on Sir Richard's great and often quixotic kindness of heart as exemplified in his behaviour at our first meeting. Before closing them I would like to give a still greater instance of his consideration for others by a reference to the last time we were together.

On the morning of October 20, 1890, at Trieste, Burton was seized with a very severe heart attack from which he succumbed within a short time. Hearing his struggles to breathe, Lady Burton rushed to his bedside, and seeing how grave his condition was, immediately started to fetch me. This, however, her husband emphatically forbade her to do, murmuring "Poor chap, he has been suffering all day from neuralgia; don't disturb him." Thus precious time was lost the while his life rapidly ebbed from him. At length, when he seemed nearly unable to breathe at all, Lady Burton hurried away to summon me. I immediately did all that I could to revive him, but, alas, it was too late, and presently he groaned "My God, I am a dead man," and falling into our supporting arms, expired. Of course it is impossible to say whether I could have saved him had I been called earlier, but I had managed to do so on several previous occasions, and it is difficult to avoid the belief that had Sir Richard been less considerate for others and thought more of his own critical condition, he might have enjoyed a further spell of life, if not of complete health and strength.

The passage of many years has in no way dimmed or destroyed the conceptions I formed of Burton's character as it manifested itself during the period of my long and close association with him.

Like Gordon, Burton was endowed with a special measure of zeal for the cause of right, justice, freedom, and sane living; so, too, he possessed his vision splendid to foresee some of Futurity's secrets, but unlike Gordon, and like Roberts and Kitchener, this, I believe, was due less to occult workings than to his extraordinary brain powers which enabled him to select and arrange causative factors and correlate the resulting stream of effects with truth and rapidity.

To me Sir Richard Burton is still the highest exponent I have ever encountered of all that is broad-minded, unselfish, honourable, and entirely lovable. And far more than this, I know from the experiences I have gathered during my many wanderings in many foreign lands, as well as while travelling in my own, that he is still held in affectionate remembrance by large numbers of people who are able to appreciate his unusual nobility of mind and distinction of character, and who can recognise his career of patriotic self-sacrifice and his lifelong enthusiasm for the work rather than for the wages of greatness.

125.   1922. Earl of Dunraven.[1]

In the course of a long life I have naturally met and known, more or less intimately, many men, and of women not a few. ... Monckton Milnes (Lord Houghton), poet, author of such sweet poems—and a good raconteur of stories, not always quite similar to his poems—a great frequenter of the Beefsteak Club. Archie Wortley, one of my best friends—the founder, I think, of the afore said Club, of which I was an original member. Bernal Osborne, most witty of men. Wilfrid Blount, with his Arab steeds and his oriental complex. Richard Burton, who prided himself on looking like Satan—as, indeed, he did, if Mephistopheles is a fair portrait—also with an oriental complex, but of a very different kind. A great linguistic scholar, with an unrivalled knowledge of the East, he was an ill-used public servant—ill-used because his invaluable services were not put to the greatest use, and because for what services he rendered he received most inadequate reward.

---

[1] Windham Thomas Wyndham-Quin *Past Times and Pastimes* Vol. 1 (London: Hodder and Stoughton, 1922) p. 178.

126. 1923. Lady Walburga Paget.[1]

… Captain Richard Burton (later on Sir Richard), the eastern traveller. Anybody might have taken him for an Arab, an illusion which was strengthened by his staining his under-eyelids with kohl. He calmly related to me how he had once killed a man in order not to be murdered himself. His wife, an Arundell of Wardour, still bore great traces of beauty, though she, too, shared the Eastern predilection for pigments. She was genial, intelligent and courageous in no ordinary way. Her defence of the poor dumb animals drew me strongly towards her. She was a friend of Ouida's, who was also sent to me during that winter.

127. 1924. Luke Ionides.[2]

I first knew Richard Burton in the year 1869. I had read several of his books and was most pleased to meet him. He was a man with great knowledge on many subjects.

One evening he told us of the various things that were smoked before tobacco was in use. Another evening he told us the stories of all the best-known gems in Europe; among other things I remember he said that the Kohinoor had a fatal reputation for the dynasty that owned it; each successive sovereign who had it was the last of his race; he also told the story of a celebrated diamond in the Russian crown, which had belonged to Charles the Bold, and was found by a peasant after the battle of Granson,[3] and sold for a few pennies.

He was consul at Damascus after we first knew him, and had trouble with the Turkish authorities, so in 1872 he was sent to Trieste as consul.

During his stay at Damascus, he and Lady Burton met the beautiful lady who had been Lady Ellenborough. The story was told that she was out riding one day with a retinue, when they were surprised by the Arabs. She escaped but her retinue was taken prisoner. The next day the Sheikh of the Arabs called on her and told her that he so admired her riding that he would free all her men if she would marry him, and marry him she did, and remained with him until her death. In 1873 Burton was in England again, and I saw a good deal of him.

Once, at Brighton, he called, and my little girl, a little over a year old, toddled up to him and put her hand on his knee. Then he said that "the last time that a child had caught hold of him, was in Africa, when he had been without food for a week, and a fat, little black child, all circles and dimples came up to him and put its hand on his knee; but his

---

[1] Lady Walburga Paget *Embassies of other days* (London: Hutchinson, 1923) p. 282.
[2] Luke Ionides "Memories" *Transatlantic Review* Vol. I (1924), pp. 22-7.
[3] Grandson (1476).

very look sent it back howling to its mother". He had lived for the whole week on tea.

After that I met him occasionally when he came to England. On one occasion something that amused him happened. He had been dining with me, and I had given him a cigar after dinner, when he asked me whether I had not anything stronger. I then remembered I had a few hundred cigars that had been saved from a wreck, and I found them so strong I could not smoke them. So I went and fetched a box, and gave him one. He said it was the best cigar he had smoked for many a long year; upon which I told him I would have the rest of the cigars put into his cab. After he left, I took one from the box which had been opened, smoked it and found it most perfect. The fact of the matter was I had kept the cigars about five years and they had mellowed in that time. A short time after that when I met him, I told him of my discovery, and added that if I had made it sooner, he would not have had the cigars. He was so amused that he never forgot the incident, and until the end of his days, whenever he met me, he used to chaff me about it.

In 1882 he came one day and in the course of conversation he told me that he was making a translation of the Arabian Nights. I said I had just received a copy of the first volume of Payne's translation. He was rather taken aback, and answered that he would now delay the publication of his own work for some years. Some few years later he told me that he was bringing out some additional Eastern stories, and that he found one in French in Paris, of which he could not trace the Arabic original. He therefore translated the French version back into Arabic, and then from Arabic into English. He knew Arabic as well as English; he also knew a large number of Eastern languages, including Persian, Turkish, Tamil and others.

He once told us the story of his expedition to Mecca disguised as an Indian pilgrim, as he was afraid that his Arabic might betray him. At one halt he was discovered by a man, who fortunately was found killed the next day. A doctor who was present said, "Oh, Burton, Burton, how do you feel after you've killed a man?" "Quite well, thank you, doctor, how do you?" he retorted.

He told me of rather a ghastly joke. Before starting on his expedition across the South American continent, he asked a lady whom he met at dinner if there were anything she would like him to bring back, and she answered, "Oh, a scalp!" So on his return he asked his former host to place the lady opposite to him at table, and when dinner was over he said to her, "I haven't forgotten what you asked, me to bring back from South America," and took from his pocket a parcel and handed it to the lady. On opening it, she discovered it contained a scalp. He brought back four bad wounds from that expedition, but I understood from Lady Burton that he had escaped easily, for he killed his four assailants. Although not a big man, he was extremely powerful, and was one of the best fencers in Europe. I saw him once walk downstairs carrying Swinburne under his arm; after putting him down on the pavement he called a hansom. Swinburne could not find the step and complained that "hansoms were getting their steps higher and higher every year."

Burton was most entertaining and every now and then scraps from his travels turned up. He was one day in an Arab village where a theft of some money had taken place. Some one appealed to the Kadi, who said that his donkey would find out the culprit, as he would order all the men who had been about, to go into his stable to pull his donkey's tail, when the donkey would discover who had committed the theft. So they all trooped in one by one, and he observed them as they came out. He caught hold of one man, and said, "You return that money or I shall have you hanged." The man confessed and returned the money. Burton asked the Kadi how he had discovered the guilty man, and the Kadi told him that he had blacked the donkey's tail and he knew that the thief would be afraid to pull the tail, so when he came out with his hands unblacked the Kadi at once knew he was the thief. Burton also told me that he once paid a visit to a man who had the reputation of being a magician. In the far end of the room there were three vases on the floor. The one to the left was filled with water. They all sat down and waited while the magician mumbled a lot, and then the vase that was full of water moved by itself and went and emptied some of its water into the middle vase. "Naturally," Burton said, "we were all hypnotized into seeing it."

One of his experiences in India was of a fakir who said that he could be buried for any length of time, a crop sown over him, and when the crop was gathered, he could be unearthed and brought to life again. So Burton and some friends agreed to try the experiment, and after the fakir had made his preparations, stopped up his nostrils, mouth and ears, he was put into a box, which was hermetically closed and sealed. It was not buried but kept in a room and Burton and his friends kept guard over it in relays. But after some days they got a little nervous for fear the man might die, and opened the box, and the man was brought to life again. They concluded that if he were able to live in a closed box without air for those several days, he might have done so had he been buried and the crop sown over him.

On one occasion, Burton went to the King of Dahomey, having volunteered to go on a quasi-official visit, to ask the King to cease his human sacrifices. The King was much flattered by his coming and sent for one of his subjects and told him, "Look here, here is a white man come from the Great White Queen, and my father never had that honour paid to him. Go and tell him all about it," on which the man's head was at once cut off. Burton reproached him very much with the deed, and told him that the Great White Queen would be very angry with him, and admonished him severely—upon which the King sent for another of his subjects, and repeated to him what he had said to the other one. He also was decapitated, "as a postscript" Burton said. (The Times rebuked him for using such a flippant expression when he wrote an account of the business.) Burton came away with a promise from the King that he would cease from making human sacrifices, but I cannot say whether the promise was kept.

One day we were talking about Livingstone, and he showed me on a map exactly where Stanley would find Livingstone of whom he had started in search, and sure enough there Stanley found him.

Burton maintained that Livingstone had a black attraction there.

He was greatly interested in anything connected with the East. He much enjoyed a story I once told him. One day in 1862 at Costanza on the Black Sea, I went into a cafe and sat down near the door, and I saw in the remote part of the room my manservant among the Turks. He told me afterwards that there was much discussion as to my nationality when I entered the cafe. At last it was settled that I must be English, on account of my clothes. Then one of the Turks said, "There are a great number of good people among the English. I remember when a lot of them were here a few years ago." "Yes," said another, "I remember too. But how did it come about?" Then the village oracle, who was in the habit of entertaining them with stories, said, "Listen to me and I will tell you. The King of England has a wife, a very good woman in every way excepting that she was most unpunctual. She never had the coffee ready at the proper time in the morning, and the pilaf was never on the table at the right hour. The King reproved her many times, but she did not mend her ways. So at last he wrote to the Padishah and complained of his wife. The Padishah wrote her such a letter that she got thoroughly scared, and improved her ways completely. Then after a time, when the Moscovite infidels attacked us, the King of England, to show his gratitude, offered to the Padishah to send some of his men to beat back the Moscovites, and they came here and they also took the Moscovite town of Sebastopol." That is the local story of the origin of the Crimean war!

Sir Henry Irving was a great friend of the Burton. One day after dinner there was a great discussion about spiritualism, when Sir Henry said he did not believe in it, but he believed in "sympathy". He said he would leave the room and if anyone in sympathy with him touched an object on the table, he would discover it on his return. As I showed him out he whispered in my ear "Sniff". So he made me an accomplice. Lady Burton said, "I feel in sympathy with him, and I will lift up this vase with some flowers." On Irving's return he stretched his long arms over the table until he heard a faint sniff, upon which he at once seized upon the vase, which had been touched by Lady Burton, to the astonishment of all present, and as we both kept the secret, the truth was never discovered.

I often saw Burton to the end of his life in 1890, and I do not believe that there is any truth in the story of his being baptized into the Roman Catholic Church on his death-bed. The religion that most appealed to him was the Mahometan, though I do not know if he ever made the Mahometan profession of faith.

Chronology

Date	RFB's Location	Event
1820/03/02	—	Captain Joseph Netterville Burton marries Martha Baker in St. James' Church, London.
1821/03/19	England	Richard Francis Burton is born at Torquay.
1823/01/18	England	Maria Catherine Eliza Burton is born at Barham House.
1824/07/03	England	Edward Joseph Netterville Burton is born.
1831/03/20	England	Isabel Arundell is born in London at 14 Great Cumberland Place.
1840/11/19	England	RFB is admitted into Trinity College Oxford.
1842/03/	England	RFB leaves Oxford.
1842/06/18	England	Granted a commission in the Army of the East India Company.
1842/06/18	England	Sails for Bombay.
1842/10/28	India	Arrives in Bombay.
1842/11/15	India	Posted to 18th Native Infantry. Stationed in Garoda in Gujerat.
1843/03/22	India	Passes Hindustani in Bombay.
1843/05/05	India	Appointed interpreter to corps.
1843/08/22	India	Passes Gujerati at Bombay.
1843/10/28	India	Passes Mahratta at Bombay.
1844/01/01	India	Leaves Bombay for Karachi. Moves from Karachi to Gharra.
1844/10/22	India	Appointed to the Scinde Survey as second assistant surveyor.
1844/12/10	India	Scinde Survey sets off for Fulayhi.
1845/04/	India	Scinde Survey returns to Karachi.
1845/05/02	India	Appointed interpreter to the 18th Native

		Infantry.
1846/01/26	India	Promoted to Lieutenant.
1847/02/20	India	Travels to Goa on sick leave.
1847/10/12	India	Appointed assistant to the Scinde Survey in Calcutta.
1847/10/23	India	Passes Persian.
1847/11/12	India	Awarded 1000 rupees for his linguistic and other accomplishments.
1848/09/07	India	Passes Sindi.
1848/12/13	India	Passes Punjabee.
1849/03/30	India	Travels back to Europe on sick leave.
1849/09/05	England	RFB arrives in England. Stays with the Bagshaws.
1849/12/?	Italy	Travels to Pisa to join family.
1850/03/?	England	Returns to England.
1850/06/?	England	Stays at Dover with sister Maria.
1851/03/17	England	*Goa and the Blue Mountains* published by Richard Bentley.
1851/04/	France	RFB relocates to Boulogne.
1851/09/30	France	*Scinde: or, the Unhappy Valley* published by Richard Bentley.
1851/10/17	France	*Sindh and the Races the Inhabit the Valley of the Indus* published by W. H. Allen.
1852/	France	RFB meets Isabel Arundell at Boulogne.
1852/06/	France	*Falconry in the Valley of the Indus* published by John van Voorst.
1853/04/04	England	RFB leaves Southampton on the *Bengal* for Alexandria, on an expedition to explore Arabia sponsored by the RGS.
1853/04/17	Egypt	RFB arrives at Alexandria in the *Bengal*. Stays with Larking at the *Sycamores*.
1853/04/	Egypt	RFB leaves Alexandria, late in the month, for Cairo.
1853/06/	Egypt	At Cairo en route to Arabia.

Chronology

1853/06/03	Egypt	*Complete System of Bayonet Exercise* published by William Clowes.
1853/07/11	Arabia	RFB is at Aqaba
1853/08/	Arabia	RFB is at Medinah
1853/09/01	Arabia	RFB joins caravan from Medinah to Mecca
1853/09/10	Arabia	RFB is at Mecca.
1853/09/20?	Arabia	RFB leaves Mecca for Jeddah.
1853/09/26	Arabia	Departs for Suez from Jeddah.
1853/10/03	Egypt	Arrives at Suez en route to Cairo.
1853/10/16	Egypt	RFB is at Cairo.
1854/01/16	Egypt	Leaves Cairo for Suez with Didier and Hamilton.
1854/02/07?	Aden	RFB arrives at Aden and spends two weeks with Steinhaueser.
1854/02/21	India	RFB Arrives at Bombay, and befriends Lumsden. He is employed by the Political Department.
1854/06/20	India	RFB leaves Bombay for Aden with permission to conduct an expedition of exploration in the interior of Somali-land, overland to Zanzibar.
1854/10/29	Aden	RFB Leaves Aden for Harar.
1854/12/10	Somalia	Martha Burton (mother of RFB) dies of heart disease.
1855/01/03	Somalia	RFB returns to Aden from Harar via Berberah.
1855/04/05	Aden	RFB leaves Aden for Berberah to initiate the overland journey to Zanzibar.
1855/04/29	Somalia	Early morning attack at Berberah in which Stroyan is killed, and RFB and Speke are badly wounded.
1855/06/28	Crimea	RFB Arrives in Crimea from London via Boulogne and joins Beatson's Horse two weeks later.

1855/07/03	Crimea	*Personal Narrative of a Pilgrimage to El-Medinah and Meccah* Vol. 1 and Vol. 2 published by Longmans.
1855/10/18	Crimea	Leaves Therapeia for England with General Beatson after his recall.
1856/01/19	England	*Pilgrimage* Vol. 3 published by Longmans.
1856/06/19	England	*First Footsteps in East Africa* published by Longman.
1856/10/03	England	RFB, appointed by the RGS to lead an expedition to discover the possible sources of the White Nile, leaves England accompanied by Speke for the overland route to Bombay.
1856/11/06	Egypt	At Shepheard's Hotel in Cairo.
1856/11/23	India	Arrives at Bombay.
1856/12/01	India	Departs Bombay for Zanzibar.
1856/12/18	East Africa	Arrives at Zanzibar.
1857/01/10	East Africa	Leaves Zanzibar for coasting voyages.
1857/06/27	East Africa	Leaves the coast for the interior.
1857/07/06	East Africa	Joseph Netterville Burton dies at age 74.
1858/02/13	East Africa	Burton and Speke reach Ujiji on Lake Tanganyika.
1858/07/10	East Africa	Speke leaves Taborah/Kazeh for the Nyanza.
1858/08/25	East Africa	Speke returns from the Nyanza.
1859/02/02	East Africa	Burton and Speke reach the coast of Konduchi.
1859/03/04	East Africa	Return to Zanzibar.
1859/03/22	East Africa	Burton and Speke leave Zanzibar for Aden.
1859/04/16	Aden	Burton and Speke arrive at Aden.
1859/04/?	Aden	Speke leaves Aden for Suez.
1859/04/19	Aden	Speke arrives in England.

Chronology

1859/04/28	Aden	RFB leaves Aden for Suez.
1859/05/20	England	RFB arrives in England.
1860/04/21	England	Leaves Liverpool for North America via Halifax.
1860/08/25	USA	RFB arrives in Salt Lake City.
1860/06/21	USA	*Lake Regions* published by Longmans.
1860/12/31	England	Arrives back in England from Panama.
1861/01/22	England	RFB and Isabel Arundell are married at Royal Bavarian Chapel, Warwick Street, London.
1861/03	England	Appointed Consul at Fernando Po.
1861/08/24	England	Departs for Fernando Po on *ASS Blackland*, Captain English.
1861/09/27	West Africa	Arrives in Fernando Po.
1861/09/29	West Africa	Departs for Oil Rivers.
1861/10/02	West Africa	Returns to F. Po.
1861/10/10	West Africa	Departs F. Po on HMS Arrogant.
1861/10/14	West Africa	Arrives in Lagos.
1861/10/29	West Africa	Departs Lagos on *HMS Prometheus* for Ogun River Abeokuta.
1861/11/07	West Africa	*City of the Saints* published by Longmans.
1861/11/08	West Africa	Leaves Abeokuta for Lagos.
1861/11/21?	West Africa	Departs Lagos on *HMS Bloodhound* to Oil Rivers incl. Brass River.
1861/11/27	West Africa	Removed from Army List.
1861/12/01	West Africa	At Brass River
1861/12/05	West Africa	At Bonny River.
1861/12/13	West Africa	Departs Brass River, arrives at F. Po that day.
1861/12/17	West Africa	Departs with Saker, Smith, Calvo to climb Cameroons Mountains, where they meet Gustav Mann.
1862/02/04	West Africa	Returns to F. Po from Cameroons.

1862/03/15	West Africa	Departs F. Po. On HMS Griffon for Gorilla-land.
1862/04/22	West Africa	Departs from Londo River for F. Po.
1862/04/25	West Africa	Arrives at F. Po.
1862/05/01	West Africa	Departs for Old Calabar River in *HMS Griffon* to investigate assault.
1862/05/04	West Africa	At Duketown in Delta.
1862/05/20?	West Africa	Returns to F. Po.
1862/07/31	West Africa	Leaves F. Po. for the Benin River to investigate an attack.
1862/08/19	West Africa	Enters Benin City after visiting Belzoni's grave.
1862/09/04	West Africa	Arrives back at F. Po.
1862/09/11	West Africa	Leaves F. Po. for Batonga.
1862/09/18	West Africa	Leaves the coast to return to F. Po. after climbing Elephant Mountain.
1862/12/04	Tenerife	RFB anchors off Tenerife but yellow fever prevents his landing.
1862/12/02	England	RFB arrives at Liverpool.
1863/01/	England	First meeting of the Anthropological Society, addressed by Hunt.
1863/01/24	England	Burtons leave for Madeira.
1863/02/02	Madeira	Burtons arrive at Madeira.
1863/04?	Tenerife	RFB leaves Tenerife for F. Po. Isabel leaves for England.
1863/05/18	West Africa	RFB arrives in Dahome.
1863/06/17	West Africa	RFB leaves Dahome.
1863/06/	West Africa	RFB arrives in F. Po.
1863/07/29	West Africa	RFB leaves for Angola.
1863/08/22	West Africa	RFB leaves Angola for the mouth of the Congo.
1863/08/30	West Africa	RFB lands at Banana Point near the mouth of the Congo.

1863/09/28	West Africa	RFB leaves Banana Point for F. Po.
1863/10/19	West Africa	*Wanderings in West Africa* anonymously published by Tinsley.
1863/10/24	West Africa	RFB arrives at F. Po.
1863/11/29	West Africa	RFB departs F. Po to Dahome via Lagos.
1863/12/14	West Africa	*Abeokuta and the Camaroons Mountains* published by Tinsley.
1863/12/16.	West Africa	Speke's *Journal of the Discovery of the Source of the Nile* (Edinburgh: Blackwood) is published.
1864/02/?	West Africa	RFB leaves Dahome.
1864/03/23	West Africa	RFB arrives at Bonny River.
1864/04/03	West Africa	RFB is at F. Po.
1864/05/07	Tenerife	RFB is at Tenerife.
1864/06/11	Tenerife	RFB is still at Tenerife.
1864/07/30	Tenerife	Speke's *What Led to the Discovery of the Source of the Nile* (Edinburgh: Blackwood) is published.
1864/08/12	England	RFB arrives in Liverpool.
1864/09/15	England	Speke dies of a self-inflicted gunshot wound near Bath.
1864/09/	England	Burton is appointed Consul at Santos, Brazil.
1864/09/27	England	*Mission to Gelele* 2 vols. published by Tinsley.
1864/11/26	England	*Nile Basin* published by Tinsley Brothers.
1865/01/13	England	*Stone Talk* published by Hardwicke.
1865/04/	England	*The Guide-book. A Pictorial Pilgrimage to Mecca and Medina* published by William Clowes, to accompany Royal Polytechnic Show.
1865/04/04	England	"Farewell Dinner for Captain Burton" held in London by the Anthropological Society.
1865/05/09	England	The Burtons leave England for Portugal.

1865/06/05	Portugal	*Wit and Wisdom of West Africa* is published by Tinsley.
1865/06/13	Portugal	RFB leaves Lisbon for Santos, Brazil via Rio. Isabel returns to London.
1865/09/08	S. America	RFB arrives at Santos.
1865/09/09	S. America	Isabel leaves England for Santos, Brazil.
1865/09/27	S. America	Isabel arrives in Recife, Brazil.
1865/11/	S. America	RFB leaves Santos for the mouth of the Rio Grande.
1866/01/16	S. America	RFB arrives back in São Paulo from the mines.
1866/03/	S. America	RFB leaves Santos for the interior of São Paulo Province.
1866/05/	S. America	RFB returns to São Paulo from the interior.
1866/08/05	S. America	RFB climbs the sugarloaf mountain of the island of São Sebastião
1866/08/12	S. America	RFB returns to São Paulo from São Sebastião
1867/06/12	S. America	Burtons leave Rio for San Fran. River via Minas Geraes.
1867/08/07	S. America	RFB sets off on a raft down the San Fran. River to the sea.
1867/08/25	S. America	Isabel sets off for Rio.
1868/01/?	S. America	RFB returns to Rio.
1868/04/?	S. America	RFB is seriously ill.
1868/07/31	S. America	RFB goes on sick leave, departs Santos for South American tour. Isabel departs Santos for England.
1868/08/06	S. America	RFB arrives at Montevideo.
1868/08/22	S. America	RFB inspects the Paraguayan war battlefields at Humaita.
1868/09/01	S. America	Isabel arrives back in England.
1868/09/05	S. America	RFB arrives in Buenos Aires, meets Arthur Orton and Wilfrid Blunt

Chronology

1868/12/03	S. America	RFB is appointed Consul at Damascus.
1868/12/	S. America	RFB Crosses the Andes with William Maxwell to Los Andes.
1869/01/?	S. America	RFB is in Santiago.
1869/01/?	S. America	RFB and Maxwell travel north to Peru.
1869/03/?	S. America	RFB and Maxwell are in Lima, Peru.
1869/03/29	S. America	RFB returns to Buenos Aires and receives appointment letter.
1869/04/05	S. America	RFB leaves by ship, up the Parana river, to the battlefields again.
1869/04/10	S. America	*Highlands of the Brazil* 2 vols. published by Tinsley.
1869/04/13	S. America	RFB is in Asunción.
1869/04/	S. America	RFB arrives back at Buenos Aires.
1869/04/26	S. America	RFB departs Buenos Aires for Rio.
1869/05/	S. America	RFB departs Rio for England via Lisbon.
1869/06/01	England	RFB arrives back in England.
1869/07/24	France	RFB arrives at Vichy with Swinburne.
1869/08/09	France	Isabel arrives at Vichy.
1869/10/	Italy	RFB leaves Brindisi for Damascus.
1869/10/03	Syria	RFB arrives in Damascus.
1869/10/29	Syria	RFB climbs Mount Hermon.
1869/12	Syria	RFB visits the eastern Hauran.
1869/12/16	Syria	Isabel leaves England for Damascus.
1870/01/01	Syria	*Vikram and the Vampire* published by Longman.
1870/02/12	Syria	*Letters from the Battlefields of Paraguay* published by Tinsley.
1871/08/18	Syria	RFB leaves Damascus for England after being recalled.
1871/09/18	England	RFB arrives in England.
1871/09/30	England	Isabel leaves the Levant for England.

1871/12/13	England	RFB testifies at the trial of Arthur Orton, the 'Tichborne Claimant'.
1872/01/06	England	*Zanzibar* 2 vols. published by Tinsley.
1872/06/04	Scotland	Sails for Iceland from Granton.
1872/06/15?	Iceland	*Unexplored Syria* 2 vols. published by Tinsley.
1872/09/05	Scotland	RFB Arrives back in Edinburgh.
1872/10/24	England	RFB leaves England for Trieste.
1872/11/18	Austria	Isabel leaves England for Trieste.
1872/12/06	Austria	Burtons arrive together at Trieste, having met in Venice.
1873/04/01	Italy	Burtons leave Trieste for Rome via Ancona and Loreto.
1873/04/25	Italy	Burtons arrive back at Trieste via Florence and Bologna.
1873/04/27	Austria	Burtons arrive in Vienna for the Great Exhibition.
1873/05/?	Austria	Burtons arrive back in Trieste from Vienna.
1873/05/?	Austria	Charles Tyrwhitt-Drake stops over in Trieste en route to the Levant.
1873/09/	Austria	*The Lands of Cazembe* published by John Murray.
1874/05/?	Austria	RFB climbs the Schneeburg.
1874/05/14	Austria	Burtons return to Trieste.
1874/05/17	Austria	RFB is seriously ill with a tumour of the groin.
1874/06/23	Austria	Charles Tyrwhitt-Drake dies of fever in Jerusalem.
1874/09/21	Austria	Burtons return to Trieste after convalescing.
1874/12/08	Austria	Isabel leaves Trieste for England.
1875/04/27	Austria	RFB leaves Trieste for England on sick leave.

1875/05/12	England	RFB is in England.
1875/07/05	Iceland	RFB leaves from Leith for Iceland
1875/07/24	Iceland	RFB returns from Iceland.
1875/09/28?	England	*Ultima Thule* published by Nimmo.
1875/12/04	England	Burtons leave England for Trieste.
1876/01/	Austria	Burtons leave Trieste for India via Suez.
1876/02/	India	*Two Trips to Gorilla Land* published by Sampson Low.
1876/02/02	India	Burtons arrive at Bombay.
1876/06/18	Austria	Burton arrive back at Trieste via Suez, Cairo and Alexandria.
1876/10/30?	Austria	*Etruscan Bologna* published by Smith & Elder.
1877/03/03	Austria	RFB leaves Trieste for Egypt and Midian.
1877/04/06	Egypt	*Sind Revisited* published by Bentley.
1877/05/06	Egypt	Leaves Alexandria for Trieste.
1877/10/19	Austria	Leaves Trieste for Egypt.
1878/04/22	Egypt	RFB returns to Cairo after Midian trip.
1878/05/02?	Egypt	*The Gold Mines of Midian* is published by Kegan Paul.
1878/05/10	Egypt	Burtons leave Cairo for Trieste.
1878/05/15	Austria	Arrive in Trieste.
1878/07/06	Austria	Burtons leave Trieste for England.
1878/08/19	Ireland	At the British Association in Dublin.
1878/11/12	England	Maria Stisted, niece of RFB, dies of TB.
1879/04/	England	RFB leaves England for Dresden, Isabel leaves for Paris
1879/04/	Austria	Isabel has bad fall in Paris Hotel.
1879/04/14	Austria	*The Land of Midian (Revisited)* 2 vols. is published by Kegan Paul.
1879/12/05	Austria	RFB leaves Trieste for Egypt.
1880/01/02	Egypt	RFB meets Gordon in Cairo.

1880/02/	Egypt	Isabel leaves Trieste from London to seek medical treatment.
1880/04/15	Egypt	Isabel meets Gordon in London.
1880/05/03	Egypt	RFB is attacked by a gang in Cairo.
1880/05/	Egypt	RFB leaves Egypt for Trieste.
1880/05/29.	Austria	RFB arrives in Trieste from Egypt. Isabel arrives in Trieste from London.
1880/05/29	Austria	Isabel returns to Trieste from London.
1880/07/	Austria	Burtons leave Trieste for Monfalcone, Tyrol.
1880/08/	Austria	Burtons are at Oberammergau.
1880/09/	Austria	Burtons arrive back in Trieste.
1880/12/	Austria	*Os Lusiadas (The Lusiads)* 2 vols. trans. Burton published by Quaritch.
1881/09/15	Italy	RFB and VL Cameron attend Geographical Congress in Venice.
1881/10/	Austria	*Camoens Life and Lusiads* 2 Vols. published by Quaritch.
1881/11/18	Austria	RFB leaves Trieste for Gold Coast via Venice.
1882/01/08	Madeira	VL Cameron joins Burton in Madeira.
1882/01/25	West Africa	Burton and Cameron arrive at the Gold Coast.
1882/03/28	West Africa	Burton leaves Gold Coast for Madeira.
1882/05/15	West Africa	Isabel arrives in London from Trieste
1882/05/20	England	RFB and Cameron arrive in London.
1882/07/15	England	RFB leaves London for Trieste via Paris and Marienbad.
1882/07/31	Austria	Burtons arrive in Trieste.
1882/11/03	Austria	RFB leaves Trieste for the Sinai in search of Palmer.
1882/11/08	Egypt	RFB arrives at Alexandria.
1882/12/10	Austria	RFB arrives back at Trieste.

1883/01/	Austria	*To the Gold Coast for Gold* published by Chatto & Windus.
1884/02/	Austria	*The Book of the Sword* published by Chatto & Windus.
1884/06/04	Austria	RFB leaves Trieste for Vienna and Marienbad etc.
1884/09	Austria	Burtons return to Trieste.
1884/11/	Austria	*Camoens: The Lyricks* 2 vols. published by Quaritch.
1885/05/19	Austria	Burtons leave Trieste for London.
1885/08/11	England	Monckton Milnes (Lord Houghton) dies.
1885/09/12	England	Volume 1 of the *Arabian Nights* is sent to subscribers.
1885/11/	England	RFB leaves for Tangier.
1886/02/	Algeria	*Iracema* published by Bickers and Sons.
1886/02/16	Algeria	RFB is awarded a KCMG.
1886/04/23	Austria	Burtons return to Trieste from Tangiers.
1886/06/04	Austria	Burtons leave Trieste for London.
1887/01/06	England	Burtons leave Folkestone for Paris and then Cannes.
1887/02/26	France	RFB has a heart attack in Cannes.
1887/04/?	Austria	Burtons return to Trieste.
1887/10/15	Austria	Dr. F. Grenfell Baker replaces Dr. Ralph Leslie as Burton's personal physician.
1887/11/22	Austria	Burtons leave Trieste for resort at Abbazia.
1888/03	Austria	The last volume of the *Supplemental Nights* is completed.
1888/05	Austria	Burtons leave Trieste for England via Switzerland and Paris.
1888/07/18	England	Burtons arrive in England, at Folkestone.
1888/10/26	England	Burtons leave Folkestone for Paris via Boulogne.
1888/11/02	France	Burtons leave Paris for Geneva.

1889/03/12	Austria	Burtons arrive back at Trieste.
1889/07/01	Austria	Burtons leave for Adelsberg.
1889/09	Austria	Burtons return to Trieste.
1889/11/15	Austria	Burtons leave Trieste for Tunis and Algiers.
1889/12/20	Tunisia	Burtons arrive at Tunis.
1890/03/	Austria	Burtons return to Trieste.
1890/07/01	Austria	Burtons leave Trieste for Switzerland.
1980/08/08	Switzerland	Burtons meet HM Stanley at Maloja in the Engadine.
1890/08/	Switzerland	*Priapeia* is published for private subscribers.
1890/09/01	Switzerland	Burtons leave Maloja for Trieste.
1890/09/07	Austria	Burtons arrive back at Trieste.
1890/10/20	Austria	RFB dies at Trieste of a heart attack.
1893/07/12	—	Isabel's *The Life of Captain Sir Richard F. Burton* is published by Chapman and Hall.
1895/01/29	—	Edward Joseph Netterville Burton dies in Springfield Asylum, Wandsworth.
1896/03/22	—	Isabel Burton dies of ovarian cancer in London.

Register: A-J

128. Abraham, Walter.

A lithographer, who was at one time superintendent of government printing.[1] He ran his own business, advertising himself as a "Copper-Plate Engraver and Printer, Die-Sinker and Embosser. Both in English and Oriental Characters, FRERE LITHOGRAPHIC PRESS, 2 Meadow Street, Bombay." He was listed as insolvent on August 28, 1873 in the *London Gazette* of 26 September 1873. His important reminiscence of

---

[1] See William Taylor *Four Years' Campaign in India* (London: Hodder and Stoughton, 1875) p. 128.

Burton, who he had known in the 1840s, is a rarity from that early period, and appears in full in Volume 1.

129. Adye, Major-General Sir John (1819-1900).

A British soldier, from a military family. He served in the Crimean War and in the Indian Mutiny, eventually rising to General. He was Governor of Gibraltar from 1883-6, and wrote several books of memoirs based on his military experiences. He met Burton in Trieste in the late 1870s and left a brief reminiscence—"I remember the Chief's annoyance at being made the object of Lady Burton's attentions at the railway station. She insisted on presenting him with a gigantic bouquet, which I am afraid he threw out of the window as soon as the train left the station".[1]

130. Arbuthnot, Forster Fitzgerald (1833-1901).

An Indian Civil Servant, born in Bombay. He was educated privately in Germany and Switzerland and then trained for the Indian Civil Service at the East India College in Haileybury. His father Sir Robert Keith Arbuthnot (1801-1873) had also been a Civil Servant in India (1819-1838). His mother Anne Fitzgerald was the daughter of Field Marshal Sir John Forster FitzGerald, from whom his first name, frequently misspelled "Foster", was derived.[2] He went out to India in 1853 and stayed there until 1878, rising to Collector of Bombay, in charge of tax assessment. His father had also been a collector and magistrate.

Arbuthnot met Burton in India, probably around 1854, and they became close friends. Burton affectionately called him "Bunny". When the Burtons visited India in 1876, they were hosted by Arbuthnot in Bombay. "Mr. F. F. Arbuthnot drove us with his own team out to Bandora, about twelve miles from Bombay, where he has a charming bungalow in a wild spot close to the sea, and where one can get a little quiet and fresh air."[3] After Arbuthnot returned to England in 1878, where he lived at Upper House Court, Guildford, they often exchanged visits in England and Trieste: "Arbuthnot's visit has quite set me up, like a whiff of London in the Pontine marshes of Trieste. He goes to-day, d--- the luck! but leaves us hopes of meeting during the summer in Switzerland or thereabouts. He is looking the picture of health and we

---

[1] See Volume 2.
[2] Isabel at one stage calls him "Frederick Foster Arbuthnot" (*Life* Vol. 2, p. 61) while even RFB calls him "Foster" in his dedication to Volume 3 of the *Nights*.
[3] Isabel Burton *AEI* (1879), p. 118.

shall return him to town undamaged."[1] He dedicated Volume 3 of the *Nights* to Arbuthnot, "whose friendship has lasted nearly a third of a century", and who had "lived long enough in the East and… observantly enough, to detect the pearl which lurks in the kitchen-midden, and to note that its lustre is not dimmed nor its value diminished by its unclean surroundings".

Arbuthnot collaborated with Burton and Edward Rehatsek on editions of Eastern exotica and erotica, through the fictitious "Hindoo Kama Shastra Society", which was financed by Arbuthnot, leading to the publication of *The Kama Sutra* (1883) and the *Ananga Ranga* (1885). These were translated by Rehatsek (1819-1891), a Hungarian resident in India, with the assistance of Sanskrit experts in India, and revised and annotated by Arbuthnot and Burton. They had tried to publish an earlier edition of the Ananga Ranga (Kama Shastra) in the early 1870s but were forced to withdraw it after objections from the printer, though some of those early copies survive.

H. S. Ashbee published the following detailed description from Arbuthnot of the process used by the Kama Shastra Society:[2]

> *The Kama Shastra, or the Hindoo Art of Love, (Ars amoris Indica)* was printed in London in 1873. In this work, at pages 46 and 59, references were made to the holy Sage Vatsyayana, and to his opinions. On my return to India in 1874 I made enquiries about Vatsyayana and his works. The pundits informed me that the *Kama Sutra of Vatsyayana* was now the standard work on love in Sanscrit literature, and that no Sanscrit library was supposed to be complete without a copy of it. They added that the work was now very rare, and that the versions of the text differed considerably in different manuscripts, and the language in many of them was obscure and difficult. It was necessary then first to prepare as complete and as correct a copy of the work as possible in Sanscrit, and after this had been accomplished, then to get it properly translated. The first thing then to be done was to find a man competent to prepare the Sanscrit text, and after that a competent translator. After some inquiry Dr. Bühler, now Sanscrit Professor in Vienna, but then employed in the Educational Department in Bombay, recommended to me the Pundit Bhugwuntlal Indraji. This Pundit had already been frequently employed by Mr. James Fergusson, and Mr. James Burgess, in copying and translating for them writings found on copper plates, on stone boundaries, and in temples in many parts of India. Not only had he been

---

[1] Wright (1906), RFB to John Payne, p. 219. Arbuthnot also lived at 18, Park Lane, London.
[2] Ashbee, *Catena Librorum Tacendorum*, pp. 458-60.

useful to the above named gentlemen, but to many others engaged in Indian archeology, and antiquities. Last year he submitted a paper to the Oriental Congress held at Leyden in Holland, and the University there conferred on him the degree of Doctor of Letters, while the Royal Asiatic Society of London elected him as an honorary member. The Pundit himself was unable to speak English fluently but understood it sufficiently, and after an interview I set him to work to compile a complete copy of the *Kama Sutra of Vatsyayana* in Sanscrit. The copy of the text he had procured in Bombay being incomplete, the pundit wrote for other copies from Calcutta, Benares, and Jeypoor, and from these prepared a complete copy of the work. With the aid then of another Brahman by name Shivaram Parshuram Bhide, then studying at the University of Bombay, and well acquainted both with Sanscrit and English, and now employed in the service of His Highness the Guicowar at Baroda, a complete translation of the above text was prepared and it is this transition which has now been printed and published in London, with the impress of Benares, 1883. The pundits obtained great assistance in their translation from a commentary on the original work, which was called *Jayamangla,* or *Sutralashya,* and which is fully alluded to in the Introduction, page 10, to the *Kama Sutra.*

Without this commentary the translation would have been most difficult, if not impossible. The original work is written in very old and difficult Sanscrit, and without the aid of the commentary it would have been in many places unintelligible.

Arbuthnot was active in the Royal Asiatic Society after his return to England, and published a number of works about Persia and the East, including *Early Ideas. A group of Hindoo Stories* (1881); *Persian Portraits* (1887); *Arabic Authors* (1890); *The Rauzat-us-safa* (1891); *The Assemblies of Al Hariri* (1898); and *The Mysteries of Chronology* (1900).[1] He also wrote an unpublished *Life of Balzac* (1902).

131. Arnold, Julian Tregenna Biddulph (1860-1945?).

An explorer and poet. Son of Sir Edwin Arnold (1832-1904). He was born 3 July 1860 at Framfield in Sussex. Toured the United States lecturing about his travels and connections. It appears though that Arnold, who practiced for a while as a solicitor, was convicted of misusing trust funds.

Old Bailey. Old court.—Friday, January 25th, 1901. Before

---

[1] Burton's annotated personal copies of *Early Ideas*, *Arabic Authors* and *Persian Portraits* survive in the collection now at the Huntington Library in the Rare Books Department.

Mr. Justice Will. ... Julian Tregenna Biddulph Arnold pleaded guilty to that he, being a trustee of £6,246 6s.3d. under the will of John Domville Taylor, did convert and appropriate £1,000 of that money to his own use and benefit; also that, being a trustee of £933 4s.11d. under the will of William Hartopp Swain, did convert it to his own use and benefit; and, Thomas Boulton Sismey to conspiring with Arnold and other persons to cheat and defraud Jane Clarke of £14,000.—Arnold—Seven years' penal servitude in respect to the Taylor case, and three years' penal servitude in respect to the Swain case, to run consecutively. Sismey—Fifteen months' hard labour.

Later he became an American. He met Burton, who also knew his father, in Egypt around 1880, and left a brief reminiscence—"Restless and adventurous, contemptuous of convention, intolerant of restraint or discipline, as reckless of himself as of others, prone to engage in a quarrel upon the slightest provocation".[1]

132. Ashbee, Charles Robert (1863-1842).

A renowned architect and member of the 'Arts and Crafts' movement, born in London and educated at Cambridge. He was the son of H. S. Ashbee (1834-1900)—see below. In his memoirs *Grannie* (1939), he included an imaginative recollection of meeting Burton as a child at his father's house (see Volume 3). Since Burton first met his father in 1885 he would in fact have been 22 or so years old at the time.

133. Ashbee, Henry Spencer (1834-1900).

A wealthy Victorian businessman with a parallel life as a renowned collector of pornography, on which he published pedantic tracts for bibliophiles as "Pisanus Fraxi, "or "White Bee": *Index Librorum Prohibitorum* (1877) *Centuria Librorum Absconditorum* (1879) and *Catena Librorum Tacendorum* (1885). He is supposed by some to have been 'Walter', the author of *My Secret Life*, a swollen piece of many-volumed erotica in which the hero inseminates large swathes of the Victorian World.[2]

Ashbee was only introduced to Burton as late as the 21st of June 1885, by F. F. Arbuthnot, over dinner with Burton's old crony Henry Edward Vaux Bellamy and Sir Reginald MacDonald at the East India Club in St James's Square. Arbuthnot had earlier been introduced to Ashbee by Bellamy, on the 29th of May 1883, though Monckton Milnes

---

[1] See Volume 3.
[2] Ian Gibson, *The Erotomaniac: The Secret Life of Henry Spencer Ashbee*, 2001.

had known him even longer, since the 5th of April 1878, and the sadist bibliophile Frederick Hankey was known to all of them—Ashbee had visited Hankey in the 1870s at his quarters in Paris, 2 Rue Laffite. Ashbee wrote in his diary that Burton "impresses one at once as a very remarkable man, whose erudition is as vast as his knowledge of the world and of humanity".[1] They went on to Ashbee's rooms at 4 Gray's Inn Square, where his large collection of offbeat *facetiae* was kept for special viewings.

Soon Burton was a guest at Ashbee's select Tuesday evening gatherings at his house in Bedford Square, had been introduced to Baron de Cosson of the Kernoozers Club, and began to exchange letters[2] and 'uncommon books' with Ashbee. On Burton's return to England in 1886, they took a train and boat together to spent a July evening in Greenwich, accompanied by F. F. Arbuthnot and Sir Charles Wingfield. Isabel innocently records a more conventional visit that September— "We had a dinner at Mr. and Mrs. Ashbee's to say good-bye to Count Teleki before going to Africa, and I gave him a talisman."[3] In 1888 Burton was able to clarify for Leonard Smithers that "Pisanus Fraxus is H. S. Ashbee of 53 Bedford Square London. I reviewed his Tunisia a few months ago. He is a well-to-do merchant and has a fine collection of facetiae."[4]

In 1888 Burton favourably reviewed Ashbee's co-authored travel narrative *Travels in Tunisia* (1888) for the *Academy*,[5] describing his curious new friend merely as a 'globe trotter.' He especially liked the book's 'truly valuable' and 'exhaustive' bibliography, 'a boon and blessing to men'—perhaps a sly reference to Ashbee's *forte* in more obscure fields. Ashbee had already known of Burton's fictitious Kama Shastra Society long before he met him, and had reviewed the *Kama Sutra* as well as the *Nights*. The productions of the Kama Shastra Society—Ashbee had snared the exceptionally rare withdrawn first issue of *Ananga Ranga* from 1873—are given fulsome coverage in *Index Librorum Prohibitorum* (1877) and *Catena Librorum Tacendorum* (1885). Ashbee had no trouble identifying the authors, Burton and Arbuthnot, by name.

134. Ashby-Sterry, Joseph (1838-1917).

An English novelist, poet and contributor to *Punch*. He knew Burton from the London clubland of the early to mid-1860s, and left a passing

---

[1] H. S. Ashbee, unpublished diary, quoted in Gibson (2001) p. 102.
[2] See Volume 3.
[3] *Life* Vol. 2, p. 329.
[4] 1888/11/14. Richard Burton to Leonard Smithers. See Volume 3.
[5] *Academy* Vol. XXXIII (1888-06-16), pp. 405-6

reminiscence—see Volume 2.

135. Aubertin, John James (1818-1900).

An author, traveller and Spanish & Portuguese scholar, who was British-born but of Huguenot descent. He was educated at King's College, London and trained as a lawyer. Later he was the Superintendent of the British-owned São Paulo Railway company, from 1860 to 1869, and a promoter of cotton cultivation in Brazil. Aubertin met the Burtons in Brazil in the mid-1860s, and travelled in the interior with RFB. Later he published his own translation of Camões' *Lusiads*[1]—which Burton described as 'workmanlike'—and travelled in Egypt with RFB in 1879-80. He recalled his friendship with Burton in his memoirs of 1893, *Wanderings & Wonderings*.[2] He was also a fellow of the Royal Astronomical Society, and had an extensive correspondence with Charles Darwin. In Burton's *Camoens: Life and Lusiads* Vol. 1 an autobiographical sketch by Aubertin appears on pp. 167 ff.

136. Austin, Richard (1832-1899).

A Vice-Consul at Rio. Burton met him soon after he arrived in 1865—"After the trial at the Custom House, where a pair of bags, the work of the great Poole, duly disappeared, I called at the British Consulate, and introduced myself to its actual tenant, Mr. Richard Austin, son of the respected chaplain of Pernam. His twenty years' experience of Brazil were invaluable. We were inseparables for a month, and he accompanied me to Bahia."[3] Austin was also a member of the Anthropological Society, no doubt encouraged by Burton—see "The Extinction of Slavery in Brazil, from a practical point of view" by A. M. Perdigão Malheiro, translated by Richard Austin, F.A.S.L..[4]

137. Babington, William.

A Captain in the Merchant Navy, and a trader in the Cameroons, where he stayed for extended periods. He was Master of the *Victory*, *Princess Royal, Moselle* and other ships. He was also a Chairman of the Court of Equity that attempted to placate the Old Calabar region, and a member of the RGS and the Anthropological Society. Based at Bonny River, he knew Rev. Alfred Saker well. His "Remarks on the general Description of the Trade on the West Coast of Africa" appeared in the

---

[1] London: Kegan Paul, 1878.
[2] London: Kegan Paul, 1893.
[3] Letters from Rio VIII (p. 168) *Fraser's Magazine*, 1866.
[4] *Anthropological Review*, No. 20, Jan. 1868.

Journal of the Royal Society of Arts in 1875.[1]

Babington met Burton on the West Coast of Africa, when Burton was Consul at Fernando Po, and got on well with him. Writing to James Hunt, Burton recommended him: "Allow me to propose as a member of the Ethnological Society Mr. William Babington a gentleman in the Merchant Navy well known in these parts, and a friend of Sir W. Hooker. His address is 'Camaroons River' and perhaps you will kindly let him have his 'little bill' ".[2]

138.   Back, Sir George (1796–1878).

An officer in the Royal Navy, who saw action in the Peninsula Wars and explored the Arctic with Franklin in the early 1820s. He later led an RGS expedition in 1833 to the Arctic to search for Captain Ross, during which he explored a great deal of new territory and experienced extreme conditions, but did not find Ross, who made it back to England on his own. Back later returned on another journey to explore Hudson Bay. He was awarded the RGS Gold Medal in 1837, knighted in 1839, and appointed an Admiral in 1857. He was also the Vice-President of the RGS and a long-standing council member, and the author of *Narrative of the Arctic Land Expedition to the Mouth of the Great Fish River, and along the Shores of the Arctic Ocean, in the Years 1833, 1834 and 1835* (London: John Murray, 1838) and, with Francis Galton, of the RGS guide *Hints to Travellers* (London: RGS, 1854). Back was a notable painter and naturalist. Burton, who knew him well through the RGS, formed a friendship with Back and kept up a correspondence with him—see Volume 1 and 2.

139.   Badger, George Percy (1815-1888).

A distinguished English Arabist and an ordained minister in the Church of England. He was Political agent at Aden in 1854, serving on the staff of Brigadier William Marcus Coghlan, and published the standard work *An English Arabic lexicon* (1881). In Burton's *Zanzibar* (1872) Badger was described as "a certain Reverend gentleman, then chaplain at Aden, who had gained for himself the honourable epithet of Shaytan Abyaz, or White Devil",[3] and associated with forces Burton blamed for thwarting his expedition to Somaliland. Badger promptly wrote to Burton to emphasize that "never, under any circumstances, did I take any part whatsoever, directly or indirectly, in your Berberah Expedition". Badger also raised the issue of Burton's Arabic Exam,

---

[1] *Journal of the Royal Society of Arts* February 12, 1875.
[2] 1862/05/25—see Volume 1.
[3] *Zanzibar* Vol. 1, p. 9.

which he had written at Aden before leaving for the interior, but which was ruled invalid by the Examination Committee in Bombay—"Outram asked me to preside and I positively declined. Why? you will ask. Well, I had heard you were very vindictive ... Playfair sent your papers to me, and after looking over them, I sent them back to him with a note eulogizing your attainments and, if I remember rightly, remarking upon the absurdity of the Bombay Committee being made the judges of your proficiency, inasmuch as I did not believe that any of them possessed a tithe of the knowledge of Arabic which you did."[1] Moreover, "I was subsequently told that the Bombay authorities would not pass you because the Examination was informal, or contrary to rule—that you ought to have passed at Bombay."[2] After this conciliation, the two corresponded on friendly terms. Isabel recalled visiting Badger in 1879: "We also saw a great deal of Dr. Percy Badger, who was always delighted (and his wife too) to get hold of Richard. Dr. Badger turned an old kitchen into a comfortable studio, and there we used to find him, working hard at his Dictionary."[3]

140. Bainton, George (1847-1925).

An English Congregationalist minister who corresponded widely with the leading authors and composers of his day, see Nigel Cross *The Common Writer: Life in Nineteenth-Century Grub Street*.[4] He corresponded with both of the Burtons on "the art of authorship" and published their responses in his *Art of Authorship* (1891)—see Volume 3.

141. Baker, Frederick Grenfell (1853-1930).

Burton's personal physician during his last years in Trieste. He was born on Lahore, the son of an Indian army officer. He trained at St George's Hospital and entered the Royal College of Surgeons in 1877. He worked for the next ten years as the surgeon at the Poplar Hospital in London. He was also a keen amateur photographer and attempted to

---

[1] 1872/02/21. George Percy Badger to Richard Burton.
[2] 1872/02/29. George Percy Badger to Richard Burton. This helps to explains Burton's statement in the *Nights* Vol. 416 that "At Aden, where I passed the official examination, Captain (now Sir R. Lambert) Playfair and the late Rev. G. Percy Badger, to whom my papers were submitted, were pleased to report favourably of my proficiency." Burton believed that he had passed the examination in *Aden* and only the technicality raised by the Bombay committee, as to place of examination, led to the certification as interpreter not being granted, though he does not explicitly say this.
[3] *Life* Vol. 2, p. 162.
[4] Cambridge University Press, 1985, p. 220.

patent "Improvements in Photographic Cameras" in 1891. The Burtons first met Baker at Cannes in 1887, where RFB had a heart attack. Poor health had forced Baker to quit his London practice, so Isabel engaged him to replace the Canadian Dr. Ralph Leslie as Burton's personal physician on October 17th 1887. He was author of *The Model Republic* (1895) on Switzerland, which Burton had helped him find a printer for, through Leonard Smithers. His photographs of the Burtons and their house in Trieste, and of the deathbed scenes there, have been widely-used, and he registered copyright for several of them.[1] Reports circulated after Burton's death that Baker was preparing a biography of Burton; however, he had fallen out with Isabel over her destruction of Burton's manuscripts. Baker left some important reminiscences of the Burtons—see Volume 3.

142. Baker, Martha Beckwith (1797?-1854.xii.10).

Mother of Richard Francis Burton, who appears to have resented her. Married Joseph Netterville Burton on March 2nd 1820, at St James Church in London. She was the second daughter of the second marriage of Richard Baker, a well-to-do businessman, of Barham House, near Elstree in Hertfordshire. Her mother was Sarah Baker née McGregor (1772-1846). Her sisters were Sarah (1795?-?), who married Joseph Netterville Burton's brother Francis Burton (1784-1828) in 1825; and Georgina (1799-1867), who married a Bagshaw. Martha received 8,000 pounds in her father's will. The inheritance was bound up in investments, from which she received the interest only, perhaps 400 pounds a year. She had a half-brother Richard George Baker (1788?-1864).

143. Baker, Richard (1762-1824.ix.16).

Maternal grandfather of Richard Burton via his daughter Martha Beckwith (see above). Married twice, the second time to Sarah McGregor (1772-1846), who was the mother of Martha Beckwith. Lived at Barham House in Hertfordshire, then a mile outside of Elstree, from 1813 until his death. Up to 1806 he had lived in St Andrews Undershaft in London, at Nine Elms Lane in Battersea (1806-9), and at Brighton (1809-13). He acquired considerable wealth, with investments in various properties and funds. A prodigal son by his first marriage, Richard George Baker (1788?-1864), studied at Trinity College, Oxford (BA, 1812) and entered at Lincoln's Inn as early as 1807.

---

[1] See The National Archives COPY 1/440/277.

144. Baker, Sir Samuel White (1821-1893).

A Nile explorer, born in London into a wealthy family of businessmen. He was educated in England and in Germany, qualifying as an engineer. In 1864 he discovered Lake Albert, travelling with his second wife Florence (1841-1916), whom he claimed to have rescued from a slave market in Vidin on the Danube in January 1859. He set off in 1861, ostensibly to explore the Blue Nile, but after a year, having exhausted the possibilities that offered, swung North down to Khartoum, then South, up the While Nile and through the marshy Sud. He reached Gondokoro, the last station on the river, in February 1863. There he encountered the Speke and Grant expedition, who were travelling down river from Lake Victoria. Speke—who had expected to find his official relief expedition, led by John Petherick, rather than Baker—suggested an exploration of the 'Luta Nzige', which his own expedition had bypassed. Baker did, and named it Lake Albert—it turned out to be a contributor to the Nile in its own right. He was knighted in 1866 for his Nile explorations, and was appointed the first Governor of Equatoria (1869-1873), preceding General Charles Gordon. He retired to Devon in 1874, though he continued to visit Egypt.

Baker was the author of many travel narratives, including *The Albert N'Yanza* 2 vols. (1866). It is not known when he first met Burton—in 1863 Burton wrote to Henry Murray "Rot your Baker—what is B. to me?"—but they were certainly well acquainted by the mid-1870s, and Burton refers to him positively in his later books, e.g. "my friend Sir Samuel Baker".[1] He appears to have kept a neutral position in the Burton-Speke-Grant quarrel.

145. Bancroft, Squire (1841-1926).

An English actor and theatre manager, eventually prospering in partnership with his wife Effie Marie Wilton. They were well-connected and produced two volumes of memoirs. They appear to have met the Burtons for the first time in Switzerland where they stayed at the same hotel at Maloja in the Engadine as Henry Morton Stanley. They left a reminiscence of Burton which appears in Volume 3.

146. Barth, Heinrich (1821-1865).

An African explorer (1850-1855) and linguist, from Hamburg, who joined and then completed a British Government expedition to explore Central North West Africa, crossing the Sahara twice. He was the author of the 5 volume description of his travels *Reisen und Entdeckungen in Nord- und Central-afrika in den Jahren 1849 bis 1855* (Gotha: J. Perthes,

---

[1] *Two Trips to Gorilla Land* Vol. 2 (1876), p. 193.

1857-8) which was translated as *Travels and Discoveries in North and Central Africa: being a Journal of an Expedition undertaken under the Auspices of H.B.M.'s Government, in the Years 1849–1855* (London: Longman, 1857-8). Burton met him in person in London when planning his East African expedition and Barth corresponded with him, offering him advice about the lakes. Burton was unimpressed with his advice—see volume 1.

147. Barnard, Charles Inman (1850-1942).

An American reporter for the *New York Tribune* who was mostly based in France. He was born in Boston, Mass. in 1850 and died at Nice, France on May 11, 1942.[1] Barnard met Burton in Cairo in the late 1870s and corresponded with him—see Volumes 2 and 3.

148. Bates, Henry Walter (1825-1892).

An explorer and naturalist, from Leicester, who was largely self-educated. He explored the Amazon between 1848 and 1850, in the company of Alfred Russel Wallace. After Wallace left in 1850, Bates stayed on till 1859, before returning to England. He later wrote a classic description of his explorations *The Naturalist on the River Amazons* (London: Murray, 1863) and provided the first accurate descriptions of adaptive mimicry in nature. Elected a Fellow of the Royal Society in 1881, he was also active in the RGS as Assistant Secretary from 1864 until his death in 1892. He had an extensive correspondence with Burton, with whom he was on good terms and knew well through the RGS—see Volume 2.

149. Bellamy, Henry Edward Vaux (1837?-1889).

A businessman and murky figure in the underworld of Victorian sexual deviance, about whom little definite is known. He may have been born in Hereford,[2] and may have been the son of Edward Vaux Bellamy of Hereford, who had worked for the British Museum. He was made a Fellow of the Anthropological Society in 1865, and lived then at 10 Duke Street, St James's, London. He may also have been a member of the Cannibal Club. No doubt he joined the Anthropological Society through Burton's influence, and he is listed as attending Burton's "Farewell Dinner" in 1865, which sent RFB off to Brazil.

---

[1] See *The United States in the Middle East: a historical dictionary* by David Shavit (New York: Greenwood Press, 1988) p. 27.

[2] According to Mendes (1993), he was educated at Oxford, graduating from St Mary Hall in 1863, but this is incorrect. *Alumni Oxiensis* lists this Bellamy as *Arthur*, son of Edward, "gent. of Oxford."

At his death Bellamy was listed, in a notice to the creditors of "Henry Edward Vaux Bellamy," as a "Secretary of Public Companies"[1] giving the addresses 1-Adam Street, Adelphi and 57 Moorgate street. He was listed previously in connection with a bewildering array of railway companies, for example as the "Secretary" of the "West London Extension Railway Company"[2] and as the "Chief Official" of the "Victoria Station and Pimlico Railway",[3] and others, including the "Calais Tramway", the "Vicksburg, Shrieveport (sic) & Pacific" etc. There was some continuity at least: in 1861 he was listed as Secretary to the "Victoria Station and Pimlico Railway", at Great-George Street, Westminster.[4]

Bellamy was associated with the Studholme Hodgson / C. Duncan Cameron / Fred Hankey set referred to in Burton's correspondence with Monckton Milnes. "I left Cameron drunk and Bellamy half sober" (1861/08/28). "Remember me with love to the amiable trio Hodgson, Bellamy and Hankey—when shall we all meet again?" (1862/04/26). "I suppose Bellamy is still fending off the angry fiend" (1863/03/29). "What of Hankey, and Bellamy?" (1863/05/07). "Monday will be a failure. We must set out at 9 P.M. not 11 and return before 12. Bellamy has promised to arrange the affair as soon as possible—probably next Monday week. Can you dine with me at 14 St James Square (7 P.M.) on that day—Monday 17th?? I will ask Cameron & Bellamy to meet you and if we don't go to the Chinese lodgings we may drop in upon our old saintly friend …" (1875). Burton also mentioned Bellamy in his description of a séance by the Davenport Brothers in 1865, apparently conducted at Bellamy's house: "On occasion I placed my foot on Mr. Fay's, while Mr. Bellamy, the master of the house, did the same to Mr. Davenport, and we measured their distance from the semicircle—10 feet."[5]

Bellamy was present in 1885 when F.F. Arbuthnot introduced H.S. Ashbee to Burton.[6] Ashbee recorded in his diary that Monckton Milnes had introduced Bellamy to him on 8th June 1878. Bellamy makes regular appearances in Ashbee's diary from there on. It was Bellamy who had introduced Arbuthnot, out of the blue, to Ashbee on the 29th May 1883. Some correspondence between Arbuthnot and Bellamy from 1884 is said to survive—e.g. "very glad to hear that you saved some of Potter's[7]

---

[1] *Law Times*, Sept. 14, 1889, p. 336.
[2] T. Skinner *The stock exchange year-book for 1883*, p. 153.
[3] *The Stock Exchange Official Intelligence*, 1882, p. xliii.
[4] *Hand-book guide to railway situations*, 1862, p. 51.
[5] Richard Burton "Captain Burton and the Brothers Davenport" *The Spiritual Magazine*, February 1865, pp. 88-9. Reproduced in Volume 1.
[6] For this and subsequent references to Ashbee's unpublished diary, see Gibson (2001).
[7] Presumably Mrs. Sarah Potter, the flagellator brothel madam, who had died

things from destruction. I saw the man they were left to, who informed me that he ought to have destroyed them all".[1] Bellamy was apparently also a subscriber to the Kamasutra, and Arbuthnot wrote to him to offer copies for circulation of the new work "by some learned Brahmans who are interested in the Humanities."[2]

On July 4 1886, Bellamy dined at the Richmond Club with Ashbee and the Anglo-Irish Catholic Sir Roland Blennerhassett. Later in July he was accompanying Ashbee, Burton and Sir Charles Wingfield to Greenwich. On the 22nd January 1888 Bellamy makes a final appearance in Ashbee's diary, at dinner in the company once again of F.F. Arbuthnot at the East India Club.

150. Bispham, David Scull (1857-1921).

An American opera singer and actor of Quaker descent, a baritone who toured extensively in Europe. See Laura Williams Macy *The Grove Book of Opera Singers*.[3] He left a reminiscence of the Burtons, though it is not clear exactly when they first met—"a wonderful couple merely to sit and watch."[4]

151. Bird, Alice "Lallah" (?-1921).

The cultured spinster sister of Dr. George Bird. She ran his household after the death of his wife, and took an active role in their circle of friends, which included the scientist William Crookes. She had an extensive correspondence with Swinburne, and also corresponded with Burton—see Volume 3.

152. Bird, Dr. George (1817-1900).

Burton's personal physician when he was in London. His obituary in the *British Medical Journal* reads:[5]

> We regret to have to announce the death of Dr. George Bird, formerly of Welbeck Street, London, which took place on May 4th at his house at Hampstead. George Bird was born in 1817. He was the eldest of a very large family. His father, James Bird,[6]

---

in 1872.

[1] Quoted in McConnachie (2007), p. 94. No citation or source is given.
[2] Quoted in McConnachie (2007), p. 151. No citation or source is given.
[3] Oxford, 2008, p. 44.
[4] See Volume 3.
[5] *British Medical Journal* May 19, 1900, p. 1266. See also the obituary in the *Lancet* June 2, 1900, p. 1619 which has some variations of detail.
[6] 'Mr. James Bird, bookseller, and extensively known as the amiable and gifted author of "The Vale of Sluughden,"—"Machin, or the Discovery of

well known in Suffolk as a poet, died in middle life, and the boys had early to turn into the world, and every one of them made some sort of mark. George was apprenticed to the doctor of the village, Dr. Wilson, known in his day as an authority on gout, and proud of the fact that he was sent for to prescribe for George IV.

In boyhood as in age Bird was always a pioneer. As a lad he wore yellow at a county election when all the neighbours were blue. Indeed he was a born Progressist; never wavered, never compromised, and was always eager for education and development in every aspect. From rural Suffolk he passed to London, and studied at University College. In 1841 he took the diploma of M.R.C.S., and in 1859 the degree of M.D. at St. Andrews.

For thirty four years he practised at 49, Welbeck Street. He always had an affinity for literature, art, and the drama, and he counted many illustrious people among his patients. He attended Leigh Hunt, and knew behind the scenes. He never lost an occasion to bear witness to the fact that the financial reproaches heaped on Leigh Hunt were undeserved. About two years ago he wrote a memorandum, which in due time will prove that Leigh Hunt was a heroic martyr. It was to shield another he stoically bore aspersions on his character. He also attended Sir Edward Bulwer Lytton, Dickens, Frank Stone, Sir Richard and Lady Burton, Thomas Woolner, R. H. Horne, Mrs. Lynn Linton, and many well-known people of the day.

An old friend of Dr. Bird sends us the following estimate of his character:

"To-the last he remained young in body and young in mind. He was always fond of athletic exercises, and in his younger days was an excellent boxer, and remained to the last an active

---

Madeira"—"Framingham,"—"Dunwich, a Tale of the Splendid City,"—"Cosmo, Duke of Tuscany, a Tragedy,"—"The Emigrant's Tale,"—"Francis Abbott," and various other works, died on the 26th of March, at the . village of Yoxford, in Suffolk, where he had been resident many years. After a long illness, in which he evinced the utmost patience, and truly Christian resignation of spirit, he fell a victim to pulmonary disease in the 51st year of his age. In the final hour he was soothed and blessed with the presence of his entire family—a bereaved wife, and twelve sons and daughters! No man was ever more beloved, or more deserving of love, than James Bird. From the pen of one of his oldest and most attached literary friends, we shall, next month, present an extended memoir of him and of his works, biographical and critical.' *The Aldine Magazine* Vol. 1 1839. See also pp 297ff of the same journal for a very full account, and *Selections from the poems of James Bird; with a brief Memoir of his life* by Thomas Harral circa 1840.

cyclist. He was also young in mind—always embraced with eagerness new ideas, and was in everything progressive. He was most kind of heart and cheerful in disposition, and had at his disposal a fund of good stories, which he narrated excellently. He thoroughly enjoyed life, and brought sunshine wherever he went to friends and patients. His patients were all his devoted friends. He leaves a happy memory behind him among his many friends who will sadly feel their loss, and will long cherish their recollection of George Bird.

Apparently Bird was also a political radical: "Mr. Goodwyn Barmby, a poet who possessed real lyrical power, an advocate of original tastes ... founded a Communist church, and gave many proofs of boldness and courage. He and Dr. George Bird, who afterwards obtained professional eminence in medicine, issued a prospectus of the London Communist Propagandist Society. Dr. Bird contributed the best literary reviews which appeared in social publications of the day."[1]

The Burtons knew the Birds and their circle well, and were married in their house at 26 Osnaburgh Street, Regent's Park, in 1861. RFB may have met Bird at some time in the 1850s, although the Birds were also known to the Arundell family.[2] They would often reunite with Swinburne and the Birds, at their new address in Welbeck Street, when they were back in London—their friend Luke Ionides married the second daughter of Dr. Bird, Elfrida-Elizabeth.

Burton used Bird as his personal physician when he was in town, and Bird was not vacationing in Egypt. Volume 5 of the *Nights* was dedicated to him—"This is not a strictly medical work, although in places treating of subjects which may modestly be called hygienic. I inscribe it to you because your knowledge of Egypt will enable you to appreciate its finer touches; and for another and a yet more cogent reason, namely, that you are one of my best and oldest friends."

In 1895 the Birds moved to Windmill Hill in Hampstead, which was their final address. Bird was over eighty when he died, and his sister was said to have passed 90.

153. Blunt, Wilfrid Scawen (1840-1922).

A diarist, politician, oriental traveler and poet, born in Sussex and inducted into the Catholic faith on the conversion of his mother.[3] Blunt was in the Consular Service between 1859 and 1869, and then married a

---

[1] *The history of co-operation* Volume 2 by George Jacob Holyoake (1879) p. 151
[2] *Romance of Isabel, Lady Burton* Vol. 1 (1897), pp. 166-7.
[3] Anthony Blunt (1907-1983) the Cambridge Traitor was his grand-nephew.

grand-daughter of Byron, the daughter of Ada Lovelace.[1] After that he wrote poetry, travelled extensively in the Middle East with his wife, dabbled in politics, adopted foreign causes, rained pamphlets, and raised Arabian horses. At the same time he was a prodigious philanderer, with a reputation for vanity, counting Lady Gregory and William Morris' wife Jane among his many and diverse trophies. His brand of politics was a mixture of Tory landowner and anti-imperialist enthusiast, a romantic nationalism-for-thee-but-not-for-me that saw him promoting Home Rule in Ireland, and Egyptian and Indian Independence, while running unsuccessfully for Parliament on a Conservative Party ticket.

In 1867 Blunt was posted to the legation in Rio de Janeiro. His cousin Walter Seymour recalled that "Wilfrid Blunt, a relation of mine, in the Legation at Buenos Ayres, turned up with his sister, a Norwegian Carriole, and a black imp whom he had purchased at St. Vincent, and who answered to the name of Pompey".[2] Blunt met Burton at Rio in the autumn of the following year. Many years later—"I unfortunately kept no notes nor journals then"—he composed the well-crafted and often quoted reminiscence which appears in Volume 2. It suggests that the Consul had gone to seed—"His dress and appearance were those suggesting a released convict". It is certain that Blunt quarreled at some stage with Burton. One biographer notes that in 1878, when the Blunts visited S. Jackson Eldridge in Beyrout, they "were delighted to learn that Richard Burton's name stank in the consulate".[3] Eldridge had been Burton's Consul General. The exact cause of the quarrel is not known.

Blunt was the author of numerous works, including several books of poetry and polemics like *The Secret History of the English Occupation of Egypt* (1907); but he is chiefly remembered now for his *My Diaries* 2 vols. (1919) and an unpublished personal journal which was embargoed until fifty years after his death.

154. Blumhardt, James Fuller (?-1922).

A Professor of Hindustani, and Reader of Hindi and Bengali, at University College London. He was also a teacher of Bengali at Oxford University. Burton met him through A. G. Ellis of the British Museum and refers to him several times in his correspondence with Ellis, and in the *Nights*.[4] Blumhardt helped to translate the manuscript of Aladdin which was eventually located in Paris, and which was in Hindustani.

---

[1] Remembered now for assisting Charles Babbage on his experiments in early computing devices.
[2] See Volume 2.
[3] Elizabeth Longford *A Pilgrimage of Passion* (1979; reprinted by I.B. Tauris in 2007) p. 131.
[4] E.g. Suppl. Vol. 3, p. viii.

155. Blackwood, John (1818-1879).

A Scottish publisher, part of the Blackwood family dynasty publishing as "William Blackwood and sons", which was founded in 1804. The firm published articles by both Burton and Speke in their widely-circulated *Blackwood's Magazine*, as well as Speke's subsequent books on his African travels. John Blackwood befriended Speke, while still maintaining cordial relations with Burton, and they had an extensive correspondence.[1] The Blackwood archives in the National Library of Scotland are now an important source of information about Speke, since few of his other papers have survived.

156. Brassey, Anna Allnutt (1839–1887).

An English travel writer. Her maiden name was Allnutt. She married Sir Thomas Brassey, a Member of Parliament, and they travelled extensively in their yacht. It is not clear when she first met Burton, but she published a brief account of "our old friend" in Trieste in the late 1870s.[2]

157. Buckley-Mathew, Sir George Benvenuto (1807-1879).

A soldier and diplomat, from a military family. After serving in the Coldstream Guards and other regiments, he was elected an MP from 1835-1841, after which he was Governor of the Bahamas in 1844, and then had diplomatic postings in Russia, Mexico, Guatemala and Argentina. Buckley-Mathew knew the Burtons through the Foreign Office. They may have met for the first time in Brazil, where they were both stationed. Buckley-Mathew was then "Minister Plenipotentiary" to the Emperor of Brazil. He is referred to often in Brazil-related correspondence by the Burtons. Later, when Burton assembled his response to his recall from Damascus, he relied on Buckley-Mathew for support—"Throughout my four years of service in the Brazil I never bad a dispute or even a difference with the authorities, and I can confidently refer your Lordship, to Her Majesty's Envoy, Mr., Buckley Mathew, C.B., for his opinion as regards the esteem in which I was held, and for the mode in which I performed my duties."[3]

158. Burke, Luke (?-1885).

A prominent member of the Anthropological Society, having been

---

[1] See Volume 1 for some examples.
[2] See Volume 2.
[3] *The Case of Captain Burton* (1872), p. 111.

one of the founders of the Ethnological Society in 1861. He also edited a journal called *The Future: a journal of philosophical research and criticism* circa 1860, and had brought out an *Ethnological Journal* as early as 1848. Earlier he had published a treatise on phrenology with a the fulsome title *Phrenological Enquiries: Being an Investigation, First of the Causes which Have Prevented the General Reception of Phrenology, Secondly, of the Nature and Advantages of the Researches of Its Advocates, and Elucidating the Imperfections of the "present System," and the Improvements and Discoveries of the Author* (1840). Burke knew and corresponded with Burton, who had been a co-founder of the break-away Anthropological Society in 1863 and its Vice-President. "With Mr. Luke Burke, I hold, as a tenet of faith, the doctrine of great ethnic centres, and their comparative gradation."[1]

159. Burton, Isabel (1831-1896).

Born Isabel Arundell, into the Anglo-Catholic aristocracy. She met RFB in Boulogne in the early 1850s, and closely followed his career after that. They were married in 1861, against the wishes of her parents. She remained in England with her parents while he was stationed in Fernando Po from 1861 to 1864, but later accompanied him to his postings in Brazil, Damascus and Trieste. They had no children, and around 1880 she told her doctor that she had "never been in the family way". She acted as Burton's hard-working literary amanuensis and business manager—at least for his mainstream works. She was the author of her own *The Inner Life of Syria, Palestine and the Holy Land* (1875) and *Arabia, Egypt, India* (1879)—though both volumes contain a substantial amount of material by RFB—as well as a two volume *Life* of Burton in 1893. Misreading her husband's audience, she had also caused the bowdlerized *Lady Burton's Edition of Her Husband's Arabian Nights* to be published in 1886.

Isabel, a pious woman, became notorious for her claim that Burton, who was notable among his friends for his atheism, had accepted the Catholic Church on his deathbed. She also burned most of his literary remains, including nearly all his diaries and letters, and the unpublished editions of erotica that she disapproved of. She interred his embalmed body in a mausoleum in Mortlake, after a second full-fledged burial service to follow on the first service performed in Trieste—Francis Galton said that it was "a ceremony quite alien to anything that I could conceive him to care for". She took a nearby cottage and held weekend séances in the tomb, which was fitted out with coloured electric lights and an altar. She died in London of ovarian cancer in 1896, after a long illness, and was interred next to RFB in Mortlake.

---

[1] *Wanderings in West Africa* vol. 1, p. 175.

Some of Burton's manuscript material was burnt by Isabel in Trieste, other parts were burnt in London, and the remainder was burnt by her literary executor after her death, on her instructions. The exact division of proportions at the various stages of this process of destruction can only be guessed at, but the staging determines only her degree of calculation, not the final outcome. As a result, many former friends like Algernon Swinburne, Lynn Linton and Ouida broke with her, as well as many members of Burton's own family. The bonfiring of this material makes it particularly difficult to evaluate her *Life*, which is now the only source for the entries from his diaries and other material represented there. Internal stylistic evidence suggests that much of it—consult, say, the entries referring to Speke—was rewritten by her.

160. Burnand, Sir Francis Cowley (1836-1917).

A playwright, author, and editor of *Punch*, the only son of a London stockbroker. He converted to Catholicism, and met Burton in the London social scene of the 1870s or 1880s, through the actor Henry Irving. He left a reminiscence of Burton, describing him as "a queer bluff man", in the old-fashioned sense—see Volume 3.

161. Burton, Edmund (1737.iv.04-1817).

Dean of Killala in Ireland from 1805 to 1817. Son of the Lake-district tenant farmer James Burton (1710-1778). Studied at St John's College, Cambridge (MA). His entry in *Alumni Cantabrigienses* reads: "BURTON, EDMUND. Adm. sizar (age 14) at ST JOHN's, Sept. 25, 1751. S. of James, farmer, of Westmorland. School, Sevenoaks, Kent. Ord[ained] deacon (Peterb.) Sept. 23, 1759; priest (Lincoln) June 6, 1762. C[urate] of Puddington (? Toddington), Beds.".[1] Became Arch-Deacon of Tuam, in West Ireland, and Vicar General of the Diocese.[2] Before that he was Prebendary of Faldown. Stanley Lane-Pool confused Edmund with his brother **Edward** (below) who was Richard Burton's grandfather rather than Edmund.[3] Pool states that there was no Rector of Tuam because the living was "impropriate" (a state in which the greater tithes had been inherited or acquired by a non-clergyman; a Rector would

---

[1] Robert Forsyth Scott *Admissions to the College of St. John* (Part III, 1903) adds that he was "bred" at Sevenoaks Kent by Mr. [Edmund] Holme, and that his tutor and surety was a Mr. [Edward] Powell.

[2] H. Cotton *Fasti ecclesiae hibernicae : the succession of the prelates and members of the cathedral bodies in Ireland* (1851) 29.

[3] Stanley Lane-Pool "Sir Richard Burton's Archdeacon", *Notes and Queries* (IIS XI 1915.vi.5), 425-6. The bizarre suggestion by Godsall (2008), 436 n 29, that this simple confusion by Poole was "probably deliberately so", is redolent of paranoia.

receive both the greater and lesser tithes directly, redistributing the lesser to the Vicar).[1] However the Church of Ireland usually (or certainly often) called Vicars "Rectors". Contemporary references to Rectors of Tuam (e.g. the son of the Archbishop of Tuam, John Beresford, 1774–1865) can be found.

162. Burton, Edward (1747.iii.10-1794).

Vicar of Annaghdown, on Lough Corrib in Ireland, from an English family. (Some sources say Rector of Annaghdown and Vicar General of Tuam, since "Vicar" and "Rector" seem to have been interchangeable in the Church of Ireland. Annaghdown had as impropriator a John Kirwan, from a prominent family in Galway). Son of James and Sarah Burton of Rossgil and Barker Hill, near Shap in Cumbria. Paternal grandfather of Richard Burton, via his son **Joseph Netterville Burton** (1782?, see below). Edward either purchased the Newgarden estate, outside Tuam, where the family lived, or inherited it from his father-in-law John Campbell (see following). Married Maria Margaretta Campbell (1752-1837?), through whom a fanciful line of descent from Louis XIV, via the Lejeunes, was traced as part of the family lore. Maria Margaretta was the daughter of John Campbell (LLD), himself a Vicar General of Tuam. His brother **Edmund** (1737.iv.04-1817, see above) was Dean of Killala in Ireland. Edward was the youngest of nine siblings. He entered Trinity College, Dublin, in 1767 (BA 1772, LLB 1776).

163. Burton, Edward Joseph Netterville (1824-1895).

The younger brother of Richard Francis Burton. He was admitted as a pensioner to Trinity College Cambridge on July 5th 1843, and matriculated, i.e. was admitted into the university as opposed to just his college, in the Michaelmas (first) term of 1843.[2] He left without a degree, joining the Army in 1845 (37th foot, purchased commission). He rose to Lieut. on 20th November 1846, then after serving in Ceylon, to Captain on 20th March 1856. He took an active part in the Indian Mutiny of 1857, where he was awarded the Indian Mutiny Medal.[3] The *New Army List* notes that he "commanded the Bickrumgee outpost, and was engaged in its defence from 1st September to 16th October 1856 against the rebel force under Ummer Singh" and was also involved in the capture

---

[1] This seems to be the source for the assertion in Godsall (2008) that the Rectorship of Tuam was impropriate, and therefore could not be held as an office.

[2] John Venn and J. A. Venn *Alumni Cantabrigiensis* (1921).

[3] On Nov 15 2015, this medal was auctioned by Lawrences Auctioneers of Crewkern.

of Judgespore.[1] He went on sick leave in 1863 and then on half-pay in 1864. Eventually he was placed in the retired list in 1881, with promotion to Major, but he was already in the Springfield Asylum, Wandsworth by then, and remained confined there until his death in 1895. Isabel mentions visiting the asylum in 1875, but omits the most relevant inmate: "Another very interesting visit we paid was to the Surrey County Lunatic Asylum, Wandsworth Common, where the doctor, who was a friend of my husband's, invited us to spend the day and dine with him, and he showed us over everything; but I know that I, for one, felt awfully glad when we left it; some of the faces that I saw there I can see now if I shut my eyes and think."[2] A family legend attributed his mental condition to a severe assault he received in Ceylon at the hands of disgruntled villagers, later followed by sunstroke during the Mutiny, but that is open to question. *The Guardian* (1895.ii.6) has a death notice: "Jan. 29, Malvern, Major Edward Joseph Netterville Burton, formerly Captain in Her Majesty's 87th Regiment of Foot."

Thomas Wright (1906) introduced several inaccuracies about E. J. N. Burton, confusing him with a cousin of RFB, Dr. Edward John Burton (1814-1897),[3] and incorrectly making him an army surgeon, errors which have been repeated many times in other biographies and cross-references: "In the meantime his brother Edward, now more Greek-looking than ever, had risen to be Surgeon-Major, and had proceeded to Ceylon, where he was quartered with his regiment, the 37th".[4]

Wright also gives the following family anecdote about the silence of Edward Burton, which he must have got from Dr. E. J. Burton himself:

> Every human device had been tried to lead him to conversation, and hitherto in vain. It seems that some years previous, and before Edward's illness, Dr. E. J. Burton had lent his cousin a small sum of money, which was duly repaid. One day Dr. Burton chose to assume the contrary, and coming upon Edward suddenly he cried:
>
> "Edward, you might just as well have paid me that money I lent you at Margate. I call it shabby, now."
>
> Edward raised his head and fixing his eyes on Dr. Burton said, with great effort, and solemnly, "Cousin, I did pay you, you must remember that I gave you a cheque."
>
> Thrilled with joy, Dr. Burton attempted to extend the conversation, but all in vain, and to his dying day Edward Burton never uttered another word.

---

[1] *New Army List* 1864.
[2] *Life*, vol. 1, p. 595.
[3] Son of the Rev. J. E. Burton, brother of Joseph Netterville Burton.
[4] Vol. 1, p. 82.

164. Burton, Joseph Netterville (1782?-1857).

Father of Richard Francis Burton, a Lieut. Colonel in the British Army. Son of Edward Burton (1747.iii.10-1794), see above. He saw action during the Napoleonic wars, in Egypt (1807) and in Italy (the taking of the heights of Genoa in 1814). He entered the 1st battalion of 31st Regiment of Foot as a Lieut. on Nov. 4th 1805, and was promoted to Captain in the 21st April 1814, as deputy assistant quartermaster general. He transferred into the 2nd battalion in 1814, but that was disbanded later in the year. After this he went on half-pay, rather than transferring back to the 1st, and went to live in Italy, where little is known of his activities. He returned to the Army only on the 20th May 1819, exchanging into the 33rd Foot, which was stationed on the Channel Islands and at Portsmouth. He married Martha Baker, second daughter of Richard Baker of Barham House Hertfordshire (see above), on March 2nd 1820, at St James Church in London.[1] (This puts to rest the elaborate speculation by Jon Godsall that the pair had eloped to Scotland to be married.) They were, as the *Morning Post* duly noted, married on a Thursday morning by the Dean of Chester.[2]

After his marriage, Joseph Netterville exchanged into the 37th Foot on Oct 19th 1820, going on half-pay. Although Jon Godsall confidently asserts that this was due to the 33rd Foot having just been posted to Jamaica, a feverish graveyard for European soldiers, this conjecture—which has no other supporting evidence—would at most explain why he *switched* regiments, and not why his new regiment agreed to put him on half pay.[3] The reason later given by his grand-daughter Georgiana Stisted, 'bronchial asthma', is more convincing.[4] With a sufficient supplement from his marriage he had no need to serve on full pay.

Joseph had a brother Francis who served as a surgeon in the army, in the 36th Regiment of Foot, and was present on St Helena with Bonaparte. Other siblings included Catherine, James Edward (who would enter the church) and John Campbell.

The Burtons produced two sons, Richard Francis (1821) and Edward Joseph Netterville (1823), and a daughter, Maria (1823).[5] The family

---

[1] *Public Ledger and Daily Advertiser* Saturday 04 March 1820, p. 4. Also, *Freeman's Journal* Thursday 09 March 1820, where the church is noted, and many other newspapers.

[2] *Morning Post* Friday 03 March 1820 p. 4. This is also stated by the *New Monthly Magazine*, Volume 13 (1820) p. 504.

[3] Godsall (2008).

[4] Stisted (1896), p. 4. Godsall is probably justified in dismissing the often-repeated family legend that the retirement was due to exceptional chivalry on the part of Joseph Netterville toward Queen Caroline, at whose trial he supposedly refused to testify.

[5] Born in Feb. 1823 at "Barnham(sic) Wood" according to *The European*

lived mostly in France and Italy, where it was cheaper, with occasional interludes in England. On the 10th January 1836, Joseph Netterville was promoted to Brevet Major.[1] (Brevet signifying that he had no actual men to command, an honorary title. His son would likewise become a Brevet Captain.) Finally he was promoted to Lieut. Colonel, on 11th Nov. 1855, in the 34th Foot.[2] He did not see active service again until his death at age 75, at his home in 20 Bennett-street, Bath, on 1857-ix-06.

165. Bushe, Charles Percy (1829-1898).

A Captain in the Royal Navy who was stationed in Paraguay.[3] He captained the *Linnet*, and left a reminiscence of Burton, who he had met there circa 1869—"he showed no active animosity against any sort of religion except one, the religion of his wife. For that he freely expressed contempt. I remember his telling me that she had a little shrine in her room, and that, on some occasion when they had a difference of opinion, he threatened that if she did not keep quiet he would 'pitch her joss-house out of the window.' "[4] Burton mentions him several times—"Mr. Gould had given me an introductory note to Lieutenant—now I am glad to say Commander C. Percy Bushe, commanding H.M.'s steamer *Linnet*. A man-of-war in miniature, and the only neutral ship here present, she is remarkable for trimness and neatness, discomfort and inutility."[5]

166. Butler, Alfred Joshua (1850-1936).

An Oxford-educated English historian, noted for his works on Egypt, especially *The Arab Conquest of Egypt and the Last Thirty Years of the Roman Dominion* (Oxford, 1902). He met Burton in Cairo circa 1880 and left a passing reminiscence—"I met him dining at Turabi's house, and Turabi afterwards told me that he was on board the same ship with Captain Burton bound for Alexandria, when the latter was about starting on his great journey."[6]

167. Butterworth, Alan (1864-1937).

An Indian Civil Servant, author of *Inscriptions on the Copper Plates*

Magazine, and London Review, Volume 83 (Feb. 1823) p. 187.

[1] He may have been in the 35th Foot at this stage.

[2] *The United Service Magazine*, Volume 79, p. 323. Godsall (2008) has the date as 1851 but that appears to be a mistake. See also *Bulletins and Other State Intelligence for the year 1855*, Part 2 p. 2391.

[3] See *Cheltenham College Register*, 1841-1889. (London: George Bell, 1890).

[4] See Volume 2.

[5] *Letters from the Battlefields of Paraguay*, p. 328.

[6] See Volume 3.

and Stones in Nellore District, *Some Madras Trees* and other books. He knew of Burton at second-hand through officers he met in India, but since Burton-sightings from this early period are rare, his hearsay is included in Volume 1.

168. Cameron, Verney Lovett (1844-1894).

A naval officer and explorer, born in Dorset. He joined the Navy in 1857, and served in the Abyssinian Campaign of 1868, and then on the East Coast anti-slavery squadron. While still a lieutenant, he volunteered to relieve Livingstone in 1873, but discovered shortly after setting out from Zanzibar that Livingstone was already dead, so he proceeded to cross Africa instead, recovering Livingstone's papers along the way, rounding the southern end of Lake Tanganyika, discovering the Lualaba River on its Western flank, and eventually reaching Angola in November 1875. He was therefore the first European explorer to cross through the middle of Africa from coast to coast, a journey he described in *Across Africa* (1877). He was promptly promoted to Commander in July 1876. This entire initiative annoyed the RGS, who did not anticipate the considerable expenses run up by Cameron, and were reluctant to reimburse him. He corresponded with Burton, who publicly pressed the RGS to reimburse the expedition, and they later formed a close friendship. Soon after his expedition, Stanley's dramatic journey down the Congo overshadowed his achievements.

Cameron later joined Burton on a gold prospecting expedition to West Africa in the early 1880s, collaborating on the book *To The Gold Coast For Gold* 2 vols. (1883). He had an extensive correspondence with Burton, and left an admiring reminiscence—"Going over ground which he explored, with his *Lake Regions of Central Africa* in my hand, I was astonished at the acuteness of his perception and the correctness of his descriptions."[1]

169. Cautley, Philip Proby.

Burton's Vice Consul in Trieste, succeeding Vice Consul Brock, who retired in 1883. He taught the now well-known author Italo Svevo (Ettore Schmitz) English, and was succeeded as a language instructor in Trieste by James Joyce. He resented the burden of work that he had to bear due to Burton's long absences from the Consulate. Cautley was also one of Thomas Wright's first-hand sources for his biography (1906).

170. Chaillé-Long, Charles (1842-1917).

An American soldier, explorer, diplomat and author from Princess

---

[1] See Volumes 2 and 3.

Anne in Maryland, the son of a planter. He was of French extraction, and due to his father's intervention had served in the Union Army during the Civil War, rather than with the Confederates.[1] Along with several ex-Confederates he joined the Khedive's Egyptian army in 1869, and was Chief of staff to General Gordon—though Gordon soon came to dislike him. He explored the upper reaches of the Nile and discovered Lake Ibrahim, but was invalided in 1877. He then studied at Columbia law school, and practiced law in Egypt—he also served as the US Consul to Korea. He wrote several books of travels, including *Central Africa: Naked Truths of Naked People* (1876) and an admiring reminiscence of Burton, with whom he had an active correspondence and a strong rapport. Chaillé Long had fallen out with the RGS after they elected to rename Lake Ibrahim to Lake Kyoga, and this 'outsider' status formed the initial basis of their attraction to each other, as well Burton's enduring hope that the Nile geography might eventually be upset.

171. Clodd, Edward (1840-1930).

An English banker and author, born at Margate, the son of a ship owner. He attended after-hours lectures at Birkbeck, University of London, becoming the sub-editor of *Knowledge* and a member of numerous London literary and scientific clubs and societies. This put him in contact with many travellers and leading scientific and literary figures of the day. He also contributed articles to several encyclopedias. Clodd knew Burton in the early 1860s through the Anthropological Society, and also through Dr. George Bird. He left a reminiscence of both men.[2]

172. Clouston, William Alexander (1843-1896).

A folklorist from Orkney, author of *The Book of Sindibad* (Privately printed, 1884) and *Popular Tales and Fictions: their Migrations and Transformations* (Edinburgh: Blackwood, 1887) which he dedicated to Burton, "the eminent scholar and world-wide traveller; whose notes to his complete translation of 'the book of the thousand nights and a night' are ample evidence of his interest in, and knowledge of, the genealogy of popular tales." Clouston also contributed notes to the *Supplemental Nights*.[3]

---

[1] See *The National Cyclopaedia of American Biography* Volume 10 by James Terry White, George Derby.
[2] See Volume 1.
[3] *Nights* Volume 6, p. 287.

173. Coghlan, William Marcus (1803-1885).

Political resident at Aden, later Commandant (1854-1863). He was the son of a Captain in the Navy, and was educated at Addiscombe, after which he joined the Bombay Artillery and served in Scinde. He succeeded James Outram at Aden in October 1854. On his retirement in 1864 he was knighted, and later promoted to General.

Burton had extensive dealings with Coghlan during the Somali Expedition of 1854-5 and several letters to him from the period survive.[1] Burton later blamed the failure of the Somali Expedition on what he described as Coghlan's apathy.[2]

174. Coimbra, Dr. Augusto Teixeira

A resident of Brazil. He was Burton's partner in a mining concession obtained from the Emperor of Brazil on 25th September 1868. This granted them mineral rights in the entire province of São Paulo. He is mentioned by Burton in *Highlands of the Brazil* in connection with diamonds: "I have only seen one in the Brazil, and that was brought from Rio Verde of São Paulo by my friend Dr. Augusto Tiexeira[3] Coimbra. It came to a bad end: he dropped it from his waistcoat pocket, and it was swallowed by a fowl." Burton referred to Coimbra often in his Brazil-related correspondence, e.g. "Coimbra I presume is heiress-hunting as usual. He'll marry some fat thing with a full pouch and a temper."[4] There is a book still extant in Burton's personal library associated with Coimbra.[5]

175. Coke, Henry John (1827-1916).

An English traveller and author, the son of the Earl of Leicester, and grandson of "Coke of Norfolk". He joined the Royal Navy as a cadet at age 11, becoming a Midshipman, and serving in China 1840-2. Wrote numerous books about his travels, including a popular account of his journey through the Rocky Mountains in 1850.[6] He knew the Burtons through Dr. George Bird, though it is not clear when they first met, and left a reminiscence—"Said he: 'I don't want to be mistaken for other

---

[1] See Volume 1.
[2] *Zanzibar* Vol. 1, p. 9.
[3] Sic. McLynn (1991), p. 114, incorrectly initials him "A. J."
[4] 1874/03/02. Richard Burton to Albert Tootal.
[5] Machado d'Oliveira, J. J. Geographia da provincia de S. Paulo ...[Sao Paulo, Typ. Imparcial de J. R. de A. Marques, 1862]. xiv, 122 pp. (A. T. Coimbra, Rio de Janeiro, n.d.). See Kirkpatrick (1978), 1849.
[6] See *Coke of Norfolk and his friends* Volume 2 by Anna Stirling (John Lane: London, 1908), pp. 502-3.

people.' 'There's not much fear of that, even without your clothes,' I replied."[1]

176. Colquhoun, Archibald Ross (1848–1914).

A colonial administrator of Scottish extraction, born in Cape Town but educated in Scotland and trained as a civil engineer. He was the first governor of Southern Rhodesia (1890-2), and was also a noted traveller and author in his own right. He met Burton through the London Social circuit in the early 1880s and left a short reminiscence—"His tales when the ladies had withdrawn—luckily in those days they always 'withdrew'—were 'scorchers' ".[2]

177. Crane, Walter (1845-1915).

An English artist and illustrator of children's literature, from an artistic family. He was associated with the William Morris' Arts and Crafts movement, and met Burton in the 1880s through Oscar Wilde, leaving a minor reminiscence—"One had the impression of a massive personality, and one with whom it would not be pleasant to quarrel".[3]

178. Davenport, The Brothers.

The Davenports, Ira Erastus (1839-1911) and William Henry (1841-1877), were American magicians from Buffalo New York who latched onto the mid Victorian craze for 'spirit phenomena.' Dr. J. B. Ferguson, part of their act, was also an American. Burton attended their performances in London, which, like most of his contemporaries he found impressive and hard to explain away. He mentioned the Davenports several times in his writings on Spiritualism and in his correspondence.[4]

179. Davey, Richard Patrick Boyle (1848-1915).

An English journalist from Norfolk, based from 1870-1880 in New York, and after that in England, where he wrote for the *Saturday Review* and the *Morning Post*. He was the author of *The Sultan and His Subjects* (1907) among other works, and appears to have met Burton in the 1880s—"You must face your true Asiatic with no sense of your own superiority, for one soon finds that he is in many ways a bigger man than

---

[1] See Volume 3.
[2] See Volume 3.
[3] See Volume 3.
[4] See for example 1864/10/12. Richard Burton to Monckton Milnes.

you. He is at least never a canting humbug."[1]

180. Dawson, Llewellyn Styles (1847-1921).

A Lieutenant in the Navy, sent by the RGS on a mission to relieve Livingstone in 1872, which was preempted by Henry Morton Stanley. After reaching Zanzibar and being told by Stanley that Livingstone had already been found, Dawson returned back to England, leading to some criticism of his conduct. Burton refers to him several times in his correspondence.

181. De Kusel, Samuel Selig (1848-1917).

A merchant and customs official at Alexandria, born in Liverpool. He was a Captain in East Surrey regiment, but was created a Baron by the Italians in 1890.[2] De Kusel met Burton on several occasions in Egypt in April 1878, and left a brief account.

182. De Leon, Edwin (1818–1891).

American diplomat and journalist of Jewish extraction. Served in the Confederate army in the US Civil War. He met the Burtons in Egypt in the late 1870s or early 1880s and left an account—"he was very superstitious, which is a common failing among people who have lived and been intimately connected with the nations of the East".[3]

183. Dennis, George (1814-1898).

A traveller and authority on the Etruscans, the self-taught son of an excise officer. He was the author of *A Summer in Andalucia* (Bentley: London, 1839) and a notable account of *The Cities and Cemeteries of Etruria* (Murray: London, 1848). He was the Consul at Crete, Sicily, and Smyrna. Burton met him in the mid-1870s when he was writing *Ultima Thule* and researching *Etruscan Bologna*, and referred to him optimistically—"the curious reader will consult my friend and colleague Mr. Dennis"—though Dennis did not take to him at all, writing snottily to his publisher John Murray "I don't feel at all honoured by being booked as his 'friend'. I only saw him once for 5 minutes when he called on me in Palermo while Lady Denman (not Isabella) was waiting in the carriage, and would not come in. He came to my backdoor, looked at my Arab horses, and was off. There is a friendship! But from what I have heard of his antecedents, he must be glad to claim any respectable

---

[1] See Volume 3.
[2] See his obituary in *Near East* Vol. 13 (1917), p. 631.
[3] See Volume 2.

individual, even tho' as insignificant as myself, as his 'friend'."[1]

184. De Ruvignes, Charles Henry Theodore Bruce (1829-1883)

A soldier and Colonial administrator. He joined the Army in 1846 and served in the Frontier Wars in South Africa, and then in Burma. He was Civil Commandant of Accra in the Gold Coast between 1857 and 1863—see *Wanderings in West Africa*.[2] Later he was involved in the Ashanti War of 1872. His name is sometimes given as 'Ruvigny,' since he was the 8th Marquis of Ruvigny & Raineval. He is often mentioned in Burton's correspondence connected with West Africa—see Volume 1.

185. De Ruvigny.

See De Ruvignes, Charles Henry Theodore Bruce, above.

186. Didier, Charles (1805-1864).

A partially-blind French traveller who encountered Burton shortly after his journey to Mecca, on his way to Aden by way of Suez. Didier's journals contain a record of this encounter—"On sighting Mr. Burton, our Indian recognised him at a glance, as he had seen him several months before on Mount Arafat, devoutly fulfilling, like himself, the ceremonies of the last pilgrimage."[3] He wrote and published poetry, novels and several travel books but committed suicide in 1864 after going completely blind.

187. Doughty, Charles Montagu (1843-1926).

A traveller and author, educated at King's College in London and at Cambridge, from where he graduated in 1864. He travelled in the Arabian Peninsula in the 1870s, proceeding south from Damascus in 1876 and ending at Jiddah in 1878. This led to his *Arabia Deserta* (Cambridge, 1888), a literary travel memoir written in an archaic style that he believed was best suited to the anachronistic subject matter, and which took him years to contrive. Doughty corresponded with Burton during the writing of the book, and his subsequent struggle to get it published.[4] Burton later wrote a critical review of *Arabia Deserta* for *The Academy*—"Mr. Doughty informed me that he has not read what I

---

[1] See D. E. Rhodes *Dennis of Etruria* (London: Wolf, 1973) pp. 113-5.
[2] Vol 2, p. 75, 153.
[3] See Volume 1.
[4] See Volume 3.

have written upon Arabia; and this I regret more for his sake than for mine".[1]

188. Drake, Charles Francis Tyrwhitt (1846–1874).

An archeologist and traveller, the son of Colonel W. Tyrwhitt Drake. He was educated at Rugby and Wellington College, and at Trinity College, Cambridge, though he did not take a degree. After he left Cambridge he travelled in Morocco, Egypt and the Sinai in the late 1860s, developing an interest in natural history and archeology He joined Professor E. H. Palmer on an expedition to Palestine in 1869. The Burtons met Drake and Palmer in Syria in July 1870, and after a joint archeological expedition Drake co-authored *Unexplored Syria* (1872) with them. He was at Nazareth with the Burtons when their party was involved in a fracas there. After Burton's recall, he visited them in Trieste. In 1874 he died suddenly of fever in Jerusalem. Burton left the affectionate reminiscence of Drake which appears in Volume 2—"He was my inseparable companion during the rest of our stay in Palestine, and never did I travel with any man whose disposition was so well adapted to make a first-rate explorer".

189. Du Chaillu, Paul Belloni (1835-1902).

An American explorer of West Africa, of French origin, who created a fierce controversy in 1861 after describing the previously-unknown Gorilla with some dramatic embroidery in his book *Explorations & adventures in equatorial Africa; with accounts of the manners and customs of the people, and of the chace of the gorilla* (New York, Harper brothers, 1861). At a meeting of the Ethnological Society in June 1861, Du Chaillu retaliated against one of his most vocal critics, T. A. Malone, from the London Institution, by spitting on him, but soon apologized in a contrite letter to *The Times*. At this time he met Burton, who came to his defence in public, and subsequently corresponded with him—"Du Chaillu showed no end of gratitude, came up from Scotland ... and accompanied me to the R.R. and en partant thrust into my hand something from which he told me to drink to his health—when opened it showed up a neat silver mug!"[2] Burton often mentions him in his correspondence, expressing far more skepticism about Du Chaillu's claims in private than he did in public—"Apropos of the latter Du Chaillu writes to propose a trading & hunting partnership with me—which I shall decline. I have now seen the very narrow field of his exploits."[3]

---

[1] Vol. XXXIV (1888-07-28), pp. 47-8.
[2] 1861/08/28. Richard Burton to Monckton Milnes.
[3] 1862/04/26. Richard Burton to Monckton Milnes.

190. Dunraven, Earl of.[1]

An Anglo-Irish newspaper correspondent and politician. He Served for a time in the Life Guards and in the Imperial Yeomanry, and was also an accomplished yachtsman. He left a brief reminiscence of Burton, though it is not certain when they first met—"Wilfrid Blount, with his Arab steeds and his oriental complex. Richard Burton, who prided himself on looking like Satan—as, indeed, he did, if Mephistopheles is a fair portrait—also with an oriental complex, but of a very different kind."[2]

191. Eames, William. James.

A surgeon in the Royal Navy, who served in the West Coast squadron on *HMS Bloodhound* and met Burton at Fernando Po. He went on to become Fleet Surgeon. Eames left a small reminiscence of Burton in a letter to a newspaper, stating that he had passed several months in his company—"He was, indeed, a man of iron will, and had a forcible manner of showing it".[3] Burton makes no mention of him.

192. Edwards, Henry Sutherland (1828-1906).

An English author and journalist who wrote for *Punch*, and collected descriptions of his travels as a correspondent in Russia, Poland and Prussia. He also wrote works of musical history and criticism. Edwards met Burton through the publisher William Tinsley in the early 1860s and left an after-dinner story—"Tinsley ... sent out for oysters and champagne, and before the second bottle was finished had agreed to give Burton (who had a head of iron) two hundred pounds more than he had originally asked".[4]

193. Edwards, John Passmore (1823-1911).

An English philanthropist and author, the son of a carpenter. He became a self-made newspaper proprietor and MP, but since he was ideologically a Manchester liberal, he declined offers of a knighthood. He claimed to have been challenged to a duel by Burton over the Du Chaillu affair, but simply ignored the challenge.[5]

---

[1] Windham Thomas Wyndham-Quin) (1841-1926).
[2] See Volume 3. Dunraven means Wilfrid Blunt.
[3] See Volume 3.
[4] See Volume 1.
[5] See Volume 1.

194. Eldridge, George Jackson (1826-?).

A solider who served in the British Army in the Crimea, and was present when Sebastopol fell. He was Consul at Kertch in 1856, and Erzeroom in 1862, then Consul-General at Beyrout from 1863 onward. He was Burton's superior when he was Consul at Damascus (1869-1871). He received the order of St. Michael and St. George in 1880, and was a Freemason in Palestine Lodge number 451. For some reason his name is often given as "S. Jackson Eldridge", even in official correspondence. Eldridge, while he kept up a friendly private correspondence with the Burtons, was critical of their activities to his superiors. RFB interpreted this as a betrayal: "I regret that I have not a single official letter from Mr. Consul-General Eldridge to put in. ... my surprise was extreme, when I found that he had been officially opposed to me on every great occasion."[1]

195. Elliot, Sir Henry (1817-1907).

A diplomat, the second son of the second Earl of Minto. He was educated at Trinity College, Cambridge, and appointed Ambassador at Constantinople between 1867 and 1877. He was Burton's superior when he was Consul at Damascus between 1969 and 1871. In 1877 Elliot was recalled from Constantinople due to concerns that he was too favourably disposed to the Turks—he was succeeded by A. H. Layard—and was placed at Vienna after this. His memoirs, which were published by his daughter as *Some revolutions and other diplomatic experiences* (1922)[2] make no reference to Burton.

196. Ellis, Alexander George (1858-1942).

Assistant-Keeper of the Oriental Books and Manuscripts collection of the British Museum, which he joined in 1883. He was the son of a civil servant and educated at Merchant Taylor's School in London. He studied semitic languages at Cambridge, gaining a first-class degree in 1881. He left the British Museum after 26 years, in 1909, to become sub-Librarian at the India Office till his retirement in 1930. See the obituary in the *Journal of the Royal Asiatic Society*.[3] Ellis corresponded with Burton about *The Arabian Nights*, *The Perfumed Garden* and related matters—see Volume 3.

---

[1] *The Case of Captain Burton* (1872), p. 16.
[2] London, John Murray.
[3] Vol. 74 (2) April 1942 pp. 153-4.

197. Erhardt, Rev. Johann Jakob (1823-1901).

A German Missionary from Württemberg, stationed at Mombas in East Africa from 1849-1855. He operated under the auspices of the Church Missionary Society, along with Johannes Rebmann, after which he went to India, 1856-1891, and then returned to Germany. Erhardt and Rebmann sketched the well-known "slug map" which combined the lakes in the African interior into one giant body of water, and was first published in the *Calwer Missionsblatt* (1855/10/01). Burton often referred to Erhardt, and corresponded with him,[1] but it is not certain if they ever met in person.

198. Faber, George Louis (1843-1915).

The British Consul at Fiume, author of *Fisheries of the Adriatic*, which was reviewed By Burton in the *Journal of the Royal Society of Arts*.[2] He was married to Alice 'Fanny' Krupp (1852-1938) of the Krupp arms manufacturing dynasty. Faber wrote a brief recollection of Burton, who he knew from nearby Trieste, in a letter to a newspaper—"he never disguised his feelings as regards the petticoat tribe, as he termed the priests".[3]

199. Fahie, John Joseph (1846-1934).

An engineer who worked for the Indo-European Government Telegraph Department, and wrote a notable *History of Wireless Telegraphy* (London: Blackwood, 1899). He corresponded extensively with Isabel Burton, and helped her to obtain subscribers to the *Arabian Nights*—"I am not surprised at what you tell me about your dream, Rich^d has a very magnetic effect upon certain temperaments, myself amongst a number of cases, but I know several people (men also) who have had dreams about him."[4] RFB put Fahie's name down for the long waiting list of the Athenaeum Club. See Eric Stanley Whitehead *A short account of the life and work of John Joseph Fahie* (Liverpool: Liverpool University Press, 1939).

200. Ferguson, Sir Samuel (1810-1886).

An Irish antiquarian and barrister, with interests in early Irish history and antiquities. He is now associated primarily with the "Irish Twilight" movement. He wrote *Ogham Inscriptions in Ireland, Wales and*

---

[1] See *First Footsteps*, p. 114.
[2] Nov. 9, 1877.
[3] See Volume 3.
[4] 1885/01/12. Isabel Burton to John Joseph Fahie. See Volume 3.

Scotland (Edinburgh: David Douglas, 1887) which was published posthumously. Burton was interested in Ogham inscriptions and corresponded with Ferguson. They may have met in 1878 when Burton was at the meeting of the British Association in Dublin.

201. Freeman, Edward August (1823-1892).

Regius Professor of Modern History at Oxford, author of *History of the Norman Conquest of England: Its Causes and Its Results* (Oxford: Clarendon Press, 1867–1879). He was notable for his political activism against the Ottoman Empire. He had been a contemporary of Burton's at Oxford in 1841[1] and corresponded extensively with him from the 1870s onward about political affairs in the Balkans.

202. Friswell, James Hain (1825-1878).

A prolific English novelist, essayist, journalist and editor, best known for his very popular collection *The Gentle Life: Essays in Aid of the Formation of Character* (London: Sampson, 1864). Friswell knew and corresponded with both of the Burtons extensively from at least the early 1860s, assisting with the production and publication of Burton's satirical poem *Stone Talk* (1865).

203. Friswell, Laura (1850-1908).

The daughter of James Hain Friswell (1825-1878), to whom Burton dedicated *Stone Talk* in 1865. She also published as Mrs. Ambrose Myall.[2] She knew the Burtons through her father in the early 1860s and left several reminiscences of them, though especially of Isabel—"there was a prince somewhere called 'dear Richard,' about whom she continually talked to my father and mother, and who was persecuted and oppressed".[3]

204. Furniss, Harry (1854-1925).

An Anglo-Irish cartoonist, illustrator and painter whose work appeared in the major London newspapers, including *Punch*. He later exhibited his own work and wrote several books of reminiscences. His connection to Burton was slight, through his brother-in-law, but he left a second-hand reminiscence which shows the long reach of Burton's popular reputation.[4]

---

[1] See Volume 1.
[2] *Times* 28 Dec. 1908, p. 9, col. C.
[3] See Volume 1.
[4] See Volume 2.

205. Galton, Sir Francis (1822-1911).

English polymath: traveller, geographer, meteorologist, statistician, geneticist and scientist.[1] Knighted in 1908. After his return from exploring South-West Africa, Galton met Burton at Dover, around January of 1853. Burton was staying there with his sister Maria Stisted. They were close friends through the 1850s and early 1860s, until the dispute between Burton and Speke produced a rift, after Galton had defended Speke in the columns of *The Reader*. They were reconciled in later years, as the correspondence reproduced in volumes 2 and 3 shows.

206. Geary, Grattan (?-1900).

A newspaperman of Irish origin, editor of the *Times of India* and later owner and editor of the *Bombay Gazette*. An Irish "Home-Ruler", he was also notable for his book *Through Asiatic Turkey* (Sampson Low: London, 1878). He was known as "The Fenian" within the European community in India.[2] Burton befriended him during his visit to India in 1876, and a substantial correspondence between the two survives. Burton used Geary extensively to place anonymous articles in the press.

207. Gerard, Cécile Jules Basile (1817-1864).

A French soldier and explorer who wrote reports from Dahome, and was later killed trying to get to Timbuktu. He styled himself the "lion killer". See his *The life and adventures of Jules Gérard* (William Lay, London, 1857). Gerard had visited Dahome in 1863, at the same time as Burton, who met him at Kana (though they had previously met on the boat from Europe to Madeira). Burton wrote that "He came to West Africa in the hope that his fame as a killer of lions had preceded him; but the only lion that can exist in that mouldy climate is the British lion, and even he is not a terrible beast to bring amongst the ladies. He expected to find Dahome a kind of Algiers, and he exchanged a good for a very bad country."[3]

208. Gessi, Romolo (1831-1881).

An Italian solider and explorer of Equatoria. He was employed by General Charles Gordon, and penetrated the upper Nile from the North, up to Lake Albert, in 1876. He caught fever on the Nile and died in Suez in 1881. His memoirs were published as *Sette anni nel Sudan egiziano* (Milano, 1891). Burton and Gordon often referred to Gessi in their

---

[1] See http://galton.org.
[2] See Pat Lovett *Journalism in India* (Calcutta: Banna, circa 1929).
[3] *Wanderings in Three Continents*, pp. 203-4.

correspondence, as Burton had pinned his hopes on Lake Albert having an influent from the South, from Lake Tanganyika.

209. Gordon, Major-General Charles George (1833–1885).

A soldier and martyr. From a military family, Gordon was educated at Woolwich in the Royal Military Academy, joining the Royal Engineers. He served in the Crimea with distinction, was promoted to Captain, but made his reputation in China, where he participated in the sack of Peking in 1860 and was promoted to Major. In the service of the Chinese government he suppressed the Taiping rebellion of 1863, and was promoted to Lieut.-Col. on his return to England in 1865. In 1873 he was given the governorship of the "equatorial regions of Central Africa", succeeding Sir Samuel Baker, taking up duties in 1874 at Gondokoro. In 1877 his authority was extended to the Sudan and Darfur, with suppression of the Slave Trade a stated goal. After enduring capture and hardship in the ensuing strife, he left the region and, after dabbling in China (again), Ireland and the Cape, was in 1883 en route to the Congo in the service of the Belgians when he was recalled and sent to the Sudan as Governor General to suppress the revolt of Madhi, a violent Islamic messianic eruption. He was killed at Khartoum in January 1885, after a long siege by the Madhi. Gordon corresponded extensively with Burton, and met both the Burtons in person several times. He attempted on several occasions to lure Burton to govern Darfur, but Burton refused.

210. Grant, James Augustus (1827-1892).

A Scottish soldier and explorer, companion of Speke on his final Nile journey (1860-3) which he described in his own account *A Walk Across Africa* (London: Blackwood, 1864). He saw service in the Sikh War of 1848-9, the Indian Mutiny of 1857, and the Abyssinian campaign of 1868, rising to Lieutenant-Colonel. Speke met him in India where they were in the Indian Army together. Grant joined the army in 1846, and became strongly attached to Speke. After the rift between Burton and Speke he maintained a life-long hostility to Burton, as the extensive correspondence with Speke and C. P. Rigby reproduced here shows. He seems never to have met Burton in person—" I have always felt bitterly towards Burton & declined to be introduced to him when asked by Mrs. Burton".[1]

211. Granville, Earl (1815–1891).

Otherwise known as Granville George Leveson-Gower, 2nd Earl

---

[1] 1890/06/26. James Augustus Grant to Sir Samuel Baker. See Volume 3.

Granville. He was leading figure in the Liberal Party, serving as Gladstone's Foreign Secretary between 1870 and 1874, and again between 1880 and 1885. He promoted a non-interventionist and conciliatory foreign policy It was Granville who recalled Burton from Damascus in 1871.

212. Graves-Sawle, Lady (1818-1914).

Born Rose Paynter. She was a friend of the poet Walter Savage Landor who dedicated works to her when she was a young woman. Later she married Charles Brune Graves-Sawle, 2nd Baronet (1816–1903). She met the Burtons in Vienna in 1873, where they were staying in the same hotel, and left a reminiscence—"She was very bright and pleasant; but her husband was generally silent, except when on the subject of his travels".[1]

213. Hale, Richard Walden (1871-1943).

An American lawyer and author, from Massachusetts. He graduated from Harvard Law School in 1895, founded the Boston law firm Hale and Dorr, and was also a friend of Oliver Wendell Holmes.[2] Hale's Great-Aunt Thesta Dana, with her husband and daughter, shared a stage coach with Burton in 1860 when he was travelling to Salt Lake City. Burton mentions the Danas several times in *City of the Saints* (e.g. p. 8, 185, 192). Sixty years later Hale published a pamphlet describing his family's memories, which he described as "private information", about the encounter.[3]

214. Hamerton, Atkins (1804-1857).

Consular Agent at Muscat in 1840 and subsequently Consul from 1841 to 1857, moving in 1843 to Zanzibar with the court of Sayyid Sa'id. He was born in Ireland at Donneycarney near Dublin, and joined the Bombay Army, in the 15th Native Infantry, as a cadet in 1824. In 1840 he made a notable journey across Northern Oman.[4] He spoke both Persian and Arabic,[5] and rose to the rank of Lieutenant-Colonel. Burton and Speke stayed at Colonel Hamerton's home in Zanzibar in 1856-7 while preparing for their East African expedition, and both later referred

---

[1] See Volume 2.
[2] See *Harvard College Class of 1892 secretary's report*, Issue 4 (1907).
[3] See Volume 1.
[4] *Bombay Secret Proceedings* 135, 1840/05/20. See Brian Marshall 'Atkins Hamerton' *New Arabian Studies*, Volume 2 (New Exeter Press, 1994), p. 26.
[5] Edouard Loarer 'Notes on Zanguebar' *Madras Journal of Literature and Science*, Volume 6 (1861), p. 91.

to him often, always in kind terms.

> I can even now distinctly see my poor friend sitting before me, a tall, broad-shouldered, and powerful figure, with square features, dark, fixed eyes, hair and beard prematurely snow-white, and a complexion once fair and ruddy, but long ago bleached ghastly pale by ennui and sickness. Such had been the effect of the burning heats of Maskat and 'the Gulf,' and the deadly damp of Zanzibar, Island and Coast. The worst symptom in his case—one which I have rarely found other than fatal—was his unwillingness to quit the place which was slowly killing him. At night he would chat merrily about a remove, about a return to Ireland; he loathed the subject in the morning. To escape seemed a physical impossibility, when he had only to order a few boxes to be packed, and to board the first home-returning ship. In this state the invalid requires the assistance of a friend, of a man who will order him away, and who will, if he refuses, carry him off by main force.[1]

After accompanying Burton's expedition to the coast, he died on board the ship *Artemise* en route back to Zanzibar, on the 5th July 1857, apparently of cirrhosis of the liver. Author of *Brief notes on His Highness the Imaum of Muskat; and the nature of his relations with the British Government &c.* Bombay: Bombay Education Society's Press, 1856.

215. Hamilton, James "Abbé" (?-1868).

Known as "Abbé Hamilton". A catholic convert, at one time he was based in Rome. Later he travelled extensively, and accompanied Charles Didier on his journey to Mecca.

> He had been born and bred a Protestant, and had turned Roman Catholic. This, he explained to me, was in the blood hereditary. For centuries his ancestors had all changed, the Catholics becoming Protestants, and the Protestants becoming Catholics. After his perversion the Abbe went to Rome, and there ran through a considerable fortune without obtaining the rank of "Monsignor," as he had desired. Shaking the dust of the Eternal City off the soles of his feet, he crossed over to Africa, and for a time became a student of the Koran, a follower of the Prophet, and lived in tents. He then settled at Tunis, and from that city journeyed to Cairo.[2]

He wrote several books of travel, including *Sinai, the Hedjaz and*

---

[1] *Zanzibar*, vol. 1, p. 35.
[2] Denis Bingham *Recollections of Paris* Vol. 2 (London: Chapman and Hall, 1896), pp. 253-4.

Soudan and *Wanderings in North Africa* (London: John Murray, 1856). He met Burton in Cairo, and Burton refers to him as 'Abbé Hamilton' in the *Pilgrimage* and elsewhere. Hamilton mentions their journey together in his *Sinai*. He is said to have been sentenced to death by the Bey of Tunis but, while en route to Istanbul for execution, bribed sailors to pass a message to the British Consul, who found him imprisoned in a barrel on the ship. Afterwards he settled in Paris, and was a noted antiquarian. He died at Pau in France, on 9th November 1868.[1] He is sometimes confused with James Hamilton (1814-1867) the Presbyterian minister and prolific author, who was not a traveller.

216. Hankey, Frederick (1821-1882).[2]

An English sado-masochist and bibliophile based in Paris, a son of Colonel Sir Frederick Hankey G.C.M.G. (1774-1855) of the 50th Foot and the Chief Secretary "Lieutenant Governor" of Malta, by his second marriage to "a lady who was a native of Corfu".[3] The Hankeys however were an extended clan of bankers, originally goldsmiths, rather than soldiers.

Frederick, who was born in Corfu, joined the Scots Fusilier Guards on 13th July 1841, after a brief spell in the Civil Service—he had been submitted for election to the Statistical Society on 19th November 1838, and was admitted as a fellow on the 19th December.[4] He purchased the rank of Lieutenant in the 63rd Regiment of Foot on 31st March 1843, and served in Malta as an aide-de-camp to Lieut.-General Sir Patrick Stuart. On the 8th of December 1846 he went on half-pay, presumably sick leave, in which state he remained until on the 16th June 1848 he switched regiments, buying into the 75th Foot as a Lieutenant. By the end of the year though he had completely resigned from the army, selling his commission. In the same year he moved to Paris, after which he must have immersed himself in bibliophilia. On the death of his father in 1855 he inherited the relatively modest sum of 4,000 pounds.

Hankey was introduced to Burton, at least as early as 1856, through Monckton Milnes, who used Hankey to procure clandestine erotic and

---

[1] See P.C. Finney, 'Abbe James Hamilton: antiquary, patron of the arts, Victorian Anglo-Catholic', in C. Entwistle (ed.), *Through a Glass Brightly: Studies in Byzantine and Medieval Art and Archaeology presented to David Buckton* (Oxford, 2003).
[2] See also Patrick Kearney 'Biographical Sketch of Frederick Hankey (1821-1882)' Scissors and Paste Biographies, June 2016.
[3] *Gentleman's Magazine*, 1855. She was a Catterina Valarmo (?-1835), sometimes given as 'Vaslamo' or 'Varlamo'. They were married in January 1819 in the Palace of Corfu.
[4] At that stage his address was Lower Berkeley Street, Portman Square.

deviant literature from Paris,[1] and who noted in his commonplace book for 1857-1860, "Hankey's love of cruel enjoyment & his strong sense of the wickedness of killing animals for food".[2] Hankey sometimes used the manager of the Covent Garden Italian Opera, Augustus Harris,[3] as a courier—Harris evaded customs officers by concealing objects in the small of his back. Burton visited Hankey when in Paris, and often referred to him, usually as "poor Hankey", in his letters to Milnes, joking about bringing him back the skin of a woman from West Africa when he was at Fernando Po. The letters to Milnes make it clear that Burton did not take Hankey too seriously. The noted collector of erotica H. S. Ashbee left the following description of him.[4]

> If ever there was a bibliomaniac in the fullest sense of the word it was Frederick Hankey. His collection was small, but most choice, and comprised objects (among others may be mentioned what he was pleased to call the sign of his house, viz., a most spirited marble by Pradier representing two tribades; he had also a beautiful bronze of a satyr caressing a woman, where caresses with the tongue are not usually bestowed; a ceinture de chasteté, an ivory dildo, &c.) and books, exclusively erotic. The former do not fall within the scope of the present work, nor did Hankey attach the same importance to them as he did to his books, which consisted of illustrated MS. the best editions and exceptional copies of the most esteemed erotic works, frequently embellished with original drawings, and clothed by the great French binders. The copies which were not in unsullied bindings of the time, he would have covered by Trautz-bauzonnet, or other binder of undoubted repute, and he designed himself appropriate toolings wherewith to embellish them. He frequently spoke of making a catalogue raisonné of his beloved books, but did not, I believe, put his project into execution.
>
> Hankey was in every respect an original; he never rose until

---

[1] See also *Ce n'est pas mon genre de livres lestes... : lettres inédites à Richard Monckton Milnes, Lord Houghton (1857-1865) / Frederick Hankey* ; édition établie, présentée et annotée par Jacques Duprilot et Jean-Paul Goujon. Miss Jenkins, 2012.

[2] James Pope-Hennessy *Monckton Milnes: the Flight of Youth* (New York: Farrar, 1851) p. 119.

[3] Augustus Frederick Glossop Harris (1825–1873) who lived at what was then 9 Pelham Place, Brompton, from 1852–63, and had once been imprisoned for bankruptcy.

[4] Pisanus Fraxi [H. S. Ashbee] *Catena Librorum Tacendorum*, pp. L ff. The confusing overly-footnoted and pedantic format used by Ashbee has been reformatted and rearranged here for clarity. Oddly, Pope-Hennessy is uncertain about the date of Hankey's death, even though it is clearly stated in Ashbee's book, which he refers to and quotes in part.

after mid-day, and his hours of reception were after 10 o'clock at night, when he was to be found among his books. He had fair hair, blue eyes, and an almost feminine expression, and answered in many respects to the descriptions which have reached us of the Marquis de Sade, his favourite author. He told me he had on one occasion recovered from a serious illness by suddenly obtaining an edition of Justine which he had long sought in vain. He had a curious habit of repeating himself, which at times rendered his conversation tedious. ...

It was the writer who had the satisfaction of introducing the editor of Le Livre[1] to the collector of the Rue Laffitte, March 9th, 1882. We had been dining together—Octave Uzanne, Felicien Rops and myself—when it was proposed to look up Hankey and spend the rest of the evening with him. We reached No 2 Rue Laffitte some time after ten o'clock, and found Hankey in his usual dishabille—short velvet coat, shirt without neck-tie, thin trowsers, thinner socks, and slippers. There was no fire or other artificial heat, in spite of the low temperature of the atmosphere. Knowing that I was in Paris, my visit was not altogether unexpected, but he would certainly have wished to receive my distinguished friends, especially the terrible creator of the Chevalier Kerhany, with more state. We were however appreciative guests, and restraint soon gave way to admiration in presence of Hankey's treasures; and our visit was protracted far into the night, or I should say following morning. ...

Son of Sir Frederick Hankey, and of his lady of Greek extraction, the subject of this notice was born at Corfu, while his father was governor of the Ionian Islands. He became captain in the Guards, and after retiring from active service, fixed his residence at Paris where he expired June 8th, 1882. A mutual friend announced to me his death in the following words: "Hankey our friend died suddenly before me last Thursday, he had begun to mend. He did not think his death imminent and he was not afraid. He suffocated, without having experienced apparent pain. We were close for 30 years, he was one of my best friends. He was buried last Saturday at the Pere Lachaise cemetery".[2]

An more unguarded reminiscence of Hankey by Ashbee was

---

[1] M. Octave Uzanne.

[2]. "Notre ami Hankey est mort subitement devant moi jeudi dernier, il avait commencé à se soigner. Il ne pensait pas sa mort si prochaine et il ne la craignait pas. ïl a été suffoqué, sans avoir éprouvé de douleur apparente. Nous étions très liés ensemble depuis 30 ans, il était un de mes meilleurs amis. Il a été enterré samedi dernier au cimetière du Père Lachaise."

recorded in his diary, in the entry for 8th April 1875:[1]

> Spent the afternoon & evening with Mr. F. Hankey among his unique volumes. His collection is small, but each vol. is a gem either of rarity or choice binding. Hankey himself is a remarkable man, quite a study, he appears to me like a second de Sade without the intellect. He has given himself up body & soul to the erotic mania, thinks of nothing else, lives for nothing else. Nothing is bawdy enough for him, whether in expression, thought or design. Besides his books, all of which are erotic, this is a sine qua non with him, he has two of the most charming erotic statues which exist, & is further surrounded with ... every other obscene object possible to be procured. Hankey himself I should take to be about 50 years old, lean, tall, with yellow hair, a white skin, & soft blue eyes, a good forehead, & yet his expression is entirely devoid of energy or determination. In his youth he must have been good-looking, but effeminate, much as the Marquis de Sade is pictured to have been.

The brothers Goncourt met Hankey in Paris in 1862, and without naming him explicitly left their own description of him in their famous Diaries, entirely unaware of the possibility that their legs were being pulled.[2]

> Monday, 7 April. - Today I visited a madman, a monster, one of those men teetering on the abyss. Through him, like a torn veil, I glimpsed an arsenal of abomination, a frightening side of an aristocracy, inured to money, the English aristocracy ferocious in lust, with that licentiousness satisfied only by the suffering of women. At the Bal de l'Opera, a young Englishman was presented to St. Victor, and to open the conversation told him simply "we do not have as much fun in Paris, London was infinitely superior, in London there was a fine house, the house of Mrs. Jenkins, where there were girls of about thirteen, who were first given lessons and then whipped, the small ones not very hard, oh! but the large ones quite hard. You could also push pins into them, not very long pins, just as long as that," and he showed us the tip of his finger. "Yes, we saw the blood! ..." The young Englishman insouciantly continued: "I am cruel by nature, but I balk at men and animals ... Once, with an acquaintance, I rented a window for a large sum, to see a murderess who was to be hanged, together with some women to assist us—his expression always very decent—at the moment

---

[1] James Pope-Hennessy *Monckton Milnes: the Flight of Youth* (New York: Farrar, 1851) pp. 119-120. The diary has never been published.

[2] Goncourt *Journal*. April 7 1862. pp. 26-29. The translation is rough and loose, as the published English edition does not include this entry.

when she would be stretched. We even suborned the executioner to yank her skirt up when he dropped her! ... But unfortunately the Queen, at the last moment, pardoned her."[1]

Today St. Victor introduced me to this novel monstrosity. He is a young man of about thirty years, balding, bulging temples like an orange, eyes clear and sharp blue, with translucent skin revealing a subcutaneous web of veins, head—it's odd—resembling one of those young priests, emaciated and ecstatic, surrounding bishops in old paintings. An elegant young man with a little stiffness in the arms and mechanical body movements, feverish as if attacked by the beginnings of a disease of the spinal cord, well-bred with fine manners and exquisite gentleness.

He opened a large, lofty cabinet, containing a curious collection of erotic books, beautifully bound, and while handing me a MEIBOMIUS, *Use of flogging in the pleasures of love and marriage*, bound by a first-rate bookbinder of Paris with interior tooling representing phalluses, skulls, and tools of torture, which he designed himself, he said: "Ah! this tooling ... no, first the bookbinder would not do it ... So I lent him my books ...Now he makes his wife very unhappy ... he chases little girls[2] ... but I had my tooling." And showing us a book ready for binding: "Yes, for this volume I still expect a skin, a skin of a girl ... a friend of mine got me ... You see the tan ... it takes six months to tan ... Do you want to see my skin? ... But that's irrelevant ... would have preferred it to be stripped from a live girl ... Fortunately, I have my friend Dr. Bartsh[3] ... you know, the one who travels in the interior of Africa ... fine, in the massacres ... he promised to procure me a skin like that ... from a living Negress."

And contemplating, with a manic look, the nails of his hands outstretched before him, he speaks on, he speaks continuously, in a small sing-song voice, stopping and faltering between you, insinuating a cannibalistic spell into your ears.

The human body is not so immutable as it appears to be. Societies and civilizations reinvent the form of the nude. The woman depicted in the Cannibal by Cranach,[4] the woman of Parmesan and Goujon, the woman of Boucher and Coustou are of three ages and three female natures. The first depiction, an

---

[1] Revealing an obvious joke.
[2] A most unlikely story.
[3] Dr. Heinrich Barth, a confusion made by the Goncourts, since Hankey had asked Burton to do this and Barth was not in Africa then.
[4] A woodcut by Lucas Cranach the Elder (1472–1553), "The Werewolf or the Cannibal".

embryonic outline, rough-hewn in Gothic sparseness, is the woman of the Middle Ages. The second form, elongated, svelte in her slenderness, with scrolls and arabesques, Daphne branching, is the Renaissance woman. The last, small, plump, dimple-grammed quail-chick, is the woman of the eighteenth century.[1]

Algernon Swinburne also knew Hankey, no doubt through Monckton Milnes, and in July 1869 wrote to a friend that "He is *the* Sadique collector of European fame. His erotic collection of books, engravings etc. is unrivalled upon earth—unequalled, I should imagine, in heaven. Nothing low, nothing that is not good and genuine in the way of art and literature is admitted. There is every edition of every work of our dear and honoured Marquis. There is a Sapphic group by Pradier of two girls in the very act—one has her tongue up où vous savez,[2] her head and massive hair buried, plunging, diving between the other's thighs. It was the sculptor's last work before he left this world of vulgar corruption for the Lesbian Hades. May we be found as fit to depart—and may our last works be like this".

In Paris Hankey appears to have had an interest in an insurance company, "Compagnie d'Assurances sur la vie Impérial", which the Hankey banking family had been involved with since at least the 1850s. By 1865 he was listed on their board in their advertisements, billed as a member "of the House of Hankey, London"—previously an "A. Hankey" had been listed by there. He was also involved with a woman named "Annie" to whom he may have been married, or perhaps she may just have been his mistress. Her full name appears to have been "Angelina Sophie Vernon Beckett." He makes a brief appearance in Felix Whitehurst's *My Private Diary during the Siege of Paris*: "saw Fred. Hankey to-day, wandering about in the original white trousers which he used to wear in the guards in 1848—period of last revolution," and "When the French advanced into the park of Malmaison, they found none thousand Prussians opposed to their three thousand selves; then, as an old Guardsman—Frederick Hankey—observed, of course 'they retired in the greatest order'."[3]

After Hankey's death, Burton dedicated Volume 6 of the *Nights* to him: "A Message to Frederick Hankey / Formerly Of No. 2, Rue Lafitte, Paris. / My Dear Fred, / If there be such a thing as 'continuation,' you will see these lines in the far Spirit-land and you will find that your old friend has not forgotten you and Annie."

---

[1] Here the Goncourts appear to have indulged in a philosophical rumination.
[2] You know where.
[3] Felix Whitehurst's *My Private Diary during the Siege of Paris* (1875) pp. 174, 268.

217. Hare, Augustus John Cuthbert (1834-1903).

English author, popular biographer and minor watercolour painter. Born in Rome, and educated at Harrow and University College, Oxford, he wrote many European travel guide books based on his tours abroad, and a prolix six-volume series of memoirs *Story of My Life* (1901). He was a lifelong bachelor, well-connected socially and known as a raconteur. He met the Burtons in the early 1870s at Lady Ashburton's,[1] and also knew of them through Mrs. Adelaide Sartoris, the actress whose recollections of meeting Burton and Swinburne in Vichy 1869 he repeated in his memoirs.

218. Harris, Frank (1856-1931).

Journalist, editor and notorious author. Born in Ireland of Welsh parents, but absconded to America as a teenager, eventually graduating in law at the University at Kansas and qualifying for the Kansas Bar. He returned to England in the early 1880s and edited the *Evening News* and the *Fortnightly Review*. Adopted socialist/anarchist politics, writing a novel, *The Bomb* (1908), romanticising anarchist violence. His imaginative book of memoirs *My Life and Loves* (1925), in which he cast himself as a sexual Olympian, was banned for some time, combining humourless pornography ("love juice", "man-root"), with colourful anecdotes about the rich and famous he claimed to have known. Harris first met Burton in the early 1880s, through Verney Lovett Cameron, after Burton returned from the Gold Coast, and later visited him in Trieste.

219. Herne, George Edward (1822?-1902).

Member of Burton's Somali Expedition of 1854-5. Served the Punjaub campaign of 1848-49, including the siege of Mooltan, and the battle of Gujerat. He was present at the surrender of the Sikh army at Bawul Pindee, and took part in the pursuit of the Afghans to the Khyber Pass (awarded the Medal with two Clasps). He was also a photographer, and many of his Indian scenes may be found in the British Library collections. Attained the rank of Lt. Colonel. His prior military career reads: Ensign 11 Dec. 40; Lt. 24 Jan. 45; Capt. 4 Aug. 55; Major, 14 June 64. Retired to Gesto Villa, Wardie, near Edinburgh.

220. Hockley, Frederick (1809-1885).

A British crystal-gazer and follower of the Occultist Francis Barrett. He was a friend of Kenneth R. H. Mackenzie and the British

---

[1] *Life*, Vol. 2 p. 135.

Rosicrucians. He met Burton in 1852 through Captain (later Rear-Admiral) Henry A. Murray, and sold him a crystal and mirror, which Burton wanted as part of 'medical' armoury, to take with him on his pilgrimage to Mecca. He claimed to have communicated with Burton remotely, from London to Cairo, through the mirror. There is a brief reference to him regarding magic mirrors in Burton's Lecture to the Spiritualists of 1878.[1]

221. Hodgson, Colonel Studholme (1805-1890).

Soldier and author, from a military family, many of whose members had confusingly similar names (he was the son of General John Hodgson). Entered the army in 1819, eventually rising "General Officer Commanding" Ceylon in 1865,[2] and the rank of General in 1876.

Hodgson also wrote the travel book *Truths from the West Indies* (William Ball: London 1838). According to *The Christian Remembrancer* the author was "a furious Whig-Radical,—a decided enemy of the Established Church,—and, for reasons best known to himself, a bitter enemy of the planter."[3] Hodgson attacked the planters for their moral conduct and sexual liaisons.

He was the (natural) father of Studholmina Letitia Marie Hodgson (1833-1902), who later gained a following as an authoress under the name Madame Bonaparte-Ratazzi (or "Cainille Bernard", "Baron Stock" etc.) and kept a literary salon in Paris. The mother was Princess Letizia Bonaparte (a daughter of Napoleon Bonaparte's brother Lucien), who had married Sir Thomas Wyse, an Irish politician, in 1822. Apparently Hodgson "rescued" the Princess from a suicide attempt, prompting the affair. In 1853 the *Gentleman's Magazine* reported the marriage of "Lieut.-Col. Studholme Hodgson, son of the late Gen. and grandson of the late Field Marshal Studholme Hodgson, to Caroline, relict of Sir John Palmer Bruce Chichester, Bart, of Arlington court, Devonshire."[4] They do not appear to have had any children by the marriage.

Hodgson is also believed to have been the clandestine author of sado-masochistic literature. It seems that he started an extensive collection of this material when he was stationed in India. It is not clear

---

[1] *Life*, Vol. 2, p. 148.
[2] Hodgson's full military record: Ens. 30 Dec. 19; Lt. 3 Feb. 25; Capt. 30 Dec. 26; Major, 28 Dec. 38; Lt. Colonel 8 Aug. 45; Colonel, 20 June 54; Major General, 11 April 60; Lieut. General,29 Aug. 68; General, 2 Feb. 76; Colonel 4th Foot, 21 Nov, 76.
[3] *The Christian Remembrancer* 1839: 74.
[4] Lady Chichester, Caroline, daughter of Thomas Thistlethwayte, of Southwick Park, Hants. Married, first. 1838, Sir John Palmer Bruce Chichester, first baronet; and second, 1853, Colonel Studholme John Hodgson. Died in 1897. (Annual Register, 1897)

exactly when he met Burton, but it was probably in the early 1850s, perhaps even earlier, in India. Hodgson, in a letter to Monckton Milnes, wrote that he had given away his collection of curiosities when he was married, and that Burton had received some of the material, which Hodgson now thought was lost.[1]

> I am sometimes sorry that I distributed among friends, on my marriage, a collection of books & sundries which no money could purchase, nor a single life gather together. I had got them mostly from persons in the higher walks of life too happy at some period or other to get rid of them. Those I presented to Burton are lost forever, being probably in the possession of the Priests of Meccah, & he poor fellow is I fear in the regions from whence no one returns. Did you hear he had been assassinated?

This was most likely part of the material that Burton later lost in the Grindlay's Warehouse fire of 1861 or 1862 and throws some light on the sources of Burtons material for the first time.[2] As Milnes recorded in his commonplace book, Burton described Hodgson to him as a sadist "delighting in cruelty", adding "[What a sheik he would have made! Which refinement of torture and pleasure wld. he have invented?".[3] Burton's correspondence with Milnes often refers to Hodgson, but show that they were not in frequent contact.

---

[1] See Volume 1, Hodgson to Milnes, 1855/—/—.

[2] Burton claimed to have lost a great number of "Eastern manuscripts" (i.e. erotica) he had stored at Grindlay's warehouse, in a fire in the early 1860s. Though Isabel later tried to show him shrugging his shoulders at this loss (she reports him saying "Well, it is a great bore, but I dare say that the world will be none the worse for some of those manuscripts having been burnt"), Hitchman has him furious instead, which was probably closer to the truth. It seems that Grindlay performed this service for many in the Indian army. The company was located at 54 Parliament Street SW1. Ironically, the Grindlay company sold fire insurance. According to Francis Hitchman, *Richard F. Burton* Volume 2 (London: Sampson Low, 1887) p. 448., "Burton's connection with Sind ended unhappily. At the sale of the Amir's Library in which the most valuable MSS. went for a song, he had bought a large stock and expended not a little time and study in preparing them for translation; but when setting out for Salt Lake City in 1860 he confided them to his then agents, Messrs. Grindlay and Co., who charged him with warehouse dues, but most improperly forgot to warn him that the goods that were warehoused were not insured. The result was a fire, which destroyed the labours and collections and costumes of nineteen years. The house was insured, but he never got any redress. One of the silly employes, seeing disgust strongly marked on his face, asked him fatuously if he had lost any plate—the only object of value he could imagine." This fire is mentioned in *Punjab Record*, Volume 8 Part 1 (WE Ball: 1873) p. 183. Civil Judgment in the case of Smallpage, November 1873.

[3] Mendes (1993) p. 11.

1862/04/26. Remember me with love to the amiable trio Hodgson, Bellamy and Hankey—when shall we all meet again?

1863/03/29. I left Hodgson the Guv'r sweating under the pangs of a balked ambition & I should be glad to hear that he has ejected the irrelevant matter.

1865/10/23. Hodgson will like Ceylon—Lady Bruce I hear has gone with him.

1871/09/26. I walked on Sunday with old Hodgson—as jolly as ever.

1873/11/05. What has become of tall Colonel?

Burton later dedicated Volume 1 of the *Supplemental Nights* to Hodgson: "To whom with more pleasure or propriety can I inscribe this volume than to my preceptor of past times ; my dear old friend, whose deep study and vast experience of such light literature as The Nights made me so often resort to him for good counsel and right direction? Accept this little token of gratitude, and believe me, with the best of wishes and the kindest of memories."

Hodgson settled at Argyll Hall, Torquay, where he died on 31st August, 1890. Isabel records in the *Life*, presumably from Burton's diaries: "On the 31st August he deplores the death of his friend, General Studholm[sic] Hodgson".[1]

Since the publication of Peter Mendes' survey of *Clandestine Erotic Fiction*[2] Hodgson has started cropping up in books which deal with Victorian pornography and sexuality, credited as the author of *An Experimental Lecture on Flagellation* by "Colonel Spanker", subtitled *Descriptive of the exciting and voluptuous pleasures to be derived from crushing and humiliating the spirit of a beautiful and modest girl, delivered in the assembly room of the society, Mayfair*. A full description of this work, which was written circa 1878, is given by HS Ashbee ("Pisanus Fraxi"). Even Ashbee, who must have read more of this sort of thing than almost anyone else, found it revolting; his full description is appended below. However, Mendes has muddled the attribution of this work, associating it in passing, on pp. 4 and 5, with Hodgson, but attributing it under his main entry for the book (p. 245) to the pornographic publisher William Lazenby, based on a note by Ashbee stating that "the publisher is the author". Likewise, Mendes' summary entry for Hodgson (p. 11-2) does **not** attribute The *Experimental Lecture* to him. He is credited instead with likely authorship, jointly, of *The Pleasures of Cruelty* (1886) and *Revelries! and Devilries!* (1867). The mistake is significant, since the *Experimental Lecture* appears to be on a different level, as far as this type of material goes. With the permission of his son, Ashbee's own copy of it was destroyed at the turn of the

---

[1] *Life* Vol. 2: p. 404.
[2] Aldershot: Scolar Press, 1993.

century by the British Museum, which kept only the French translation in its private case of forbidden material. One should note also that the attribution of the *Pleasures* to Hodgson does not have any specific evidence to support it, though it is surely plausible.

The use others have made of this misattribution is enlightening. James McConnachie confidently tells us that Hodgson "gloried under the sobriquet of Colonel Spanker—at least until promoted to the rank of General"[1]. No citation is given, but Mendes was probably the basis for this embroidery. Ian Gibson repeats it more cautiously, stating that Hodgson *appears* to have been the author, and cites Mendes explicitly.[2]

Ashbee describes *Revelries and Develries* as follows, attributing it to "four Oxford men and an officer in the army".

> Revelries! and Develries!! or Scenes in the Life of Sir Lionel Heythorp, Bt. His Voluptuous Emotions, and Emissions : His Amorous Peculiarities : His Peccant Penchants, for the Bottoms of Bleeding Beauties : and many other strange diversions, never before narrated and now selected, from the Private Diary of the Baronet. With fine Coloured Engravings. London:-Printed for the Booksellers.
>
> 8vo. ; size of paper 6s by 44, of letter-press a by 3 inches ; two lines on the title-page; pp. 123 in all; 7 coloured plates, and a frontispiece with two naked women holding birches, and five bare buttocks ; all badly done, and most obscene ; published by W. DUGDALE, in 1867.
>
> It is the joint production of four Oxford men and an officer in the army, whose names must not be divulged; they each wrote a story and then patched them together, making a continuous narrative in three chapters.
>
> In Revelries and Devilries there is, as the title promises abundance of flogging, besides other episodes of the most disgusting nature, not the least remarkable and revolting of which is a visit to a lunatic asylum, in which the erotic idiosyncrasies of the patients are portrayed in the crudest fashion. The volume terminates with A Night in the Borough, chapter the third, an orgie as filthy and crapulous as any dreamed by DE SADE in his wildest moments. Although the obscenest words and expressions are employed, the style is rather above the average of such books.

Ashbee also gives the following description of *An Experimental Lecture on Flagellation* by "Colonel Spanker",[3] for those who have the

---

[1] James McConnachie *The Book of Love*: p. 89.
[2] Ian Gibson *The Erotomaniac*: p. 66.
[3] Pisanus Fraxi [H. S. Ashbee]. *Catena Librorum Tacendorum*.

stomach.

Size of paper 5 1/2 by 4 1/8, of letter-press 4 5/8 by 2 7/8 inches; no signatures; pp. 81; toned paper; a line on the title-page; a frontispiece with portrait of the heroine, under which are her name and four lines of verse, and 11 coloured, obscene plates, in outline, rough in drawing and execution, by four different artists; price £4 4S.; issue 75 copies; date incorrect, the book having been issued in 1878-79. The work is comprised in two parts, although a third part was contemplated, to provide for which the last page, p. 81, was struck off in duplicate, the one terminating with "End of Part the Second," the other with three additional lines marrying the heroine, and the word "Finis." It is from the pen of the publisher.

Of this strange performance, "done for a peculiar school of flagellants, who delight in extreme torture," and "written to order, in obedience to a regular framework of instructions."

He then gives a description by a third party: "I offer, in preference to any further description of my own, a very thorough analysis kindly furnished me by a brother bibliophile".

The Experimental Lecture treats, as its title denotes, of the extasy which is supposed to be found in cruelty, both moral and physical.

The emotion of voluptuousness can only be excited by two causes, firstly, when we imagine that the object of our desire approaches our ideal of beauty, or when we see this person experiencing the strongest possible sensations. No feeling is more vivid than that of pain, its shock is true and certain. It never misleads like the comedy of pleasure eternally played by women, and seldom really felt. He who can create upon a woman the most tumultuous impression, he who can best trouble and agitate the female organisation to the utmost, will have succeeded in procuring for himself the highest dole of sensual pleasure.

These remarks contain the quintessence of the whole philosophy which is found argued to exhaustion in the notorious volumes of the Marquis de Sade, where he, in his wild dreams of bloody orgies, phlebotomy, vivisection and torture of all kinds, accompanied by blasphemy, lays so much stress upon the moral humiliation of the victims employed. What he craves for is physical enjoyment caused by the lingering torture to which his unfortunate patients should be subjected, and which generally ends in their death. In this little work, our flagellants succeed in reducing their experiment to the customs of the present day, embracing a long series of torments that are wilfully inflicted upon one person, a sensitive and highly educated young lady. In Justine and Juliette, the number of individuals employed in the orgies and the constant murders, preclude all idea of reality, while here the whole process is so methodically and tersely set out, that we may almost fancy that all is founded on strong facts, the story being so graphically brought home to the astonished reader.

Are we thus to believe that we daily rub shoulders with men who take a secret delight in torturing weak and confiding women, and by so doing can produce erection and consequent emission? Experience proves this to be so, and we could unfortunately quote several recent cases where girls have been tied up to ladders, strapped down to sofas, and brutally flogged, either with birch rods, the bard hand, the buckle-end of a strap, and even a bunch of keys! Some have been warned beforehand that they will be beaten till "the blood comes," pecuniary rewards being agreed upon, others have been cajoled into yielding up their limbs to the bonds and gags by the promise that it is "only a piece of fun." Once fairly helpless in the hands of the flagellating libertine, woe betide them. These cowards are bent on inflicting the greatest amount of agony possible, and their pleasure is in proportion to the damage done. They seem sometimes at that moment like devils unchained, and howl with delight almost as loudly as the poor girl cries out in pain. And yet immediately their paroxysm is over, they will treat their wretched victim with the utmost kindness, and buttoning up their frock-coats, appear once more as affable, kind gentlemen, for they are all gentlemen by birth who indulge in this awful mania.

Such proceedings are bad enough in all conscience, but what can be said of one who derives pleasure "in crushing and humiliating the spirit," besides the body? According to Colonel Spanker's horrible theory, we may suppose that no enjoyment can be found in whipping the callous posterior of a match girl, who has been used to rude corrections at the hands of her parents, but only from exposing the delicate nakedness of a real tenderly-nurtured lady, whose mind has been carefully cultured. In order to carry out this diabolical idea, the Colonel rents a house in Mayfair and forms the Society of Aristocratic Flagellants which includes "at least half-a-dozen of the most beautiful and fashionable ladies of the day."

So we see that the author considers that females are also pleased with a little occasional cruelty practised upon one of their own sex. Our blueblooded viragoes are tired of vulgar, consenting victims, who submit to be tortured for the sake of lucre, so the Spanker fiend decoys "a young lady known to most of them, Miss Julia Ponsonby, a lovely young blonde of seventeen, whose widowed mother being compelled to go abroad for a time, is seeking for a suitable lady to whose charge she can entrust her daughter during her absence." The suitable lady is merely a procuress to the Society, and Miss Julia soon finds herself a prisoner in the house in Mayfair, the conservatory of which is fitted up as a Lecture Hall, where in the midst of flowering plants, fountains, and other luxurious surroundings, stands the apparatus "something like a large pair of steps, only made of mahogany," to which the victims are attached when undergoing punishment. [Similar in construction to The Berkeley Horse, of which an engraving will be found at p. xliv of *Index Librorum Prohibitorum*] The Colonel appears on the scene, and after tantalizing Julia, who treats him with the scorn he deserves, begins by terrifically slapping her naked bottom, then takes other "dreadful liberties," and sends her to bed. The next morning he awakes her, rod in hand, and despite her shame and terror, assists at her toilette, which he aids by sundry cuts with the birch. When half dressed, he forces her to walk up a ladder, holding open her own drawers, while strokes of the merciless birch enforce obedience. Her executioner makes her stand on her head against the wall, and then leaves her. She is now decked out in an elegant ball costume, and after being flogged with a ladies' riding whip on the bare shoulders, is presented to the eagerly expectant company of flagellants: six ladies in masks and dominoes, and four gentlemen with false beards. The Colonel now expounds his ideas and theories, interspersed with blows, to which Julia has to submit, and he gives the whole secret of the delight of flagellation, much more fully explained than we have ever met with it before. She is now forced to submit to the indecent caresses of all the company, the little whip is put into requisition once more, and she is slowly undressed, being still tortured at every stage of her toilette. She is pricked with a pin, pinched, and made to recount several erotic experiences of her school-days. Miss Debrette, one of the company, is now placed upon the horse, and Julia is forced to flog the lady, who likes it exceedingly, although ill-treated until she bleeds all over. More frightful indecencies, to prove that "the floggee as well as the flogger experiences voluptuous pleasure," are perpetrated, and now begins what the Colonel grimly calls "flagellation in earnest." Julia is tied up to the ladder with her back to the rungs, and this concludes the first part. The second portion opens by the relation of Miss Debrette's experiences of flagellation. A male member of the company follows suit, and after their cynical and extraordinary confessions, Julia is tortured again, a bundle of stinging nettles being now used. Her position on the ladder denotes the manner in which this vile description is given. She is turned with her back to her pitiless audience, and after more tales of torture related by the Colonel, she undergoes fresh anguish from a kind of cowhide, until she almost faints. They play leap-frog over her poor bruised back, and after that variety to their disgusting entertainment, we are treated to a story of a wife who was humiliated and brutalized on her wedding night. Now a leather scourge tipped with fine steel points is called into play while the victim is turned upside down on the ladder. A general melee takes place, which is utterly impossible to describe; suffice it to say that each gentleman flagellant satisfies the lascivious feelings which all this cruelty is supposed to excite, of course at Julia's expense. She has again to suffer a fearful onslaught with a heavy riding-whip, and a still greater torture than all-she is brutally ravished, with every addition of bitter humiliation and savage cruelty.

This book, which we can fairly assert is the most coldly cruel and unblushingly indecent of any we have ever read, stands entirely alone in the English language. It seems to be the wild dream, or rather nightmare, of some vicious, used-up, old rake, who, positively worn out, and his hide tanned and whipped to insensibility by diurnal flogging, has gone mad on the subject of beastly flagellation. The above analysis only gives the scaffolding of the work, as we have avoided copying any of the details, which are too minutely erotic for our pen. The boldest descriptions are given, and every stage of the poor girl's agony, every movement, blush and shriek are dwelt and expatiated upon. Her beauty forms the subject of the most violently crude remarks, and nothing seems left undone to prove that only a Nero or a de Sade can really enjoy the slightest sensual enjoyment. We may console ourselves by thinking that the book is too deliberately horrible to be dangerous, for this mixture of gloating debauchery, inseparable from mental anguish, and bodily, cold-blooded, slaughter-house ill-usage, is merely a highly-coloured, over-wrought phantasy of obscene ideas. It is well written, and the author has evidently taken great pains to bring out every point into proper relief, as if he intended to convince the reader of the absolute reality of the repulsive system he so amply expounds.

222. Hooker, William Jackson (1785-1865).

Eminent Botanist, traveller, Gentleman-scientist, and Fellow of the Royal Society. Author of many scientific books, and the scientific travel narrative *Tour in Iceland* (1809). Burton corresponded with Hooker, being known to him since at least the early 1850s, when still in India, and sent him botanical specimens and queries. Hooker had no formal botanical training before becoming Professor of Botany at Glasgow University, between 1820 and 1840, through the influence of Sir Joseph Banks. Subsequently he was Director of Kew Gardens, where he was succeeded by his son Joseph Dalton Hooker (see below).

223. Hooker, Joseph Dalton (1817-1911).

An eminent English botanist and explorer, who trained in medicine at Glasgow University, and was the son of the botanist Sir William Jackson Hooker (1785-1865), whom he succeeded as Director of the Royal Botanical Gardens at Kew. After qualifying as a doctor at Glasgow he joined the Ross Expedition to the Arctic, between 1839 and 1843. He was elected a Fellow of the Royal Society and became a close confidant of Charles Darwin. Burton mentioned both Hookers frequently in his works and corresponded with Joseph Dalton Hooker about plant specimens, but the principal connection between the two was a result of the Gustav Mann affair (see the entry for Mann below).

224. Hunt, George Samuel Lennon.

British Consul at Pernambuco and Rio de Janeiro. He was a member of the Anthropological Society and the Royal Geographical Society (1861). "Lennon" is sometimes given as "Lennox". Burton uses "Lennon"—see *Highlands of the Brazil* vol. 1, p. 20. Burton met Hunt in Brazil and mentioned him often in his correspondence with Albert Tootal (see Volume 2).

225. Hutchinson, Thomas Joseph (1820-1885).

Consul at Callao in Peru, previously Governor of Fernando Po in 1857, then Consul (and briefly acting Governor) till Burton replaced him. Burton had crossed his path in South America in 1868, see Hutchinson's reminiscence in Volume 2, from his memoir *Two Years in Peru* (London: Sampson Low, 1873). Hutchinson published several other books, including *Impressions of Western Africa* (London: Longmans, 1858), dealing with his time at Fernando Po.

226. Hyndman, Henry Mayers (1842-1921).

English journalist and socialist, son of a barrister. He remembered meeting Burton several times in the company of George Percy Badger, most likely in the late 1870s or early 1880s (see Volume 3). Isabel Burton mentions him in her AEI "Mr. Hyndman has lately startled the India House by his shocking details concerning the semi-starvation of India. In English society people say, 'Nonsense ! India poor! why, it was never richer.' But this certainly will be altered and remedied as soon as it is made known. I am John Bull enough to believe that England never sins with her eyes open."[1]

227. Ionides, Luke (1837–1924).

Stockbroker, from a wealthy Greek family in London who were known as patrons of the arts. Son of Alexander Constantine Ionides (1810-1890). Ionides knew Whistler, William Morris, Swinburne and others. Married Elfrida Elizabeth Bird, a daughter of Dr. George Bird, who had been raised by Bird's sister Alice "Lallah" Bird. Burton met him in London in 1869, most likely through Dr. Bird, shortly before going to Damascus, and both Burtons maintained a long correspondence with him. The Burtons tried to interest Ionides in their Gold mining scheme in Midian, hoping that he would put up capital for a stock-boosting exercise. He left an important memoir of the Burtons (see Volume 3).

228. Iturburu, Atilano Calvo.

Assistant Judge and Secretary to the Spanish Government of Fernando Po. Translated Prescott's *Ferdinand and Isabella*, and Livingstone's *Missionary Travels and Researches in South Africa*, into Spanish. Accompanied Mann and Burton on their December 1861 to January 1862 climbing expedition in the Cameroons mountains, described in Burton's *Abeokuta* (1863). Burton often mentioned him in his correspondence with Frank Wilson (see Volumes 1) and part-dedicated *Mission to Gelele* (1864) to him.

229. James, Frank Linsly (1851-1890).

An explorer and botanist from Liverpool, of American parentage. Between 1884 and 1885 James travelled in the horn of Africa with James Godfrey Thrupp (1849-1913), a surgeon known for his service in the Zulu wars, collecting botanical specimens. They met Burton in Cairo en route to the horn, describing the encounter in their subsequent book *The*

---

[1] Isabel Burton, AEI, p. 144.

Unknown Horn of Africa (1888, see Volume 3), which Burton had an annotated copy of in his personal library.[1]

230. Johnston, Sir Harry (1858-1927).

Explorer and colonial administrator of Scottish extraction, who had studied at King's College in London at the Royal Academy. He received the gold medal of the RGS, and while serving as a colonial administrator became a prolific travel writer, colonial historian and novelist. He was the first Commissioner of Nyasaland (modern day Malawi) and briefly administered Uganda at the turn of the 19th century. He met Burton in London in 1885, through Oswald Crawfurd, and idolized him, leaving an affectionate reminiscence in his memoirs (see Volume 3). Isabel recorded that on their visit to London in 1888 "we had the pleasure of seeing our friend H. H. Johnston, Consul in West Africa and artist, one of the most charming and sympathetic of men."[2]

231. Jones, Herbert (?–1928).

Of Irish extraction. Originally intended to train as an artist but his eyesight failed. Chief Librarian at the Central Library in Kensington, 1887-1924. Began his career at James Heywood Library, 106 Notting Hill Gate as an assistant. See the obituary in *The Library World*, 1929. Jones left a notable description of Burton's personal library and his activities as a book collector (see Volume 3), though it is not clear if he ever met him.

---

[1] Kirkpatrick (1978), 1604.
[2] *Life* Vol. 2, p. 362.

Portraits

Figure 1. Wilfrid Scawen Blunt

Figure 2. Dr. F. Grenfell Baker.

Figure 3. Samuel Selig de Kusel.

Figure 4. Earl of Dunraven.

Figure 5. Frank Wilson.

Figure 6. James Hain Friswell.

Figure 7. Joseph Dalton Hooker.

Figure 8. Sir Harry Johnston.

Figure 9. Colonel Chaillé Long.

Figure 10. Edward Thomas McCarthy.

Figure 11. Justin McCarthy.

Figure 12. The Tichborne Claimant.

Figure 13. Ouida.

Figure 14. Albert Leighton Rawson.

Figure 15. Algernon Swinburne.

Figure 16. Frederick James Stevenson.

Figure 17. Cecil John Rhodes and protégés, including Alex. Colquhoun.

Photograph taken at Kimberley, May, 1890.

Some pioneers in making South Central Africa British:
Left to right standing: J. A. Grant, John Moir, Joseph Thomson.
Left to right sitting: Rochfort Maguire, H. H. Johnston, Cecil Rhodes, Alex. Colquhoun.

Figure 18. Gustav Mann.

Figure 19. Julian Arnold.

Figure 20. Armin Vambery.

266 Portraits

Figure 21. John Passmore Edwards.

Figure 22. Verney Lovett Cameron

Figure 23. Verney Lovett Cameron.

Figure 24. Francis Galton.

Figure 25. Lord Houghton (Monckton Milnes).

Figure 26. John Hanning Speke.

Figure 27. Lord Redesdale (Bertram Mitford).

Figure 28. Charles Francis Tyrwhitt Drake.

Figure 29. Dr. Norton Shaw of the RGS.

Register: K-Z

232. Kingsford, Anna Bonus (1846-1888).

Animal rights campaigner, vegetarian, feminist and theosophist, closely associated with Edward Maitland (1824-1897). She studied medicine in Paris and obtained a qualification there, but suffered from poor health herself. Kingsford and Maitland met the Burton in the late 1880s in London, and Maitland left a brief reminiscence (see Volume 3).

233. Kirby, William Forsell (1844-1912).

A self-educated lepidopterist, linguist and folklorist from Leicester, who worked in the Natural History Department of the British Museum from 1879 until his retirement in 1909. He was the son of a banker. Author of a translation of a Finnish epic *Kalevala: The Land of Heroes* (1907), *An Elementary Text-book of Entomology* (1885) and several other scientific works. He assisted Burton when he was writing the *Arabian Nights*, supplying the Bibliography of the various editions of the Nights which appears in the tenth volume, and other appendices.

Kirby had written to Burton in 1885 to volunteer information about the Nights and they developed a productive working relationship. However Kirby was not overawed by Burton and complained to Thomas Wright that "At the British Museum, Burton seemed more inclined to talk than to work. I thought him weak in German and when I once asked him to help me with a Russian book, he was unable to do so. ... He told me that he once sat between Sir Henry Rawlinson and a man who had been Ambassador at St. Petersburg, and he spoke to one in Persian, and the other in Russian, but neither of them could understand him. I have never, however, been able to make up my mind whether the point of the story told against him or against them. Although Burton was a student of occult science, I could never lead him to talk about crystals or kindred subjects ; and this gave me the idea that he was perhaps pledged to secrecy. Still, he related his experiences freely in print."[1]

234. Kirk, John (1832-1922).

A physician, naturalist and explorer from Scotland, trained at the University of Edinburgh. Kirk served in the Crimean War as a physician, then accompanied Livingstone on his Second Zambezi expedition from 1858 to 1863. Went to Zanzibar as medical officer, eventually becoming Consul General in 1873. Vice-President of the RGS 1891-4. Published widely on Botany and Zoology. Burton maintained a friendly correspondence with Kirk (see Volume 2) and mentioned him frequently

---

[1] Wright Vol. 2 (1906), pp 79-80.

in his works concerning Africa.

235. Kirkwood, Roy.

Possibly from Glasgow. In charge of English Factories at Glasstown and Olomi in West Africa. Also resident agent for the Glasgow firm of Taylor and Laughland in West Africa. Burton had extensive contact with him when he was consul at Fernando Po and mentions him frequently in his correspondence with Frank Wilson; he is also mentioned in *Two Trips To Gorilla Land* (1876).[1] Apparently the factories burned down in a rum fire, which a missionary interpreted as just reward for Sabbath trading: "You will recollect that in my letter of last month I noted the landing of goods on the Sabbath. The same week, a vessel belonging to the same firm landed ten thousand gallons of rum. Last Monday night, or rather at half-past one o'clock Tuesday morning, we were startled from sleep by an unusual sound. I thought for a moment that it was on the mission premises, but looked out and saw a factory on fire. Three and a half tons of powder had exploded, and in a few moments that 10,000 gallons of rum was sending fiery flames towards heaven, and pouring streams of fire into the river. Blessed flames those, which kept the people at a distance, or I know not what would have been the consequence! In the course of one half hour, Taylor, Laughland, & Co.'s factory was entirely consumed. To the leeward of this was R. Kirkwood's factory, which went, and Dolluer, Potter, & Co.'s followed,—all in ashes in less than one hour; more than $50,000!".[2]

236. Krapf, Johann Ludwig (1810-1881).

German missionary, traveler and linguist, a Lutheran trained at the Basel Missionary Institute, from Tübingen in the Protestant dominated Württemberg, His book *Travels, Researches, and Missionary Labours in Eastern Africa* (Stuttgart, 1858; London, 1860) described his time in Ethiopia (1937-1842) and the Mombas Mission (1844-1845), under the auspices of the Church Missionary Society.

At Mombas Johannes Rebmann was a colleague, and after Rebmann saw a snow capped mountain when travelling in the interior in 1848, Krapf travelled to see Mount Kenya and Kilimanjaro the following year. Their reports caused prolonged controversy in Europe, where it was thought that snow was unlikely in the Tropics, and some proposed that the missionaries had only seen sun glinting off rocks.

The Mombas Missionaries were ultimately vindicated, but they had less success in the sphere of religious conversion than they did in the

---

[1] pp. 6, 17.
[2] *The Missionary Herald at Home and Abroad*, Volume 66 (1870), p. 219.

geographical, and Krapf returned home, discouraged, to settle in Germany in the late 1850s, though he continued to make occasional trips back to Africa until his death in 1881.

Burton met Krapf in Cairo in 1853, when Krapf was en route to Europe, and mentions him several times in correspondence with Norton Shaw (see Volume 1). That meeting encouraged Burton's first serious interest in the Nile sources.

237. Larking, John Wingfield (1801-1891).

Merchant at Alexandria, Consul from 1838-1841, succeeding Robert Thurburn, a relative by marriage. He was son of John Larking (1755-1838) of Clare-house, Maidstone, Kent, who had been Sherif of Kent in 1808 and had married Dorothy Style. Larking was also an Egyptologist, collecting antiquities, and a keen gardener. On his retirement to England in 1858, he settled in semi-Oriental style in "The Firs," Lee, Kent.[1] Burton stayed with Larking in Alexandria on his journey to Mecca in 1853, in a "little detached pavilion" in the large garden of the Larking/Thurburn residence "The Sycamores", on the Mahmudiyah canal, having met him en route to Alexandria onboard the *Bengal*.[2] It was Larking who got him a passport "Through ignorance which might have cost me dear but for friend Larking's weight with the local authorities, I had neglected to provide myself with a passport in England."[3] Larking was married to Rosina Teresa Elizabetta Tibaldi (1805-1866) who died in England at the Firs.[4]

Burton frequently mentions Larking, a fellow member of the Athenaeum Club, in correspondence, and Volume VII of the Nights is dedicated to him, as "an old and valued friend". Thus to Norton Shaw he wrote "If you see Larking pray give him my best salaams & tell him my throat is all safe still. What fun we had on board the steamer!" (1853/11/16).

See the obituary by his gardener in *The Gardeners' Chronicle*.[5]

238. Laughland, Edward.

A trader at Fernando Po, employed as the West African agent of the Glasgow firm of Taylor and Laughland, though according to Burton he was actually no relation to John Laughland, a partner in the firm. John Laughland had been Acting Consul in 1861 before Burton's arrival, with Edward as his Secretary, but had gone back home to Glasgow, leaving

---

[1] Boase *Modern English Biography* 1898.
[2] *Wanderings in Three Continents* (1901), p. 11.
[3] *Pilgrimage* Vol. 1, p. 19.
[4] *The Gentleman's Magazine*, Volume 220 (1866), p. 929.
[5] May 23, 1891, p. 653.

Edward as the firm representative for West Africa.[1] Edward Laughland was subsequently a Vice-Consul for Burton in Fernando Po during his frequent absences, and is most notable for his role in the "Brig Harriett" affair.

The "Harriett" had been the property of William Johnson, a British subject from Sierra Leone, and on his death in May 1863 was put up for sale by his heirs—Pratt, Taylor and Jarrett, all of Sierra Leone—to recover claims against the estate. The ship had put into Fernando Po in distress in May 1863 and had been declared unseaworthy. Laughland was Acting Consul at the time and assumed charge of staffing and provisioning the ship himself while it was laid up in the harbour. In August of 1863 Burton was mailed Power of Attorney by the heirs to sell it, but it is not clear exactly when he saw the request, as he was away for most of this period. He sold the ship at auction on November 21st, just after returning from the Congo, with his factotum Selim Aga acting as auctioneer, then left for Dahome It was bought by none other than Edward Laughland himself, ostensibly acting for William Brash and James Dick of the firm William Taylor and Company, Glasgow. He paid just 280 pounds for it.[2] Brash and Taylor were apparently proxies for the firm of Laughland and Taylor, and so it had really been sold to the Laughland business network.

Laughland however paid no money to the ship's owners, taking possession of the ship and refitting it. After the heirs repeatedly demanded payment, through the Foreign Office and Burton, Laughland countered with a list of expenses he claimed, on behalf of Taylor and Laughland, for provisioning the ship from May 2 to November 23,

---

[1] Godsall (2008) insists on truncating his name to "Laughlan", and proposes to correct Burton's own spelling of it, a mistake copied by Newman (2011), but his name was certainly Laughland with a 'd', as the Foreign Office documents in the National Archive show (FO 84/1147), and that is also how Burton always referred to him in his correspondence (see Volume 1)

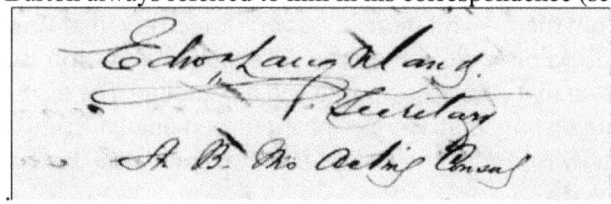

[2] A notarized *copy* of the bill of sale is in the National Archives records (FO 97-438). Both Mary Lovell (1998) and James Newman (2011) state that the signature on the document is not in Burton's hand, but it is not the *original* document, so that is a non sequitur. It is also not the case, contrary to Lovell, that Burton claimed to have simply deputized the sale to Laughland and therefore was not involved in it. His submissions to the F. O. show that he was directly involved in it, and that the part played by Laughland was as buyer, not seller.

including salmon, lobster, claret, brandy, potted meats and other items.[1] The list of expenses, which stretched back before the death of Johnson, amounting to just over 309 pounds, with another 11 pounds in commission. This meant that the heirs actually *owed* 40 pounds to Laughland and Taylor. In effect, he had seized their asset. The heirs promptly engaged a lawyer, William Rainy, to fight the case. Rainy, who was of mixed race, was hostile to Burton, having taken strong exception to his comments about Sierra Leone and (what he described as) its litigious population, in *Wanderings in West Africa*.

The F. O. held Burton liable for the 280 pounds and docked his salary to get the money back. After appeals and counter-appeals to the Foreign Secretary, the West Coast Commodore was asked to conduct an enquiry at Fernando Po, and his report strongly argued that Laughland had contrived to deliberately overcharge for the maintenance of the Harriet, also suggesting that the auction itself was rigged, since the ship was soon back at sea with minimal refitting after Laughland had bought it, despite its advertised unseaworthiness. All this was an abuse of Laughland's role as Vice Consul. The report did not find Burton in any way personally connected with any of this. Before the auction, Burton had been away on private business (his trip to the Congo River), during which time he was responsible for the actions of his Vice Consul. However, the problem for the Foreign Office was that after the auction was concluded, during the time the purchase money was at issue, Burton was away at Dahome on *official* business, making the claim that he was solely responsible for the actions of his Vice Consul problematic.

A compromise was ultimately reached whereby the Foreign Office agreed to repay Burton 400 pounds for repairs he had made out of his own pocket to the run-down Consulate at Fernando Po, from which the 280 pound charge from the "Harriett" sale was deducted. Laughland was also barred from acting as Consul ever again. Burton responded furiously that both he and Laughland had acted properly at all times, and that neither he nor Laughland were asked to submit evidence at the inquiry—they were not there—and moreover, very forcefully, that Rainy was scoring political points out of the case. Technically Burton may have had a point, given that Rainy had published a pamphlet *The Censor Censured* (1865) suggesting that Burton profited personally from the transaction, but that was irrelevant to the issue at hand, as the F.O. immediately concluded.

From the evidence in the Foreign Office files, which is all we have to go on, it is hard to avoid the conclusion that Edward Laughland deliberately abused his official position to make a windfall—the ship's Captain during this period was actually one of his own employees, and moreover denied receiving more than a portion of the wages that

---

[1] The complete list of expenses is given in Rainy (1865)

Laughland expensed for him. There is no reason to believe that Burton received any money himself from the affair, which the F.O. accepted at all stages. The problem was that Burton was responsible for Laughland's actions when he appointed him to act in his name while away on private business.

239. Leighton, Frederic (1830-1896).

Wealthy and highly regarded English painter and sculptor, associated with the Pre-Raphaelites, who had studied art on the Continent and was the son and grandson of physicians. President of the Royal Academy in 1878, he was accorded the title of Baron Leighton of Stretton in 1896. He is noted for his portrait of Burton, which was painted at various sittings at Leighton's house in 2 Holland Park Road between 1872 and 1875, and finished in 1876. Leighton holidayed with Swinburne and the Burtons at Vichy in 1869, and later visited the Burton's former cottage at Salihiyyah, outside Damascus, with Charles Tyrwhitt Drake, in 1873—after they had been recalled to London. It is possible that Swinburne, who was closely connected with the Pre-Raphaelites, introduced the Burtons to Leighton, or that they first met in Vichy through Mrs. Sartoris; Leighton may have thought of painting Burton as early as that meeting of 1869.

Leighton started his well-known portrait, now on display in the National Portrait Gallery, in 1872, for no fee. Isabel remembered that "Sir Frederick Leighton began to paint Richard on the 26th of April, and it was very amusing. Richard was so anxious that he should paint his necktie and his pin, and kept saying to him every now and then, 'Don't make me ugly, don't, there's a good fellow;' and Sir Frederick kept chaffing him about his vanity, and appealing to me to know if he was not making him pretty enough."[1]

According to Edgcumbe Staley, "Leighton made up his mind—firmly as was his wont—how he meant to paint his subject. Burton's will was no less inflexible; so, to put Leighton on his mettle, he kept on looking up from the position in which he had been placed, and by violent contortions of the face jeopardized the idea Leighton had formulated. Now and then he interrupted the solemnity of the sitting by remarking with mock gravity, 'Mind you make me nice!' Leighton responded by hearty laughter."[2]

Leighton only completed the portrait in 1876 and exhibited it at the Royal Academy. Burton also helped Leighton to procure the Arabic tiles he used to decorate his unusual house in Kensington, now a museum, and when they were in London often visited him. Correspondence

---

[1] *Life*, Vol. 1, p. 596.
[2] E. Staley *Lord Leighton of Stretton* (London: Walter Scott, 1906) pp. 106-7.

survives between the two men (see Volume 2).

240. Levant Herald.

Burton liked to place articles in newspapers under pseudonyms, a practice he started in India (or perhaps earlier) and kept up all through his career. While stationed in Damascus he published a stream of articles as "Our Correspondent" in the *Levant Herald*. These articles were full of inside information and had Burton's fingerprints all over them ("Holy Land on the brain", the war in Paraguay etc.) despite some obfuscation. Isabel helped to write many of these, and kept copies with spelling corrections by Burton and her own annotations (one such annotation is "not from us", indicating that the others were). An intriguing sequence of these articles, several of which are about a violent altercation involving Isabel, is given in Volume 2.

241. Leveson, Henry Astbury (1828-1875).

English sportsman, author and soldier, attaining the rank of Major. Fought in the Crimean War, but criticised its conduct. Served with Garibaldi in 1860, and raised a native corps in Lagos in 1863. Invalided by a bullet wound which never healed, but nevertheless accompanied Napier's expedition to Abyssinia in 1868. Wrote many accounts of his hunting exploits as "H. A. L., the Old Shekarry". See the Memoir of Leveson by "H.F." in Leveson's *Sport in Many Lands* [1] Leveson visited Burton at the consulate in Fernando Po in the 1860s and left a reminiscence, see Volume 1.

242. Lynslager, James (1810-1864).

A Governor (Superintendent) of Fernando Po, 1854-1855. Burton refers to him several times by his nickname "Daddy Jim". According to the trader John Whitford:[2]

> The successor to Governor Beecroft, who officiated until the Spaniards took charge, was called sometimes Governor James Lynslager, but oftener "Daddy Jim." He was a native of Holland, was wrecked when a boy and cast forth from the sea with a broken leg, and therefore became addicted to a wooden one. He waxed wealthy, married a black wife, in accordance with the rites of the Church of England, of which he was a strict member, and, as a mark of welcome and friendship to his numerous acquaintances, was

---

[1] Volume 1 (Chapman and Hall: London, 1877).

[2] *Trading Life in Western and Central Africa* (Porcupine: Liverpool, 1877), pp. 309-10. See also Cecil Holt 'A Note on the John Holt Archives' in *Journal of the Historical Society of Nigeria* Vol. 1, 1957, pp. 154-5.

wont to suddenly unship his timber limb and throw it at their heads. He was a most hospitable but very eccentric host. If a dinner prepared for guests did not suit his idea of correctness, he did not hesitate to destroy it, which spoliation invariably caused at first surprise, followed by merriment. After this he naturally insisted upon "pot luck," which was thoroughly enjoyed. It did not matter whether those whom he entertained were admirals or skippers; if anything went wrong "Daddy Jim" drew the cloth, and nobody could prevent subsequent assault and battery upon somebody blameable, unless, by stealing his loose leg, he was reduced to hopping about like a lame rooster. I met him shortly before his death at the '62 Exhibition, and waited to catch the leg, as, upon observing African features, he at once, full of joy, reclined upon a sofa and placed his hands convenient to loosen his missile, but, suddenly recalling to mind that he had mounted a cork substitute, curiously fastened and concealed by a broadcloth cover corresponding with the genuine article, his display of feeling found vent and satisfaction in the nearest refreshment-room. When the Spaniards came, "Daddy Jim" retired into private life, after which Hutchinson, Burton, Charles Livingstone, brother to the great African explorer, and Hopkins, succeeded as British consuls […]

243. Mackenzie, Kenneth Robert Henderson (1833-1886).

Kenneth Robert Henderson Mackenzie was a Freemason from Deptford in London, the son of a surgeon. He was a member of both the Anthropological Society and the Royal Asiatic Society, and is often mentioned in their journals. He also knew the spiritualist Frederick Hockley. Author of *Burmah and the Burmese* (2 volumes, 1853), a *Life of Bismarck* (1870), and the *Royal Masonic Encyclopedia* (1877). Mackenzie was a member of the Cannibal Club, but may have known Burton at an earlier date, possibly through Hockley. He claimed that many of the Cannibal Club members were Freemasons.

244. Mann, Gustav (1836–1916).

German botanist, originally from Hanover, who was employed at Kew Gardens. Mann took part in an expedition to West Africa to collect specimens, in the early 1860s, at the direction of Sir William Jackson Hooker, the Director of Kew Gardens. Mann met Burton in Lagos, when Burton had just arrived on the West Coast in 1861, and they agreed to explore the volcanic Cameroons mountains together. In December of 1861 to January 1862 a joint expedition with the Rev. Albert Saker was successfully made, but led to a minor controversy between the two men when Mann claimed that Burton had unfairly understated Mann's role in the expedition, and Burton claimed that Mann had tried to steal the honour by breaking an agreement to set off together to climb the highest peak. Mann later returned to Germany in 1892 after working for nearly 30 years in the Indian Forest Service (1863-1892).

245. Markham, Sir Clements Robert (1830-1916).

English Artic explorer, author, and geographer, the son of a Vicar. He joined the Royal Navy as a cadet in 1844, and served on the relief mission of 1850 to search for Sir John Franklin, whose doomed expedition of 1845 had tried to find the Northwest Passage. He left the Navy to work in the India Office, leading an expedition to Peru in search of cinchona quinine-bark, and joining the Abyssinia Expedition of 1867, among others. He was an influential member of the Royal Geographical Society, replacing Norton Shaw as Secretary in 1863, and eventually becoming the president in 1893. His is chiefly remembered for his enthusiastic support of exploration expeditions, rather than educational initiatives he considered "doctrinaire". Author of many books, including *Franklin's Footsteps* (1852), *Travels in Peru and India* (1862), and *The fifty years' work of the Royal geographical society* (1881).

Markham knew Burton well through the RGS and left an important reminiscence (see Volume 3) in his unpublished history of the RGS. He also collaborated with Burton through the Hakluyt Society. Some correspondence between the two men survives (see Volume 2).

246. Martin, Sir James Ranald FRS (1796-1874).

Founding Fellow of the Royal College of Surgeons. Born in the Isle of Skye, trained at St George's Hospital and the Windmill Street School of Medicine. Influential Surgeon in the Bengal Army, 1817-1842. He retired to London, was knighted in 1860, and died of bronchitis at Upper Brook Street in 1874. Author of, among other works, *On the Influence of Tropical Climates on European Constitutions* (1841). See J. Fayrer *Inspector-general Sir James Ranald Martin* (London: A. D. Innes, 1897). Burton met Martin at Bathurst and mentions him in *Wanderings*.[1] The extant correspondence suggests they were on friendly terms (see Volume 1).

247. Massey, Gerald (1828-1907).

Poet, Journalist, autodidact and amateur Egyptologist who was interested in psychic talk and spiritualism. Born in Tring to an illiterate labourer and a pious mother, he was forced to earn a living in the mills

---

[1] pp. 148,155,166,169,182.

at an early age. After moving to London, where he worked as an errand boy and at other menial jobs, he educated himself entirely through reading on and off the job. In early adulthood he was attracted to Chartism and to the Christian Socialism of F. D. Maurice. He initially made his name through multiple books of politically-aware poetry, but could not earn a living and was only financially secure after he was awarded a Civil List pension in 1863. By then he had moved to Edinburgh, and taken up Spiritualism. In later years he switched to long theosophical treatises on the supposed Ancient History of Egypt, starting with the *Book of Beginnings* (London: Williams & Norgate, 1881) and culminating in the twelve volume *Ancient Egypt: The Light of the World* (London: T. Fisher Unwin, 1907). Burton and Massey corresponded extensively about Camoens and Egyptology, and he appears often in the *Book of the Sword*. Several annotated copies of Massey's books were retained in Burton's personal library. Burton may have met him through meetings of the Spiritualist Society, which Burton was invited to address, and occasionally contacted (in more traditional ways, i.e. written letters).

248. McCarthy, Edward Thomas (1856?–1943).

English mining engineer, graduated from the Royal School of Mines in 1877. Died at age 86 in Swindon, after a long career in mining North America, West Africa, China, Australia, New Zealand, South America and South Africa. Met Burton in West Africa in the early 1880s when Burton and Cameron were in search of Gold Mines, and left an unflattering impressions of Burtons' practical knowledge of mining engineering (see Volume 3). He is quoted briefly in *To the Gold Coast for Gold*,[1] and some manuscript material by him can be found in Burton's personal library.

249. McCarthy, Justin (1830–1912).

Catholic Anglo-Irish author, journalist and politician. He was born and educated in Cork City. In the 1850s and 1860s he worked in Liverpool and London as a journalist, becoming a parliamentary reporter, a public lecturer and a frequent magazine contributor. He was a Member of Parliament for Longford and other constituencies, as a moderate Home Rule Liberal (1879-1896) and Parnellite. He was also the author of various novels, biographies and popular histories. McCarthy knew Burton through the London clubs of the 1860s, and left more than one affectionate reminiscence (see Volume 2).

---

[1] Vol. 2, p. 148. His name is given there as Edward L. McCarthy, a mistake copied by Kirkpatrick (1978) and others.

250. McCarthy, Justin Huntly (1859-1936).

Son of Justin McCarthy (1830-1912, see above), educated at University College London, who also became an MP (1884-1892), Home Ruler, historian, novelist and poet. He published prolifically, and collaborated with Isabel Burton, and wrote verses on the death of RFB which appear on the tomb in Mortlake.

251. Milnes, Monckton (Lord Houghton) (1809-1885).

Poet and politician, educated at Trinity College, Cambridge, where he was an early member of the secretive Apostles. He travelled in the East in the 1840s, running into Mansfield Parkyns, recently sent down from Cambridge, on the Nile. Florence Nightingale refused his offers of marriage. He was made Lord Houghton in 1863.

Milnes met Burton at some time in the early 1850s—either through the RGS itself, or perhaps later through Admiral Henry Murray's sessions for travellers in his Monday evenings at home at "D4, the Albany"—and they formed a lasting and intimate friendship. Milnes, who had a special interest in travelers—he took up Francis Galton for a while on his return from Africa in 1852—hosted a regular "10 o'clock breakfast" for the like-minded at his house in 16 Upper Brook street, London. He brought Burton into contact with figures like Swinburne, Hankey and others. In turn Burton introduced him to characters like Colonel Studholme Hodgson, and possibly Edward Vaux Bellamy (or the other way around). Milnes' now mostly forgotten poetry included an anonymous set of verses from 1871 on flagellation, the *Rodiad*, a subject he corresponded extensively with Swinburne about. Burton suggested a better name for its earlier version, the "Betuliad": "Hankey ... showed me also a little poem entitled the Betuliad. I liked much every part except the name—you are writing for a very very small section who combine the enjoyment of verse with the practice of flagellation and the remembrance that betula is a birch. Why not call it the Birchiad? If you want it corrected here I can do so. Hankey and I looked over the copy made at Paris and corrected the several errors."[1]

Isabel Burton later wrote a reminiscence of Milnes' country home Fryston in Yorkshire, which the Burtons visited regularly was well-attended by a network of society, as well as literary and bohemian, figures.[2]

The hospitalities of Lord Houghton have long since made

---

[1] Burton to Monckton Milnes 1860/01/22 (see Volume 1).
[2] Isabel Burton 'Lord Houghton at Fryston Hall.' *Celebrities at Home* Series 2 (London: Office of 'The World', 1878). Reprinted from *The World* (20 June, 1877).

Fryston famous. None of those who have had that pleasant experience will forget the hearty reception which awaited them after their drive to the Hall—the figure of the host just about the middle height, his brown hair flowing carelessly from his broad forehead, his blue eyes beaming with gladness at the arrival of his friends, as he stood on the top of the stone steps, in front of the house, with both hands extended. Then followed the cup of tea in the library, a long, handsome, comfortable room, soft carpeted, and replete with ottoman and sofa luxury, but walled with books, as indeed was the whole house, not in formal rows, but in separate cases, each with its own subject—Poetry, Magic, French Revolution, Oriental Thought, Theology and Anti-theology, Criminal Trials, Fiction, from Manon Lescaut to George Eliot. ...

In August 1859, soon after Monckton Milnes had become proprietor, there met at Fryston, Mansfield Parkyns of Abyssinia; Robert Curzon of the Monasteries; Richard Burton, just returned from discovering the Lake Tanganyika, Central Africa; Petherick of Khartoum ... and other travellers in distant fields and in many paths of practical and ideal life

She does not mention Milnes' special collection of erotica, much of it supplied by Frederick Hankey, which Milnes liked to show to his guests. In her *Life* she recalled "Richard cross-legged on a cushion, reciting and reading 'Omar el Khayyam' alternately in Persian and English, and chanting the call to prayer, 'Allahhu Akbar.'" Later the house burned down and Milnes lost his unique collection.

An extensive and revealing correspondence between Burton and Milnes survives in the Houghton Papers at Trinity College Cambridge, see Volumes 1 and 2. The Burtons regularly called on his political influence. Burton dedicated *City of the Saints* to him—Milnes repaid the favour by reviewing it glowingly, though anonymously, in the Edinburgh Review—and named a peak in the Cameroons *Mount Milnes*, though the name did not stick.

252. Mitchell, Roland Lyon Nosworthy (1847-1931).

A colonial administrator, born in Oxford and educated at Christ Church College, Oxford. Met Burton in Egypt, where Mitchell was tutor to the Khedive's son, who he had met at Oxford, from 1873-1878. He worked briefly in the Statistical Department of the Revenue Survey in Cairo the following year before becoming Commissioner of Limassol in Cyprus between 1879 and 1911. Author of *An Egyptian Calendar for the Koptic Year 1617* (1900) and *An Egyptian Calendar for the year 1395 AH* (1877). Mitchell left an unpublished reminiscence of Burton in his memoirs, which survive in manuscript. He is mentioned by Isabel in *AEI*,[1] and in the *Arabian Nights*.[2]

253. Mitford, Bertram (Lord Redesdale) (1837-1916).

English diplomat and author, member of the well-known Mitford family which later produced the Mitford sisters, and a cousin of Algernon Swinburne. According to the *DNB* "As a human being, Lord Redesdale was a sort of Prince Charming; with his fine features, sparkling eyes, erect and elastic figure, and, in the last years, his burnished silver curls, he was a universal favourite, a gallant figure of a gentleman, solidly English in reality, but polished and sharpened by travel and foreign society. To see him stroll down Pall Mall, exquisitely dressed, his hat a little on one side, with a smile and a nod for every one, was to watch the survival of a type never frequent and now extinct." Mitford first met Burton when he was working for the Slave Trade Department in 1861, and was almost persuaded by Burton to join him in Africa at Fernando Po, pulling out at the last minute. He visited them in Damascus (Isabel calls him "Barty Mitford"[3] was "pleasantly surprised" and "showed him the sights"[4]) and later, in 1890, the Burtons ran into him again in Algiers.[5]

254. Mohl, Mary Elizabeth (1793-1883).

A bluestocking, popularly known as Clarkey from her maiden name, born in Westminster, from a family of Irish Jacobites. Educated at a convent in Toulouse. She ran a literary salon in Paris, where her mother had retired in 1831 on becoming a widow. She was well-connected socially. Past middle age, she married Julius Mohl, the orientalist who had helped to locate Nineveh. She knew Lord Houghton (Monckton Milnes) and left a brief but sharp mention of Burton, who she met in the Autumn of 1864, in a letter to Houghton (see Volume 1).

255. Money, Edward James (1822-1889).

An Indian Army officer, born in Calcutta, who served in the Crimea with the Bashi-Bazouks, commanded by William Beatson, and also known as "Beatson's Horse." He later served in the Imperial Ottoman army. Burton served in the same regiment in the Crimean War, as Beatson's Chief of Staff. The Bazouks were composed of irregular cavalry, "Bashi-Bazouk" meaning "leaderless" or "madcap"; they were

---

[1] p. 405.
[2] Volume 5 (1885), p. 231.
[3] *Life* Vol. 1, p. 470.
[4] *Romance*, Vol. 2 p. 468.
[5] *Life*, Vol. 2, p. 391.

mainly Albanian mercenaries who caused a great deal of trouble without seeing action before they were removed from Beatson's command by Lord Panmure. This led to a bitter dispute between Beatson and his superiors, which Burton was party to. Money left an interesting reminiscence of Burton in his book on the *Twelve Months with the Bashi-Bazouks* (1857), see Volume 1 here. Money wrote several other books, including *The Tea Controversy* (1884) and *The Truth about America* (1886)—where the tea was apparently no good.

256. Moore, Noel Temple (1833-1903).

Consul at Damascus, succeeding Burton there in 1871. His father Niven Moore (1799-1889) had been Consul-General in Syria. Noel Temple Moore, who was married to Emma Churchill, eventually went on to become Consul General at Tripoli in 1890, retiring in 1894. Previously he was Consul at Jerusalem, 1862-1871, and had been at the Beyrout Consulate in the 1850s. Burton mentions him in Unexplored Syria.[1]

257. Murchison, Sir Roderick FRS (1792-1871).

Geologist, Fellow of the Royal Society and President of the Royal Geographical Society 1843–1845 and subsequently for most of the period in which Burton's connections to the Society were strongest (1851–1853, 1856–1859, 1862–1871). See the reminiscence by Clements Markham for the uneasy relationship between Murchison and Burton.

258. Murray, Rear-Admiral Henry Anthony (1810-1865).

An officer in the Royal Navy who was actively involved in the RGS in the 1850s and early 1860s, and was a lifelong bachelor. Third and youngest son of George, fifth Earl of Dunmore, and Lady Susan Hamilton. Joined the navy in 1823, obtaining his commission in 1831. Murray published a travelogue describing his trip through the Americas in *Lands of the Slave and the Free* (London: John Parker, 1855). He cultivated explorers and befriended Burton early in the 1850s, hosting him at well-attended Monday evening gatherings at his bachelor's quarters in D4, the Albany—other attendees included Francis Galton, John Petherick, Mansfield Parkyns, Samuel Baker and Tom Hughes. Jocular correspondence between the two survives which suggests an extensive association (see Volume 1). Burton dedicated *Wit and Wisdom of West Africa* (1865) to Murray, who had just died, describing himself

---

[1] Vol. 2, pp. 293, 306.

as one of Murray's "reclaimed"—he addressed Murray in his letters as "Imperious Reclaimer".

259. Nichols, Harry Sidney (1865-1941?).

Publisher, born in Leeds. Operated a business as a publisher in Sheffield, and then the bookshop "Nichols' Book Emporium and Literary Lounge", in Gladstone Buildings, quickly expanding from more traditional antiquarian books to erotica—but he had moved on by 1889, when the shop and its stock of 12,000 volumes were sold, and was established in London at Wardour Street by the early 1890s. He became a partner of Leonard Smithers in the "Erotika Biblion Society" and thus involved with Burton. The partnership with Smithers broke up in 1895. Also published Georgiana Stisted's *The True Life of Capt. Sir Richard F. Burton* (1896). First exiled to Paris in 1900, when charged with obscenity for publishing *Kalogynomia* by Stockdale and Roberton—Sotheby's promptly auctioned off his London stock—and subsequently fled from there to New York City in 1908, to avoid possible extradition to England. In America he went on to publish titles such as *Fifty Drawings By Aubrey Beardsley, Selected from the Collection Owned by Mr. H. S. Nichols* (1920). He died in Bellevue Psychiatric Hospital—some sources give his date of death as 1939, the year he was admitted there. Nichols is often mentioned in the extensive correspondence between Smithers and Burton still extant (see Volume 3), which shows that Burton was initially leery of his motives and the safety of any partnership with him.

260. Nicolson, Harold (1886-1968).

English diplomat and author, born in Tehran, the son of a diplomat, Arthur Nicolson (1849-1928) who was the Consul-General at Budapest between 1888 and 1893. An Oxford graduate, he was married to Vita Sackville-West, an odd union described memorably by their son when he published their diaries.[1] Nicholson met Burton, who knew his father, as a very young child and left a reminiscence which showed that he retained a strong impression of the explorer—see Volume 3.

261. Neville, Amelia Ransome (1837-1927).

San Francisco socialite, originally from Connecticut. She arrived in San Francisco in 1852. She met Burton in San Francisco on his way back from Salt Lake City in 1860, and left a brief reminiscence of a dinner with him—see Volume 1.

---

[1] Nigel Nicolson *Portrait of a Marriage* (1973).

262. Notcutt, Oliver.

Burton's agent in England in the late 1880s. Notcutt was with the publishing firms Waterlow & Sons and Partridge & Cooper, who had printed the *Nights* for the Burtons. He also wrote lyrics for musicals. Correspondence between Notcutt and Isabel survives in the Huntington Library.

263. Orton, Arthur (the 'Tichborne Claimant') (1834-1898).

Orton claimed to be the lost son Roger, heir of the Tichborne family, who were wealthy Anglo Catholic aristocracy. Although he managed to convince Mrs. Tichborne's that he was her long lost son, he was ultimately convicted of perjury after a sensational trial. Orton was born in London but spent time in South America and Australia, under various names. Burton testified at his trial in December of 1871 and claimed to have barely known him, but in fact knew him well during his time in South America. Correspondence between the two was published at the time of the Tichborne trial, as were diary entries by Orton referring to Burton—see Volume 2.

264. Ouida (Marie Louise de la Ramée) (1839-1908).

Popular novelist, born in England at Bury St Edmunds, the daughter of a French teacher. After publishing her first (romantic) novel in 1863, she went on to conducted a salon at the Langham Hotel in London, where she continued to write successful novels. She lived abroad in Florence from the early 1870s, producing occasional novels, and then took to topical periodical writing later in life. Eventually destitute, she accepted a pension. "Cynical, petulant, and prejudiced, she was quick at repartee. … Slightly built, fair, with an oval face, she had large dark blue eyes, and golden brown hair."[1] It is not clear when she first met RFB, though it may have been through Swinburne, who was associated with her salons, or Monckton Milnes. She corresponded with both the Burtons, and also wrote an important reminiscence of RFB for the Fortnightly Review—see Volume 3. She was highly critical of Isabel's destruction of Burton's manuscripts and diaries, and broke with her after that.

265. Outram, Sir James (1803-1863).

Highly distinguished Lieut.-General in the Indian Army, which he joined in 1819. He was the son of Civil Engineer, and was educated in Aberdeen at Marischal College. Outram, who had made a name in the

---

[1] Dictionary of National Biography.

Afghan war of 1838, had a highly public row in the 1840s with General Charles Napier, when Outram was still a Major, and Political Agent in Lower Sindh. He opposed Napier's annexation of Sindh, and the two fought a long battle in the press. Burton, like many of Napier's officers, sided with Napier in this quarrel. He encountered Outram again at Aden in 1854 when he conducted his mission to Somali-land—"I applied officially to the Political Resident of Aden, the late Colonel, afterwards Sir James, Outram, of whose 'generous kind nature' and of whose 'frank and characteristic ardour' my personal experience do not permit me to speak with certainty."[1] Outram went on to serve with distinction in the Indian Mutiny of 1857, after which he was promoted to Lieutenant-General, and was buried in Westminster Abbey on his death in 1863. Burton later wrote a set of unflattering biographical notes on Outram, which are now in the British Library.

266. Paget, Lady Walburga (1839-1929).

German diarist and writer, born in Berlin, with connections to Queen Victoria—she had been her lady in waiting. She was married to the British Ambassador to Rome, Sir Augustus Berkeley Paget (1823-1896). She died of burns after falling asleep next to a fire at home. The Pagets were well-known to the Burtons, who would run into them in Vienna on holiday. Lady Paget also corresponded with Isabel, see Volume 3. She wrote several books of memoirs and other productions, including *Embassies of Other Days* (1923) and *In My Tower* (1924).

267. Palgrave, William Gifford (1826-1888).

A traveller and Orientalist, born in Westminster and educated at Charterhouse and Trinity College, Oxford. He was a son of Sir Francis Palgrave. He joined the East India Company in 1847, and converted to Catholicism in India, where he was ordained as Jesuit priest. Later he renounced the religion—"We visited Mr. Palgrave's old quarters, a monastery of fifty or sixty Jesuits, where Mr. Palgrave was a Jesuit for seventeen years. Here we all got fever."[2] In 1862 he travelled through Central Arabia, recorded in his book *Personal Narrative of a Year's Journey through Central and Eastern Arabia* (1863). After this he took up various consular postings, for example Trebizond In Turkey, and authored a number of books, including *Essays on Eastern Questions* (London: Macmillan, 1872) and *A Vision of Life: Semblance and Reality* (London: Macmillan, 1891). Burton mentions Palgrave several times, in his correspondence and in his books, and his personal library contains

---

[1] *Zanzibar* Vol. 2, p. 380.
[2] *Life* Vol. 1, p. 501.

several works by him, with written annotations.[1]

268. Parkinson, Joseph Charles (1833-1908).

Journalist, civil servant and social reformer. Parkinson left a reminiscence of Ali the Pilot, who had been on the ship with Burton in the Red Sea on his journey to Mecca in 1853—see Volume 1.

269. Paull, George (1837-1865).

An American Presbyterian Missionary in West Africa. Originally from Pennsylvania, he was educated at Jefferson College and the Western Theological Seminary, graduating in 1862. He died at his mission in 1865.[2] Paull left a detailed reminiscence of Burton on the slopes of Fernando Po 1864, climbing up six miles to the salubrious cottage at Buena Vista that Burton learned to prefer to the consulate on the coast—see Volume 1.

270. Payne, John (1842-1916).

English poet, Arabist and prolific author, born in Bloomsbury. He was the son of John Edward Hawkins-Payne, a linguist and inventor, and Betsy Rogers, the daughter of a wealthy merchant from Bristol. Although he trained and alter practiced as a solicitor, he took up poetry on the side, befriending the Rossettis and Swinburne. In the late 1870s he helped to found the Villon Society, along with Justin Huntly McCarthy (see above) for bringing out translations of works not in the mainstream of publishing. He is chiefly remembered now for his translation of the *Arabian Nights*, which he started in 1881 and completed in 1884. Burton corresponded with Payne extensively when he discovered that Payne was working on *Nights* project, which he had been toying with himself. They continued to collaborate through the production of Burton's unexpurgated 'literal' version, which Payne later claimed not to approve of, and met many times in person. Payne left several unflattering impressions of Burton which are reproduced by Payne's biographer, Thomas Wright—see Volume 3.[3] Payne went on to produce, among many other works, *The Decameron by Giovanni Boccaccio* (1886), *The Quatrains of Omar Kheyyam of Nisahpour* (1898) and *Poems of Master François Villon of Paris* (1900).

---

[1] Kirkpatrick, 1878: 1915, 2043.
[2] *Memorials of foreign missionaries of the Presbyterian church, U. S. A.* by William Rankin (Presbyterian Church in the U.S.A. Board of Publication, 1895) pp. 264-9.
[3] The same Wright who had previously written a biography of Burton, see Wright 1906.

271. Quaritch, Bernard (1819-1899).

Publisher, successful antiquarian dealer and bookseller, of Prussian Wendish origin, who naturalized in England. "Fond of airing his views on politics and sociology in catalogue notes" with "a somewhat squat and awkward figure, occasionally rough manners, irrepressible egotism, pithy sayings, half humorous, half sardonic, delivered in a grating voice, combined to form an interesting if not a very attractive personality".[1] He was the author of several works on bibliophilia. His son Bernard continued the family business after his father's death, and it continues on today. Quaritch had extensive dealings with Burton from an early stage, no later than his preparations for his journey to Mecca in 1853, and left a reminiscence—see Volume 1. He remembered then supplying Burton with a disguised copy of Freytag's Dictionary of Arabic, "bound like a pair of Oriental MSS". He also published Burton's *Kasidah* (1880, anonymously) and his 6-volume *Camoens* set (1880-1884). Burton mentions him several times in his works, e.g. *Ultima Thule* and the *Nights*.[2]

272. Rashid Pasha, Mehmet (?-1876).

Governor of Syria from 1866 to 1872, during Burton's Consulship at Damascus, which Rashid opposed from the start—see the letters in Volume 2. Ultimately he insisted on Burton's recall in 1871. After a change of government in Istanbul in 1872, Rashid was dismissed from his governorship, which Burton considered a personal vindication, but was later made Minister of Public Works and Foreign Affairs at Istanbul. Not long after, he was killed by a shot in the dark during the affray in the Council Chamber which followed the assassination of the Minister of War, Hussein Avni Pasha, on the 15th of June 1876. Opinions vary about the quality of his administration of Syria.

273. Rathborne, Anthony Blake (1811?-1885).

Magistrate and Revenue Collector in Hyderabad in the 1840s, when Burton was stationed in Scinde. Son of Captain Wilson Rathborne (1748-1831) of the Royal Navy, of Anglo-Irish descent, who distinguished himself in Napoleonic naval engagements, including the aftermath of Trafalgar.[3] Studied at Ushant. Joined the East Indian army, at age 16, serving in the 24th Native Infantry. He described his family background as follows:[4]

---

[1] DNB.
[2] *Ultima Thule* Vol. 1, p. 245. *Nights* Vol. 7, p. 156.
[3] See DNB.
[4] *Mr. Disraeli, Colonel Rathborne and the Council of India* (1860), pp. 8-10.

I am the son, then, of a man belonging to the middle classes—my grandfather having been a beneficed clergyman of the Church of Ireland. His fathers, again, had filled positions of honour and credit there, from the time of the first of them crossing over from Lancashire in the reign of James the Second; by a party of whose officers he was set upon and assassinated, during that monarch's invasion of Ireland in the endeavour to recover his crown, From early associations, my mind was pretty much divided between the claims of letters, politics, and arms. For my father was an officer of the Royal Navy, of conspicuous bravery, and who had served his sovereign with as much distinction as the rank of captain, in which he died, allowed. He had been in many general actions, as well as engagements of lesser consequence; he had lost his eye, and had had his shoulder shot away, while contributing as first lieutenant of a line-of-battleship to one of our greatest naval victories. He had had presented to him a sword of some value from the Patriotic Fund, at Lloyd's, for his share in the action under Sir Richard Strachan, which put the finishing blow to the destruction, by Nelson at Trafalgar, of the fleets of France; and on the remodelling of the Order of the Bath, in 1815, he was made one of the first companions of it, when the honour was much more sparingly bestowed, and thought much more of a distinction than it is at present. On the other hand, politics and political literature drew me towards them by the example ever present to my mind, of three among my nearest relatives and connections who had built themselves up a name in these departments of public service entirely by their own unaided talents. One of these, Mr. Blake, my mother's cousin, was Chief Remembrancer of Ireland, appointed to the office by the Marquis Wellesley; and was, I have no doubt, known to many of the older members of your Honourable House. The second, my first cousin, by my father's side, the late Mr. Croker, must also have been well known to all who were members of the House before the passing of the Reform Bill, as well as to many who have entered it since. Last, not least, was the great Edmund Burke, nearly allied to my mother, who had spent many of her earlier days under his roof; and my veneration for whose character and writings first imbued me with those sentiments of hostility to the Company's rule, which, long before 1 had had any difference with its officials or directors, filled my breast.

Burton referred to Rathborne as his 'old friend'[1] and recalled,

---

[1] Isabel Burton *Life*, Vol. 1, p. 145. The letters from Rathborne actually appeared in *The Bombay Gentleman's Gazette and Commercial Advertiser* of

somewhat inaccurately, that 'The Karrachee Advertiser presently appeared in the modest shape of a lithographed sheet on Government foolscap, and, through Sir William Napier, its most spicy articles had the honour of a reprint in London. Of these, the best were "the letters of Omega," by my late friend Rathborne, then Collector at Hyderabad, and they described the vices of the Sind Amirs in language the reverse of ambiguous. I did not keep copies, nor, unfortunately, did the clever and genial author.'[1]

Rathborne went on to author many books, including a collaboration with General Charles Napier's brother William, the lengthily-titled *Comments by Lieut.-General Sir William Napier, K.C.B., upon a memorandum of the Duke of Wellington, and other documents, censuring Lieut.-General Charles James Napier, G.C.B. with a defence of Sir C. Napier's government of Scinde, by Captain Rathborne, Collector of Scinde* (London: C. Westerton, 1854), and his own running battle with Bartle Frere *Mr. Disraeli, Colonel Rathborne and the Council of India* (London: C. Westerton, 1860) and *Supplement to Mr. Disraeli, Colonel Rathborne, and the Council of India.* (London: C. Westerton, 1861), *Mr. Disraeli and the "Unknown Envoy." A letter to Viscount Palmerston* (London, 1861), and the more practical *A Few Words of advice on the subject of making Wills.* (London: M. Pillay & Co., 1879) and another political broadside that Burton would have approved of, *Turkey and the victims of its bad faith and its mis-government, financial, religious and political.* (London: J. G. Taylor, 1875). He also wrote widely for the reviews and journals, and was active in the East India Association. He retired from the Indian Army in 1856 and practiced at the bar in London after studying law at the Middle Temple, where his address was 5 Brick Court. Some correspondence between Burton and Rathborne survives, see Volume 2.

274. Rawson, Albert Leighton (1829-1902).

Born in Chester Vermont but raised in Weedsport outside Syracuse New York, Rawson is chiefly remembered today as a painter, theosophist and "freethinker". He published many books on biblical and religious subjects and listed fanciful academic degrees, including an honorary LLD from Oxford. He styled himself as "Professor Rawson", and claimed to have visited Mecca disguised as a medical student in 1851-2. None of these claims has ever been supported, but there is evidence that he was a bigamist, and that he was once convicted of larceny. His entries in contemporary biographical listings contain many stupendous feats, most likely based on information he supplied himself.

1845.
[1] There is also a letter from Rathborne to Burton in *Life*, Vol 2, p. 245.

Rawson's "reminiscence" of Burton appears in Volume 3 and appears to be an outright invention.

275. Reade, William Winwood (1838-1875).

Traveller, journalist and novelist. Born in Oxfordshire and educated at Magdalen Hall, Oxford (1856), though he did not take a degree. He was a nephew of the novelist Charles Reade, and made some efforts to write novels himself. After Du Chaillu's controversial reports of the Gorilla, he travelled to The Gaboon in 1861 to search for it, then on to Angola and the Cameroons, but he did not find it. This trip is described in his book *Savage Africa* (London: Smith, Elder & Co., 1864). He returned to West Africa in 1869 on behalf of the RGS, and later covered the Ashanti War of 1873 as a newspaper correspondent. He went on to write several other novels, travelogues and attacks on religion. Isabel tried to convert him as he was dying: "During all the month of April I was very sad about Winwood Reade, who was living, or rather dying, alone in a wretched little room at the top of a house. I used to go and see him every day and try and cheer him, and take him anything I fancied he could touch. I asked him if money could be of any use to him, but he told me he had quite enough to last him for the time he had to live. What distressed me the most of all, was the state he was dying in, which to me was dreadful, because he said he had no belief, and it seemed true. Of course it was useless—it was no business of mine; but I could not help doing my best during the last fortnight of his life to induce him to believe in God, and to be sorry before he died."[1]

Burton had been on friendly terms with Reade since 1864, when they met in England, and frequently refers to him in his books and in his correspondence.[2] Reade missed meeting him at Fernando Po in 1862 "I was disappointed of an interview with Richard Burton, who was up the Cameroons, a volcanic mountain as high as the Peak of Teneriffe. However, during the few days which I spent at Fernando Po, I was located at his house, and had at my disposal a library of which the profound and varied nature was an index to that great mind."[3] In *Two Trips to Gorilla Land*, Burton lauds Reade: "I deplore his loss. The highest type of Englishman, brave and fearless as he was gentle and loving, his short life of thirty-seven years shows how much may be done by the honest, thorough worker. He had emphatically the courage of his

---

[1] *Life* Vol. 2, p. 44.
[2] See for example *Mission to Gelele* Vol. 1, p. 22, where Burton refers to Reade as "the author of an amusing and picturesque book", suggesting that they had not yet met. Reade reviewed *Mission to Gelele* very positively for the *Anthropological Review* Vol. 2 No 7 (Nov. 1864), pp. 335-343.
[3] Reade, *Savage Africa* (1864) p. 66.

opinions, and he towered a cubit above the crowd by telling not only the truth, as most of us do, but the whole truth, which so few can afford to do. His personal courage in battle during the Ashanti campaign, where the author of 'Savage Africa' became correspondent of the 'Times,' is a matter of history. His noble candour in publishing the 'Martyrdom of Man' is an example and a model to us who survive him. And he died calmly and courageously as he lived, died in harness, died as he had resolved to die, like the good and gallant gentleman of ancient lineage that he was." There are annotated copies of *Savage Africa* and *The Martyrdom of Man* in Burton's personal library.[1]

276. Rebmann, Johannes (1820-1876).

Missionary for the Church Missionary Society, active in East Africa from 1846 to 1875. Born in Württemberg in Germany, the son of a farmer, and trained in Basel and at the Church Missionary Society College in London. A colleague of Johann Krapf, the pair discovered Mount Kilimanjaro and Kenya and sent back reports of 'eternal snows' to the *Church Missionary Intelligencer* in London, which regularly published letters and extracts from Rebmann's journal from May of 1849 onward.

> The mountains of Jagga gradually rose more distinctly to our sight. At about ten o'clock (I had no watch with me) I observed something remarkably white on the top of a high mountain, and first supposed that it was a very white cloud, in which supposition my guide also confirmed me; but having gone a few paces more I could no more rest satisfied with that explanation; and while I was asking my guide a second time whether that white thing was indeed a cloud, and scarcely listening to his answer that yonder was a cloud, but what that white was he did not know, but supposed it was coldness, the most delightful recognition took place in my mind of an old well-known European guest called snow. All the strange stories we had so often heard about the gold and silver mountain Kilimandjaro in Jagga, supposed to be inaccessible on account of evil spirits, which had killed a great many of those who had attempted to ascend it, were now at once rendered intelligible to me, as of course the extreme cold, to which the poor Natives are perfect strangers, would soon chill and kill the half-naked visitors. I endeavoured to explain to my people the nature of that "white thing," for which no name exists even in the language of Jagga itself; but they at first appeared as if they were not to trust my words at once. Soon after we sat down to rest a little, when I

---

[1] Kirkpatrick (1978): 1664, 295.

read the 111th Psalm, at which I had just arrived in my daily reading. It made a singular impression on my mind in the view of the beautiful snow mountain so near to the Equator, and gave, especially the sixth verse, the best expression to the feelings and anticipations I was moved with.[1]

Later, their interpretation of reports they heard about the interior, brought back to Europe in 1855 by another colleague Jacob Erhardt, led to the publication in the *Calwer Missionsblatt* of the prototype of the famous "slug map", which conflated the lakes of the interior into one enormous continuous body of water—see Volume 1. Rebmann met and corresponded with Burton as a result of the East African Expedition of 1856-9. Burton considered adding him to his expedition, but soon changed his mind, explaining to Sir George Back that "I am resolved not to take Mr. Rebmann, he would never stand the climate suffers from spleen and appears to have a kind of longing for martyrdom which you know would not suit the R. G. Soc.".[2] Some correspondence between the two survives—Rebmann writes that "I am a little afraid, as you are rather a facetious writer, that you might misrepresent my views about the cause of colour, as indeed you have already done, though only in a joking way, when I was in conversation with you."[3] Rebmann returned to Europe in 1875, dying of pneumonia the following year.

277. Rhys, Ernest Percival (1859-1946).

Poet, folklorist, critic and long-time editor of J. M. Dent's "Everyman's Library". Born in London, the son of a publisher's assistant who became a wine merchant, John Rhys, of Welsh descent, and Emma Percival. He qualified as a mining engineer but preferred writing, an inclination he credited to his mother's ancestry. Rhys was exceptionally well-connected in literary circles, and knew Burton at first-hand, through Dr. George Bird, his sister Alice "Lallah" Bird, and Swinburne. Rhys had met Dr. Bird when staying in (what was believed to be) Leigh Hunt's cottage—Bird, who had known Hunt, stopped to stare at it and was invited in.[4]

Rhys left an interesting Boswellian reminiscence of an evening spent with Swinburne, the Birds and Burton: "I sat down and wrote what I could remember of the conversation. So what is here recorded is red hot. I wish I had taken notes of other equally wonderful evenings with Swinburne and Burton."—see Volume 2. Among his many works was

---

[1] Church Missionary Intelligencer, May 1849, p. 17.
[2] 1857/04/09, Burton to Back—see Volume 1.
[3] 1859/03/21. Johannes Rebmann to Richard Burton—see Volume 1.
[4] Ernest Rhys *Everyman Remembers* (New York: Cosmopolitan, 1931) pp 196-7.

a set of memoirs of his literary connections, *Everyman Remembers* (1931).

278. Ricci, Dr. Hermann Robert (R. H. R.).

Very little seems to be definitely known about the traveller and author "R.H.R.," whose *Rambles in Istria* (1875), which contains a reminiscence of Burton, is highly collectable today—see Volume 2. His real name is hard to determine, some suggest "Robert Hole Ricci" or "Richard Hole Ricci" instead.[1] The best known source lists "Dr. de Ricci" as the author.[2] This is presumably Dr. Hermann Robert de Ricci, a physician from Dublin, listed by the *Gentleman's Magazine* as the only son of Adj.-Gen. and Lady Jane De Ricci.[3] De Ricci published widely in the Medical and Scientific press. There is a copy of *Rambles in Istria* in Burton's personal library.[4]

279. Richards, Alfred Bate (1820-1876).

English journalist, dramatist and novelist, the son of a Yorkshire MP. Richards was a contemporary of Burton at Oxford.

> This is a curious reflection at school for any boy or any master, "what will become of the boy? Who will turn out well, who ill? who will distinguish himself, who remain in obscurity? who live, who die?" I am sure, although Burton was brilliant, rather wild, and very popular, none of us foresaw his future greatness, nor knew what a treasure we had amongst us.[5]

In his reminiscences written for Francis Hitchman, Burton recalled first meeting Richards: "At the fencing rooms Richard made an acquaintance which afterwards ripened into friendship with poor Alfred Bate Richards. He was upwards of six feet high, broad in proportion and very muscular. Richard found it unadvisable to box with him, but could easily master him with foil and broadsword."[6]

Richards graduated from Exeter College in 1841, and remained a life-long friend. Shortly after leaving Oxford, Richards published the polemic *Oxford Unmasked* (1841). He briefly practiced law at Lincoln's

---

[1] See Trevor R. Shaw *Foreign travellers in the Slovene Karst: 1486-1900* (ZRC, 2008): p. 267.
[2] Alnwick Mercury, Saturday 03 March 1883, p. 3. "Dr. de Ricci in his admirable book, "Rambles Istria," &c, 1875".
[3] June 1843, p. 643. Lady Jane was a daughter of Robert King, the 2nd Earl of Kingston, and had previously married Count de Winzengerode.
[4] Kirkpatrick (1978): 2107.
[5] Alfred Bate Richards *A sketch of the career of Richard F. Burton* (1880 / 1886) pp. 2-3.
[6] F. Hitchman *Richard F. Burton* (1887) p. 87.

Inn, but was attracted to drama and journalism instead, editing the *Morning Advertiser*. In 1859 he helped to found a rifle corps of working men, who volunteered to protect England from the threat of a French Invasion. Richards later became a Colonel in the resulting "3rd City of London Rifle Corps". His biographical writings about Burton were published after his death as *A Sketch of the Career of Richard F. Burton* (1880), an expanded and revised version of which was published in 1886. His name is often misspelled as "Bates Richards".

Burton later wrote, regarding the *Morning Advertiser*, that the "journal was ever friendly to me during the long reign of Mr. James Grant, and became especially so when the editorial chair was so worthily filled by my old familiar of Oxford days, the late Alfred Bate Richards, a man who made the 'Organ of the Licensed Victuallers' a power in the state and was warmly thanked for his good services by that model conservative, Lord Beaconsfield."[1] Burton also dedicated The *Book of the Sword* to Richards, "my old and dear college friend".

280. Rigby, Christopher Palmer (1820-1885).

An officer and accomplished linguist in the Indian Army. Born at Yately Lodge in Hampshire, son of Tipping Thomas Rigby, a barrister in the Inner Temple and recorder of Wallingford. After a bleak childhood spent mainly in spartan boarding schools, with a mother who appeared to actively dislike him, Rigby trained at the Addiscombe Military College of the East India Company, entering at the early age of 14. He arrived in Bombay in 1836, in the 16th Native Infantry, at age 16, and passed in Hindoostanee, Maharatta, Canarese, Guzerati, Persian and Arabic. He was then posted to Aden for 4 years, where he compiled grammars of the Somali and Sathpoora languages. His outstanding language skills led to his appointment as President of the Military and Civil Examination Committee at the Bombay Presidency in 1854, and he served as interpreter on the Persian Expedition of 1856-7.

Rigby was appointed Company Agent and then British Consul at Zanzibar, serving from 27th July 1858 to 5th September 1861, succeeding Atkins Hamerton. He opposed an attempted coup by two brothers of the Sultan of Zanzibar, and is credited with promoting the suppression of the slave trade there. This led to a serious dispute with Captain Richard Borough Crawford of the *Sidon*, who was accused by Rigby of knowingly impounding a Turkish ship and destroying it, on the pretext that it was a slaver, of lying to Rigby about the flag it was flying, of disobeying orders from Rigby to not release the crew, of visiting and irregularly accepting gifts from the Sultan without Rigby's permission, and of subsequently sending Rigby an insulting message. After Rigby

---

[1] *Suppl. Nights*, Vol. 6., p. 398.

spread these reports in official circles, Crawford—who resented what he saw as presumption, since he outranked Rigby—insisted on a court-martial to clear his name. When the court-martial was held at Portsmouth in February of 1862, Rigby was compelled to travel back to England to attend in person, and Crawford was largely vindicated, and in the words of a modern Naval historian, "accused Rigby of having spared no pains 'to rake up into one huge heap' all the gossip which could have tarnished his image".[1]

After his retirement to England in 1866, with rank of Major-General, Rigby was active in the RGS, the Royal Asiatic Society and the Anti-Slavery Society. He married a Miss Prater in 1867 and had two sons who both served in the Boer War—Gerard Christopher Rigby, born in 1868, who emigrated to Canada, and Percy George Rigby, who was killed in the First World War—and a daughter, Lillian, who would later write his biography. He died of pneumonia.

Rigby was closely allied with John Hanning Speke in his controversy with Burton, to whom Rigby took a violent dislike. The original source of the quarrel is hard to disentangle now. Isabel Burton promoted the idea that Rigby was jealous of Burton having, she claimed, beaten him in some of the language examinations they both took in India, and this has been repeated by many authors ever since. Likewise, Burton accused Rigby of an unspecified "personal pique". However, the examinations were qualifying and not competitive, with no ranking of candidates, and neither Isabel nor RFB could not have had any personal knowledge of Rigby's motivations.

In earlier years, Burton referred with mixed praise to Rigby's paper "Outline of the Somauli Language, with Vocabulary",[2] which he said "supplied a great lacuna in the dialects of Eastern Africa" but "asserts that the dialect of which he is writing 'has not the slightest similarity to Arabic in construction.' A comparison of the singular persons of the pronouns will, I believe, lead to a different conclusion."[3] But Burton only met up with Rigby again—they had apparently known each other in India—on his return to Zanzibar, eight months after Rigby had succeeded Hamerton. Before they got there, however, Burton had been sending desperate notes to the British Consul for supplies, and the trouble between them may have started with these. In a letter to Norton Shaw, written on June 24, 1858, Burton warned that "unless Col. Ham.'s

---

[1] Raymond Howell *The Royal Navy and the Slave Trade*, p. 33. Howell cites records of the court-martial in the National Archives, ADM 1/5808. There is no mention of this intriguing dispute in the memoir by Rigby's daughter, *General Rigby* (1931).

[2] *Transactions of the Bombay Asiatic Society* IX (May 1949 to August 1850), p. 129.

[3] *First Footsteps in East Africa* Vol. 2, p. 153.

promises be fulfilled by his successor, we shall be placed in a most disagreeable position at Zanzibar" and that he had received some help from the Sultan of Zanzibar and his officials, but only after they were "urged on by the Consul de France, M. Lad. Cochet, who after Lt.-Col. Ham.'s unfortunate decease, has proved himself an active & energetic friend".[1] Burton had addressed his requests for help to both the British Consul and to Cochet "in case of accidents".[2] He also mentioned having received "friendly letters" from Cochet, who "supplied me with the local news".[3]

Ladislas Cochet was apparently a Russian Pole, but had served the French on Zanzibar since 1855. He was suspected at the time of Burton's return—by the Sultan's administration, and by Rigby—of conspiring with rebels to stage a revolt in Zanzibar, hoping to move it into the French sphere of influence.[4] Rigby was by then conducting a protracted personal campaign against the French, whom he alleged were carrying on a disguised form of slavery through their indentured labour system—he tried to seize their ships when he could find a pretext. The situation got hot enough on the island for four warships to be summoned by the British and two by the French.[5]

When Burton and Speke returned to Zanzibar in March 1859, they stayed for a month with Rigby, at the Consul's house overlooking the harbour, until their return to Aden. Burton remained on friendly terms with Cochet, visiting him often. Rigby's daughter later suggested that this angered her father: "Contrast Rigby's scruples as a host with Burton's absence of proper feeling as a guest when he forgathered on friendly terms with a man not on visiting terms with the said host, viz. M. Cochet."[6] Later, in his *Lake Regions*, Burton kept stirring the pot, referring to Cochet as an "uninterested spectator" in the rebellion who nevertheless "thought favourably" of their cause, a rival claim by the elder brother of the Sultan.[7] Given that Rigby was also an earnest and committed Christian, he was unlikely to have warmed to Burton's personality and manners.

Speke had approached Rigby at the Consulate with complaints about Burton failing to pay some of the porters who had been engaged to the expedition. At first Rigby had declined to get involved, but after Speke raised the issue again in correspondence, en route to Aden, he became more interested. Speke obsessively returned to this issue, at

---

[1] 1858/06/24. Burton to Norton Shaw.
[2] *Lake Regions*, p. 77.
[3] *Lake Regions*, p. 361.
[4] Lyne, 1905: 53.
[5] Nwulia, 1975: 69.
[6] *General Rigby*, p. 247.
[7] *Lake Regions*, pp. 523-4.

ever greater length, whenever he wrote to Rigby, and both men went on to use it as a weapon against Burton.

Here Rigby was much more damaging to Burton than Speke, since he was able to make written complaints to the East India Company and the RGS in his official capacity as the Consul on the spot. The letters in Volume 1 show that Speke and Rigby fed on their shared hostility to Burton, while remaining in ostensibly friendly contact with him. It was over 8 months before he was made aware of this covert hostility by a letter from Rigby to the RGS, passed on to him by Norton Shaw, after which Burton wrote an open letter to Rigby, concluding "I shall at all times, in all companies, even in print if it suits me, use the same freedom in discussing your character and conduct that you have presumed to exercise in discussing mine".[1]

It is obvious from this correspondence that the rift with Rigby long pre-dated comments that Burton eventually made in print about both men, after relations had already broken down between them. Consider this remark by Speke to Rigby, written on the 17th Oct 1859: "I am sincerely obliged to you for the very long and highly amusing letter that you have sent to me. It has gone the rounds of the family circle and has been much chuckled over, especially that part descriptive of great Burton and his big boots. The boots were worn day and night until he arrived at Aden when Sharam alone induced his dropping them & then he took to quiet slippers—an article much better adapted to the miserable condition of his weak legs and rotten gut." This also suggests that their hostility was not really based on righteous indignation, self-persuaded or not, over payments to porters,.

After the dispute with the Speke/Rigby/Grant alliance became public, both sides took every chance to warm it over. At meetings of the RGS he was able to confront Rigby in occasional heated debates. According to Isabel, he also used to leave mocking calling cards in the rooms of the RGS, inscribed:

> Two loves the Row of Savile haunt,
>   Who both by nature big be;
> The fool is Colonel (Barren) Grant,
>   The rogue is General Rigby.[2]

Rigby reciprocated, raging in letters to Grant "I see that fellow Burton is going to Santos in Brazil. I was sorry to see Sir Roderick[3] call such a man his friend for he must know his true character"[4] and "I noticed the yelping of that cur Burton in the papers. It makes me quite savage to

---

[1] 1860/01/16, Burton to Rigby—see Volume 1.

[2] *Life* Vol. 1, p. 389. By "barren" Burton meant that Grant was not permitted to see the falls where the Nile flowed out of the Victoria Nyanza.

[3] Murchison.

[4] 1864/11/06, Rigby to Grant—see Volume 1.

see how the Geographical listen to a man who is such a habitual liar; I don't believe he could speak a word of truth if he tried."[1]

An anonymous reviewer of Isabel's *Life* in the *Edinburgh Review*—most likely Laurence Oliphant, who knew both men—recalled the dispute: "Rigby was a man well known and esteemed, a man of ability and prudence; but to the end of his life the mere name of Burton was enough to rouse him to fury—an effect similar to that which his name had on Burton".[2]

281. Roscher, Dr. Albrecht (1836-1860).

German explorer, sent by the King of Bavaria to explore East Africa. Author of *Ptolemaeus und die Handelsstrassen in Central-Afrika* (Gotha, J. Perthes, 1857). He was already in Zanzibar in September 1858, and in early 1859 met Burton's party, returning from the interior, on an excursion to the mainland. Burton left a barbed portrait of him:

> One day we were surprised by the abrupt entrance of a youth, eminently North German in aspect, with sandy hair, smooth face, and protruding eyes, flat occiput and projecting ears, he announced himself as Dr. Albrecht Roscher, of Hamburg, and he made himself doubly welcome by bringing from Zanzibar the wished-for supplies, letters, and newspapers .... The traveller, who appeared at most 22, applied himself forthwith to the magnetic survey, for which he had been engaged by the Prussian Government. A visit to Mozambique, and a run up coast, had taught him everything learnable about East Africa. He despised the dangers of climate, against which he was cautioned: having hitherto escaped fever, he held himself malaria-proof, and he especially derided our advice about not wandering over the country unarmed. He lauded to the skies his fellow-townsman Dr. Barth. He severely criticised Dr. Livingstone; he patronized, in a comical way, Herr Petermann; he highly extolled his own book; and he wrote to Zanzibar—so we afterwards heard—a far from flattering estimate of our qualifications as travellers. He stayed with us two days, and then departed northwards ... .[3]

Roscher left Zanzibar in June 1859 for Lake Nyassa, joining a caravan at Kilwa. He was murdered on the 19th of March 1860, near Lake Nyassa (Lake Malawi) which he had reached by the 19th November

---

[1] January 1865, Rigby to Grant. Extract in the Mary Lovell Collection, Orleans House, stated to be from the original letter in the National Library of Scotland.
[2] *Edinburgh Review* Oct. 1893, p. 459.
[3] *Zanzibar*, pp. 332-3.

1859. Consul C. P. Rigby reported from Zanzibar that "on the third day they arrived at the village of 'Kisoongoonee,' about midday, and Dr. Roscher was invited by the head man of the village to his house. About 4 o'clock P.m. Dr. Roscher was sleeping in this house, and one servant was lying at the door, the other servant had gone to a stream some distance from the village to bring water. On his return he heard the other servant, who was his own brother, calling to him to come quick as the villagers were about to attack them. On reaching the village he saw a number of men armed with bows and arrows in front of the house, and at the same moment his brother was shot. Dr. Roscher just then appeared at the door of the house and was instantly shot with two arrows, one striking him in the breast, the other in the throat. He fell and expired almost immediately."[1]

282. Rossetti, Dante Gabriel (1828-1882).

Pre-Raphaelite poet and painter. Born in London to an Italian immigrant from Naples, who later became a professor of Italian in King's College—and an eccentric Dante specialist. Educated at Kings College, where he was a child prodigy. Trained at Cary's Drawing Academy for four years, and then at the Royal Academy. He knew Burton through the Bohemian set in London, perhaps originally through Swinburne, and they corresponded about Italian poetry—see Volume 2. In his edition of the "Lyricks" of *Camoens*, Burton wrote

> I have borne in mind Rosetti's[2] dictum—"the life-blood of rhythmical translation is, that a good poem should not be turned into a bad one."[3]

He descended in middle life into a spiral of drug and alcohol addiction, which increased his production of poetry. Rossetti translated *The Early Italian Poets* (1861; 1874, as 'Dante and His Circle'), and produced *Poems* (1870) and other works, including many picture/poem combinations. His sister Christina and brother William were also notable in their own right: they were all known to Burton from his greater London circle.

283. Russell, Katherine Louisa (1844-1874).

Mother of the philosopher and public figure Bertrand Russell, known informally as Kate. She was a daughter of Edward Stanley (1802-1869), and married Lord John Russell, Viscount Amberley (1842-1876) the son of the former Liberal Prime Minister Lord Russell (1792-1878), who was

---

[1] See CP Rigby Political Dispatch 43 of 1860, *Transactions of the Bombay Geographical Society* Vol. 16 (1863), p. xlvi ff.
[2] Dante Gabriel Rossetti.
[3] *Camoens: the Lyricks*, p. 2.

later Earl Russell—and the Foreign Secretary when Burton was Consul at Fernando Po. The Russells met the Burtons at Alderley, the country estate of Kate's brother Henry Edward John Stanley, 3rd Baron Stanley of Alderley (1827–1903). Her brother had converted to Islam in 1862. Both Russells left important reminiscences of the Burtons in their diaries—see Volume 2. She died at a young age of diphtheria, and is chiefly remembered today as an early advocate of female suffrage and related ideas.

284. Russell, Lord John, Viscount Amberley (1842-1876).

Father of the philosopher and public figure Bertrand Russell. Married Kate Stanley (see above). Educated at Trinity College, Cambridge, but did not receive a degree. He was briefly a Member of Parliament, as a Liberal (1866-8). He was an epileptic, and died a few years after his wife, of bronchitis.

285. Russell, Odo William Leopold (1829-1884).

Nephew of Lord Russell (1792-1878), educated at home. He became a professional diplomat, and was Assistant Under-secretary in the Foreign Office in 1870-1871. Later he became Ambassador to Germany in 1871, as Lord Ampthill. Russell dealt with Burton extensively during his tenure as Consul at Damascus, but was known to him much earlier, when Russell was Secretary to Lord Stratford de Redcliffe in Constantinople, during the Crimean War. Isabel later wrote that "It was, by-the-by, no bad idea to appoint this high-bred and average talented English gentleman to the Court of Prince Bismarck, who disliked and despised nothing more thoroughly than the pert little political, the 'Foreign Office pet' of modern days."[1] Russell's nickname "O Don't" seems to have come from *Punch*, when he was stationed at the Vatican in the 1860s.[2]

> *As all ladies confess*
> *That their "no" oft means yes,*
> *Mr. Russell but followed men's wont,*
> *When the Pope's reply, too,*
> *He construed, "O, do,"*
> *Though the Cardinal swears 'twas, "O, don't."*

---

[1] *Life* Vol. 1, p. 231.
[2] *Punch* Feb 21, 1863, p. 74. "Rome and Russell".

286. Saker, Rev. Alfred (1814-1880).

A Missionary from Kent, a member of the Baptist Missionary Society. He was the son of a millwright and engineer, under whom he apprenticed as a shipyard engineer. He was active on Fernando Po from 1844 to 1858, and after that, when the Baptists were expelled by the Spanish from Fernando Po, in the Cameroons at Victoria, which he founded with a congregation of resettled slaves from Jamaica. Burton met Saker in the Cameroons, in October 1861, soon after arriving as Consul for Fernando Po: "Mr. Saker Baptist missionary called upon me today, he appears a long hearted man, not unlike a petit Townsend."[1] Saker later accompanied Burton and Gustav Mann on their expedition to climb the Cameroons Mountains in December 1861 to January 1862. The expedition started from Saker's base in Victoria, from where the mountains could clearly be seen, as they could from Fernando Po. Saker's diary entries from the expedition appear in Volume 1. Burton and Saker appear to have rubbed along well. He returned to England in 1878.

287. Sartoris, Adelaide Kemble (1815-1879).

An Opera singer and occasional authoress, born at Covent Garden, a sister of the actress Fanny Kemble, from the famous Kemble family of actors and singers. She was married to Edward John Sartoris, MP, but they lived mostly abroad, in Italy. Mrs. Sartoris was with Burton, Swinburne and Frederick Leighton in Vichy in September 1869 and left a reminiscence, known to us at second-hand. Leighton was rumoured to be her lover. She was the author of *A Week in a French Country House* (1867)

288. Sayce, Archibald Henry (1845-1933).

An English Orientalist and philologist, the son of a curate. He graduated from Queen's College, Oxford, in 1869, and later became professor of Comparative Philology there. A lifelong bachelor, he published extensively on archeology and philology, and travelled often to Greece and the Levant. It is not clear when he first met Burton, but Sayce later remembered that they planned a journey in North Africa together in the early 1880s, which did not come off. Burton often refers to Sayce in his later books, from *Etruscan Bologna* onwards. His personal library contains several works by Sayce, e.g. *An Assyrian grammar, for comparative purposes* (London, Trubner, 1872) and *The Hittites: the story of a forgotten empire* (London, The Religious Tract Society, 1888). Some correspondence also survives.

---

[1] 1861/10/01. Richard Burton to William Henry Wylde—see Volume 1.

289. Schroeder, Seaton (1849-1922).

An American naval officer, rising to Admiral. He was the son of the US Ambassador to Sweden and was educated at the Naval Academy. He served in the far east and in the Spanish-American war. He met Burton in Trieste in the early 1870s—his brief reminiscence of the encounter appears in Volume 2.

290. Schweinfurth, Georg August (1836-1925).

A German-speaking African explorer from Riga in Latvia. Received the Gold Medal of the RGS, in 1874, for his exploration of the Nile region between 1868 and 1871. Author of *Im Herzen von Afrika (The Heart of Africa)* (Leipzig, 1873). Burton refers to him in his books and in his correspondence, but it is not known if they met in person. A presentation copy of Schweinfurth's book *Die altesten Kloster der Christenheit (St. Antonius und St. Paulus)* (Cairo, October 1877) survives in Burton's personal library, with his annotations.[1]

291. Scully, William (?-1885).

Irish-born owner and editor of the weekly *Anglo-Brazilian Times* (1865-1884). Often referred to as "Misther Scully" in Burton's correspondence. Emigrated to Brazil in the 1850s. Author of *Brazil: Its Provinces and Chief Cities; the Manners and Customs of the People; Agricultural, Commercial and other Statistics, etc.* (Rio de Janeiro: 1865; London: Murray, 1866), and *A New Map of Brazil* (London: George Philip & Son, 1866). "Mr. William Scully kindly printed in his paper, the *Anglo-Brazilian Times* (February, 1867), a biographical sketch [of Camoens] borrowed from Viscount Juromenha, and specimens of Canto i."[2]

292. Seymour, Walter Richard (1838-1922).

Travelling gentleman, son of an English Canon, Rev. Richard Seymour. Travelled in South America. His brother Richard wrote *Pioneering in the Pampas or, The first four years of a settler's experience* (Longmans: London, 1869). He met both Wilfrid Blunt and Burton in South America, in the company of the Tichborne Claimant (Arthur Orton), and left an intriguing mention of this meeting, which is confirmed by Arthur Orton's diary entry, both of which appear in Volume 2. He was later, like Burton, subpoenaed to testify at Orton's trial in London.

---

[1] Kirkpatrick (1978), 1668.
[2] *Camoens: Life and Lusiads*, vol. 1 p. 186.

293. Seymour, Sir Edward Hobart (1840-1929).

Admiral of the fleet, from a family with distinguished naval connections. Considered a good linguist, he served in the Crimean War and the far east, where he saw action in the Boxer Rebellion. He never married. Isabel Burton mentions him often in her *Life*, e.g. as the Captain of the *Iris*, and RFB noted that the Egyptians called him "samur", Arabic for dog.[1] Seymour left a brief reminiscence of the Burtons at Trieste in his memoirs—see Volume 3.

294. Shand, Alexander Innes (1832-1907).

Scottish lawyer, journalist, critic, novelist, travel writer and biographer, educated at the University of Aberdeen. He met Burton at the Athenaeum Club in London, and his description of him is given in Volume 3: "At the club he lunched alone, and generally with a book before him". His many publications are now mostly forgotten. The acquaintance seems to have been slight: no correspondence between the two is known to survive, and Burton does not mention him in any of his books.

295. Shaw, Dr. Henry Norton (?-1868).

Assistant-Secretary of the RGS from 1849 until 1863, a position that was salaried. He was born in the Danish West Indies, the son of a Danish General, and was partly educated in New York. He became an Assistant Surgeon in the Merchant Navy, retiring to work for the RGS. He was known for his success in recruiting Fellows to the society, improving its financial footing. He also founded the Kosmos Dining Club, which Burton was a member of. A personality clash with Francis Galton, an Honorary Secretary, led to the resignation of both men in 1863, after which Shaw left the Society altogether and was Consul at Sante-Croix in the West Indies (under Danish jurisdiction) until his death there. The Kosmos Dining Club was continued after his departure by H.W. Bates. He produced a revised edition of J. R. Jackson's *What to Observe; or, the Traveller's Remembrancer* (London: Houlston & Wright, 1861)—an annotated copy of the third edition survives in Burton's personal library—and also edited many other books of travel, e.g. *Narrative of a Voyage to the West Indies and Mexico in the Years 1599-1602* by Samuel de Champlain (1859).

Shaw was Secretary of the West Indian Association and was an active organizer in the annual meetings of the British Association for the Advancement of Science. Although he was never a Fellow of the RGS, he was very active and influential in editing their publications; they

---

[1] *Nights* Vol.4, p. 57.

granted him 500 pounds on his retirement and a "Norton Shaw Testimonial Fund" was started to gather donations. See the notice by Sir Roderick Murchison in the *Journal of the Royal Geographical Society of London*.[1] His brother Geronimo Shaw also had dealings with the RGS.

Shaw knew Burton since 1852 at the latest, and put him in touch with many figures who were influential in geographical circles. They maintained an active, warm and extensive correspondence, both personally and in an official capacity, which appears in Volume 1. After the break with Speke, Shaw was placed, much like Francis Galton, in the difficult position of maintaining friendly relations with both men, without appearing to choose sides.

Many years after the death of Shaw, Karl Pearson stumbled on rumours still circulating within the RGS that some indelicate scandal was associated with Norton Shaw's departure, vaguely involving a woman and an apartment.[2]

296. Shelley, Major Edward (1827-1890).

Soldier and restless traveller, a nephew of the poet Percy Byshe Shelley. He joined the Hussars in 1844 at age 17, but in 1847 transferred to the Lancers, and was promoted to Captain in 1848. He had the urge to travel, and some independent means, so he resigned his commission in 1849, and travelled to Africa in search of Lake Ngami, leaving on the 23rd July that year for the Cape. On May 1st 1850, in the company of fellow officers Charles Bethune Ewart and Bushe,[3] he was arrested and turned back at the Malopa River by the Boers, who resented British incursions into the interior—news of this and similar incidents persuaded Francis Galton's expedition to seek Ngami through South-West Africa instead. After some more years wandering around the Kalahari, and South America, Shelley joined up with Beatson's Bashi-Bazouks during the Crimean War. There he met Burton, who was Beatson's Chief of Staff, and was drawn in to the bitter Beatson-Vivian controversy, which started when the fractious Bazouks were transferred by Lord Panmure from Beatson to General Smith, and it was rumoured that Beatson, with Burton's encouragement, urged his officers and soldiers to resist the transfer—Beatson viewed the Bazouks as his personal creation. Shelley himself was reluctant to support allegations of mutiny against either Beatson or Burton—his letter stating so is in Volume 1.

He later travelled continuously, with no particular purpose, in China and Australia, and in South, Central and North America. He visited

---

[1] Volume 39 (1869), p. cxlviii.
[2] Karl Pearson Papers relating to his *Life Letters and Labours of Francis Galton*, UCL. Communication from the RGS.
[3] Possibly Charles Percy Bushe, who later met Burton in Paraguay.

many of the places in South America that Burton would later visit when he was stationed in Brazil. Stopping off in San Francisco, en route to Honolulu, he encountered Amelia Ransom Neville,[1] who would later meet Burton in 1860, and leave memoirs of both men—see Volume 1 for her encounter with Burton. In 1866 he was back in England, where he finally settled down, and inherited his Uncle's baronetcy shortly before he died in 1890. Shelley's surviving travel journals have now been published—see Lawrence Woods *Edward Shelley's Journal, 1856-61*.[2]

297. Shepheard, Samuel (1816-1866).

Hotel proprietor in Cairo, where Shepheard's British Hotel became the first resort for any traveler of the mid-19th Century. Burton stayed there when he was recovering from his Mecca journey in 1853-4, and on the way through to East Africa. Burton befriended Shepheard and corresponded with him, though Shepheard's biographer records that 'tradition has it that he considered Burton somewhat of a poseur.'[3]

298. Sheridan, Richard Brinsley (1806?-1888).

Grandson of his namesake the playwright Richard Brinsley Sheridan (1751-1816). Son of Thomas Sheridan (1775-1813). Based at Frampton House, near Dorchester, which he had inherited by marriage and became known as a literary salon during his tenure. Whig MP for Shaftesbury (1845-52) and Dorchester (1852-68). The racy society beauty and authoress Caroline Sheridan, Mrs. Norton, was his younger sister. The Burtons knew the "Brinsley Sheridans" well, visiting them whenever they were in England. Isabel mentions them in her correspondence several times, and in her *Life*.

299. Skene, James Henry (1812-1886).

Scottish soldier, traveller and diplomat. Served in the 73rd Perthshire Regiment. From 1852 onward he was Vice-Consul, then Consul, and finally Consul-General at Aleppo. Author of *Anadol: the Last Home of the Faithful* (London 1853) and *The Frontier Lands of the Christian and the Turk, Comprising Travel in the Regions of the Lower Danube in 1850 and 1851* (London 1853) and *With Lord Stratford in the Crimean war* (London: R. Bentley, 1883), among other works. During the Crimean war he served Stratford de Redcliffe, the British Ambassador to the

---

[1] See Amelia Ransome Neville *The Fantastic City: Memoirs of the Social and Romantic Life of Old San Francisco* (1935). She called him "Sir Edward Shelley".

[2] Authorhouse, 2005.

[3] Michael Bird *Samuel Shepheard of Cairo* (London: Michael Joseph, 1957).

Ottoman Empire, and became embroiled in a dispute with General Beatson and the Bashi-Bazouks. Skene was highly critical of Beatson's conduct when in charge of the Bashi-Bazouks, and therefore at odds with Burton, who later wrote of Skene that "he was known on the spot to be taking notes, that every malignant won his ear, and that he did not cease to gratify the Ambassador's prejudices by reporting the worst. General Beatson was peppery, like most old Indians, and instead of keeping diplomatically on terms with Mr. Skene, he chose to have a violent personal quarrel with him."[1] One of Skene's reports to Stratford de Redcliffe about the Bazouks, which includes a section about a multiple duel challenge involving Burton, is included in Volume 1.

300. Sladen, Douglas Brooke Wheelton (1856-1947).

English author, son of a solicitor. An Oxford graduate, he spent some time in Australia. Returned to London and edited *Who's Who*. Sladen recalled meeting Burton at an Oxford event in the 1880s—see Volume 3.

301. Smalley, George Washburn (1833-1916).

Foreign Correspondent for the *New York Tribune* in London, after making a name as a reporter during the American Civil War. He met Burton in London at a party in Belgravia and left a detailed description of the evening—see Volume 3.

302. Smith, Laura A.

Journalist, who published in the *Paternoster Review* and the *Nineteenth Century*, sometimes as "Miss Laura A. Smith" (possibly "Alexandrine"). She wrote a worshipful profile of Burton, whom she knew briefly at Tangiers circa 1886, describing him as "a Hercules of literary power and universal tact"—see Volume 3.

303. Smith, William Robertson (1846-1894).

Polymath from Aberdeenshire, son of a church minister, educated at home and at Aberdeen University. Minister of the Free Church of Scotland and Professor of Hebrew at Aberdeen Free Church College until his trial for heresy in the late 1870s, after questioning the liberal truth of the Bible in articles ("Angel", "Bible") in the Encyclopædia Britannica. He was suspended and then dismissed from Aberdeen Free Church College, after a vote of no confidence. Instead he became Professor of Arabic at Cambridge, succeeding the murdered E. H.

---

[1] *Life* Vol. 1, p. 239.

Palmer, and later the editor of the Encyclopædia Britannica. While he was suspended from his chair at Aberdeen, between 1879 and 1881, he travelled in Egypt, Palestine and Arabia, going as far as Taif. He was the author of *The Prophets of Israel and their place in history, to the close of the 8th century B.C.* (Edinburgh: Black 1882), *Kinship and Marriage in Early Arabia* (Cambridge University Press, 1885) and many other related works. Robertson Smith travelled with Burton in Egypt— "On April 10, 1880, Professor W. Robertson Smith, of Aberdeen, and I, set out together with the view of visiting the Coptic convents in the Desert about the Natron Lakes to the north-west of Cairo"[1]. They seem to have corresponded extensively—see Volume 3. Smith died at age 47 of tuberculosis.

304. Smithers, Leonard (1861-1907).

A solicitor from Sheffield, an author, translator and all-round entrepreneur of erotica, and late 19th century avant-garde literature. His father was a dentist in Sheffield, from a family said to have emigrated to England from France after the Revolution. Though he practised as a solicitor from the early 1880s, Smithers was increasingly drawn to the world of rare book collecting, more especially to erotica. In Sheffield he met Harry Sidney Nichols, a book dealer and printer, who dealt in under the counter material. Together they formed the Erotika Biblion Society as a means for maintaining plausible deniability when publishing illicit material, in the same way that Burton had started the fictitious Kama Shastra Society.

Smithers became known to the Burtons in 1885, as a subscriber to the *Arabian Nights*. He soon developed a friendship with RFB, channeling rarities from his rapidly expanding personal collection to him. Burton was delighted, being well-versed in off-beat literature of the sort that Smithers was interested in. The first product of the Erotika Biblion Society, by Smithers alone, was an edition of *Priapeia*, a collection of scatological Latin epigrams, threatening would-be burglars with unmanly violation and emasculation. Burton offered some helpful criticism, leading to a joint second edition, for which Burton supplied verse translations. The work was complete by early 1890, and was published toward the end of the year. However, Burton suppressed his association with it at the last minute, out of fear for his Consular pension, at the insistence of Isabel and (most likely) on the advice of F. F Arbuthnot.

Smithers and Nichols moved down to London in 1891, setting themselves up as high-end rare book dealers and niche publishers. They

---

[1] "How to deal with the Slave Scandal in Egypt," reprinted in *Life* Vol. 2, p. 197.

went on to issue Burton's verse translation of the *Carmina* by Catullus, which he had been collaborating with Smithers on before his death—or at least as much as Isabel decided was decent, after she burnt the manuscript. Smithers supplied his own notes and annotations. He also reissued Burton's *Kasidah* and the *Arabian Nights*, in several variant editions, and helped with the production of Isabel's uniform edition of Burton's works. After his partnership with Nichols dissolved in 1895, Smithers published Aubrey Beardsley and Oscar Wilde (e.g. *A Ballad of Reading Gaol*) along with other 'decadents' of the 1890s. He became known for sumptuous book production, with fine materials and craftsmanship. However, a grandiose lifestyle and overly ambitious publishing ventures involving hard-to-sell avant-garde literature led to his bankruptcy in 1900. A downward spiral into poverty, drink and opiates followed, during which he supported himself through increasingly desperate scams and pirated editions; and, finally, an early death in 1907, at age 46. His son Jack left an account of his father's life and his own unusual childhood in *The Early Life & Vicissitudes of Jack Smithers* (London: Martin Secker, 1939). An extensive correspondence between Burton and Smithers survives and appears in Volume 3, covering their collaboration on the Priapeia and Catullus translations, and showing their growing friendship.

305. Soldene, Emily (1838-1912).

An English singer, actress and novelist. Her memoirs created a minor sensation when they were first published, and include a brief account of a meeting with Burton in the early 1870s—see Volume 2.

306. Speke, John Hanning (1827-1864).

An officer in the Indian Army. Born in Devon, at Orleigh Court near Bideford. His father was Captain William Speke, of the 14th Dragoons, his mother Georgina Hanning, from a family which had made money in business. Educated at Barnstaple Grammar school and a college near Blackheath in London. From a young age he suffered from ophthalmia, possibly due to tuberculosis. Very little else is known about his early life, as no documents survive. The family knew the Duke of Wellington, who recommended him for a position in the Indian Army, which he joined as a cadet in the Bengal Native Infantry, arriving in June 1844. Promoted to Lieutenant in 1850, and Captain in 1858, seeing action in the Sikh War of 1849. During this period he used frequent leaves of absence to go on trophy and specimen-hunting trips to Tibet, as the sole officer, mapping regions of the hill country he crossed.[1]

---

[1] See for example, *Allen's Indian Mail* p. 415, who note a leave of absence to

Speke stopped at Aden on furlough in September 1854, intending to go hunting in Somali-land, and ran into Burton's expedition. Burton officially enrolled him and had his leave cancelled. *Allen's Indian Mail* reported a little enigmatically that Speke had "obtained three years' leave of absence, to count as service, in order to join Lieut. Burton in his expedition to the Somalee country. ... with the conviction on his mind that he will never return, from sheer weariness of civilization."[1] His first task on the expedition, to explore the previously unreached Wady Nogal in the interior, ended in failure—which he attributed to his duplicitous guides and interpreter—and he was forced to return to Aden. After this he was severely wounded at the incident in Berberah, where the expedition had camped to prepare for departure, in the early hours of April 19th 1854. Although he was captured and then stabbed multiple times with a spear while tied up, his relatively easy escape after this suggests that, as with Burton and his companions, the attackers were more interested in plunder than murder—notwithstanding the death of his fellow expeditionist Lieut. Stroyan in the heat of the raid.

After Speke recovered more rapidly than expected—he said that his wounds 'literally closed as wounds do in an India-rubber ball after prickings with a penknife'[2]—he served in the Crimean War through 1855, in the Turkish Contingent commanded by Vivian. Then after the war he once again accompanied Burton on the East African expedition of 1856 to 1859, abandoning plans for a private hunting expedition in the Caucasus at Burton's request. Continually tormented by malaria and ophthalmia, they discovered Lake Tanganyika in the interior on Feb. 13th 1858, after six months of travel, but they were forced to cut their journey short by a lack of supplies. During their return to the coast Speke discovered Lake Victoria on July 30th 1858, after setting off to the north with Burton's agreement on his own trip from the Arab trading station Taborah,[3] while Burton stayed behind to organize their return and to recuperate his health. Speke correctly supposed that the Lake he had discovered was the headwaters of the White Nile. Though both men later stated that Burton was immediately skeptical, a letter from Burton to the RGS from Aden, on the way home, suggests of the Nyanza that "there are grave reasons for believing it to be the source of the principal feeder of the White Nile".[4] Here Burton appears to have been accommodating—as the leader of the expedition—the views of his fellow participant Speke, rather than his own.

Simla for April 25 to July 25, 1851. Speke's MS map of Tibet is in the Grant Papers in the National Library of Scotland.

[1] *Allen's Indian Mail* Vol. XIII 1855, p. 64.
[2] *What Led to the Discovery of the Source of the Nile* (1864), p. 149.
[3] Called "Kazeh" by both men, but Taborah by all others.
[4] 1859/04/19. Richard Burton to RGS.

In the aftermath of the journey a rift emerged between Speke and Burton. The correspondence reproduced here shows that Speke never accepted Burton's authority and rankled under his leadership, costively accumulating grievances at what he thought were past slights, and actively seeking opportunities to break free from Burton's influence. When Burton refused to pay some of the porters on their return to Zanzibar in March 1859—citing mutinous behaviour on the trip and placing responsibility for additional bonuses on the former Zanzibar Consul Atkins Hamerton—Speke encouraged the new Consul C. P. Rigby to submit a formal complaint to the East India Company about Burton, which Speke endorsed. Rigby, who was initially reluctant, appears to have had his own reasons for disliking and distrusting Burton, who was friendly with Rigby's arch-enemy at Zanzibar, the French Ambassador Ladislas Cochet. Whatever the merits of this case were, Speke and Rigby pursued and returned to it relentlessly, using it as a weapon against Burton in years to come. Before the charge was filed, however, Speke exploited a two-week stopover at Aden by Burton, en route to London, to beat him to the capital and present his discovery of the Nyanza to the RGS. It is likely that Speke, immediately on his arrival, privately complained to the President of the RGS about Burton's conduct.

Ostensibly maintaining friendly relations with Burton throughout 1859, Speke continued to cultivate Rigby during this period, and their correspondence shows fostering of a shared and virulent dislike for Burton, in private. Before this was revealed in Rigby's official charges against Burton, a dispute also arose about the financing of the Expedition, which had overspent its allowance of 1,000 pounds. Burton had borne the extra cost and requested that Speke help him defray it. Speke took the position that while he had indeed promised to pay half, he would only do so if and when the Bombay government refused to refund the extra money, whereas Burton argued that Speke ought to first pay his portion and then wait for his share of any refund, instead of expecting Burton to carry the entire cost till then. This dispute escalated and was inflamed by the revelation of the complaint about the porters, which Burton interpreted as a duplicitous conspiracy on the part of Speke and Rigby. Ultimately it was only toward the end of the following year that Speke paid his share of the cost overrun, via his brother William, many months after the refund was refused.

Speke returned to Africa in command of his own RGS and Government-sponsored Nile expedition on the 17th August 1860, accompanied by an old friend from India, James A. Grant. On his triumphant return in 1863 he claimed to have shown beyond any doubt that Victoria was the Nile source, having retraced the route of the first expedition to the lake, travelled up close to its western shore, and then journeyed down the Nile from Victoria to Egypt. But his route and other observations left a lot of room for criticism, which he exacerbated by declining to publish a detailed description through the RGS, preferring to publish a book of his own through Blackwood, who were prepared to pay 2,000 pounds for it. He now became involved in a renewal of his bitter dispute with Burton, who along with many other geographers doubted his results, which were only vindicated by Stanley and other explorers in the mid-1870s. On top of this he became involved in a separate public dispute with John Petherick, a Consul and explorer who had been sponsored by public subscription to relieve Speke at Gondokoro, the last southward station on the Nile, but had been delayed—Speke considered his support grossly negligent, refusing to accept his help when they met, and implied in public that Petherick had been using the money subscribed to dabble in the slave trade. A furious response from Petherick and his relatives followed.

By mid-1864 Speke had isolated himself, even courting the Emperor of France to sponsor a scheme he had drawn up for Christianizing the benighted in Central Africa. In the meantime he continued to spread complaints about both Petherick and Burton, who he now accused to trying to poison him in Africa. After he addressed some of these wild allegations to the Anthropological Society, they barred him from entering their premises. Sir Roderick Murchison at the RGS complained that he had assembled a pile of letters labelled "Speke's ravings". Many years later Speke's companion James Grant revived these allegations with former Council members of the RGS, and hinted at them in the press.

Speke wrote two books covering his trips to Africa, *Journal of the Discovery of the Source of the Nile* (Edinburgh: Blackwood, 16th December 1863) and *What Led to the Discovery of the Source of the Nile* (Edinburgh: Blackwood, 30th July 1864)[1]. As with Burton's published accounts after their quarrel, the events described in these are distorted by the dispute between the two men, and Speke attempted to minimize Burton's roles and capabilities wherever possible—a favour reciprocated by Burton's own accounts of Speke.

On Sept. 15th 1864, during an afternoon's partridge shooting near Bath, with his cousin George Pargiter Fuller—the day before a meeting of the British Association at Bath, at which he was scheduled to debate Burton on the Nile sources—Speke died of a self-inflicted gunshot wound. The shot entered his body on his left side, below the chest, passing close to his heart and through his lungs, severing the major

---

[1] A few privately distributed copies of this book include an additional "tail" in which Speke floats a novel theory about Burton's stopover at Aden after the end of East African expedition. Speke claims Burton told him he intended to go on to Jerusalem. This is contradicted by Burton's own letters to the RGS.

vessels. At the time Speke had climbed on to a low loose stone wall, following his cousin, who was some 60 yards ahead. The left barrel only of the gun had discharged. A formal inquest held the next day ruled that the shooting was an accident.

A memorial was subsequently erected to Speke in Hyde Park, and a subscription fund was started, to which Burton—who was never a wealthy man—contributed more generously than most. Almost all of Speke's critics discreetly dropped the subject after his death, except Burton, who not only published a swingeing attack on Speke in *The Nile Basin* (1864) but went on to return to the subject of the Nile and his 'quondam friend' many times afterward, in the columns of journals and the footnotes of his books, even devoting a dismissive postscript to 'Captain Speke' in *Zanzibar* Vol. 2 (1872).

307. Spencer, Walter Thomas (1863-1936).

An Antiquarian book dealer and Dickens specialist, whose store was in New Oxford Street. He knew Leonard Smithers well. Burton was apparently one of his customers, and Spencer left a brief sighting of Burton and the Wilde-Whistler set in his memoirs—see Volume 3. He was also one of Thomas Wright's sources for his biography of Burton.

308. Stanley, Henry Morton (1841-1904).

African explorer, newspaper correspondent and travel writer of Welsh descent (christened "John Rowlands"). Started his early career in America,[1] but made his name by relieving Livingstone at Ujiji in 1871, to the annoyance of the RGS, who distrusted his motives and disliked his methods. Subsequently crossed the African continent in an epic journey from 1874-7, confirming Speke's description of Lake Victoria, by circumnavigating it, and tracing the Congo from Lake Tanganyika to the sea. He later founded the Congo Free State as a Belgian dependency. Stanley's hostility to the RGS, which was never at ease with him, established a bond between himself and Burton. They first met in London in 1872—Stanley thought he showed "savage independence"— and established a correspondence. In 1990 they met by chance in Switzerland, at Maloja, where they were staying in the same hotel, and several group photographs from this occasion survive. Stanley also left an interesting reminiscence of Burton in his autobiography, which appears in Volume 3.

---

[1] See also Stanley's diary entries on Burton, held in the archives in Belgium cited in Tim Jeal, *Stanley* (New Haven: Yale University Press, 2008). Early biographies of Stanley are grossly inaccurate, largely because of his own determination to obfuscate his origins.

309. Steinhaüser, Dr. John Frederick (1814-1866).[1]

A close friend of Burton's from his Indian days, with the Dickensian nickname "Stiggins". He entered the Royal College of Surgeons in May 1838, but after that he became a surgeon in the Bombay Artillery, arriving in December of 1845. Posted to Scinde in 1846, where he spent time in Hyderabad and Karachi, and first met Burton. He served in the Second Sikh War of 1848 to 1849, and took part in the Siege of Mooltan. Subsequently he qualified as an interpreter in Hindustani in 1852, and then became the Civil Surgeon at Aden on the 19th May 1853. Burton recalled that "It may be permitted me also to note that this translation is a natural outcome of my Pilgrimage to Al-Medinah and Meccah. Arriving at Aden in the (so-called) winter of 1852, I put up with my old and dear friend, Steinhaeuser, to whose memory this volume is inscribed; and, when talking over Arabia and the Arabs, we at once came to the same conclusion that, while the name of this wondrous treasury of Moslem folk-lore is familiar to almost every English child, no general reader is aware of the valuables it contains, nor indeed will the door open to any but Arabists. Before parting we agreed to 'collaborate' and produce a full, complete, unvarnished, uncastrated copy of the great original, my friend taking the prose and I the metrical part; and we corresponded upon the subject for years. But whilst I was in the Brazil, Steinhaeuser died suddenly of apoplexy at Berne in Switzerland and, after the fashion of Anglo-India, his valuable MSS. left at Aden were dispersed, and very little of his labours came into my hands."[2] And "Steinhaeuser and I began and ended our work with the first Bulak ('Bui.') Edition printed at the port of Cairo in A.H. 1251 =A.D. 1835. But when preparing my MSS. for print I found the text incomplete, many of the stories being given in epitome and not a few ruthlessly mutilated with head or feet wanting."[3]

Burton intended "Stiggins" to accompany the East Africa Expedition of 1857-1859, but Steinhaüser could not get a passage to Zanzibar in time. On the way back to England after the expedition, Burton and Speke stopped off at Aden and both stayed with Steinhaüser. "We afterwards wandered together over the United States, and it is my comfort, now that he also is gone, to think that no unkind thought, much less an unfriendly word, ever broke our fair companionship. His memory is doubly dear to me".[4] Stiggins did not accompany him to Salt Lake City. Burton described him as a "sound scholar, good naturalist, skilful practitioner, with rare personal qualities".[5] He died, Burton said of apoplexy, at Berne

---

[1] Sometimes spelled 'Steinhaueser' or 'Steinhauser' due to the umlaut.
[2] *Nights* Vol. 1, p. 9.
[3] Nights Vol. 1 p. xix.
[4] *Zanzibar* Vol. 1, pp. 14-15.
[5] *Life* Vol 1, p. 172.

in Switzerland.¹

310. Stevenson, Frederick James (1835-1926).

Engineer and explorer, born in London of Scottish parents, William Stevenson (1795-1854) and Louisa Rudd, and educated in Ayrshire, on Free Church of Scotland principles. He was articled to an engineer, working on canal construction. Between 1863 and 1869 he travelled in North and South America. He first worked on railway construction in North America, some time before the Civil War, memorably employing Thomas Edison as a train newsboy and vendor in Detroit. But in 1863 he left the business to embark on private expeditions to the Mammoth Caves of Kentucky, and to Havana. He went on to South America, including Brazil, the Argentine and Patagonia (1867-1868), and then Chile, Peru and Bolivia (1868-1869). Various specimens he collected on his travels are still held by the British Museum. He returned to England in 1870, but not before stopping off to explore the West Indies en route. Arriving in Europe he set off to witness the Franco Prussian War. After this little is known, beyond that he educated and ran a camp for schoolboys from around 1890 onward—"it became his constant practice to entertain parties of schoolboys to enormous teas".² Stevenson was given letters to deliver to Burton in Brazil, in November 1867, and left an interesting account of the meeting in his diary, describing the Consul as "resolute and determined" but "reckless in conversation"—see Volume 2. Stevenson's complete travel diaries, which were only published in abbreviated form, are held at the RGS, and may contain more material about Burton.

311. Stisted, Georgiana Martha (1846?-1903).

"Miss G. M. Stisted of Norwood", a niece of Burton, the daughter of his sister Maria (1823–1894), who had married Sir Henry William Stisted (1817-1885), the first Lieutenant-Governor of Ontario (1867-8). Georgiana, who was unmarried, left a reminiscence of her uncle in *Temple Bar*,³ and later wrote a worshipful biography (Stisted, 1896) claiming to represent the position of the Burton family against Isabel's *Life*. In this, Isabel—"handsome, fascinating Isabel Arundell"— worships but is not worshipped, nor is her pursuit of her religion, to

---

¹ See also 'Births and Deaths' *Pall Mall Gazette* Saturday 04 August 1866, p. 6.
² Douglas Timins, preface to Stevenson *A Traveller of the Sixties* (London: Constable, 1929) pp. 76, 95. Timins appears to be the only extant source of information about Stevenson, outside of the MS diaries.
³ The novel sections of this reminiscence are included here by their date of occurrence.

which Georgiana attributes Burton's recall from Damascus. In particular, she scoffs at the supposed deathbed conversion of Burton. Aside from that and a few scattered anecdotes there is surprisingly little that is new in her biography, large chunks of which were just paraphrased or quoted from Burton's own works, and the attacks on Isabel were not well-received. She had earlier published an angry 3-volume novel, *A Fireside King* (Tinsley, 1880), which the *Athenaeum* thought "by no means badly put together",[1] while the *Spectator* wondered "It is difficult to believe that any writer can have continued to be in a rage during all the time that must have been consumed in the production of a novel in three volumes".[2] Her sister Maria "Minnie" Stisted had died in 1878. She bred pedigreed cats, and died in 1903 at her home Grazeley in Norwood, after a long seclusion due to illness. She was buried in Chirbury Churchyard in West Shropshire.[3]

312. Stocks, John Ellerton (1822-1854).

A doctor and botanist from Hull, in the service of the East India Company, where he was an assistant surgeon. He had trained at University College London. T.H. Huxley had been a classmate of Stocks, and recalled:[4] "The examination began at eleven. At two they brought in lunch. It was a good meal enough, but the circumstances were not particularly favourable to enjoyment, so after a short delay we resumed our work. It began to be evident between whom the contest lay, and the others determined that I was one man's competitor and Stocks (he is now in the East India service) the other. Scratch, scratch, scratch! Four o'clock came, the usual hour of closing the examination, but Stocks and I had not half done, so with the consent of the others we petitioned for an extension. The examiner was willing to let us go on as long as we liked. Never did I see man write like Stocks; one might have taken him for an attorney's clerk writing for his dinner. We went on. I had finished a little after eight, he went on till near nine, and then we had tea and dispersed."

While stationed in Sindh, where he was appointed vaccinator and collector of drugs, he co-authored a notable early paper on the region with Burton, which was submitted to the Pringle Commission of 1847-8: "Division of Time, Articles of Cultivation, and Modes of Intoxication,

---

[1] *Athenaeum*, May 1 1880, pp. 563-4.
[2] *Spectator*, Aug 14 1880, p. 1044.
[3] *Bye-gones: relating to Wales and the border counties* 1903-4 (London: Oswestry & Wrexham, 1905), p. 48. See also Thomas Wright's *The Life of Sir Richard Burton* (London: Everett, 1906), p. 186.
[4] *Life and Letters of Thomas Henry Huxley* by Leonard Huxley (New York, Appleton, 1901) Vol. 1, p. 19.

in Scinde".[1] Stocks, "whose brilliant attainments as a botanist, whose long and enterprising journeys, and whose eminently practical bent of mind had twice recommended him for the honors and trials of African exploration" was originally intended to join the Somali Expedition.

Stocks had returned to England on Furlough in 1853 to deposit and arrange his collection of botanical specimens at Kew, and complete a long memoir on Sindh. En route, he ran into Burton at Shepheard's Hotel in Cairo, and they discussed an abandoned Government project from 1851 to explore the Somali-land interior, which Stocks had volunteered to join—Burton invited him to join forces to complete it. Cheerfully notifying Norton Shaw at the RGS, he wrote "Anent Stocks. I gave him a note to you ... The fellow writes well but is modest—shameful defect! I intended him to accompany me to Zanzibar, and I verily believe he would still do it. Above all things he's an excellent chap, but a mad bitch. Very mad."[2] In 1854, at Cottingham near Hull, during a "stay with some very intimate friends at the place of his birth, he was seized with an apoplectic stroke, from which he partially recovered; but a second, after an interval of ten days, carried him off."[3] He had died on Wednesday 30th August, shortly after permission to proceed with the Expedition had been received from the East India Company.

313. Stoker, Abraham "Bram" (1847-1912).

Athletic Irish novelist, born in Dublin of parents who were originally from Sligo. He is popularly remembered as the author of the enduring horror story *Dracula* and tales like *The Lair of the White Worm*. He graduated from Trinity College, Dublin, where he studied mathematics. Although he qualified as a barrister, he never practiced, turning to journalism instead. He managed the legendary actor Henry Irving for many years, after one of his positive reviews of the actor had attracted Irving's notice; through him Stoker came to know Burton, leaving vivid descriptions in his memoirs of several encounters between 1878 and 1885—see Volumes 2 and 3. Burton dedicated Volume III of the Nights to Irving, who he had first met in London in 1875. It may have been through Burton that Stoker first met the Hungarian explorer Ármin Vámbéry,[4] whose Transylvanian table-talk has been suggested as a source of inspiration for *Dracula*. He died of syphilis in 1912, not long

---

[1] Later reissued as "Brief Notes Relative to the Division of Time, and Articles of Cultivation in Sind; to Which Are Appended Remarks on the Modes of Intoxication in That Province." *Bombay Government Records*. New Series No. 17, Part 2, pp. 613-36.
[2] 1853/11/16. Richard Burton to Norton Shaw.
[3] *The Gentleman's Magazine and Historical Review* July 1854, 401.
[4] See the entry for Vámbéry below.

after the Titanic sunk.

314. Stokes, Sir John (1825–1902).

Soldier in the Royal Engineers, born at Cobham in Kent. He trained at the Woolwich Academy, and was involved in the War of the Axe (1846-7) in South Africa and the Crimean War. Later he was a Vice President of the Suez Canal Company. He briefly met Burton at Alexandria in 1881, and left the mention which appears in Volume 3— "He was an interesting man but I was so disgusted with his language that I took an early opportunity of leaving the table". Isabel, who he met at Trieste, made a better impression on him—"almost as eccentric as her husband, but a fine looking woman and very tall".

315. Stroyan, William (1825?-1855).

Lieutenant in the Indian Navy, joining on the 5th March 1842. Received his commission on 8th Feb. 1848. Served on the "Elphinstone" in 1848 and on the *Palinurus* surveying expedition of 1850. Surveyed the Punjaub river system in 1853. Accompanied Burton on the Somali Expedition of 1854-5. Burton had known Stroyan on the Sindh Survey, and later wrote that he "applied to the Bombay Government for the assistance of Lieut. William Stroyan, I. N., an officer distinguished by his surveys on the coast of Western India, in Sindh, and on the Panjab Rivers. It was not without difficulty that such valuable services were spared for the deadly purpose of penetrating into Eastern Africa. All obstacles, however, were removed by their ceaseless and energetic efforts, who had fostered the author's plans, and early in the autumn of 1854, Lieut. Stroyan received leave to join the Expedition."[1] He was killed, aged 30, during the attack on Burton's party at Berberah in the early hours of April 19th 1855. His heart was speared through, and his skull was crushed by a blow from a club or a stone.

316. Swinburne, Algernon (1837-1909).[2]

Lyrical Poet, the son of Admiral Charles Henry Swinburne (1797-1877), and Lady Jane Henrietta Ashburnham (1809-1896). Largely raised on the Isle of Wight, he was educated at Eton, but left for reasons now thought to be related to a growing fondness for the flogging inflicted on him there. He was at Balliol College in Oxford from 1856 to 1861, but left without taking a degree. During his time there he had fallen in

---

[1] *First Footsteps*, p. xxiii.
[2] There is a cottage industry devoted to Swinburne's poetry and general life, with 6 Volumes of *Letters* (Lang, 1956) and a further three of *Uncollected Letters* (Myers, 2004).

with Dante Gabriel Rossetti and the Pre-Raphaelites, but had found the gateway to a much wider circle of influence through an invitation to meet Monckton Milnes some time in May 1861. At one of Milnes' 10 o'clock breakfasts, on the 5th of June 1861, he was introduced to Burton and the two men took to each other at once.

On the 12th of August 1861 the Burtons and Swinburne were invited to Milnes' country estate at Fryston in Yorkshire. They were joined by the Parisian Bluestocking Mary Clarke Mohl, Holman Hunt, Francis Turner Palgrave, and the array of emerging and established travellers, artists, political and literary figures that Milnes liked to mix with and bump into each other. This was the first of many Swinburne visits to Fryston, where he developed a habit of staying on long after the other company had left. By this time he had already shown signs of dissipation, a process which was not reversed by his new introductions to Burton, Frederick Hankey, Edward Vaux Bellamy, Colonel John Studholme Hodgson and the rest of the Milnes-Burton coterie. Even though Burton soon left for Fernando Po, he kept in touch with both Swinburne and Milnes, and whenever he returned to London on leave over the coming years, the coterie reunited.

In 1865 Burton induced Swinburne to join the Anthropological Society that he had co-founded two years earlier. With an inner circle of self-styled 'Cannibals' they dined together as the at Bertolini's Hotel[1] near Leicester Square where Swinburne sardonically intoned a Catechism, piously pleading for the roasting, boiling, squeezing and jamming of all the 'milky, vegetable race', apostates to the Cannibal Faith:[2]

> Preserve us from our enemies,
> Thou who art Lord of suns & skies,
> Whose meat & drink is flesh in pies
>   And blood in bowls!
> Of thy sweet mercy, damn their eyes,
>   And damn their souls!
>
> The cannibal of just behaviour
> Acknowledges the Lord his saviour,
> With gifts of whose especial favour
>   He hath been crammed,
> To whom an offering of sweet savour
>   Are all the damned.
>
> O Lord, thy people know full well
> That all who eat not flesh & fell,

---

[1] 34 St Martin's Street, on the corner of Orange. Sometimes misspelled as 'Bartolini's'. It was later pulled down.

[2] *The Cannibal Catechism* (London: Privately Printed, 1913).

Who cannot rightly speak or spell
    Thy various names,
Shall be for ever boiled in hell
    Among the flames.

Glad tidings of great exhultation
Proclaim we to the chosen nation;
To all men else in every station
    The joyful story
That they are going to damnation
    And we to glory.

In pits of sulfur thou wilt cram them,
In chains of burning brimstone jam them,
Squeeze them like figs, like wadding ram them,
    With flame surround them;
O Lord of love, confound and damn them
    Damn & confound them!

Grind them to pieces small & gritty,
O thou whose names are love & pity!
Roast brown all faces that were pretty,
    All black even blacker;
Strip off the trappings of their city,
    Paint, plumes, & lacquer.

The foes thy people seek to kill,
Even as a devil do thou grill!
O let thy stormy anger still
    Shake them like jellies!
Give thou their carcases to fill
    Thy servants' bellies!

The heathen, whose ungodly lip
Doth in ungodly pewter dip,
Curse his gin, whiskey, rum & flip,
    Strong ale & bumbo![1]
Scourge him with anger as a whip
    O Mumbo-Jumbo!

The men who eat their neighbours not,
For all such has the Lord made hot
(To boil their souls as in a pot)
    The fire of hell:
But if thou leave not me to rot
    Then all is well.

The milky, vegetable race
Of such as have not seen thy face,

---

[1] A drink made from rum, flavoured with sugar-water and nutmeg.

> Lord, damn them by thy special grace
>   Thou who art gracious.
> And raise into the holy place
>   Me, Athanasius.[1]

A mace was placed on the dinner table, next to the President, in the shape of a negro head in ebony chewing a thigh bone in ivory—Swinburne called it "Ecce Homo". But Burton was soon off again, in April 1865, to his posting at Santos in Brazil. Swinburne teasingly wrote to his fellow-flagellant Milnes, "As my tempter and favourite audience has gone to Santos I may hope to be a good boy again, after such a 'jolly good swishing' as Rodin alone can and dare administer. ... The Captain was too many for me; and I may have shaken the thyrsus[2] in your face. But after this half I mean to be no end good."

Houghton must have said something about dissipation under Burton's influence, to which Swinburne unflappably responded "As to anything you have fished (how I say not) out of Mrs. Burton to the discredit of my 'temperance, soberness and chastity' as the Catechism puts it—how can she who believes in the excellence of 'Richard' fail to disbelieve in the virtues of any other man? En moi vous voyez Les Malheurs de la Vertu; en lui Les Prospérités du Vice.[3] In effect it is not given to all his juniors to tenir tête à[4] Burton—but I deny that his hospitality ever succeeded in upsetting me—as he himself on the morrow of a latish séance admitted with approbation, allowing that he had thought to get me off my legs, but my native virtue and circumspection were too much for him."[5] But as Edmund Gosse remarked, nothing was easier than to get Swinburne "off his legs".

From Brazil Burton kept up a bantering correspondence with Swinburne (2 letters survive and are given in Volume 2), whose book *Poems and Ballads* (1866) was attracting increasingly hostile attention: "One anonymous letter from Dublin threatened me, if I did not suppress my book within six weeks from that date, with castration ... he had seen his gamekeeper do it with cats." He promised Burton that "I have in hand a scheme of mixed verse and prose—a sort of etude a la Balzac plus the poetry—which I flatter myself will be more offensive and objectionable to Britannia than anything I have yet done". Burton replied that "I fairly warn you that at the least sign not of movement retrograde but of remission in advancing you will be bellowed by the British hound". By now Swinburne had (privately) tired of Monckton

---

[1] Father of Orthodoxy, Contra Mundum, the 4th Century Bishop of Alexandria.
[2] A wand of giant fennel topped with a pinecone that was a symbol of hedonism.
[3] In me you see The Misfortunes of Virtue; in him the prosperity of Vice.
[4] To stand up to.
[5] Swinburne to Lord Houghton, Lang Vol. 1 (1959), pp. 124-5.

Milnes, whose gentle advice about reigning in his drinking he found tedious, and Burton sympathized: "I fear that unless you pall with abject poverty or paralysis you will see no more of our mutual friend Houghton.[1] I hope to arouse his wrath by a Canto of Camões which I have sent to Macmillan".[2] At the same time Isabel was writing to Houghton asking after "poor little Swinburne,"—"I am sorry for him as far as the drinking propensities go. He is simply possessed by an 'unclean imp'".[3]

When Burton returned in 1869 to Europe, en route to his new posting in Damascus, he met up with Swinburne at the end of July for a water cure at Vichy through the month of August. Swinburne may have been looking for a cure for his chronic dysentery. Together Burton and Swinburne tramped over the hilly countryside, returning spent in the evenings to the Hotel de France. They climbed the steep Puy de Dôme, 5000 ft. above sea level, investigated the cathedrals and gathered wild flowers to press. Swinburne, whose mother disapproved of Burton, tried to change her mind with enthusiastic reports home: "I feel now as if I knew for the first time what it was to have an elder brother." Two weeks after they arrived they were joined by Isabel, and by Adelaide Sartoris, who looked Swinburne up in the hotel register. With Mrs. Sartoris was her close friend Frederick Leighton, and this may have been the first time that Burton met his best-known portrayer. When the month-long water cure was over—"The waters did me some good but I was delighted to leave the hideous hole with its jaundices gout and diabetes. Out of Paris the French are perfect savages"[4]—the Burtons toured the Auvergne with Swinburne. At the end of August they were off overland through Italy to take their boat to the Levant, while Swinburne headed north to drop in on Frederick Hankey and Victor Hugo in Paris, and after that back to England.

In subsequent years Burton would always reunite with Swinburne whenever he was back in London. By 1872, in the long interlude between Burton's recall from Damascus and his posting in Trieste, Swinburne had already been expelled from the Arts club, either for dancing or for stomping on the hats of other members, depending on who told the story; so they were back at the Cannibal Club—"I shall come and bring my friend (Simeon) Solomon. Yours in the Cannibal Faith, A. C. Swinburne."[5] The two maintained a steady and affectionate

---

[1] Monckton Milnes, see Register.
[2] 1867/04/05. Richard Burton to Algernon Swinburne.
[3] 1867/11/23 and 1868/04/18. Isabel Burton to Monckton Milnes.
[4] 1869/09/01. Richard Burton to Monckton Milnes.
[5] Lang Viol. II (1859), p. 135. This undated note is tagged February 1871 by Lang but that is a mistake, since Burton was still in Damascus then. It could only be 1872.

correspondence, and Burton appears often in Swinburne's letters to others, usually as an exemplar of ruggedness, sometimes as the whole cloth from which to cut a red flag to wave at propriety: "that lost love of Burton's, the beloved and blue object of his Central African Affections, whose caudal charms and simious seductions were too strong for the narrow laws of Levitical or Mosaic prudery which would confine the jewel of a man to the lotus of a merely human female by the most odious and unnatural of priestly restrictions."[1]

Monckton Milnes must have complained about Swinburne's downward spiral to Isabel, who carefully cultivated him—"I don't like Swinburne for neglecting you ... I abominate ingratitude".[2] But as Swinburne later wrote to Burton, he had tired of inoffense—"I got a pathetically pressing invitation to luncheon from our common Houghton. I'm afraid the poor old Thermometer is getting very shaky—but the quicksilver though running low will keep time with the weather to the last."[3]

Alice "Lallah" Bird left a vivid description of an evening spent in 1878 in the company of the Burtons and Swinburne, at the Welbeck Street house she shared with her brother Dr. George Bird. By then Swinburne was in the closing stages of the alcoholism that he would soon be rescued from by Theodore Watts Dunton, by force—"He looked ill and worn, and older. He had a haggard expression as if his nerves were out of tune. He and Captain Burton were the chief talkers".[4] Dante Gabriel Rossetti had long given up on him. In 1879 Watts-Dunton removed him to his house *The Pines*, to be kept on a short leash, prolonged but dampened.

Over the succeeding years there are occasional glints of Swinburne in the company of one or more of the Burtons. Isabel lunched with him in March 1880, introducing him to Lynn Linton, and both Burtons dined with him in the company of the Birds in July 1882. Swinburne later wrote admiringly of Burton's translation of Camoens' *Lyricks* (1884), which was dedicated to him, reciprocating Swinburne's dedication of his *Poems and Ballads Second Series* (1878). There was another reunion on Aug. 12, 1885, while the Burtons were in England to arrange the Nights, but that may have been their last meeting.

Swinburne publicly—very bitterly—fell out with Isabel after the death of Burton, specifically over the deathbed conversion act and the destruction of Burton's manuscripts, attacking her in verse in his 'Auvergne Elegy' to Burton.[5] His private sniping was salted with

---

[1] Lang Vol. III (1959), p. 61.
[2] 1874/08/12. Isabel Burton to Monckton Milnes.
[3] 1884/11/27. Algernon Swinburne to Richard Burton.
[4] See Volume 2.
[5] *Fortnightly Review* July, 1892.

peculiarly old-fashioned anti-popery. He wrote to Theodore Watts-Dunton in July 1891 of "Lady B. or her fellow-conspirators against a deathbed on behalf of the Oly Catholic Church" and in November 1892 to their former lunch partner Lynn Linton, of "the popish mendacities of that poor liar Lady Burton ... she has befouled Richard Burton's memory like a harpy".[1]

But it was Swinburne who was Isabel's "clever friend" who said that Burton projected the "jaw of a Devil and the brow of a God". And when Edmund Gosse contacted him about writing a precis of Burton's life ten years after his death (possibly for the DNB) Swinburne could not imagine being that terse, but assured Gosse "from personal experience" that "no more delightful companion can be imagined, either in his most serious or his most humorous moods".[2]

317. Sykes, Colonel William Henry (1790-1872).

British Naturalist from Yorkshire, a founder member of the Royal Statistical Society and the Asiatic Society of Bombay, and a Fellow of the Royal Society. He was a Bombay Army officer, having joined the East India Company in 1803. He rose to the Board of the Company in 1840, becoming Vice Chairman in 1855 and Chairman in 1856. Burton dedicated Volume 1 of his *Pilgrimage* to Sykes. Isabel describes him as an early friend of RFB, and he was an influential early supporter of Burton's expeditions to Arabia and to Africa, although in 1853 Sykes supposedly "sharply rebuked him with printing a book that would do far more harm than good"[3]—*A Complete System of Bayonet Exercise* (1853), whose contents seem wholly uninteresting now. Sykes, his thermometers and his statistics are mentioned several times by Burton in *Lake Regions* and *Zanzibar*, even popping up again in the *Nights*—"We are not told that the Prince was thereby salivated like the late Colonel Sykes when boiling his mercury for thermometric experiments".[4] After retiring from the Company Board in 1857 Sykes became a Liberal Member of Parliament for Aberdeen until his death in 1872, but kept up his scientific involvement—he was with Burton and Speke at Bath for the British Association of 1864. He was the author of a number of papers and books, including *Notes on the Religious, Moral and Political State of Ancient India* (1841).

---

[1] Lang Vol. VI (1859) pp. 10, 45. July 23, 1891 and November 24, 1892. Although Swinburne sent many presentation copies of his works to Burton, the only surviving volume in Burton's personal library is *Essays and Studies* (1875).
[2] Lang Vol. VI (1959), p. 147.
[3] *Life* Vol. 1 p. 97.
[4] *Nights* Vol. 3, p. 344.

318. Thorndike, Rev. Charles Faunce (1821-1915).

"On the 12th of August arrived our new Consular Chaplain (the Rev. Mr. Thorndike), a charming, gentlemanly, and devout man, who had been in the army."[1] Retired from Trieste in 1905 and became Chaplain at Fiume. He left an admiring reminiscence of Burton for *Chamber's Journal* (see Volume 3)—" 'Do you know, you are the only padre Richard has ever taken to,' said Lady Burton to me as I sat by her side at dinner." Oddly, Thorndike make no mention of Burton in his slim booklet of memoirs *Some Memories of Ninety Years. The recollections of Charles Faunce Thorndike of Trieste, gunner and priest.* (William Clowes: Canterbury, 1912).[2] Thorndike started his career in the Royal Artillery, and retired to the Villa Freeland, Trieste.

319. Tinsley, William (1831-1902).

An English publisher born at South Mimms in Hertfordshire, the self-educated son of an illiterate gamekeeper who had married the daughter of a veterinarian. After following his brother Edward to London in 1852 to work on the railways, the two soon quit their regular jobs to found their own publishing firm 'Tinsley Brothers' in 1854— "Later on Tinsley's health was drunk, and he replied in characteristic fashion, detailing among other things his first arrival in the great metropolis on the top of a haycart, with the traditional three half-pence in his pocket."[3] Eventually the Tinsley authors ranged from Ouida to Wilkie Collins, Thomas Hardy, G. A. Henty and Richard Burton. Edward died of a stroke in 1866, but William continued on, founding *Tinsley's Magazine* the following year. The magazine made no money, the books sold inconsistently, and the firm was driven to bankruptcy in the late 1880s.

Tinsley's memoirs *Random Recollections of an old Publisher* contain a substantial section on Burton (see Volume 3), since Tinsley had published most of Burton's output from the 1860s, including all his travel writing: *Abeokuta and the Camaroons Mountains* (1863), *Wanderings in West Africa* (1863), *A Mission to Gelele* (1864), *The Nile Basin* (1864), *Wit and Wisdom from West Africa* (1865), *Explorations of The Highlands of the Brazil* (1869), *Letters from the Battlefields of Paraguay* (1870), *Unexplored Syria* (1872) and finally *Zanzibar; City, Island, and Coast* (1872). It was an uneasy relationship, as the following remark, from a letter Burton wrote to his Brazil-based friend Albert Tootal, shows—"I want the stupid editor Tinsley to get up a S. American

---

[1] *Life* Vol. 2, p. 253. This was 1883.
[2] This is held by the British Library, shelf mark 4908.g.17. 15 pages.
[3] Henry Vizetelly *Glances back through seventy years*—see Volume 2.

clientèle, but like other Britishers he is too slow. They will probably not translate my 'Highlands of the B.', but if that is done I should like to correct the copy & to cut out about half, in fact all that suits only Britishers."[1]

None of his Burton titles, according to Tinsley, made much money, but their sales were persistent and perennial. He had a poor opinion of the *Arabian Night*s and the Erotica of the later years—"it seems hard to believe that any truly noble-minded man or woman could, or would, lend their name to literature full of innuendo, if not worse matter."

320.   Tootal, Albert (1838?-1893).

A clerk in Rio de Janeiro who eventually rose to head the Brazilian branch of the firm John Bradshaw & Co. The Burtons met him when they were stationed at Santos in the late 1860s, and a number of important letters between both of the Burtons and Tootal survive—see Volume 2. Tootal was fluent in German and collaborated with Burton in producing the first translation into English of *The Captivity of Hans Stade of Hesse* (London: Hakluyt Society, 1874), a memoir of South American cannibalism which Tootal translated and Burton annotated— to which he added a long description of his own travels in the area associated with Hans Stade, amounting to a third of the whole book.

Tootal was a member of the Anthropological Society, which he joined in 1867 as a result of Burton's encouragement. After *Hans Stade*, Burton urged him to keep on: "hundreds of business men (e.g. John Lubbock) find time for study, and change of occupation [to] an active mind like yours is the best of rest. Why should you not go in regularly for anthropology, get all the books from Wilson downwards and read them carefully making notes in the margin? A couple of hours a day (regular) soon makes a giant hole in a subject. Your translation of Hans Stade will be noticed vy favourably and your name will have made its first appearance in public. The anthropology of the Brazil requires a completely modern treatment and you have not a soul as rival."[2] Tootal, who shared Isabel's interests in music and was a founder of the 'Club Beethoven' in Rio, does not appear to have acted on this advice. He died in 1893 in Hampstead at age 55, 'after a few hours illness'.[3]

321.   Tussaud, John Theodore (1858-1943).

A member of the "Madame Tussaud" waxworks dynasty. He was brought into the business at a young age and later became the chief modeller. After Burton's death, he had duly received his place in

---

[1] 1870/05/16. Richard Burton to Albert Tootal.
[2] 1874/10/29. Richard Burton to Albert Tootal.
[3] *London Evening Standard*, Tuesday 05 December 1893, p. 1.

Tussaud's collection by 1894, apparently with the help of Isabel—"his handsome and stately widow", who said that though she "gave them the real clothes and the real weapons, and dressed him myself" she nevertheless "always had a trouble with Tussaud about a certain stoop which he declares is artistic, and which I say was not natural to him."[1] Although the reliability of his memoirs has been questioned,[2] Tussaud left an admiring reminiscence of Isabel that appears in Volume 3.

322. Vámbéry, Ármin (1832-1913).

A Jewish-Hungarian traveller, author, linguist and orientalist. He was born in Hungary and educated in Vienna and Budapest, showing marked linguistic abilities. After a stint as an Ottoman official in the late 1850s, he travelled, disguised as a Dervish, through Central Asia to Samarkand, from 1861 to 1864. This trip is described in his *Travels in Central Asia* (1865). He was later appointed to a professorship at the University of Budapest.

In 1864, after his travels as a dervish, Vámbéry met Burton at Fryston, the Yorkshire estate of Monckton Milnes, a scene he described fondly in his memoirs.[3] Later he also attended the fateful meeting of the British Association at Bath in September 1864—"At the request of the President,[4] M. Vambery convulsed the audience by pronouncing the Mahomadan blessing, which as a holy beggar pilgrim he was constantly called upon to utter."[5] The affection between the two was qualified in later years, since Burton did not approve of Vámbéry's supposed Turcophilia—"You will therefore regard M. Vambery's opinions upon the subject of Turkey with suspicion, and reserve all your respect for his invaluable publications upon the Turanian dialects, his specialite."[6]

323. Viator.

Pseudonym of Richard Burton e.g. in letters of 1848 to the *Bombay Times* about the language examination system in India—see Volume 1. Others were known to use the pseudonym too over the years, but it is certain the Burton used it again himself. Burton is known to have published letters and articles under many other pseudonyms, in the *Daily News* and other papers.

---

[1] Wright Vol. 2 (1906), p 275.
[2] See *Madame Tussaud: And the History of Waxworks* by Pamela M. Pilbeam (Hambledon: London, 2003), p. 174.
[3] See Volume 1.
[4] Sir Roderick Murchison.
[5] *The British Association at Bath, 1864. Authorised reprint of the reports in the special daily editions of the Bath Chronicle* (1864), p. 238.
[6] AEI, p. 47.

324. Villiers, Frederick (1851-1922).

British newspaper correspondent and war illustrator, born in London but educated in France. He reported for the *Graphic* and the *Illustrated London News*, and produced several books of memoirs based on his first-hand experience of the minor wars of the late Victorian Era—he is said to have covered 21 campaigns in total. He may have been the first war correspondent to use a film camera on a battlefield, during the Sudan Campaign of 1897. He met Burton in Cairo in 1880 and left a reminiscence—" 'Excuse me!' I said, 'but are you not the Consul of Trieste?' ".[1]

325. Vizetelly, Henry Richard (1820-1894).

A London journalist, author and publisher whose firm Vizetelly and Company brought out English translations of Emile Zola's novels, including *La Terre* (The Earth, 1887) in 1888. When prosecuted by the National Vigilance Association for obscenity, he eventually pleaded guilty and was convicted and fined 100 pounds. The court did not accept his argument that the translations had been expurgated. See the detailed description of the trial by Ernest Alfred Vizetelly *Émile Zola, Novelist and Reformer: An Account of His Life & Work* (London: John Lane, 1904). Vizetelly knew Burton from the 1860s and left a reminiscence of him.[2] Burton made frequent references to Vizetelly in his correspondence with Leonard Smithers, as Vizetelly's legal difficulties, over obscenity, coincided with their own collaboration, which ran similar risks.

326. Whistler, James McNeill (1834-1903).

American-born painter and wit living in England. He was a friend of Swinburne, through whom he may have met Burton, possibly as early as 1869. Isabel also recalled running into him in Italy towards the end of 1879—"we went off to Chioggia, the fishing village near Venice, and we had the pleasure of unearthing Mr. Jemmy Whistler and Dr. George Bird. Mr. Whistler was a great find for us."[3] They met up again in the 1880s through Luke Ionides—see the anecdote in Volume 3. Whistler was also connected to Burton through the Oscar Wilde set, which circulated through his Tite Street house. This is confirmed by a brief note by Burton, written from the Athenaeum Club, to Whistler, which is still extant: "Last Sunday I drove in hurried and pleasurable anticipation

---

[1] See Volume 3.
[2] See Volume 2.
[3] *Life* Vol. 2, p. 174.

to Tite St. Chelsea ... Where and when can I see you?".[1]

327. Wilson, Charles Rivers (1831-1916).

An English civil servant and financier, born in London and educated at Eton and Oxford. He was a Director of the Suez Canal Company, and met the Burtons briefly in the late 1870s—"He is less a ruffian than I expected, but it is true, as Vivian[2] says, that he has a hard and cruel face, and Mrs. Vivian says he frightens her. Mrs. Burton is what you might expect from her book, rather a gusher".[3] Isabel hoped at the time they met to involve him in her campaign against cruelty to animals.[4]

328. Wilson, Frank.

Burton's vice-consul at Fernando Po, possibly of Scottish descent, though very little is known for sure about him. They were already friends when Burton got him the job, perhaps having met in London. Wilson was temporary Consul after Burton's departure, before Charles Livingstone got the job in 1865, and intermittently after that till at least 1874. When the missionary Henry Roe arrived on Fernando Po in 1870, Wilson was there to greet him.[5] In 1866 Wilson's address at the Anthropological Society was "41 Arlington Street, Glasgow and Fernando Po" and he appears to have been there till 1870. One source describes his career as "very short and inglorious", due to his "having fallen victim to the temptations of the climate"[6] but this appears to be a mistake—extant correspondence with Burton shows that he returned to London and went to work for the Education Department in Whitehall, at the very least between 1875 and 1880, and married, living at one time in South Hackney, London. He took a leave of absence from the Education Department in 1880 to pursue a mining venture in Sierra Leone.[7] Burton and Wilson kept up a lively correspondence, which appears in Volume 1 and Volume 2.

---

[1] 30 July, probably 1885. Whistler Correspondence, Glasgow.
[2] The British Consul General at Cairo.
[3] See Volume 2. The book was Isabel's *Inner Life* (1875).
[4] *AEI* (1879), p. 245.
[5] Henry Roe *West African Scenes* (1874), p. 32.
[6] Harry Cotterel "Reminiscences of one connected with the West African Trade from 1863 to 1910" in *Trading in West Africa, 1840-1920* ed. by Peter N. Davies (New York: Africana Publishing Company, 1976). See also Noel Matthews *A guide to manuscripts and documents in the British Isles relating to Africa* (London: Oxford University Press, 1971) page 207.
[7] Huntington Library, RFB 1315-1318, letters from Frank Wilson to Richard F. Burton.

329. Wood, Sir Charles (1800–1885).

A British Member of Parliament for the Liberal Party and Cabinet Minister, educated at Eton and Oxford. He was Chancellor of the Exchequer in Lord John Russell's government between 1846 and 1852, and later Secretary of State for India under Palmerston between 1859 and 1866. It was in the latter capacity that Burton came into direct contact with him, as the complaint made in 1859 by C. P. Rigby, concerning the unpaid porters of the East Africa Expedition, came to Wood's attention—"Sir Charles Wood especially desires to be informed why you took no steps to bring the services of the men who accompanied you, and your obligations to them, to the notice of the Bombay Government".[1] It was Wood who ultimately censured Burton as a result of this complaint. Moreover, Isabel attributed Burton's "coming under the reduction" in 1861, when he was retrenched from the Army, to Wood—"In 1861 [Burton] was compelled to leave, without pay or pension, by Sir Charles Wood, for accepting the Consulship of Fernando Po."[2] Unsurprisingly, Burton referred to him as the "unlearned Sir Charles Wood" in *Sind Revisited*.[3]

330. Wright, William [Salih] (1837-1899).

An Irish Presbyterian missionary and author from County Down in Northern Ireland, educated at Queen's College in Belfast. He was influenced by the preacher Spurgeon to become a missionary. Wright spent ten years as a missionary at Damascus, where he met the Burtons when they were stationed there between 1869 and 1871. He returned to England in 1875. Under the pseudonym 'Salih' he wrote a lengthy and highly affectionate reminiscence of Burton at Damascus—"He was always saying things to frighten old women of both sexes, and to make servant-maids stare"[4] When Burton was recalled from Damascus, Wright was one of many Damascus associates who wrote a testimonial in his defense, which was submitted to the Foreign Office.

Wright also published books on *The Empire of the Hittites* (1884), *The Brontes in Ireland* (1893) and *Account of Palmyra and Zenobia, with Travels and Adventures in Bashan and the Desert* (1895). The latter book described an exploration of Palmyra that was suggested to him by Burton, whose own exploration of the ruins was published in *Unexplored Syria* (1872)—"Sir Richard Burton, who had visited the ruins before me, urged me to take ladders and ropes and grappling-irons, for the ascent of the towers, which he had been unable to examine for lack of such

---

[1] *Life*, Vol. 2, p. 567.
[2] *Life* Vol. 2, p. 325.
[3] Vol. 1 (1877), p. 117.
[4] See Volume 2.

appliances."[1]

331. Wylde, William Henry (1819-1909).

A civil servant in the Foreign Office, the eldest son of Major-General William Wylde of Chiswick (1788-1877). He was educated at a private school, then served for a while as private secretary to his father, before entering the Civil Service in 1838. He was the Superintendent of the Commercial, Consular, and Slave Trade Department of the Foreign Office between 1869 and 1880. In 1872 he was on the Commission of Inquiry into Consular Establishments.

Burton knew both William Henry and his father, as well as William Henry's sons Everard William (1847-1911) and Augustus[2] Blandy (1849?-1909), who were in the Foreign Office and Consular service respectively. He maintained an active correspondence with Wylde, who was in the Foreign Office and actively involved with West African Affairs when Burton was stationed at Fernando Po. They were both members of the Athenaeum Club, and Wylde was also a Fellow of the RGS. A decent portion of their correspondence survives and appears in Volumes 1 and 2.

---

[1] Wright *Account of Palmyra and Zenobia* (1895), p. 74.
[2] To whom Isabel refers as 'Gustavus', for no clear reason. *Life* Vol. 2, p. 55.

Sources

Archives

Manuscript-derived material from the following archives and libraries appears in this collection.

Boston Athenaeum, Boston, USA.

British Library, London, UK.	Rare Books and Manuscripts India Office Records
Durham University, Durham, UK.	Wylde Papers
Huntington Library, San Marino, California, USA.	Sir Richard Francis Burton Papers. Sir Richard Burton Manuscripts Collection. Burke E. Casari Collection. Burton-Smithers Papers. Rare Books (Burton's Personal Library).
Kew Gardens, London.	Correspondence Collection.
National Archives, Kew, UK.	Foreign Office Records (FO). Military Records (MIL).
National Library of Scotland, Edinburgh, UK.	Grant Papers. Murray Papers. Kirk Papers.
Orleans House Gallery, Richmond, UK.	Mary Lovell Collection.
Royal Anthropological Institute, London, UK.	Burton Collection. Minutes.
Royal Asiatic Society, London, UK.	Burton Collection.
Royal Geographical Society, London, UK.	Correspondence Blocks CB4, CB5, CB6. Burton Collection. John Hanning Speke Collection. George Back Collection. Gordon Collection. Spiro Collection.

Smithsonian Institute, Washington DC, USA.	Russell E. Train Africana Collection.
Cambridge University.	Trinity College, Houghton Papers. Manuscripts and Archives, Robertson-Smith Papers.
University College London	Galton Papers. Greenough Papers.
University of Texas at Austin	Harry Ransom Center.
Wiltshire and Swindon Record Office.	Arundell Family Collection.

Microfilms

- *The papers of Sir Richard Burton (1821-1890) from the Wiltshire and Swindon Record Office (Colonial discourses., Series 2, Imperial adventurers and explorers, part 1.).* Marlborough: Adam Matthew, 2001.
- *Colonial discourses. Series two, Imperial adventurers and explorers. Part 2, Papers of James Augustus Grant (1827-92) and John Hanning Speke (1827-64) from the National Library of Scotland.* Marlborough, Wiltshire, England: Adam Matthew Publications, 2003.

Electronic Collections.

- *India, Raj and empire.* Marlborough, Wiltshire: Adam Matthew, 2013.
- *JSTOR Global Plants.* JSTOR.ORG

Bibliography

Books by Richard Burton

1851.	*Goa, and the Blue Mountains; or Six Months of Sick Leave.* London, Richard Bentley.
1851.	*Scinde; or, The Unhappy Valley* (2 volumes). London, Richard Bentley.
1851.	*Sindh, and the Races that Inhabit the Valley of the Indus.* London, W. H. Allen.
1852.	*Falconry in the Valley of the Indus.* London, John van Voorst.
1853.	*A Complete System of Bayonet Exercise.* London, William Clowes.
1855-6.	*Personal Narrative of a Pilgrimage to El-Medinah and Meccah* (3 volumes). London, Longman.
1856.	*First Footsteps in East Africa; or, An exploration of Harar.* London, Longman.
1860.	*The Lake Regions of Central Africa, A Picture of exploration* (2 volumes). London, Longman.
1861.	*The City of the Saints and Across the Rocky Mountains to California.* London, Longman.
1863.	(ed.) *The Prairie Traveler, a Hand-book for Overland Expeditions by Randolph B. Marcy.* London, Trubner.
1863.	*Abeokuta and the Camaroons Mountains. An Exploration.* (2 volumes) London, Tinsley.
1863.	*Wanderings in West Africa, From Liverpool to Fernando Po.* (Anon. by F.R.G.S.) (2 volumes) London, Tinsley.
1864.	*A Mission to Gelele, King of Dahome* (2 volumes). London, Tinsley.
1864.	*The Nile Basin.* London, Tinsley.
1865.	*Wit and Wisdom from West Africa.* London, Tinsley.
1865.	*The Guide-book. A Pictorial Pilgrimage to Mecca and Medina.* London, William Clowes.
1865.	*Stone Talk.* London, Robert Hardwicke.
1869.	*Explorations of The Highlands of the Brazil* (2 volumes). London, Tinsley.
1870.	*Vikram and the Vampire, or Tales of Hindu Devilry.* London, Longman.
1870.	*Letters from the Battlefields of Paraguay.* London, Tinsley.
1872.	*Unexplored Syria* (2 vols.) London, Tinsley.

1872.	*Zanzibar; City, Island, and Coast* (2 volumes). London, Tinsley.
1872.	*The Case of Captain Burton, Late H. B. M.'s Consul at Damascus.* Clayton & Co, London.
1873.	(transl.) *The Lands of Cazembe. Lacerda's Journey to Cazembe in 1798.* London, John Murray.
1874.	(ed.) *The Captivity of Hans Stade of Hesse, in A.D. 1547-1555, Among the Wild Tribes of Eastern Brazil.* London, Hakluyt Society.
1875.	*Ultima Thule; or A Summer in Iceland* (2 volumes). London, William P. Nimmo.
1876.	*Etruscan Bologna: A Study.* London, Smith, Elder & Co.
1876.	*A New System of Sword Exercise for Infantry.* London, William Clowes.
1876.	*Two Trips to Gorilla Land and the Cataracts of the Congo* (2 volumes). London, Sampson Low.
1877.	*Sind Revisited* (2 volumes). London, Richard Bentley.
1878.	*The Gold-Mines of Midian and The Ruined Midianite Cities.* London, C. Kegan Paul.
1879.	*The Land of Midian* (revisited) (2 volumes). London, C. Kegan Paul.
1880.	*The Kasidah of Haji Abdu El-Yezdi a Lay of the Higher Law.* London, Bernard Quaritch.
1880.	(transl.) *Os Lusiadas* (The Lusiads) (2 volumes). London, Bernard Quaritch.
1881.	*Camoens: His Life and His Lusiads* (2 volumes). London, Bernard Quaritch.
1881.	*A Glance at the "Passion-Play".* London, W. H. Harrison.
1883.	*To the Gold Coast for Gold* (2 volumes). London, Chatto & Windus.
1883.	(ed.) *The Kama Sutra of Vatsyayana.* London, Kama Shastra Society.
1884.	(transl.) *Camoens. The Lyricks* (2 volumes). London, Bernard Quaritch.
1884.	*The Book of the Sword.* London, Chatto & Windus.
1885.	(ed.) *Ananga Ranga.* Cosmopoli, Kama Shastra Society.
1885.	(transl. and ed.) *A Plain and Literal Translation of the Arabian Nights' Entertainments* (10 volumes). Benares, Kama-Shastra Society.
1886-8.	(transl. and ed.) *Supplemental Nights to the Book of The Thousand Nights and a Night* (6 volumes). Benares,

	Kama-Shastra Society
1886.	(transl.) *Iracema, The Honey-lips and Manuel de Mores.* London, Bickers and Son.
1886.	(transl.) *The Perfumed Garden of the Cheikh Nefzaoui.* London and Benares, Kama Shastra Society.
1887.	(ed.) *The Beharistan (Abode of Spring).* London and Benares, Kama Shastra Society.
1888.	(ed.) *The Gulistan or Rose Garden of Sa'di.* Benares, Kama Shastra Society.
1890	(transl.) Priapeia or the Sportive Epigrams of divers Poets on Priapus. Cosmopoli.
1891.	(ed.) *Marocco and the Moors. by Arthur Leared.* London, Sampson Low.
1893.	(transl.) *Il Pentamerone; or, the Tale of Tales.* London, Henry and Co.
1894.	(transl.) *The Carmina of Gaius Valerius Catullus.* London, Privately printed.
1898.	*The Jew, The Gypsy, and El Islam.* Ed. W. H. Wilkins. London, Hutchinson.
1901.	*Wanderings in Three Continents.* Ed. W. H. Wilkins. London, Hutchinson.
1911.	*The Sentiment of the Sword: A Country-House Dialogue.* London, Horace Cox.
1982.	*The Uruguay: A Historical Romance of South America.* Berkeley, University of California Press.
1990.	*Sir Richard Burton's Travels in Arabia and Africa: Four Lectures from a Huntington Library Manuscript.* Edited by John Hayman. Huntington Library Press.
2003.	(transl.) *Pilpay's Fables.* Bangkok: Orchid Press, 2003.

Books by Isabel Burton

1875.	*The Inner Life of Syria, Palestine and the Holy Land.* London, Henry S. King.
1879.	*A. E. I.: Arabia Egypt India. A Narrative of Travel.* London: William Mullan. RFB is known to have contributed to this book.
1893.	*The Life of Captain Sir Richard F. Burton K. C. M. G., F. R. G. S.* London, Chapman and Hall.

Auction Catalogues

Spink and Son Ltd. 1976. *Sir Richard Burton KCMG 1821-1890. Catalogue of valuable books, manuscripts & autographs letters of Sir*

Richard Francis Burton, 1821-1890: many recorded for the first time including a fine portrait in oils. London.

Sothebys Sale, *Fine Books and Manuscripts, #6515*, 1993. New York.

Maggs Bros. Ltd. 1996. *Sir Richard Burton. Books from a Private Collection with Drawings & Related Material.* London.

Christies, London. 2004. *The Quentin Keynes Collection, Part I. Important Travel Books and Manuscripts.*

General

Ashbee, H. S. as "Pisanus Fraxi".
    Index Librorum Prohibitorum. London, 1877.
    Centuria Librorum Absconditorum. London, 1879.
    Catena Librorum Tacendorum. London, 1885.

Casada, James A.
    1990. *Sir Richard F. Burton: a Biobibliographical Study.* London, Mansell.

Digby, Simon.
    2006. *Richard Burton: the Indian Making of an Arabist.* Jersey, Orient Monographs.

Gibson, Ian.
    2001. *The Erotomaniac: the Secret Life of Henry Spencer Ashbee.* New York, Da Capo.

Godsall, Jon.
    2008. *The Tangled Web.* Leicester, Troubadour.

Hitchman, Francis
    1887. *Richard F. Burton: K.C.M.G. His Early, Private and Public Life.* 2 volumes. London, Sampson Low.

Jutzi, Alan H.
    1993. *In Search of Sir Richard Burton: Papers from a Huntington Library Symposium.* San Marino, Huntington.

Keynes, Simon, ed.
    2004 *Quentin Keynes: Explorer, film-maker, lecturer and book-collector, 1921-2003.* Cambridge, Privately Printed.

Kirkpatrick, B. J.
    1978. *A Catalogue of the Library of Sir Richard Burton, K.C.M.G. held by the Royal Anthropological Institute.* Royal Anthropological Institute. This collection is now housed at the Huntington Library.

Lang, Cecil.
    1959. *The Swinburne Letters*. 6 volumes. New Haven, Yale.

Lovell, Mary.
    1998. *A Rage to Live. a Biography of Richard and Isabel Burton*. New York, Norton.

McCarthy, James.
    2006. *Selim Aga: A Slave's Odyssey*. Edinburgh, Luath Press.

McConnachie, James.
    2007. The Book of Love: the Story of the Kamasutra. New York, Metropolitan Books.

McLynn, Frank
    1991. *From the Sierras to the Pampas: Richard Burton's Travels in the Americas 1860-69*. London, Century.

Mendes, Peter
    1993. *Clandestine Erotic Fiction*. Aldershot, Scolar Press.

Maitland, Alexander.
    1973. *Speke and the Discovery of the Source of the Nile*. Newton Abbott, Victorian & Modern History Book Club.

Moore-Harell, Alice.
    2001. *Gordon and the Sudan: Prologue to the Mahdiyya, 1877-1880*. New York, Frank Cass [London: Routledge, 2014].

Myers, Terry L.
    2004. *The Uncollected Letters of Algernon Charles Swinburne*. New York, Routledge.

Penzer, Norman.
    1923. *An Annotated Bibliography of Sir Richard Francis Burton K.C.M.G.* London, A.M. Philpot.

Rainy, William.
    1865. *The Censor Censured, or the Calumnies of Captain Burton*. London, privately printed for the author by Geo. Chalfont.

Russell, Mrs. Charles E. B.
    1935. *General Rigby, Zanzibar and the Slave Trade with Journals, Dispatches etc.* London, George Allen & Unwin. The author was Rigby's daughter.

Simpson, Donald.
    1976. *Dark Companions: The African Contribution to the*

European Exploration of East Africa. London, Paul Elek.

Stevenson, Richard.
2015. *Beatson's Mutiny: the Turbulent Career of a Victorian Soldier.* London, I. B. Tauris.

Stisted, Georgiana.
1896. *The True Life of Captain Richard F. Burton.* London, H. S. Nichols.

Waterfield, Gordon.
1964. *First Footsteps in East Africa by Sir Richard Burton.* London, Praeger. This contains a great deal of new material and commentary by Waterfield.

Wright, Thomas.
1906. *The Life of Sir Richard Burton.* 2 vols. London, Everett.

Young, Donald.
1979. *The Selected Correspondence of Sir Richard Burton 1848-1890.* MA Thesis. Nebraska.

Young, Donald and Quentin Keynes.
1999. *The search for the source of the Nile: correspondence between Captain Richard Burton, Captain John Speke and others, from Burton's unpublished East African letter book; together with other related letters and papers in the collection of Quentin Keynes, esq.* London, Roxburghe Club.

Plates

Miscellaneous

Figure 30. Sporting Truth.

Figure 31. Allen's Indian Mail Dec. 6th 1843.

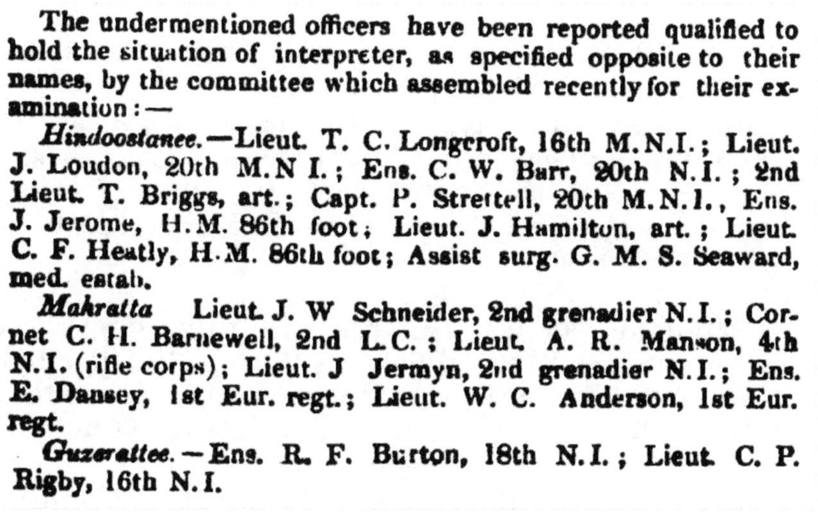

The undermentioned officers have been reported qualified to hold the situation of interpreter, as specified opposite to their names, by the committee which assembled recently for their examination:—

Hindoostanee.—Lieut. T. C. Longcroft, 16th M.N.I.; Lieut. J. Loudon, 20th M.N I.; Ens. C. W. Barr, 20th N.I.; 2nd Lieut. T. Briggs, art.; Capt. P. Strettell, 20th M.N.I., Ens. J. Jerome, H.M. 86th foot; Lieut. J. Hamilton, art.; Lieut. C. F. Heatly, H.M. 86th foot; Assist surg. G. M. S. Seaward, med. estab.

Mahratta Lieut. J. W Schneider, 2nd grenadier N.I.; Cornet C. H. Barnewell, 2nd L.C.; Lieut. A. R. Manson, 4th N.I. (rifle corps); Lieut. J Jermyn, 2nd grenadier N.I.; Ens. E. Dansey, 1st Eur. regt.; Lieut. W. C. Anderson, 1st Eur. regt.

Guzerattee.—Ens. R. F. Burton, 18th N.I.; Lieut. C. P. Rigby, 16th N.I.

Figure 32. Calling Card of H. S. Ashbee.

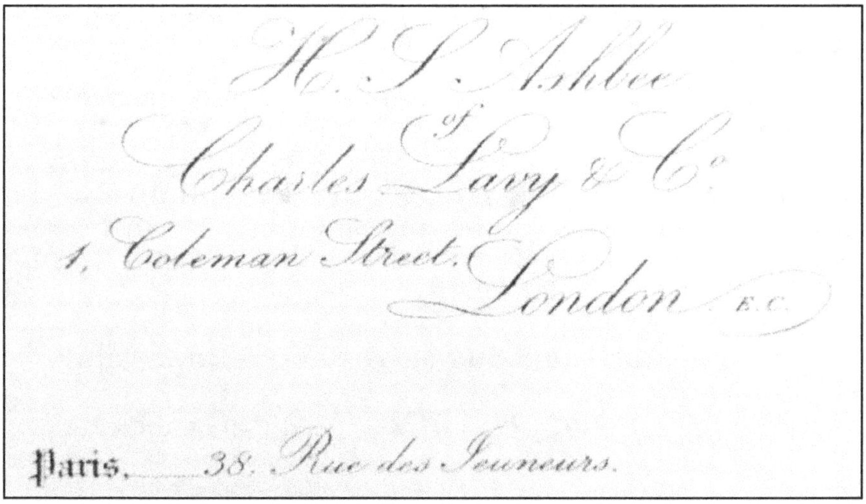

Figure 33. Mining Concession granted to Burton and Teixeira.

DECRETO N. 4255 — DE 25 DE SETEMBRO DE 1868.

Proroga por 20 mezes o prazo de dous annos concedido a Augusto Teixeira Coimbra e Richard Francis Burton na clausula 2.ª do Decreto n.º 3706 de 26 de Setembro de 1866, para a execução de trabalhos referentes á exploração de mineraes na Provincia de S. Paulo.

Attendendo ao que Me requerêrão Augusto Teixeira Coimbra e Richard Francis Burton, Hei por bem Prorogar por 20 mezes, contados do dia 27 do corrente mez, o prazo de dous annos, que lhes foi concedido

na clausula 2.ª do Decreto n.º 3706 de 26 de Setembro de 1866 para a execução de trabalhos referentes á exploração das minas de chumbo, estanho e outros mineraes na serra do Iporanga, da Provincia de S. Paulo.

Joaquim Antão Fernandes Leão, do Meu Conselho, Ministro e Secretario de Estado dos Negocios da Agricultura, Commercio e Obras Publicas, assim o tenha entendido e faça executar. Palacio do Rio de Janeiro, em vinte cinco de Setembro de mil oitocentos sessenta e oito, quadragesimo setimo da Independencia e do Imperio.

Com a rubrica de Sua Magestade o Imperador.

Joaquim Antão Fernandes Leão.

Figure 34. Speke Memorial Fund.[1]

SPEKE MEMORIAL.— In remembrance of the intrepid and lamented SPEKE, who discovered the great Equatorial Lake of Africa, the Victoria Nyanza, and, with his gallant companion Grant, followed its waters to the mouth of the Nile, it has been resolved to erect a Monument.

List of Subscribers.

	£.	s.		£.	s.
Sir Roderick I. Murchison, K.C.B., Pres. Roy. Geo. Soc.	20	0	G. E. Eyre, Esq.	1	1
			E. Stanford, Esq.	1	1
Lady Murchison	2	0	Henry Salt, Esq.	1	1
Capt. J. A. Grant	10	0	Capt. Sherard Osborn, C.B. R.N.	1	1
Capt. R. F. Burton	5	0	Charles Ratcliffe, Esq.	1	1
William Spottiswoode, Esq., F.R.S.	1	1	Major W. E. Hay	2	2
Admiral R. Collinson, C.B.	1	1	Lieut.-Col. F. J. Goldsmid	2	0
C. R. Markham, Esq., F.S.A.	1	1	Dr. Karl von Scherzer	1	1
Mrs. Markham	1	1	Sir Henry Rawlinson, K.C.B.	2	0
John Crawfurd, Esq., F.R.S.	5	0	Charles White, Esq.	1	1
			Capt. Allen Young	1	1
Francis Galton, Esq., F.R.S.	2	0	Capt. E. A. Porcher, R.N.	1	1
			Capt. Malcolm	1	0
Sir George Back, F.R.S.	5	0	W. R. Sandbach, Esq.	1	0
Dr. David Livingstone	1	1	S. Van Capellen	1	0
Lady Franklin	3	3	Mrs. Ford	1	0
Viscount Milton	5	0	Rev. E. H. M. Sladen	1	1
His Grace the Duke of Wellington	5	0	George H. Fitz-Roy, Esq.	10	0
			John Murray, Esq.	2	2
His Excellency Baron de Brunnow	5	0	James Heywood, Esq., F.R.S.	1	1
W. J. Hamilton, Esq., F.R.S.	1	1	John Blackwood, Esq.	15	0
			William Blackwood, Esq.	10	0
Commendatore Cristoforo Negri	2	0	T. Hamilton, Esq.	1	0
			Col. P. T. French	1	0
General Alfonso De La Marmora	4	0	Capt. T. B. Heathorn	1	0
			Capt. W. Gosling	1	0
Laurence Oliphant, Esq.	2	2	James Harris, Esq.	1	0
Lieut.-Gen. Charles Fox	2	2	Gen. J. Holms	1	0
Right Hon. H. U. Addington	5	5	R. Chatfield, Esq.	1	0
			Capt. Miller	1	0
John Hogg, Esq., F.R.S.	1	0	H. M. S. Graeme, Esq.	1	0
Sir William Miles, Bart., M.P.	5	0	Col. Showers	1	0
			Thomas Prendergast, Esq.	1	0
James Fergusson, Esq.	1	1	Col. A. Park	1	0
Edward Porter, Esq.	1	1	Col. J. Cameron	1	0
Rev. W. B. Beaumont	5	0	Capt. C. E. Bates	1	0
Sir Peregrine Acland, Bart.	5	0	A. Purvis, Esq.	1	0
			Capt. S. D. Turner	1	0
Sir Alexander Acland Wood, Bart., M.P.	5	0	Capt. W. H. Blowers	1	0
			A. S. Mathison, Esq.	1	0
Arthur G. Puller, Esq.	10	10	Geographical Society of Paris	10	0
Sir Justin Sheil, K.C.B.	2	0	Capt. F. R. Aikman	1	0
Admiral W. H. Hall, C.B. F.R.S.	1	1	Gen. Sir A. Boyle	1	0
			Capt. W. D. Hoste	1	0
Peter Sharp, Esq.	1	1	Gen. A. W. Lawrence	1	0
R. Jasper More, Esq.	1	1	J. W. Kaye, Esq.	1	0
Sir Andrew S. Waugh, F.R.S.	1	0	Capt. G. Jenkins, C.B. I.N.	5	0
Col. G. Balfour, R.A. C.B.	1	0	John Arrowsmith, Esq.	1	0
J. M. Ziegler, Esq.	2	2	Capt. B. Carter	5	0
Reginald T. Cocks, Esq.	2	2	D. B. Chapman, Esq.	5	0
Joseph Hambleton, Esq.	1	0	J. R. Dorrington, Esq., jun.	5	0
Col. Honeywood	1	0			
Francis Beckford, Esq.	1	0	Rev. W. Bilton	5	0
W. F. Webb, Esq.	5	0	W. Gladstone, Esq.	5	0
Henry D. Seymour, Esq. M.P.	5	0	F. F. Tuckett, Esq.	1	1

Subscriptions received by Messrs. Coutts & Co., 57, Strand, W.C.; Messrs. Cocks, Biddulph & Co., 43, Charing Cross, S.W.; Messrs. Grindlay & Co., 55, Parliament-street, S.W.; and the Office of the Royal Geographical Society, 15, Whitehall-place, S.W.

Figure 35. The Burton Exhibit at Madame Tussaud's.

---
[1] *Athenaeum* Jan. 14 1865, p. 34.

Figure 36. Axim from the Gold Coast.

Figure 37: Illustration by Albert Letchford to Burton's Arabian Nights.

The East African Expedition.

Figure 38. Zanzibar Town from the Sea.

Figure 39. Fuga, sketched by Burton.

Figure 40. Pangany Falls, sketched by Burton.

Figure 41. Pemba Island, sketched by Burton.

Figure 42. Mombas, sketched by Burton.

Plates 351

Figure 43. Shamba, sketched by Burton.

Figure 44. The Town of Wasim, sketched by Burton.

Figure 45. Fort of Tongway, sketched by Burton.

Figure 46. The Hills of Usumbara, sketched by Burton.

Figure 47. East Coast Scene, sketched by Burton.

Figure 48. A 'Savage of the Nyika', sketched by Burton.

Figure 49. The Ivory Porter.

Figure 50. Party of Wak'Hutu Women.

Figure 51. The Wazaramo Tribe.[1]

---

[1] "Their distinctive mark is the peculiarity of dressing their hair. The thick wool is plastered over with a cap-like coating of ochreish and micaceous clay, brought from the hills, and mixed to the consistency of honey with the oil of the sesamum or the castor-bean. The pomatum, before drying, is pulled out with the fingers to the ends of many little twists, which circle the head horizontally, and the mass is separated into a single or a double line of knobs, the upper being above, and the lower below, the ears, both look stiff and matted, as if affected with a bad plica polonica. The contrast between these garlands of small red dilberries and the glossy black skin is, however, effective." Lake Regions Vol. 1, p. 108.

Figure 52. A Village in Khutu. The Silk Cotton Tree.

Figure 53. Sycamore in the Dhun of Ugogi.

Figure 54. Explorers in East Africa.

Figure 55. The East African Ghauts.

Figure 56. Majiya W'heta, or the Jetting Fountain in K'hutu.

Figure 57. Ugogo.

Figure 58. Usagara Mountains, seen from Ugogo.

Figure 59. View in Unyamwezi.

Figure 60. Ladies' Smoking Party. [1]

---

[1] "Every evening there is a smoking party, which particularly attracts my attention. All the feminine part of the population, from wrinkled grandmother to the maiden scarcely in her teens, assemble together … . Amongst the fair of Yombo, there were no less than three beauties—women who would be deemed beautiful in any part of the world. Their faces were purely Grecian; they had laughing eyes, their figures were models for an artist … ." Lake Regions Vol. 1, p. 388.

Figure 61. African House Building.

Figure 62. Land of the Moon. Loom and public house.

Figure 63. Navigation on the Tanganyika Lake.

Figure 64. View in Usagara.

Figure 65. My Tembe near the Tanganyika.

Figure 66. Head Dresses of Wanyamwezi.

Figure 67. African Types.

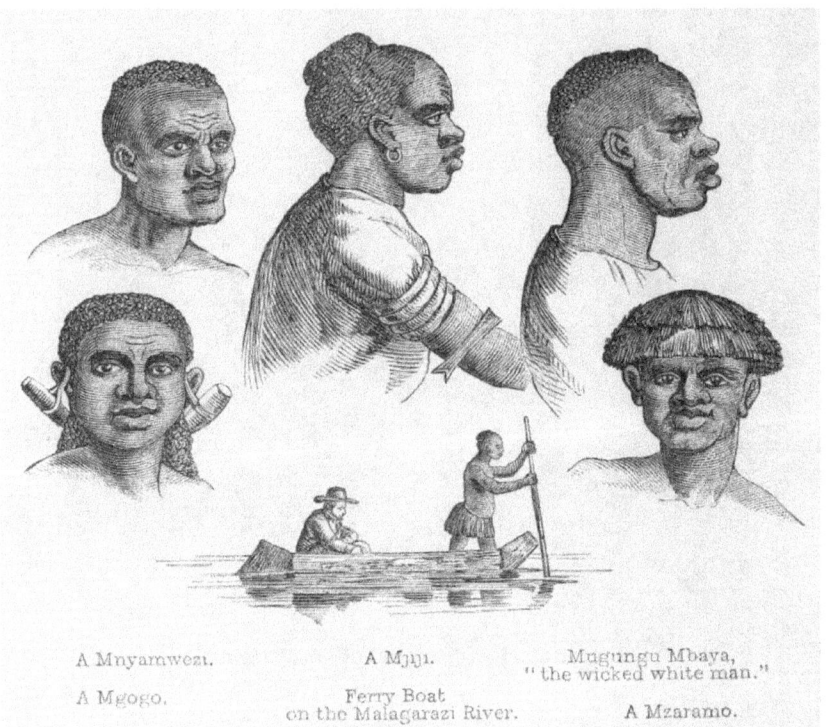

A Mnyamwezi.   A Mjiji.   Mugungu Mbaya, "the wicked white man."
A Mgogo.   Ferry Boat on the Malagarazi River.   A Mzaramo.

Mganga, or medicine man.   The porter.   The Kirangozi, or guide.
Muinyi Kidogo.   Mother and child.

Figure 68. Snay Bin Amir's House.

Figure 69. Saydumi. a Native of Uganda.

Figure 70. Mgongo Thembo, or the Elephant's Back.

Figure 71. Jiwe la Mkoa, the Round Rock.

Figure 72. The Basin of Maroro.

Figure 73. The Basin of Kisanga.

Figure 74. Rufita Pass in Usagara.

Figure 75. The Ivory Porter, the Cloth Porter, and Woman, in Usagara.

Figure 76. African Implements.

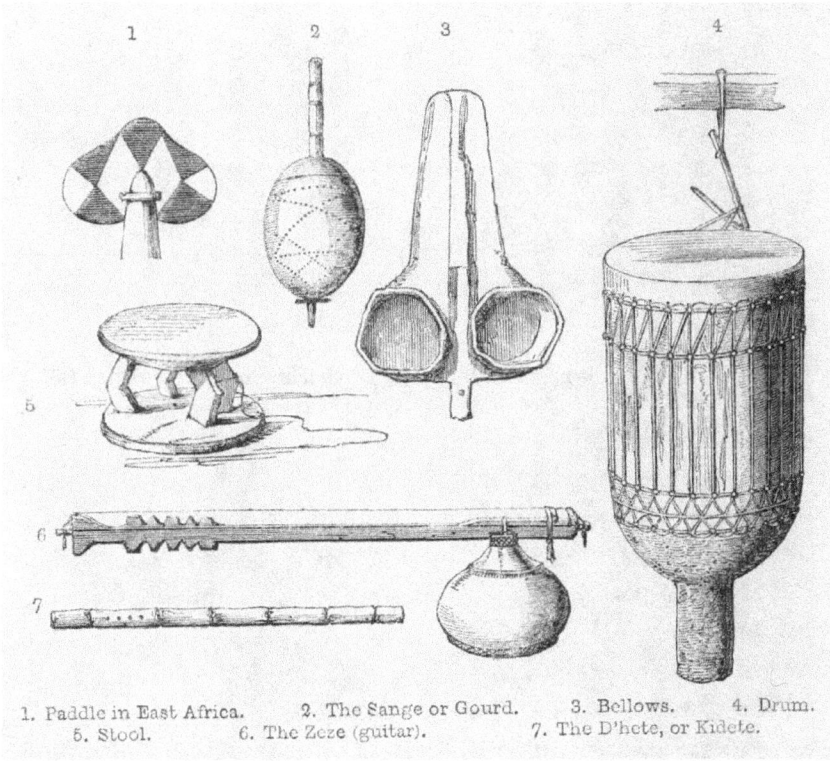

1. Paddle in East Africa. 2. The Sange or Gourd. 3. Bellows. 4. Drum.
5. Stool. 6. The Zeze (guitar). 7. The D'hete, or Kidete.

Figure 77. Gourds.

Figure 78. A Mnyamwezi (l). A Mhela (r).

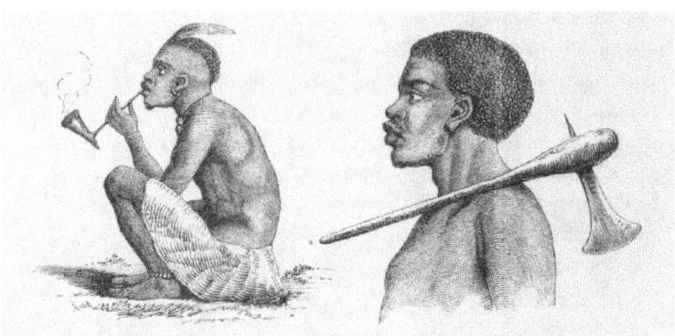

Figure 79. The Bull-headed Mabruki (l). African Standing Position (r).

Figure 80. Elephant Rock.

The Elephant Rock (Ἀκρωτήριον Ἐλέφας, Periplus II. رأس الفيل), seen from fifteen miles at sea, direction S.W.

Trieste.

Figure 81. Burton, Baker, and Isabel at Folkestone, 1888.

Figure 82. Burton at work in his study, Villa Gosleth, Trieste.

Figure 83. Isabel at work, Villa Gosleth, Trieste.

Figure 84. Isabel, F. F. Arbuthnot and RFB in the garden, Villa Gosleth, Trieste.

Figure 85. Isabel talking to Richard in the Garden, Villa Gosleth, Trieste.

Figure 86. In the Garden, near the end. Villa Gosleth, Trieste.

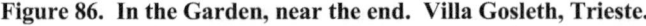

Figure 87: Burton on his death bed.

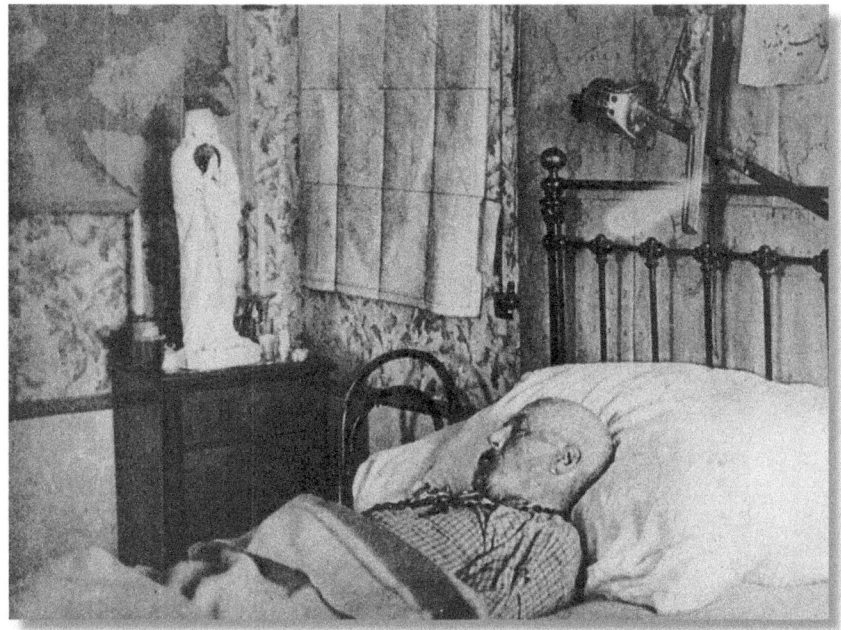

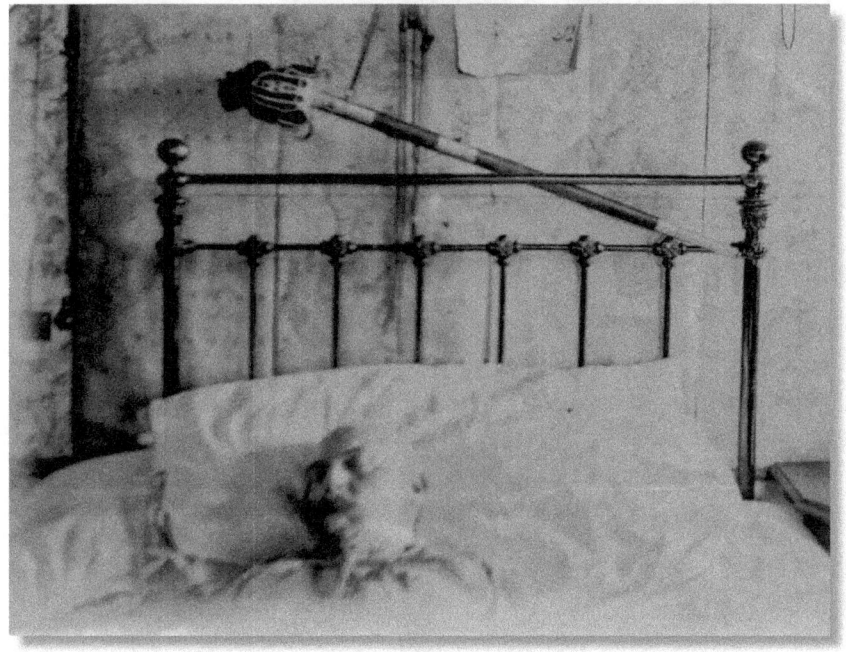

Figure 88. Death mask and casts of Burton.

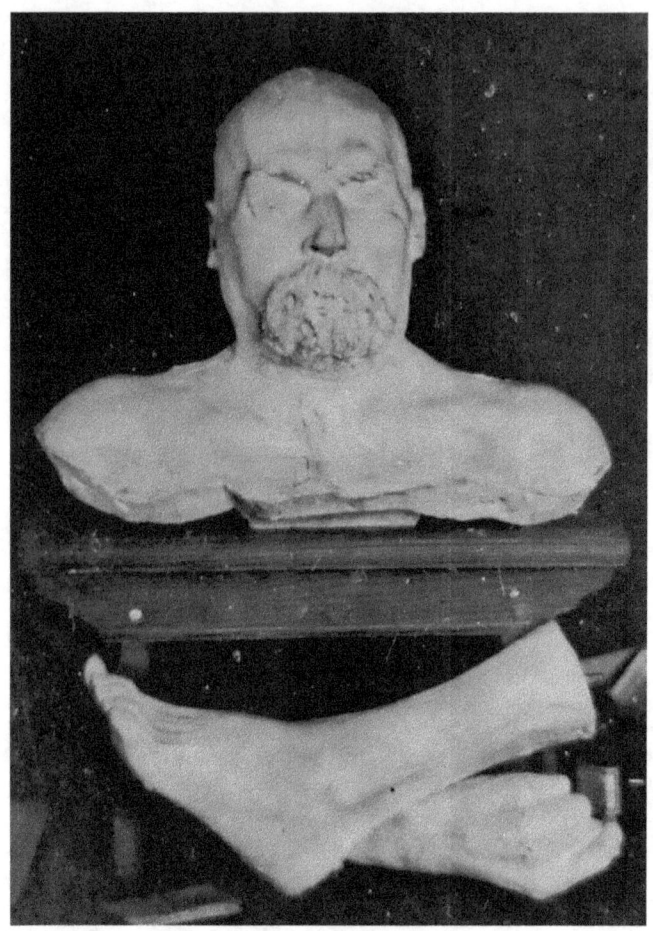

Figure 89. The Wake in Villa Gosleth.

Figure 90. The Smoking Divan in Villa Gosleth, Trieste, by Albert Letchford.

Figure 91. Room in Villa Gosleth, Trieste, by Albert Letchford.

Figure 92. Isabel Burton's Study in Villa Gosleth, by Albert Letchford.

Figure 93. Isabel Burton's Bedroom in Villa Gosleth, by Albert Letchford.

Figure 94. View of the Bay of Trieste from Villa Gosleth, by Albert Letchford.

Figure 95. Villa Gosleth, Trieste, scene by Albert Letchford.

Figure 96. View from Villa Gosleth, Trieste, by Albert Letchford.

Figure 97. View of the Bay of Trieste by Albert Letchford.

Figure 98. Burton, Letchford, and Isabel in the Dining Room at Trieste.

Figure 99. Alternative view of the dining room, with Burton, Letchford and Isabel.

Figure 100. Drawing Room, Villa Gosleth, Trieste.

Figure 101. The study, Villa Gosleth, Trieste.

Figure 102. Villa Gosleth, Trieste, in the 1830s, from an old print.

Figure 103. Burton in the 1880s.

Figure 104. Portrait of Burton by Madame de Benvenuti, Trieste, 1879. [1]

---

[1] "We had a most charming family of neighbours, who were some of our best friends in Trieste; they had a lovely property, an old castle called Weixelstein, near Steinbruck (Monsieur and Madame Gutmansthal de Benvenuti). He was a Trieste-Italian gentleman, and she was the daughter of a Russian, by an American wife, and is far away the most charming woman I know, and so clever."—Isabel Burton. *Life* Vol.2 p. 168.

Credits

By kind permission of the London Borough of Richmond upon Thames, Orleans House Gallery:[1]

    The Wake in Villa Gosleth, by F. Grenfell Baker;

    Death mask and casts of Burton, by F. Grenfell Baker;

    In the Garden, near the end, Villa Gosleth, Trieste, by F. Grenfell Baker;

    Burton, Baker, and Isabel at Folkestone, 1888;

    Isabel talking to Richard in the Garden, Villa Gosleth, Trieste, by F. Grenfell Baker;

    Isabel, F. F. Arbuthnot and RFB in the garden, Villa Gosleth, Trieste;

    Burton at work in his study, Villa Gosleth, Trieste, by F. Grenfell Baker;

    Isabel at work, Villa Gosleth, Trieste.

    Cover: Burton at work in his study, by Albert Letchford.

    The Smoking Divan in Villa Gosleth, Trieste, by Albert Letchford.

    Room in Villa Gosleth, Trieste, by Albert Letchford.

    Burton, Letchford, and Isabel in the Dining Room at Trieste.

    Isabel Burton's Study in Villa Gosleth, by Albert Letchford.

    Isabel Burton's Bedroom in Villa Gosleth, by Albert Letchford.

    Villa Gosleth, Trieste, scene by Albert Letchford.

    View from Villa Gosleth, Trieste, by Albert Letchford.

    View of the Bay of Trieste, by Albert Letchford.

    View of the Bay of Trieste, by Albert Letchford.

    Drawing Room, Villa Gosleth, Trieste.

    Burton, Letchford, and Isabel in the Dining Room at Trieste.

    Alternative view of the dining room, with Burton, Letchford and Isabel.

    Burton in the 1880s.

---

[1] http://www.richmond.gov.uk/orleans_house_gallery.

Smithsonian:

> Fuga, sketched by Burton.
>
> Pangany Falls, sketched by Burton.
>
> A 'Savage of the Nyika', sketched by Burton.

University of London, SOAS:

> Portrait of Burton by Madame de Benvenuti, Trieste, 1879.

Index to Authors and Correspondents

A

Anonymous, 76
Ashbee, H. S., 13, 28
Auberton, John James, 82

B

Bainton, George, 17
Baker, Dr. Frederick Grenfell, 168
Baker, Samuel, 58
Bancroft, Squire, 63
Bispham, David Scull, 166
Blathwayt, Raymond, 141
Burton, Isabel, 5, 6, 19, 66, 94, 96,
    115, 130, 131, 134, 137, 140
Burton, Richard Francis, 1, 2, 4, 6, 7, 8,
    9, 10, 11, 12, 13, 14, 15, 19, 20, 21,
    22, 23, 24, 25, 26, 27, 28, 29, 30,
    31, 32, 35, 36, 37, 39, 40, 41, 42,
    43, 44, 45, 46, 47, 48, 50, 51, 52,
    53, 54, 55, 56, 57, 59, 60, 61, 64,
    65, 68, 69, 71, 72, 73

C

Cameron, Verney Lovett, 16, 84
Chaillé-Long, Colonel, 8, 20, 69, 70, 94
Clodd, Edward, 138

D

Davey, Richard Patrick Boyle, 162
De Leon, Edwin, 88
Doughty, Charles Montagu, 4
Dunraven, Earl of, 179

E

Eames, W. J., 145
Ellis, A. G., 2, 11, 12, 28, 47, 51

G

Galton, Francis, 83, 163
Grant, James Augustus, 58, 75

H

Hare, Augustus John Cuthbert, 139

I

Ionides, Luke, 180

J

Jones, Herbert, 146

K

Kingsford, Anna Bonus, 1

L

Linton, Lynn, 19, 145

M

Markham, Clements Robert, 156

N

Nicolson, Harold, 17

O

Ouida, 5, 6, 7, 156

P

Paget, Lady Walburga, 131, 140, 180
Payne, John, 1, 6, 13, 21, 22, 45, 54,
    152, 164

Q

Quaritch, Bernard, 144

R

Rawson, Albert Leighton, 97

S

Sayce, A. H., 16
Sayce, Archibald Henry, 167
Smalley, G. W., 78
Smithers, Leonard, 2, 4, 9, 10, 12, 14, 15, 19, 21, 23, 24, 25, 26, 27, 29, 30, 31, 32, 35, 36, 37, 39, 40, 41, 42, 43, 46, 48, 50, 52, 53, 54, 55, 56, 57, 59, 60, 65, 68, 71, 72, 73
Spencer, Walter, 3
Sporting Truth, 76
Stanley, Henry Morton, 62
Stisted, Georgiana, 95, 145
Symonds, John Addington, 63, 64

T

Thayer, Alexander Wheelock, 44, 61, 94, 96, 130, 134, 137
Tinsley, William, 152
Tussaud, John Theodore, 136

W

Wright, Thomas, 164

www.ingramcontent.com/pod-product-compliance
Lightning Source LLC
Chambersburg PA
CBHW080723230426
43665CB00020B/2596